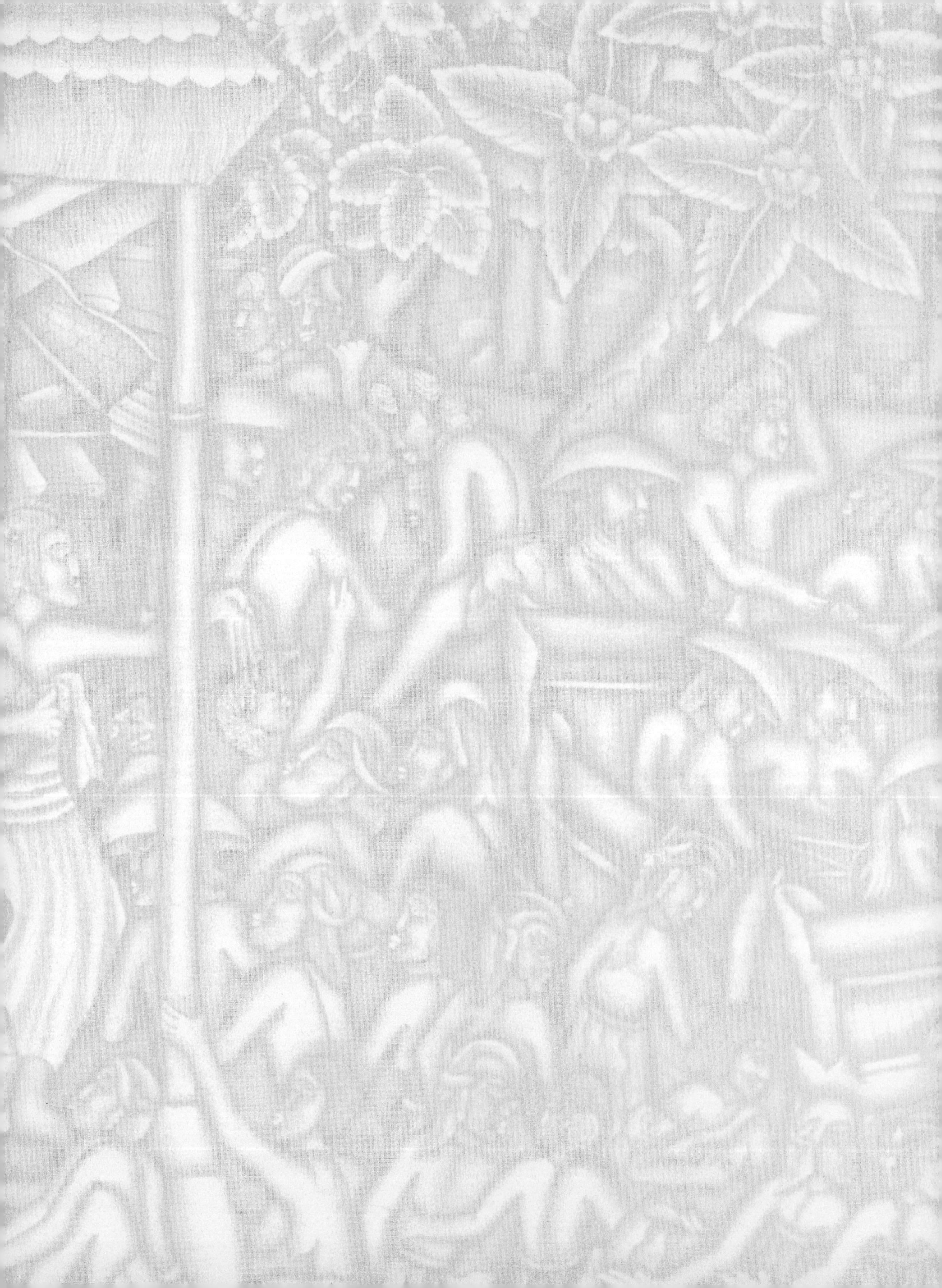

IMAGES *of* POWER

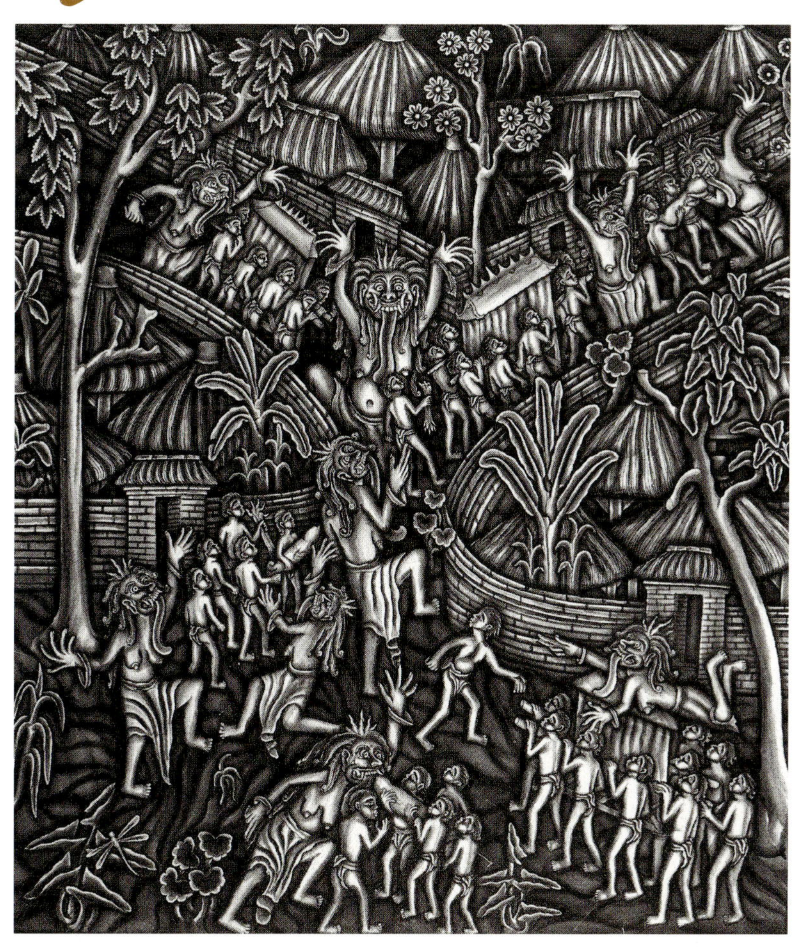

IMAGES

of POWER

Balinese Paintings Made for Gregory Bateson and Margaret Mead

Hildred Geertz

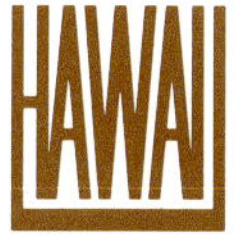

University of Hawaii Press/Honolulu

Published on the occasion of the exhibition *Images of Power: Balinese Paintings Made for Gregory Bateson and Margaret Mead*, organized and circulated by EducArt Projects, Inc., Davis, California.

Book design by Marquand Books, Inc.

Cover: *The Tale of Little Képét*, Ida Bagus Ketut Sawa
Endpapers: *Temple Festival*, Ida Bagus Nyoman Sanoer Tampi
Page i: *Epidemic*, Ida Bagus Nyoman Tjeta
Page ii: *Amad Defeated by Seroja's Magic Snake*, Ida Bagus Madé Djatasoera

Library of Congress Cataloging-in-Publication Data

Geertz, Hildred.
Images of power: Balinese paintings made for Gregory Bateson and Margaret Mead / Hildred Geertz.
p. cm.
Published on the occasion of a touring exhibition held in New York, Australia, and elsewhere.
Includes bibliographical references (p. 131) and index.
ISBN 0-8248-1646-3. — ISBN 0-8248-1679-X (pbk.)
1. Pen-and-ink painting, Balinese—Indonesia—Batuan—Exhibitions. 2. Pen-and-ink painting—20th century—Indonesia—Batuan—Exhibitions. 3. Bateson, Gregory—Art collections—Exhibitions. 4. Mead, Margaret, 1901–1978—Art collections—Exhibitions. 5. Pen-and-ink painting—Private collections—Exhibitions. 6. Bali Island (Indonesia) in art—Exhibitions. 7. Folklore in art—Indonesia—Exhibitions. 8. Spirituality in art. 9. Art and anthropology. I. Title.
ND2060.B38G44 1995
759.9598'6—dc20 94-13675
CIP

Printed in Singapore
99 98 97 96 95 94 5 4 3 2 1

Illustration Credits

Illustrations in the main text—with the exception of those on pages 46, 71, and 74, and those credited here—were photographed by Philip W. Smith.

Page 7. Basel Museum of Ethnography, IIC 16096, 1518, 14236. Photos by Colorphoto Hans Hinz.

Page 8. National Museum of Ethnology, Leiden, catalogue numbers 556 816, 556 587, and 556 528.

Page 9. Basel Museum of Ethnography, IIC 15327, 1717a–f. Photos by Colorphoto Hans Hinz.

Page 10. Rudolf Bonnet Archives. In H. de Roever-Bonnet, *Rudolf Bonnet: Een zondagskind.*

Page 11. Royal Tropical Institute, Amsterdam.

Page 13. Leiden University, Bonnet Coll. Br 135–78.

Page 18. Margaret Mead Archives, Manuscript Division, Library of Congress, Washington, D.C.

Page 19. Margaret Mead Archives, Manuscript Division, Library of Congress, Washington, D.C.

To the People of Batuan

Buku hasil penelitian puniki kaatur mantuka ring ida dané sareng sami ring Désa Batuan sané lédang ngicénin titiang kasuksman kayun. Kirang langkung antuk titiang nunas geng rena sinempura.

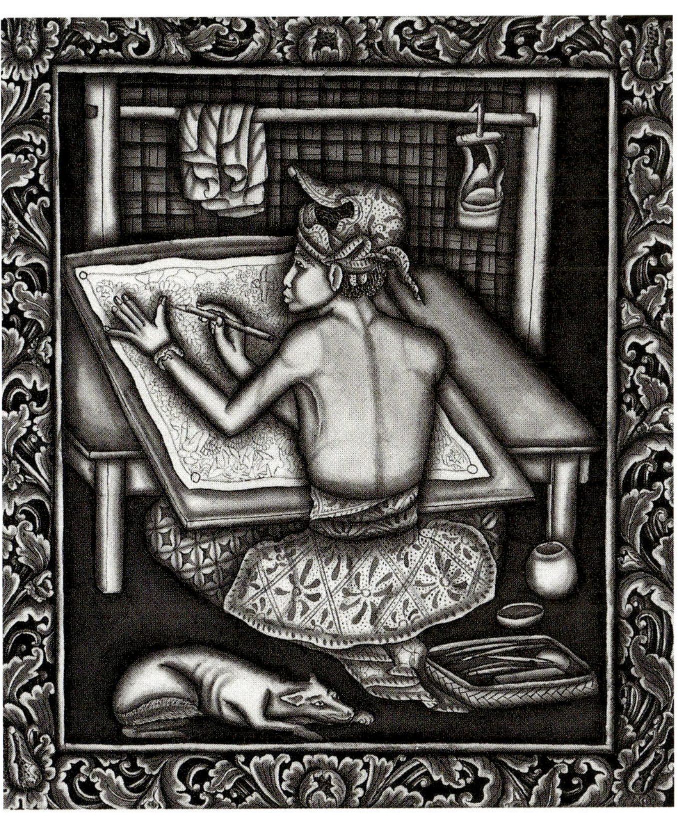

Self-Portrait
I Madé Djata

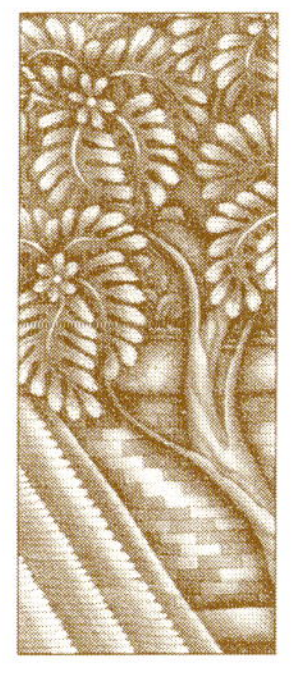

Contents

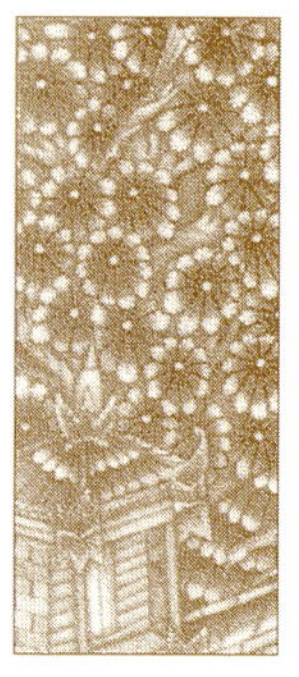

Acknowledgments

This study would not have been possible without the extensive help of many Balinese, most particularly the inhabitants of Batuan. There is no adequate way that I can express my gratitude to them for their trust, tolerance, and goodwill. I hope they will forgive me for my errors.

In Bali, Professor Gusti Ngurah Bagus was a constant source of support, collegiality, and friendship. In addition, my two research assistants, I Wayan Suparto and I Nyoman Dhana, deserve many thanks. Kristina Melcher provided thoughtful help, warm friendship, and delightful amusement over the years. In Batuan, the following were of particular assistance: Déwa Putu Bratha, Déwa Ketut Baroe, Ida Bagus Ketut Alit, I Madé Djata, the late Ida Bagus Madé Togog and his son, Ida Bagus Putu Gedé, but there were also countless others.

My intellectual debts are even more numerous and widespread. Most important is that to Clifford Geertz with whom I first attempted to understand Bali and to think through what it means to interpret cultural phenomena. My ideas about Bali have been greatly influenced by the writings of and discussions with James Boon, Ann McCauley, Henk Schulte Nordholt, Adrian Vickers, Margaret Wiener, and also A. L. Becker, Judith Becker, Frederik deBoer, William Cole, Linda Connor, A. A. M. Djelantik, Shelly Errington, Anthony Forge, Jean-François Guermonprez, Hedi Hinzler, Angela Hobart, Mark Hobart, Ward Keeler, J. Stephen Lansing, Barbara Lovric, Michel Picard, Raechelle Rubinstein, Abby Ruddick, John Stowell, David Stuart-Fox, Carol Warren, and Mary Zurbuchen.

I owe thanks to Margaret Mead, who in 1972 first showed me the paintings, still packed in their original wrappings of the *London Times* for April 1938. I am also grateful to Lois Bateson, who owns the pictures, and to Mary Catharine Bateson, literary executor for both Bateson and Mead, for long-term loan of the pictures and permission to exhibit them, and for access to Bateson and Mead's field notes and permission to quote from them. The field notes are stored in the Margaret Mead Archives, Manuscript Division of the U.S. Library of Congress, and I am grateful to Mary Wolfskil of the library, for her assistance in finding my way among them. The Institute for Intercultural Education, founded by Margaret Mead, which administers Mead's enormous legacy, not only assisted me financially, but also made access to the files much easier.

For their work in cataloging and organizing the Bateson-Mead Collection, I am indebted to Carl Thune, Mark Whitaker, Kirsten Scheid, Pauline Caulk, and many undergraduates. For compiling a sample of photographed paintings from Bali in 1971, and for an early study of them, I owe gratitude to Uwe Hamilton.

The staffs of a number of museums and libraries were helpful: in Leiden, the Rijksmuseum voor Volkenkunde; in Basel, the Museum für Völkerkunde; in Amsterdam, the Tropenmuseum; in New York, the American Museum of Natural History. The Cornell University Indonesia Project started me off by showing me Claire Holt's slides of prewar Balinese paintings.

This manuscript was read, generously and perceptively, by Patsy Asch, Benjamin Geertz, Fred Eiseman, Ann McCauley, Raechelle Rubinstein, Kirsten Scheid, Adrian Vickers, and four anonymous readers from the University of California Press and the University of Hawaii Press. I have profited from their critiques and their warm support.

My sponsors through all this research were the Indonesian Institute of the Sciences (LIPI) and the University of Udayana in Bali. Funding was given by the Social Science Research Council, the National Science Foundation (grant nos. BNS 81-12418, BNS 84-05549, and BNS 83-14361), the Wenner-Gren Foundation, the American Council of Learned Societies, and the Princeton University Committee on Research. I am deeply grateful to all of them.

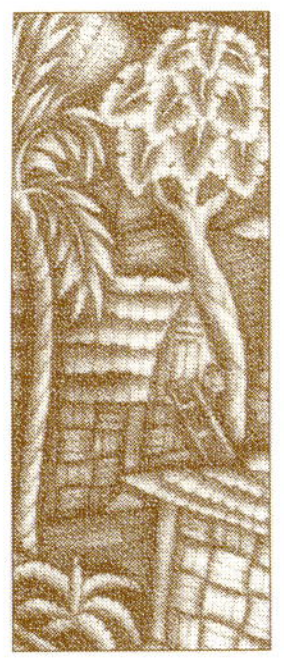

Balinese Names and Terms

Balinese names have three main parts, the person's title, a birth-order name, and a personal name. Titles include I, indicating that the person is a commoner; Ida Bagus, indicating a noble of priestly rank; and Déwa (for a man) or Désak (for a woman), indicating a noble person of Déwa (Satria) rank. Gedé indicates that the person is of an important line within his clan. Another title, Anak Agung, was given to those Satria who held official positions in the Dutch government. The birth-order name gives the relation of the person to his or her siblings. First-born people are called Wayan or Putu, second-born Nyoman, third-born Madé, and fourth-born Ketut. The cycle begins again with the fifth-born, who is called Wayan or Putu again. The last name in the series is a personal name, of which some people have two for various reasons. There is only slight differentiation by name of men and women, and a woman does not change her name at marriage. Thus, I Madé Kalér is a commoner, third-born, named Kalér.

In Bali it is very impolite to refer to someone by his or her personal name alone. However, in keeping with Western customs, and to make it easier for the Western reader, I have done so after the first reference. Full names with titles are given with the pictures and in the appendix.

Spelling conventions for Indonesian languages were changed in 1963, but many people kept the old spelling of their names. I have modernized the spelling of titles and birth-order names, but retained the 1930s spelling of the personal names. The changes were (old spelling first): *dj* = *j*, *j* = *y*, *oe* = *u*, *tj* = *c*. For instance Djatasoera would now be written Jatasura, Njoman is now written Nyoman, and Tjeta is now Ceta.

In spelling Balinese terms I have followed the authority of the major Balinese dictionary, *Kamus Bali-Indonesia*, published by Dinas Pendidikan Dasar, Propinsi DATI I BALI, 1978/1989.

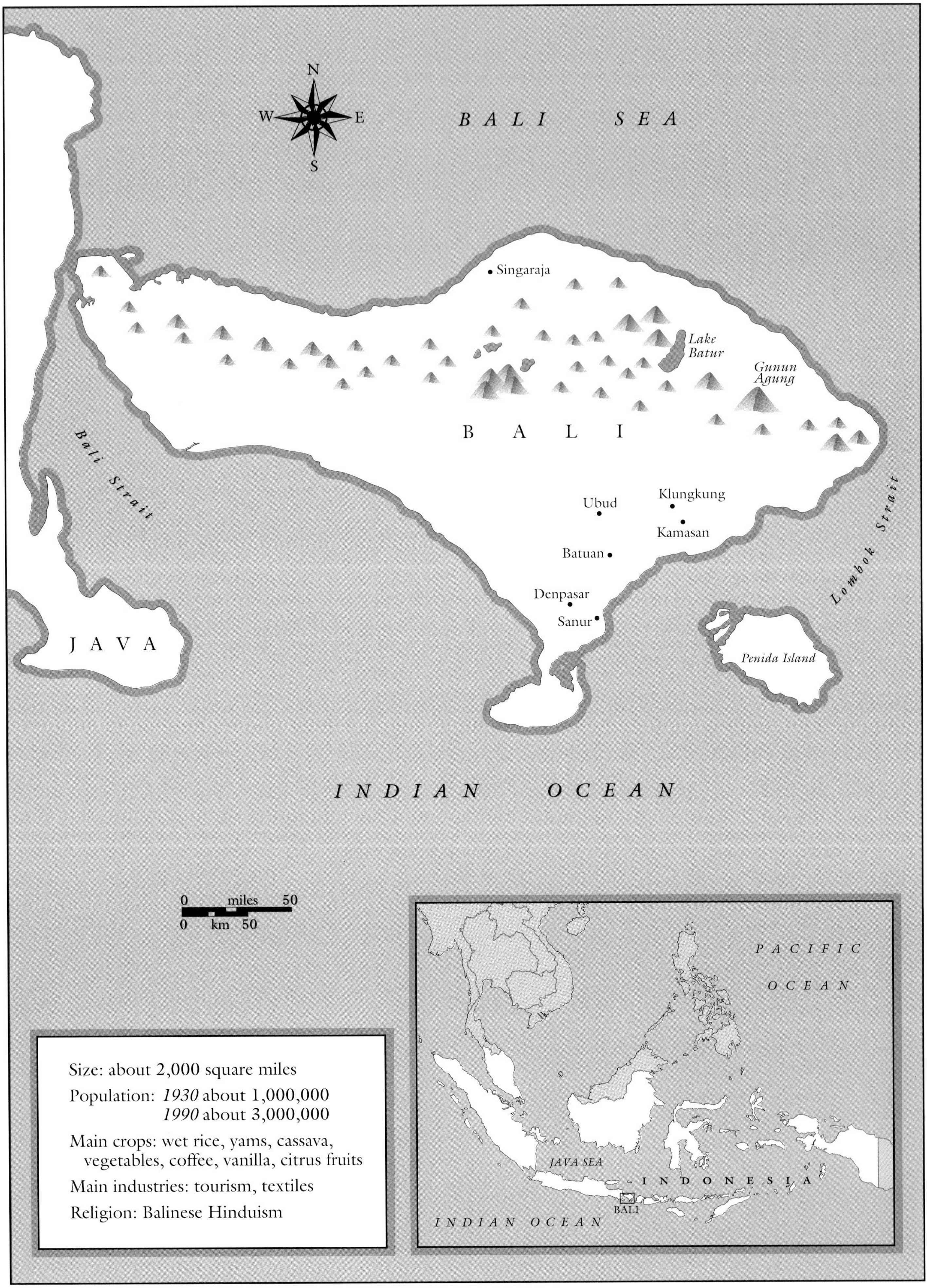

N
W
E
S

BALI SEA

Singaraja

Lake Batur

Gunun Agung

B A L I

Bali Strait

Ubud

Klungkung

Kamasan

Batuan

Denpasar

Sanur

Lombok Strait

J A V A

Penida Island

INDIAN OCEAN

0 miles 50
0 km 50

Size: about 2,000 square miles

Population: *1930* about 1,000,000
1990 about 3,000,000

Main crops: wet rice, yams, cassava, vegetables, coffee, vanilla, citrus fruits

Main industries: tourism, textiles

Religion: Balinese Hinduism

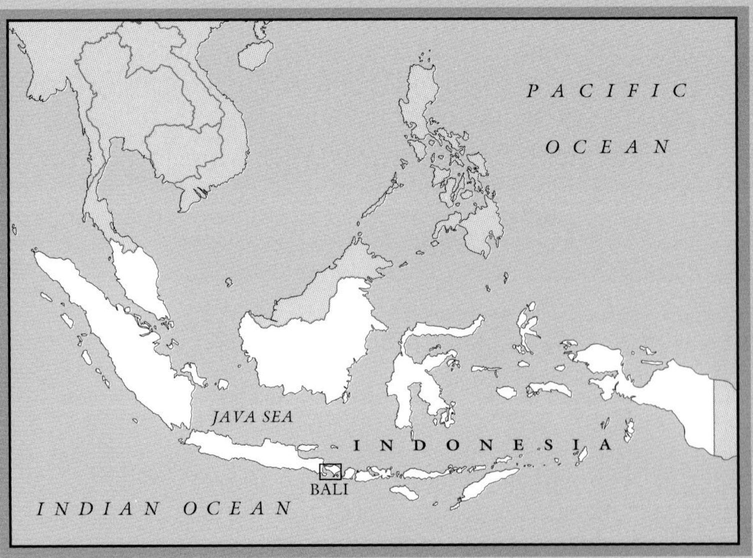

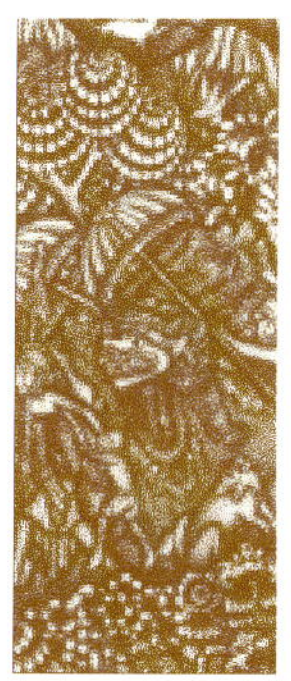

Introduction

Around 1931, a couple of young Balinese peasants tried their hands at painting Western-style pictures on paper. They had seen visiting European artists at work, borrowed their materials, and tentatively created a few paintings of their own. The foreign tourists bought them eagerly, so these young men made more and taught their friends the new craft as well. They drew tropical landscapes of rice paddies and volcanoes, Hindu festivals, highly stylized dances, and busy, crowded villages—all the colorful spectacles that foreigners saw and enjoyed. These 1930s pictures were the precursors of today's tourist art.

In 1936, the anthropologists Gregory Bateson and Margaret Mead arrived in Bali with plans for a two-year study of Balinese character. Seeing some of the new Western-style paintings, they decided to study them and their makers for evidence of their psychological tendencies. Bateson and Mead collected more than twelve hundred paintings and made documentary notes on most of them.

During the years of Mead and Bateson's research (1936–1938, with a brief visit in 1939), Bali formed part of a Dutch colony, the Netherlands East Indies. The Dutch had gained sovereignty over Bali through a series of bloody wars between 1846 and 1908. With colonial rule came the building of roads, government offices, elementary schools, and hotels. By the 1930s a small community of Western artists was living permanently in Bali, and a small but steady flow of tourists passed through. Several of the resident artists began to urge their young Balinese friends to paint and, later, helped sell the pictures to other visitors.

World War II interrupted the Balinese experiments with painting. After the war, a politically turbulent period ensued during which the present autonomous Republic of Indonesia was established and new governing and commercial institutions were set up. In the late 1960s tourists again began flooding into Bali, and picture making, which had dwindled in the interim, suddenly swelled with that tide. The look of the postwar products, however, is very different from that of the prewar period. The pictures that travelers purchase today are, for the most part, brighter and larger, and although there are many different styles and genres, the subject matter is much more standardized.

In the 1930s three main villages were producing paintings on paper. One was Ubud, up in the cool foothills, where most of the resident foreign artists settled. Another was Sanur, on the beach, where a few foreigners had built houses, and others came to swim. The paintings produced in Ubud and Sanur were more specifically tailored to Westerners' tastes than were the paintings made in the third village, Batuan, where tourists rarely visited. Remaining somewhat apart from Westerners, the Batuan painters followed a different route. My curiosity about where they went with their paintings led me to center my own research and this book on the work of the painters of Batuan.

Making drawings with paper, pen, and brush was foreign to these Balinese in the 1930s, for there was little in their traditional art forms that resembled this European genre. The Western artists who stimulated the Balinese to draw and paint saw a painting as something made to stand alone, sharply cut off from the life around it, hanging on a wall. But the few Balinese paintings that existed at the time had been made to contribute to ritual activities, primarily as cloth hangings in temples. Most Balinese artworks, unlike their Western counterparts, are made as elements in rituals, with the elaborate musical and dramatic dance performances leading the way. These new paintings had nothing to do with such religious activities.

Because of its freedom from ritual responsibility, this new art did not draw directly on older Balinese painting styles. Furthermore, there were few exemplars of traditional Balinese painting for the novice painters to study by the 1930s, since most temple congregations had already replaced their older temple hangings with imported fabrics of brighter colors. The one village that continued to make temple paintings, Kamasan, lay quite distant from Batuan. For all these reasons, few of the images in the new genre were adopted from traditional Balinese paintings. The Batuan paintings were novel in manner even when they depicted old folktales and myths.

Though stimulated by naturalistic Western photographs and paintings of scenes of Bali, these works from Batuan cannot be viewed as simple reports on the visible characteristics of Balinese society, for with some exceptions their makers did not attempt self-conscious depictions of the externals of their life. In addition, their coverage of their world is very selective. Rather than providing materials for an ethnography of Bali, the paintings from the village of Batuan give instead an ethnography of Balinese imaginations.

Each painting is an individual statement by a young person of Bali at a particular historical moment. Most of them are phrased within a language of narratives—of folktales about princes and princesses but also of eventful actual confrontations with spirits and sorcerers—that needs translation and interpretation. They have put their lives before our eyes, if we can find the means to see them.

As personal documents, many of the Batuan paintings reveal a profound concern with disaster and suffering (crop failure, illness, moral breakdown of the community). Anyone who has lived in Bali for any length of time knows that the fear of the sorcery of fellow villagers, and the dread of godly or ancestral wrath governs much of everyday life. These works, in sometimes horrifying ways, give vivid images of this pervasive anxiety, which is normally hidden behind a happy facade of courtesy. The usual idea of Bali as a paradise of contented sensualism or balanced equanimity is given a jarring challenge.

At the same time, the paintings tell about the formidable powers that healers, priests, and kings have for averting or curing such afflictions. They can do this through a special kind of mystical "power," which is, in Balinese thought, a capacity to harm, heal, protect, or benefit individuals or communities through techniques that I call, for want of a better English term, "sorcery." That spiritual power is sometimes referred to by Balinese as *sakti.*

The people of Bali today call their religion "Balinese Hinduism" after a major strand in a complexly woven web of symbols, ideas, and ceremonies. The names of Hindu deities, demons, and heroes—Siva and Durga, Vishnu and Brahma, Rama and Ravana, Arjuna and his brothers, Ganesha, and others—appear frequently in the prayers, songs, dramas, temple carvings, and paintings. A knowledge of their original significance can help only partially in interpreting contemporary Balinese religious life, for they have been absorbed and reinterpreted within Balinese thought and ritual. Blended with indigenous cosmological conceptions, with important augmentations from Tantric Buddhism, and even, in the present century, with indirect influences from Islam and Christianity, these Hindu traces today have very different meanings than in India.

The Batuan pictures, taken as an interconnected whole and against the background of Balinese culture in general, have suggested to me that an inner purpose of all Balinese rituals is the mobilization of the mystical power called *sakti.* To my own surprise, as a long-time student of Balinese religious life, these pictures have given me an entirely new view of it through a recognition of the central motivating importance of sorcery, a complex of ideas that most Western writings have assumed to be peripheral to Balinese religion.

Balinese temple rituals are, in this view, best understood as ways to use *sakti* to protect the temple congregation. These ceremonies are carried out largely by local communities and family groups, and involve works of music, drama, dance, costume making, literature, painting, and sculpture. They aim to build protective walls and attract spiritual guardians against the predations of all those—humans as well as nonhumans—who can use their magical potency to afflict others with dire sufferings and death. The Batuan pictures portray all sorts of what I call "sorcerers"—holy men, priests, kings, warriors, and witches—sometimes in violent conflict with one another. The images portray terror, but also courage; defeat, but also victory; war, but also peace; weakness, but also strength. Their settings are not merely the magical worlds of stories and myths, but also, by implication, the real world of everyday life. This "real" world, for the Balinese, is pervaded by invisible spirits, both malevolent and benevolent, all in combat with one another and with human beings.

Strong evidence that the subjects of these paintings were closely related to personal dread of other people's malevolent potency appears in an unusual set of illustrations of the dreams of one of the artists. Bateson and Mead invited Ida Bagus Madé Togog to illustrate his own dreams and to dictate an account of each one. They may have intended to perform a psychoanalytic analysis of his dreams, but they never did so. I have not attempted to interpret the concealed meanings of Togog's dreams, but rather have studied their manifest subject matter, which in itself reveals much about Togog's daily life and conscious concerns. Many of his dreams are about demonic beings and the dreamer's ability, through his own inner mystical strength, to vanquish them. At least one dream concerns the dreamer's spiritual training to become a sorcerer capable of healing or harming others. Any Balinese who had such dreams would assume that they were signs of his own increasing mystical competence. It is striking that the other paintings produced by Togog at the same time as his dream accounts are also about struggles among various kinds of sorcerers.

It might seem ironic that these young peasant men who were illustrating their fantasies about acquiring the power to harm or help their fellows lived in a colonial situation where they were essentially powerless. Some of the tales they illustrated are of their former kings, who reigned in Bali until this century, each one endowed with, or with access to, the mystical power of *sakti.* By the time the pictures were made, all those former kings were considered to have lost their mystical power, as proven by their defeat in this century by what were considered to be spiritually weak foreigners, the Dutch. But the term *sakti* cannot properly be translated as "power" if taken as merely the capacity to control other people's actions, as in the usual Western political sense of the word. Rather, *sakti* is the capacity to join in the mortal combat of the competing forces of the universe in order to secure an envelope of safety around oneself and those near one. The greatest of Balinese kings all had this mystical potency, but so did many others, even commoners.

In writing about Balinese conceptions of the world in a language as foreign to them as English, I am handicapped by the available terminology, which is itself enmeshed in associations long related to Western philosophy and theology. Thus the terms "mystical," "magical," and "spiritual" for many readers have connotations of imaginary, unscientific, and impractical. Other terms such as "gods," "demons," and "sorcerers" imply either essential goodness or evilness, an idea that is quite contrary to Balinese notions, for whom all beings are capable of both. When I use such terms, and others such as "spirit," "deity," and "witch," the reader should keep in mind that they signify ambivalent beings who in Balinese thinking are capable of *both* harming and healing, attacking and protecting, according to particular circumstances. The nature of the various spiritual beings with whom Balinese traffic, as well as the notion of the kinds of "power" that can be had over them, will become clearer in later chapters.

The pictures Bateson and Mead collected are best understood as bicultural products, bound up in the meaning systems and aesthetic ideas of several cultures at once. Made within Western pictorial conventions, they draw almost entirely from Balinese culture for their images. This dual ancestry had uneven effects on the pictures, since their makers did not understand the Western tradition of pictorial art very deeply. They saw the few examples of European drawing and painting that made their way to Bali, but through eyes that had been complexly trained within their own culture. Yet, for the painters of the village of Batuan at least, adoption of certain Western conventions seems to have given them a new way to look at themselves and their lives.

These Batuan paintings are intricate works, which can be read only through an understanding of the complex multicultural situation of their making and of both enfolding cultures—that of their foreign viewers and that of their makers. The dilemma for those who look long at these drawings and paintings today has its source in their ambiguous bicultural nature. We uneasily ask ourselves questions: What in them comes from the desire of their makers to please foreigners? What derives from their own cultural preoccupations, their own aesthetic values, and their own ways of seeing? How much did these painters simplify their subjects and prettify the images they confected in order to satisfy purchasers whom they saw as ignorant, godless, and tasteless? When I look at their works, am I projecting onto them my own, perhaps romantic, notions of what Bali and the Balinese are, or were at that time? I have met these concerns in the only way that I know—through a redoubling of my efforts as an anthropologist to get at implicit Balinese views of life and the world.[1]

A selection of paintings from the Bateson-Mead Collection forms the backbone of this book, which is organized according to its developing story. As I guide the reader through this imaginary gallery, I provide some of the contextual information needed for a deeper understanding of each work.[2]

Chapter 1, "Inventing an Art—Both Balinese and Western," describes the origin of the pictures, their relationship to traditional Balinese pictorial arts and to the paintings and drawings of the Western patrons whom the Batuan painters watched at work, and the influence of the anthropologists who bought the paintings.

Chapter 2, "The Everyday World of (Mere) Appearances," presents the paintings made by the Batuan people that were closest to the European expectations of a "folk art." Through these pictures, a preliminary understanding of Balinese life can be reached.[3] Most of these "scenes of everyday life" are, in fact, of rituals and dance-drama performances central to Balinese experience. And the most important source of images and themes of the Batuan paintings was precisely there: in the meanings of the rituals and in the commentaries on them that the accompanying dance-dramas provided.

Chapter 3, "The Magical Story World," tells a number of stories from Balinese dance-dramas and family tale tellings that the Batuan painters illustrated. These stories and their illustrations reveal a great deal about Balinese notions of mystical power and the means that human beings have to gain access to it.

Chapter 4, "The Real World of Dangerous Powers," takes the reader further into the heart of Balinese imaginations through an examination of one central narrative, the story of the Sorcerer-Queen, Calon Arang, and a key set of rituals having to do with sorcerers and sorcery.

Chapter 5, "Masters of *Sakti* Powers," explores the painters' reflections on the human power to triumph over death and destruction in the world.

Chapter 6, "Crossing Cultures," returns to the problems involved in studying bicultural pictures, and the painters' awareness of the anomalous nature of their works. Taken all together, these paintings provide complex interpretations of the deeper meanings underlying the outer visible shell of Balinese life.

I am convinced that it would be a mistake to dismiss these early Balinese pictures as mere tourist art, manufactured "souvenirs" of a Bali that exists only in tourists' eyes. It would be an equally serious mistake to assume that they are directly expressive, that they speak to us simply and intimately across the cultural barriers. Only through careful explication of the major references and allusions of these images can we outsiders begin to understand the worlds that they invoke and, at the same time, create.

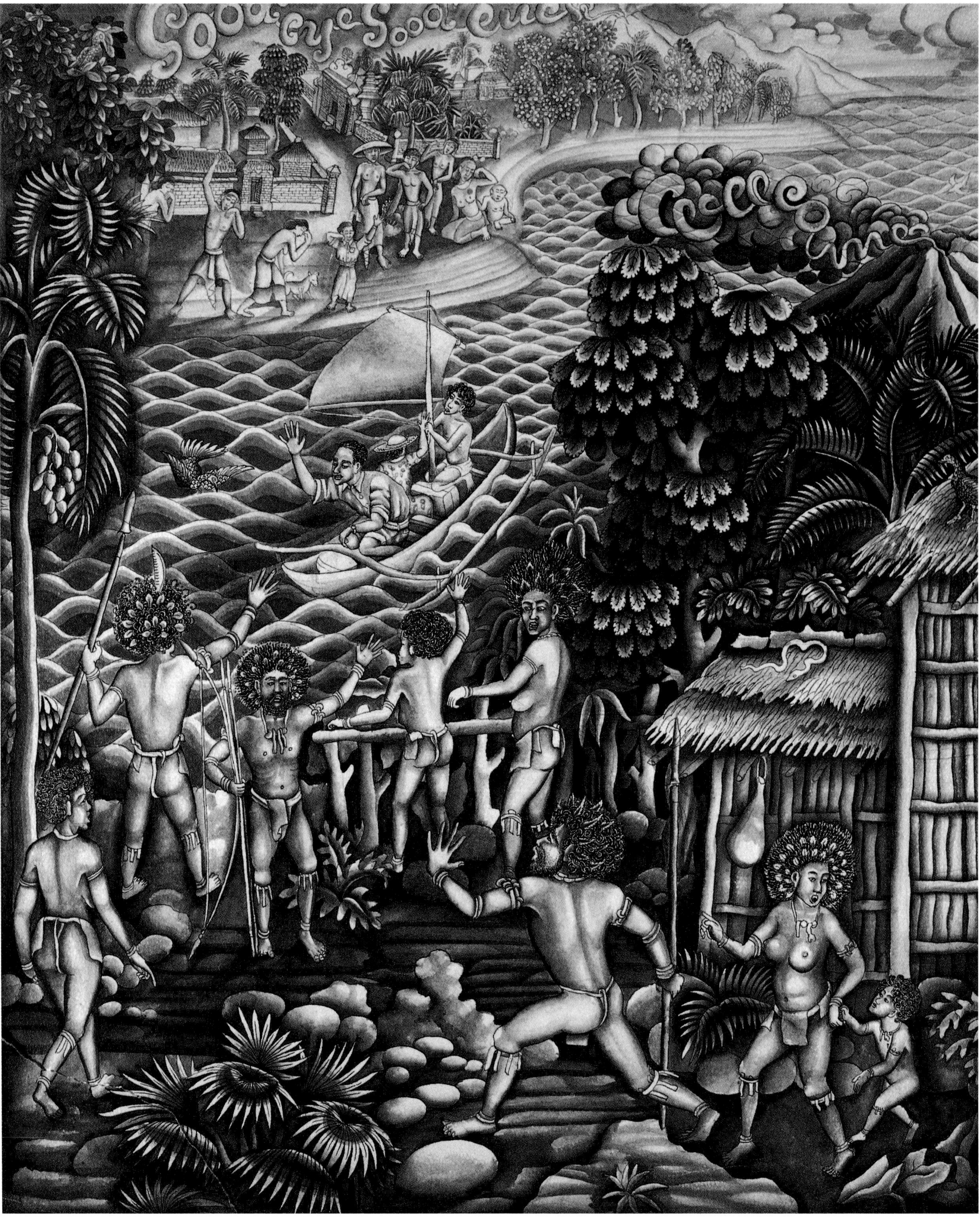

Chapter 1

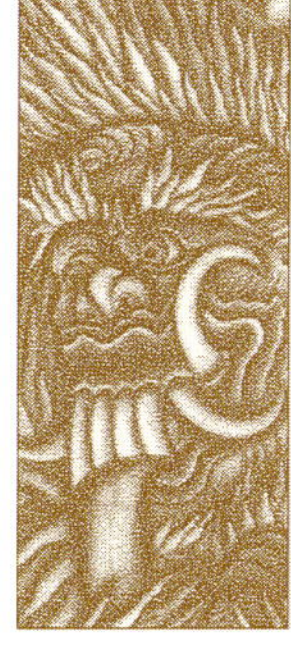

Inventing an Art—Both Balinese and Western

The picture facing, created by I Ketut Ngéndon, one of the leaders of the Batuan painters, shows Gregory Bateson and Margaret Mead in a small boat leaving Bali for a new research site in New Guinea. It was commissioned as a going-away present by their Balinese field assistant who had worked with them for two years.

Ngéndon drew the assistant standing on the Balinese shore, in a Western shirt but a Balinese skirtlike sarong, wiping away his tears and waving. Near him are other Balinese in dramatically mournful stances.

Ngéndon and several of his friends, a few years before making this painting, learned the techniques of using pen and brush to put ink on paper from two European artists, Walter Spies and Rudolf Bonnet, who had made their homes in Bali in the late 1920s. These two modern Gauguins found in Bali a delightful paradise, marveling at the "artistic genius" of the culture and reveling in its sensuousness and grace. They persuaded their Balinese acquaintances that they, too, could make paintings; provided the young peasants with paper, pens, and brushes; and later marketed their pictures to Western travelers in Bali. By the time Mead and Bateson arrived, this tourist art was well underway.

The pair of anthropologists had gone to Bali in March 1936 with plans to spend two years studying the nature and formation of "Balinese character." Mead, an American, and Bateson, an Englishman, had met while doing research in New Guinea, and had worked out together a theory of human personality types and their relation to cultural differences. They had decided that Bali would provide a crucial comparative test case with the cultures of New Guinea, as the Balinese had a personality type not found in New Guinea. They had heard of the European artist Walter Spies, who, while not painting, was doing an ethnography of dance and drama in Bali, and they asked him for help in locating a site for study.

When Bateson and Mead first disembarked in Bali, they at once motored over the central volcanic massif directly to Spies' village home in Ubud. They stayed there for two months while studying the Balinese language and arranging to move into the mountain village where they were to spend a year. Soon Spies introduced them to the new Balinese paintings from various villages. Those from the lowland village of Batuan attracted Bateson and Mead's particular attention, and they quickly decided to make a side study of the paintings and their makers, hoping through them to find insight into the inner feelings of Balinese.

Over a period of three years they collected 1,288 pictures, of which 845 came from the village of Batuan. Each painting was given a date, and its maker identified and usually also interviewed about its content. Toward the end of their stay in Bali, the anthropologists decided to move down from the mountain village where they had concentrated their psychological researches to Batuan in the lowlands for several months. While there, they intensified their study of the picture makers. Their assistant, I Madé Kalér, administered a detailed questionnaire to twenty-three painters about their artistic training and life situations. Bateson and Mead wrote little on their study of the painters of Batuan.[1] In 1981 I went to Batuan to build on their research. Some of the painters were still alive, and I could talk with them and study the social and cultural contexts within which they worked.

In the Bateson-Mead Collection from Batuan there are paintings and drawings by seventy-one different people, but only about thirty of them made more than one crude and simple picture. Some were mere children, copying the work of their elders. However, there was a core group of about twenty-two serious painters who made numerous paintings and, over the period of study, exhibited considerable growth in skill and originality of vision. These painters, who all knew one another and often painted together, are the people whose work appears in this book.

The Batuan painters made highly diverse pictures of even more variety than could be shown here. In large part the diversity was due to the novelty of the form. They had not yet

OPPOSITE: *Goodbye and Good Luck to Margaret Mead and Gregory Bateson*
I Ketut Ngéndon

The anthropologists Margaret Mead and Gregory Bateson are imagined seated in a catamaran, crossing the sea between the two cultures they were studying. Commissioned in 1938 as a parting gift from their Balinese research assistant, this picture shows the Balinese, in the background, waving farewell, while a group of New Guinea people, in the foreground, happily greet them.

Behind the beach of Bali are palm trees, village walls, and volcanoes looming above. The smoke from the volcanoes of Bali at the top of the picture spells out the words "goodbye" and "good luck," while the smoke from the volcano in New Guinea says "welcome." The New Guinea village must have been modeled on photographs borrowed from the anthropologists, for the artist could not otherwise have known what it looked like.

developed strong craft-wide norms for what the paintings should look like, nor clear ideas as to what would or would not sell. After World War II a greater standardization of topic and style would develop in Batuan. The high variation in the kinds of pictures made in Batuan came in part from the artists' different family backgrounds. Some were sons of high Brahmana families (from which the traditional priests and scholars of Bali come) and consequently had detailed experience with religious practice and imagery. Others had dancers and musicians in their families and were familiar with the narratives and characters of the dance-dramas. Four had had training in making the ornate cut-out shadow puppets of deities and demons, the iconography of which they used in their pictures, but most had no training at all in the pictorial arts.[2] Some, like Togog, made paintings of folktales, revealing a rich knowledge of many different ones, while others were content to repeat a few well-known tales.

Made expressly for Westerners, the new paintings are like briefly overheard fragments from ongoing conversations between the Balinese and the foreigners in an intercultural situation in which each side only partially understood the expectations of the other. As communications the paintings were given form by presuppositions of both cultures. Each picture was an experiment, often clumsy and ill-conceived, in pulling images and themes from both sides, but joined together in an expressive whole. The Balinese were guessing what might please their customers, yet having to please themselves as well. Just as the anthropologists were crossing the boundaries between cultures, so too were their Balinese protégés, who were in the midst of inventing a bicultural art.

Indigenous Models

What were the models the Balinese looked to in concocting these new drawings? What exactly did they take from their own pictorial traditions? And what from the Westerners? The first and most obvious places to go for answers to these questions are to temple hangings, large painted cloths illustrating sacred narratives that used to festoon the walls and eaves of temple and palace buildings.[3] Surprisingly, the new painters, whether from Batuan or elsewhere, took little directly from these temple paintings, either for style or for subject matter.

In the traditional paintings shown on page 7, stiff figures stand against white backgrounds, their faces presented in a standard three-quarters view. There is no differentiation between foreground and background; all the figures are on one plane. Single trees stand alone between ornately dressed personages rather than as in the 1930s Batuan works, in clumps around the edges of a scene. The white spaces are filled in with little teardrop-like motifs standing for atmosphere. Several different episodes in the story are given, each separated by decorative borders, resulting in a highly segmented overall composition. These paintings, as with all the traditional hangings, have a limited range of colors, bright red, blue, and gold. The stories in temple hangings are primarily highly respected myths from the heroic age of the Mahabharata and the Ramayana, Hindu epics from India. And within these stories, the episodes most often illustrated are those of royal ceremony. There are exceptions of course, such as depictions of war or rowdy commoner festivals, but even the most furious battle scenes have a repetitive and decorative quality.

In contrast, the paintings of the 1930s have agile figures moving about in naturalistic settings. Architectural forms are drawn with a simple perspective, even when the picture is not consistently organized from a single viewpoint. Most of the Batuan paintings are in black and white, but when color was employed, the artists used a much wider palette than the restricted traditional one.

Why is there this great difference between the traditional and the new pictures? In part, for the simple reason that very few examples of traditional paintings were around for young people to study in the 1930s. The few that were still being made came from a distant village, Kamasan near Klungkung. A case can be made that by the 1920s traditional cloth paintings were in little demand, having been replaced by cheaper, brighter, imported calicoes.

Another traditional kind of picture, which, however, could hardly ever be seen by laymen, were those found in the book-like manuscripts called *lontar.* These small strips of palm leaves were inscribed with a knife and the scratched letters then blackened with soot. *Lontar* made up libraries of classic texts of Balinese literature, healers' medical handbooks, and priests' ritual guides. Only occasionally were these writings illustrated. In Batuan several priestly houses had large collections of such books, but only a few consecrated priests and learned scholars were allowed to look at them.

Shadow puppets, for some of the painters, were a direct source of imagery. There was a shadow puppet maker in Batuan itself, named Déwa Putu Kebés, with whom several of the young picture makers had studied. (Making these puppets, and the decorated leather headdresses of dancers that resemble them, requires considerable training.) Few of the artists, however, chose this mode of drawing, preferring more naturalistic figures. One skilled puppet maker, I Reneh, used shadow puppet forms in some of his works. Ngéndon made one of this sort early in his career, but since he had no training, he must have asked someone else to make the basic sketch, which he then completed and sold. For most, the new genre of pictures provided the opportunity of a much freer mode of drawing figures, a mode that was not only easier but more expressive. But in drawing demons the Batuan people did turn to their memories of shadow puppets, as demons were one type of puppet that was already very free in form.

Other traditional arts that were generally available to the new painters were textiles and bas-relief temple carvings in stone. Here, too, the new painters were highly selective, and did not make mere transpositions from them. Instead, they seem to have adopted certain highly general stylistic features.

The marked reliance on line as opposed to the use of color or texture to delineate form is seen in all these paintings and is found in all traditional visual arts, from the Kamasan-type temple hangings to the temple wall carvings.

Another general characteristic of the new paintings is what might be called linear interweave. This is the pervasive style used in the decoration of stone and brick walls, wood architectural carvings, textiles, and gold and silver work. Intricately interwoven elements, such as plant forms, produce a lively

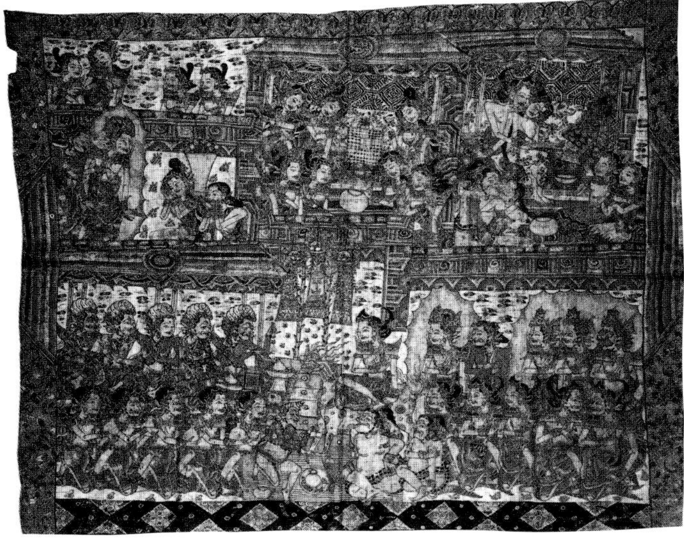

Traditional Painting
Artist unknown, from Kamasan, Klungkung, probably late 18th century
65.74 × 52.36 in.

The story of Arjuna Wiwaha. In the lower section, the hero Arjuna (center, seated on horse-like creature, wearing headdress with tail of hair arched up over top of head) is being praised by members of the royal court. At his feet are his two companions/servants. At the upper right Arjuna is making love with one of his wives, while below him his servant is doing the same with another servant.[4]

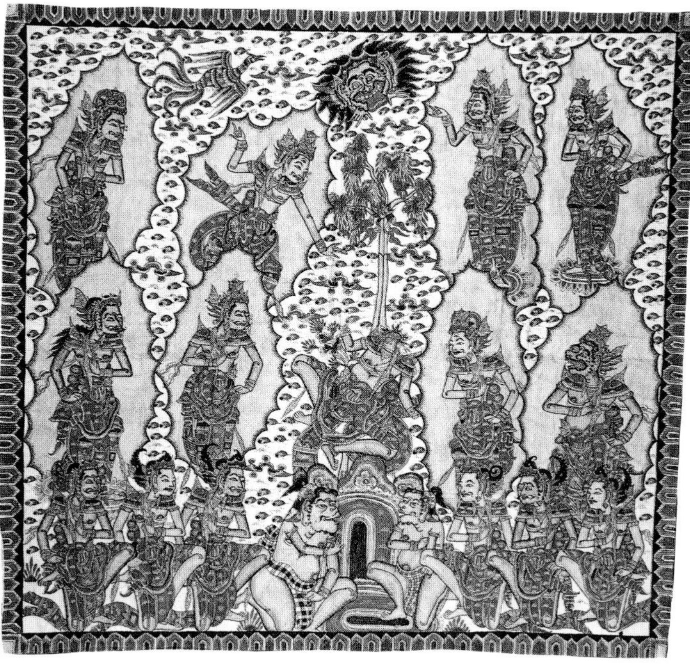

Traditional Painting
Artist unknown, from Kamasan, Klungkung
49.6 × 47.63 in.

The decapitation of the demon Kala Rahu. The figures surrounded by scalloped halos are gods. Wisnu, with arm extended, has just thrown his circular weapon, a *cakra*, at Kala Rahu, lower center, and cut off his head. The head is at the top center. This is an episode from an important myth that accounts for eclipses of the moon and sun, in which the demon, now reduced in form to his head, but still alive, periodically attempts to eat them.[5]

Traditional Drawing Etched on Dried Palm Leaf
Artist unknown, from Saba, Gianyar, date unknown
1.33 × 15.35 in.

Two episodes from an illustrated book of the story of the romantic hero, Panji. The picture on the left shows a princess on her bed in the palace. The one on the right shows the king of Koripan speaking with his bodyguard.[6]

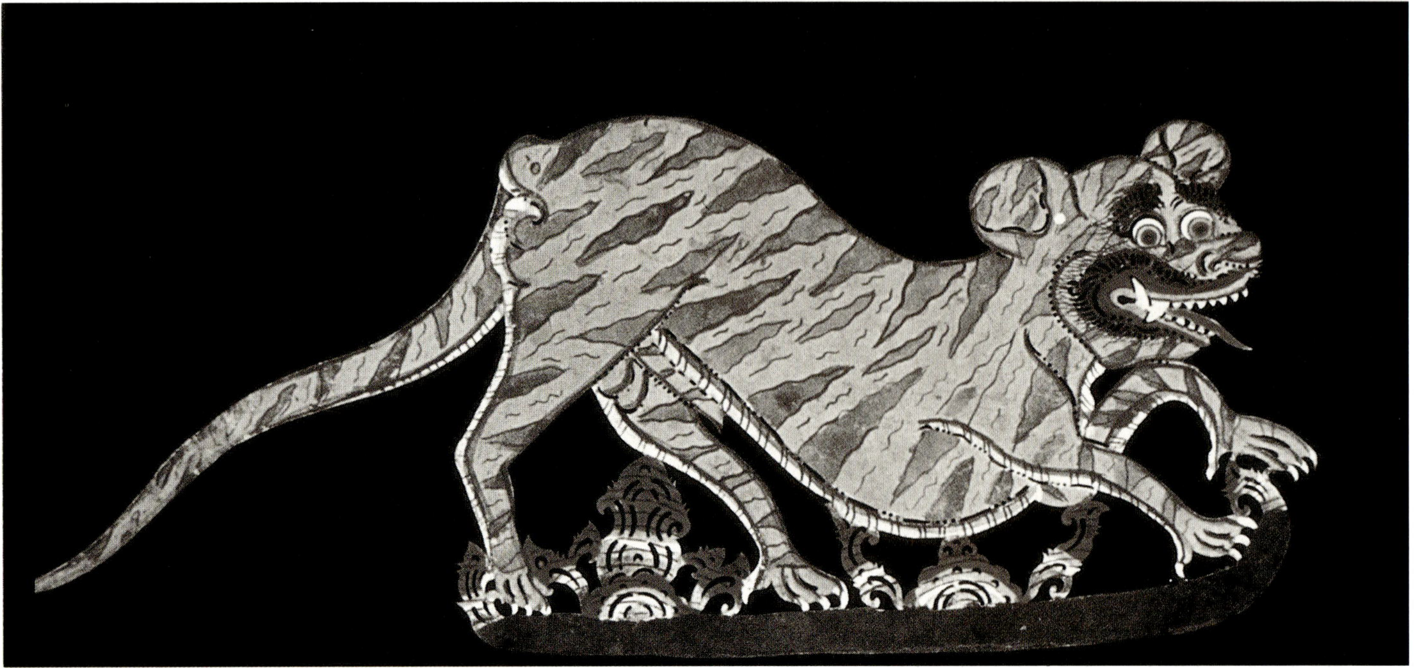

A tiger.

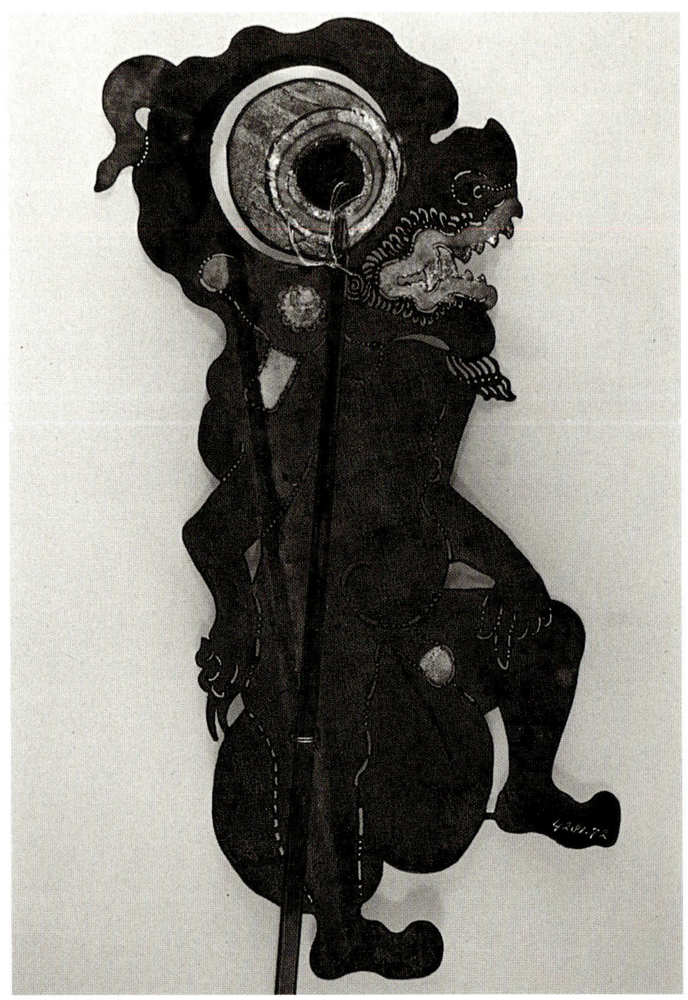

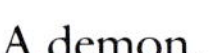

A demon.

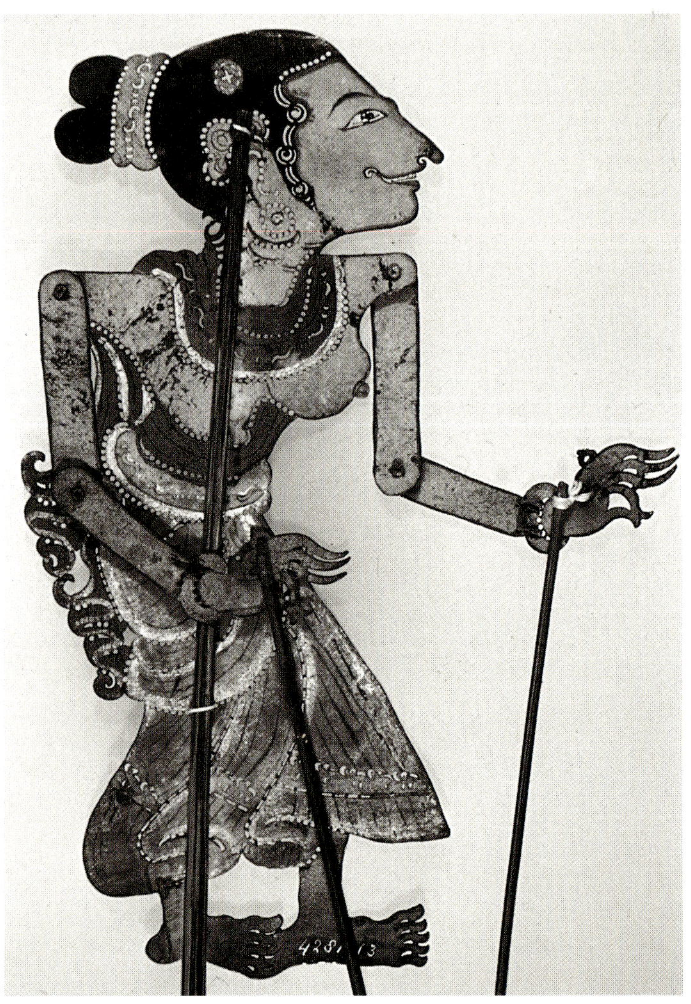

A servant woman *(condong)*.

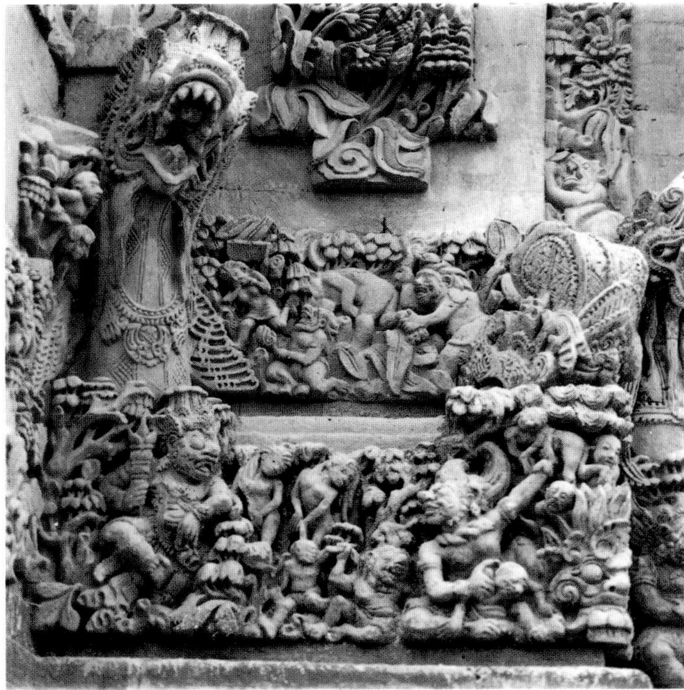

Stone Temple Carving
Artist unknown, from temple Pura Dalem in Lukluk, Badung, date unknown

The story of the god-like hero, Bima, who went into the other world *(suarga)* to rescue the souls of his dead father and mother. Bima is the figure with arm outstretched holding a woman (presumably his mother) aloft. The other figures near him are the demons who guard and torment their victims, all people who have done something wrong while in life. Compare with the picture on page 56.[7]

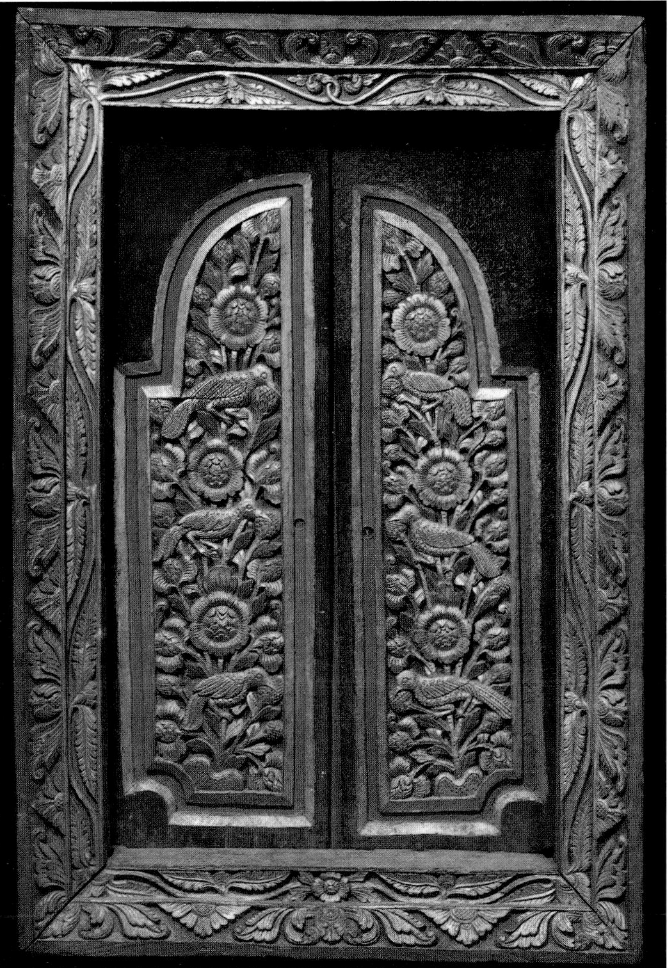

Carved Wooden Window Frame and Shutter, Painted with Gold Leaf
19.29 × 29.13 in.[9]

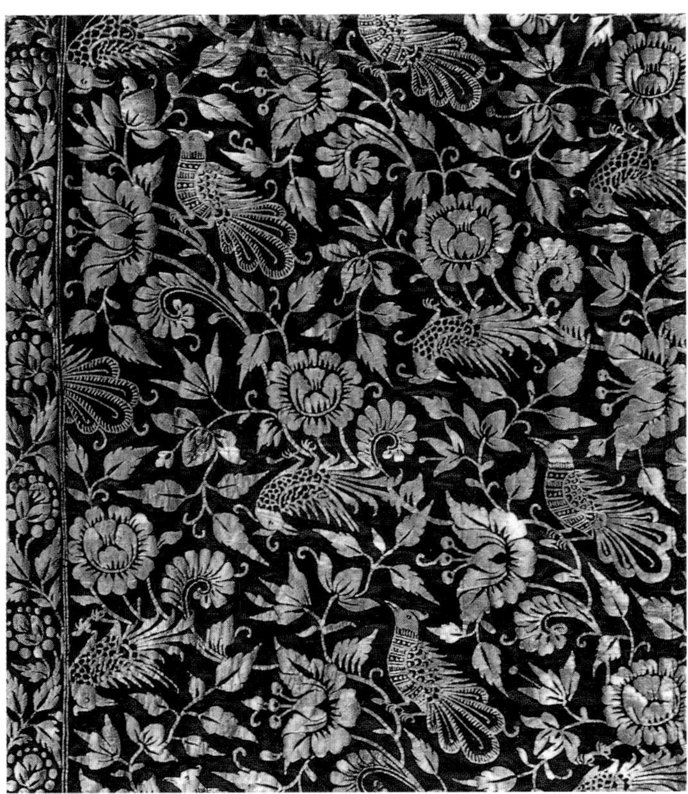

Ceremonial Cloth Painted with Gold Leaf Designs (perada)
Probably from Kamasan near Klungkung
63.77 × 54.72 in.[8]

filigree or arabesque effect. This feature of Balinese art is closely related to similar styles in other parts of Southeast Asia.

Examples of linear interweave can be found in the *perada*, or painted textiles. These cotton cloths on which designs were traced in gold paint are part of most costumes in Balinese drama. Several of the Batuan artists had been trained to make them. Their complicated floral patterns were a source of leaf, blossom, and bird forms used throughout the Batuan pictures. Their overall patterning effects may have also been an inspiration for the general look of the paintings.

Most of the new drawings are highly detailed and have repeated, rhythmic patterns of leaves and human forms spread over the entire paper. This stylistic characteristic mirrors the strong patterning in Balinese textiles and temple wall carvings. I believe it is based on a general Balinese value, what they call *ramé* and I call "copiousness." The Balinese word could also be translated as "plenitude," or as "busy, crowded sociability," or "excitement and fun." From their social life, much of which is organized to maximize the pleasant cooperation of many people, to their religious rituals, which entail preparing great numbers of identical offerings to the swarms of deities and demons that come for them, the Balinese make sure that there is always a constant buzz of activity around them. Their pleasure in being members of a crowd is always apparent. This pleasure in multiplicity and complexity marks almost every Balinese expressive form, not only the new genre of foreign-style drawings.[10]

Imported Models

The Batuan painters had seen some Western pictures, but how many and how often is uncertain. Important, perhaps, were the occasional small commercial pictures—advertising images on objects like matchboxes, illustrations in foreign magazines, and drawings in the new Balinese children's schoolbooks. More immediately significant for the making of the new art, however, were the paintings of the two European artists who were the main links to the outside world, Walter Spies and Rudolf Bonnet. A look at their works may shed light on the example they set. In addition, since Spies and Bonnet were the first viewers and purchasers of the new art, and as such could have had a strong formative influence in the kinds of paintings they selected for praise, a study of their own paintings may give us a glimpse of their taste in pictures in general.

Walter Spies was a German who spent his formative years in Moscow and was closely involved in the aesthetic ferment of Europe just before and after World War I. In a period when many painters were caught up in expressionism and abstractionism, Spies found his strongest early affinities in the work of Henri Rousseau and Marc Chagall. Interned as an enemy alien during World War I in a Tatar village in the Russian Caucasus, he developed an interest in folk music, lore, and art.

In 1922 Spies despaired of living a free life in a Europe that he felt was stuffy and bourgeois and fled to the Dutch East Indies. In 1927, he decided to live permanently in Bali. There he painted, studied the flora and fauna, and wrote an important book on Balinese dance and drama.[11] Spies' paintings show a strong mystical interest, and it is likely that he encouraged the Balinese to make pictures of their folktales and myths, as well as their everyday life.

A German art critic of the time termed Spies' painting style "magical realism."[12] I suspect that those Balinese who saw Spies' paintings did not see them as "magical" in any sense, and that they were more interested in their "realistic" aspects. The way that Spies painted leaves, each one independently, in great masses, which he may have adopted from Rousseau, could have influenced the Balinese. However, they had examples of their own in textiles. It seems to have been a case of a coincidental affinity, from which both Spies and the Batuan artists were reinforced in their predilection for the patterns made by leaves.

The other important European artist in the early development of the Balinese paintings was Rudolf Bonnet. Dutch born and academically trained in Haarlem and Amsterdam, Bonnet came to Bali soon after Spies, first briefly in 1929 and then permanently in 1931. Bonnet's pictures were much more naturalistic than Spies', and in fact Bonnet took it upon himself to teach several of the painters how to draw figures and buildings in perspective.

How much and what kind of influence Spies and Bonnet had on the painters of Batuan is debatable. A few painters of Ubud, the village region where Spies and Bonnet lived, were strongly affected.[13] In Batuan, only Ngéndon's drawings show clearly that he had studied their pictures, as for instance his picture of the tiger in the forest. And a number of the Batuan painters reported that Bonnet had given them advice on how to draw figures. An incomplete drawing by Togog shows evidence of the hand of a foreigner, most likely Bonnet, in the drawing of the nude woman. But none of Togog's other drawings show that he learned the anatomy lesson given him. The fact that the pictures made in Batuan and in other villages at the time have such a great variety shows that the European painters probably directly influenced only a small number of people.

What the Batuan artists did learn from Spies and Bonnet they could have picked up from looking at almost any Western picture: that is, how to make "naturalistic" pictures. This is a term that can be applied only in a relative sense in contrast to the "nonnaturalistic" modes of traditional Balinese art. Here I use it to refer to the manner of making rounded moving bodies and indicating distance through diminution of size and lightening of tone. "Naturalistic" here also refers

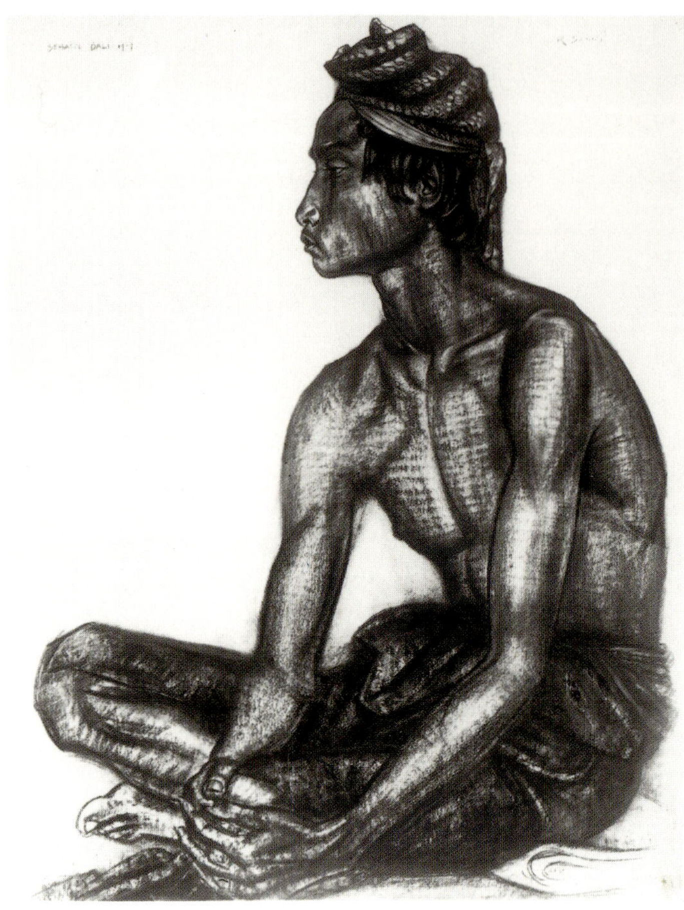

Seated Farmer in Sebatu (Bali)
Rudolf Bonnet, 1929
Pastel chalk on paper
Rudolf Bonnet Archives

OPPOSITE: *Tiger and Snake in Combat in a Primeval Forest*
Walter Spies, 1928–1929
Oil on canvas, 31.88 × 25.59 in.
Private Collection

This picture may depict a Balinese legend of a fight between a tiger and a snake. Neither the deer, the goat, nor the baboon is native to Bali. Spies referred to it in a letter as "a picture of a deer, an ape, a tiger, and a snake: a primeval forest with mangrove trees" (Feb. 1928, Rhodius [1964?], p. 258).

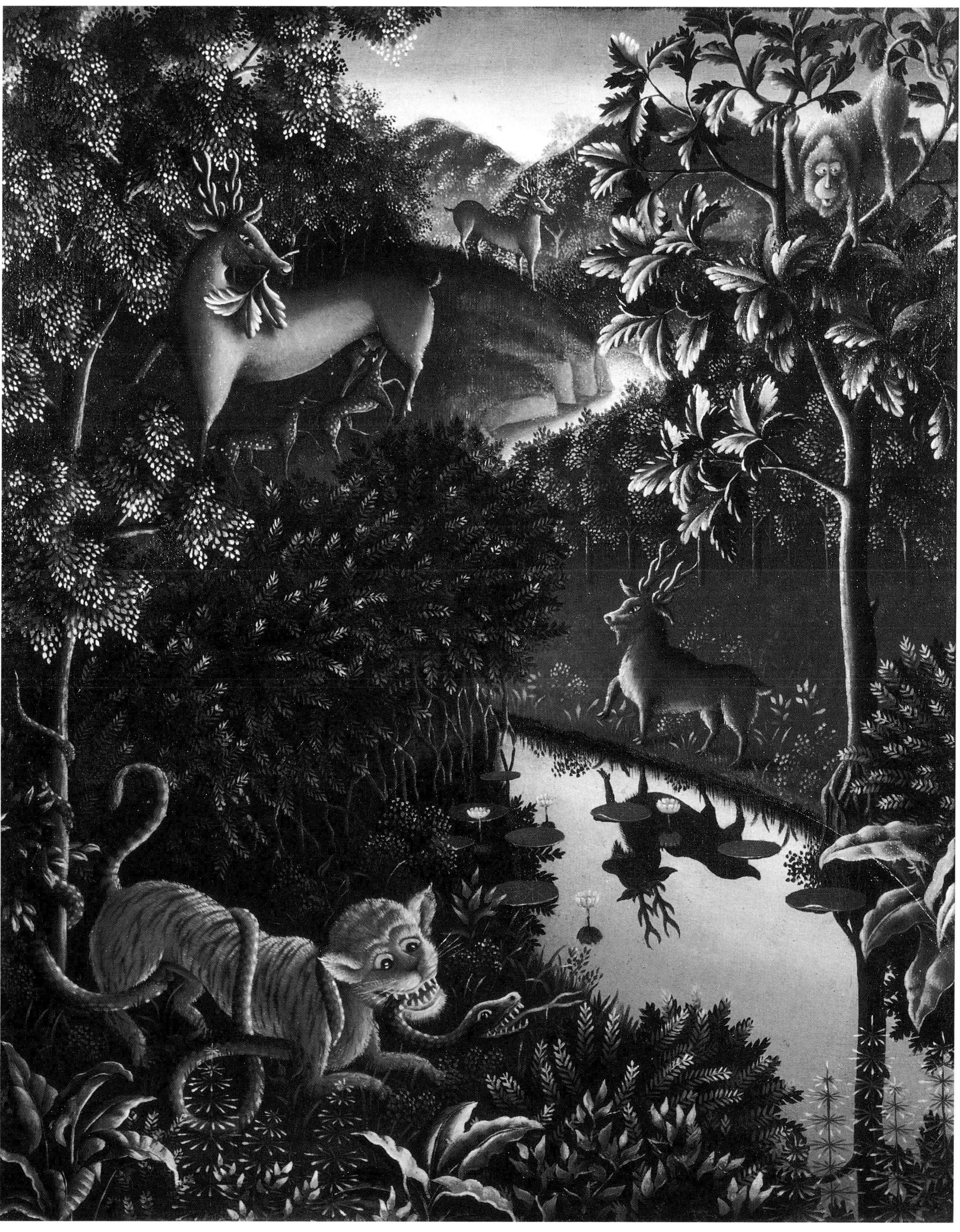

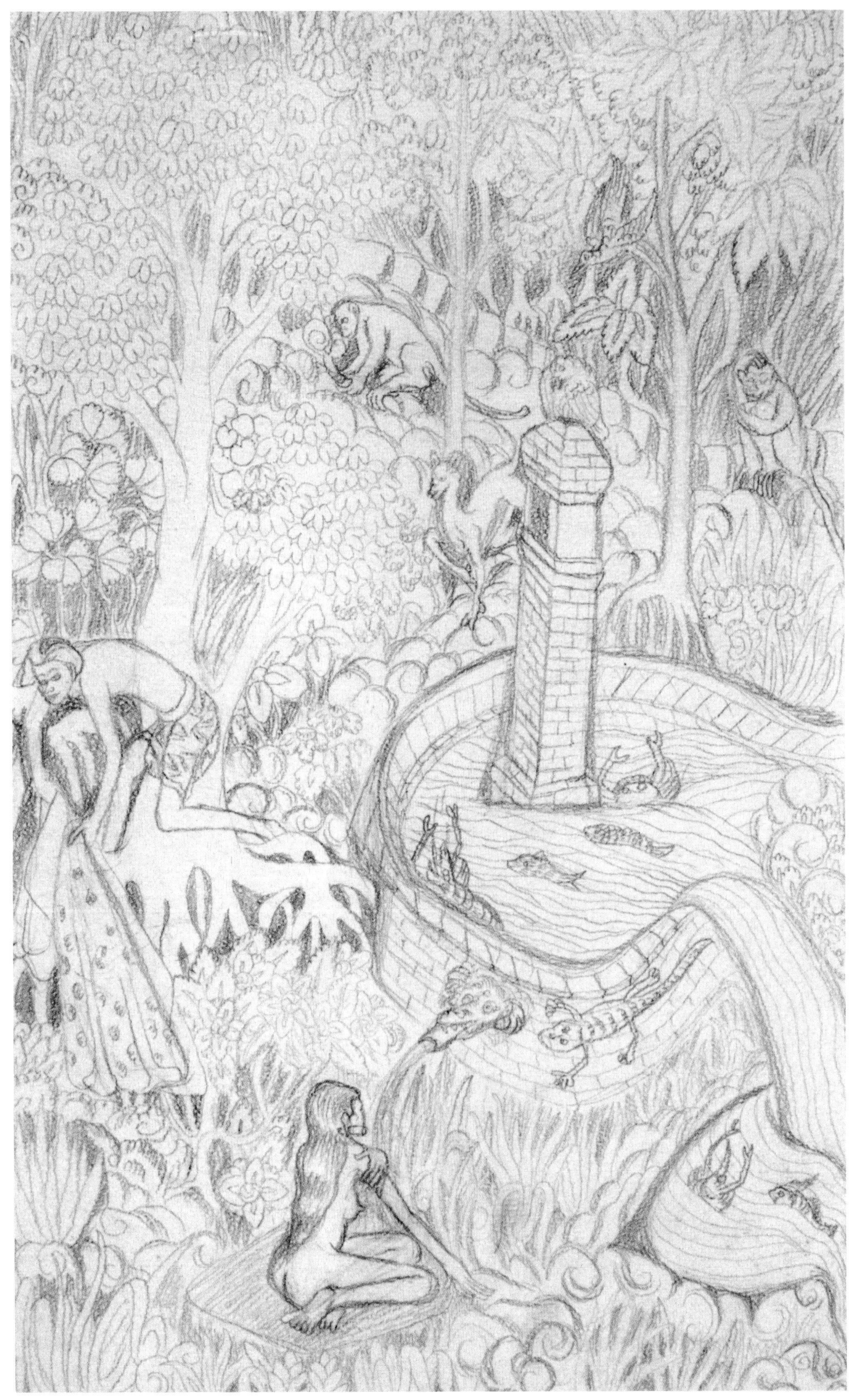

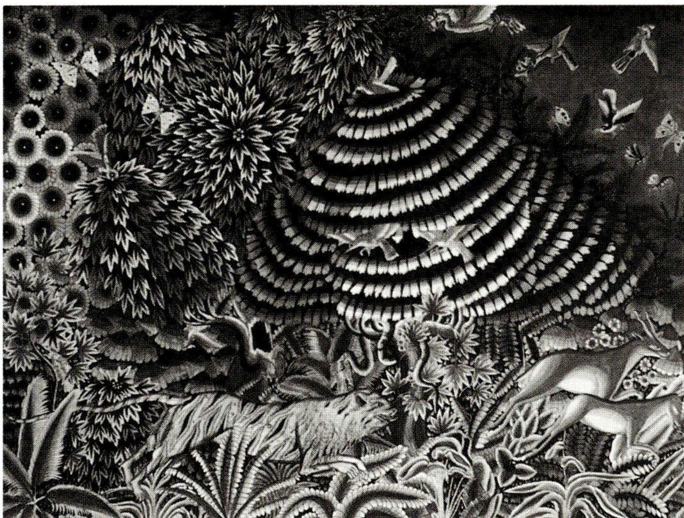

ABOVE: *The Tiger in the Forest*
I Ketut Ngéndon

This may be one of the first of Ngéndon's works. The tiger in this drawing resembles that of Spies' painting of a tiger. The sheep at top right seems to descend from one painted by Bonnet (not illustrated). There are no sheep in Bali.

to placing figures in settings that use Western notions of space so as to give an impression of "scenes" looked at from points outside the pictures. The use of perspective, no matter how clumsy, is a way of suggesting to the viewer that what is shown is an event that may have actually taken place, in a world that may have actually existed. Sometimes the picture makers took from Western pictures the compositional idea of a tree in the foreground, which frames the scene, or a river winding from the lower border to the upper part of the picture, which unites its various parts. These devices serve to connect the event portrayed with the world around it. In drawing folktales or myths, this naturalistic mode led the people of Batuan to depict princes and princesses as though they were ordinary people, dressed in ordinary clothing and doing ordinary activities. From a Western point of view these are hardly "naturalistic," and instead, perhaps, naive, but from a Balinese position they were revolutionary and sophisticated.

The Batuan painters' use of black and white alone may also have derived from foreign models. The consequent "darkness" of the pictures cannot be traced to Balinese traditional pictures, nor to some general Balinese value or personality characteristic, since Balinese taste always favors bright colors. Their temple festivals are riots of color, their clothing is bright, and their indigenous artworks, including sculpture, are almost always painted. After World War II, when access to imported tempera paints became easy, even the Batuan artists took up color.

The darkness of these paintings may have been encouraged by the Westerners. In fact, there is some evidence that Bonnet pressed the Batuan painters to keep working in black and white, possibly on the academic art-school principle that they would develop a firm grounding in good draftsmanship through several years of pen and pencil practice. Other Westerners apparently liked the Batuan black and white paintings too, perhaps because they were easily understood within their longstanding European traditions of black and white etchings, woodcuts, and charcoal drawings.

Then, too, the picture makers of Batuan were very poor, and tempera colors were too expensive for them to purchase. While picture makers from villages that lay near the residences of the Western painters had access to colored paints, the people of Batuan did not. When Mead and Bateson arrived in Bali in the late 1930s, their own funds were extremely limited because of the economic depression, and they bought only a few of the more expensive colored paintings.

Whatever their reasons, when the Batuan painters made their dark and moody monochrome drawings, they found that the works sold, and they continued to develop their art within this mode. If Westerners had not purchased the dark paintings, I am certain that the Batuan people would not have continued to make them. In fact, in postwar Bali, tempera paints were much more easily available, and most of the painters of Batuan made brightly colored works. After the war, Togog became known for sunny pictures of village festivities, as did nearly everyone else.

In the 1930s, the painters seem to have responded strongly to the blackness itself and to have sought subject matter appropriate to it. The choice of dark and violent themes may have been suggested to them by the ink's blackness, which evokes night and all the evil things that happen then. The pictures of ferocious combat and of terrible dangers may have come about, to some extent at least, through the historical accident of the unavailability of colored paints.

Tourists' Expectations

Ngéndon's "goodbye" drawing at the beginning of this chapter is typical of the most Westernized of these bicultural paintings. In fact, it presages a kind of picture that became especially important in Balinese tourist art after World War II: paintings portraying landscapes with figures that were largely slick in technique and shallow in substance, successful as colorful and decorative souvenirs of Balinese sights.

Ngéndon's picture, with its strong differentiation of foreground and background, use of perspective, lively portrayal of bodies in motion, and foliage forms, follows somewhat

OPPOSITE: *The Story of Truna Tua Stealing the Clothes of the Sky Nymph*
Ida Bagus Madé Togog

This is one of the first drawings by Togog that Bateson and Mead bought. At the bottom is a nude woman bathing, with penciled corrections of the anatomy made probably by Bonnet. Togog must have taken it to Bonnet for his help, and then to Mead and Bateson with more finished pictures. Bateson was very interested in purchasing incomplete works and probably asked Togog to give it to him unfinished.

The story, which Togog identified but did not tell, is a popular one among the Ubud painters because it gives a good opportunity to show a nude. It tells of an old bachelor who could not get any woman to marry him. He came upon a pool in the forest where a group of nymphs was bathing and stole the clothing of one of them so that she could not fly up to the sky where she lived. He forced her to agree to marry him before giving back her clothing.

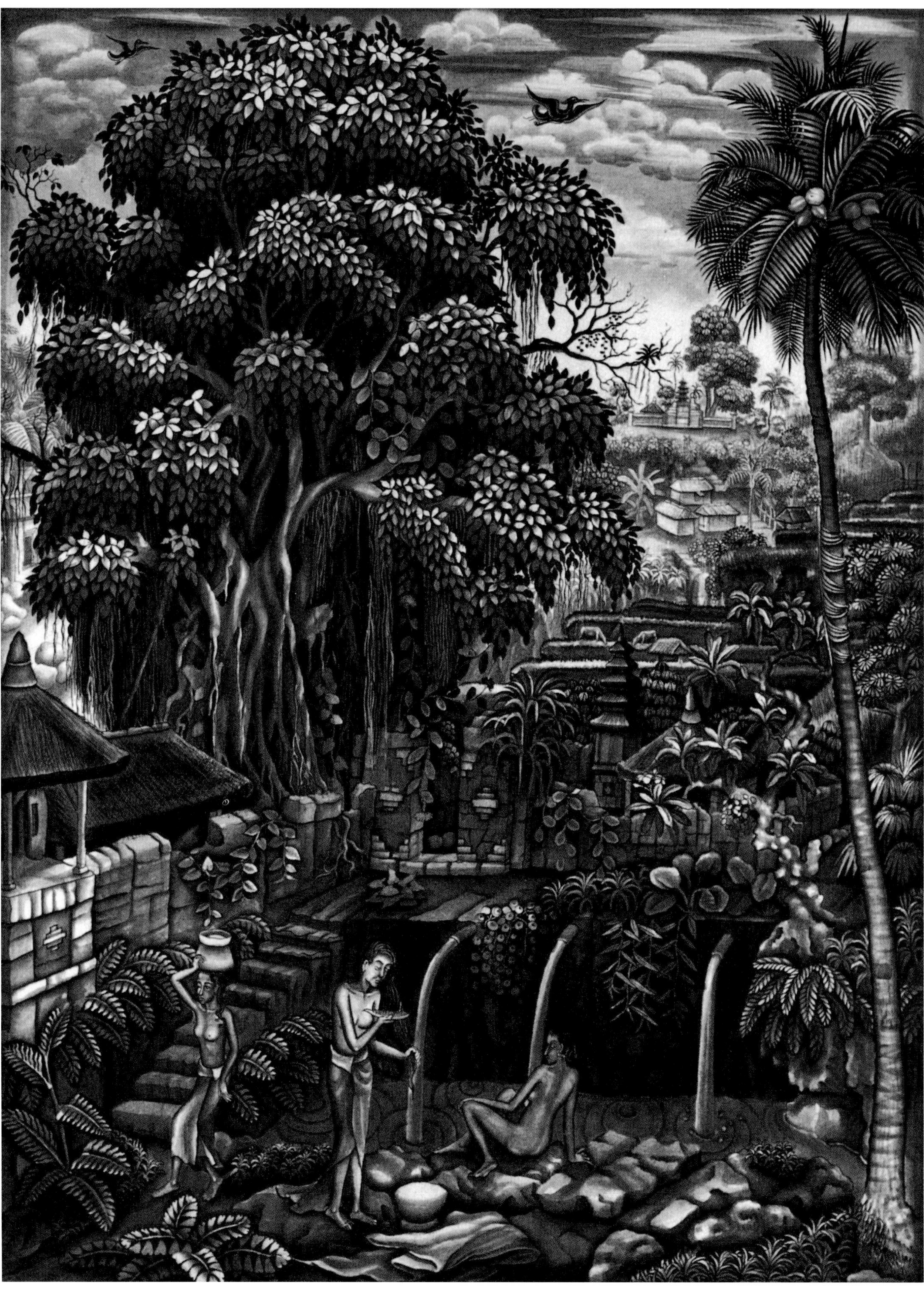

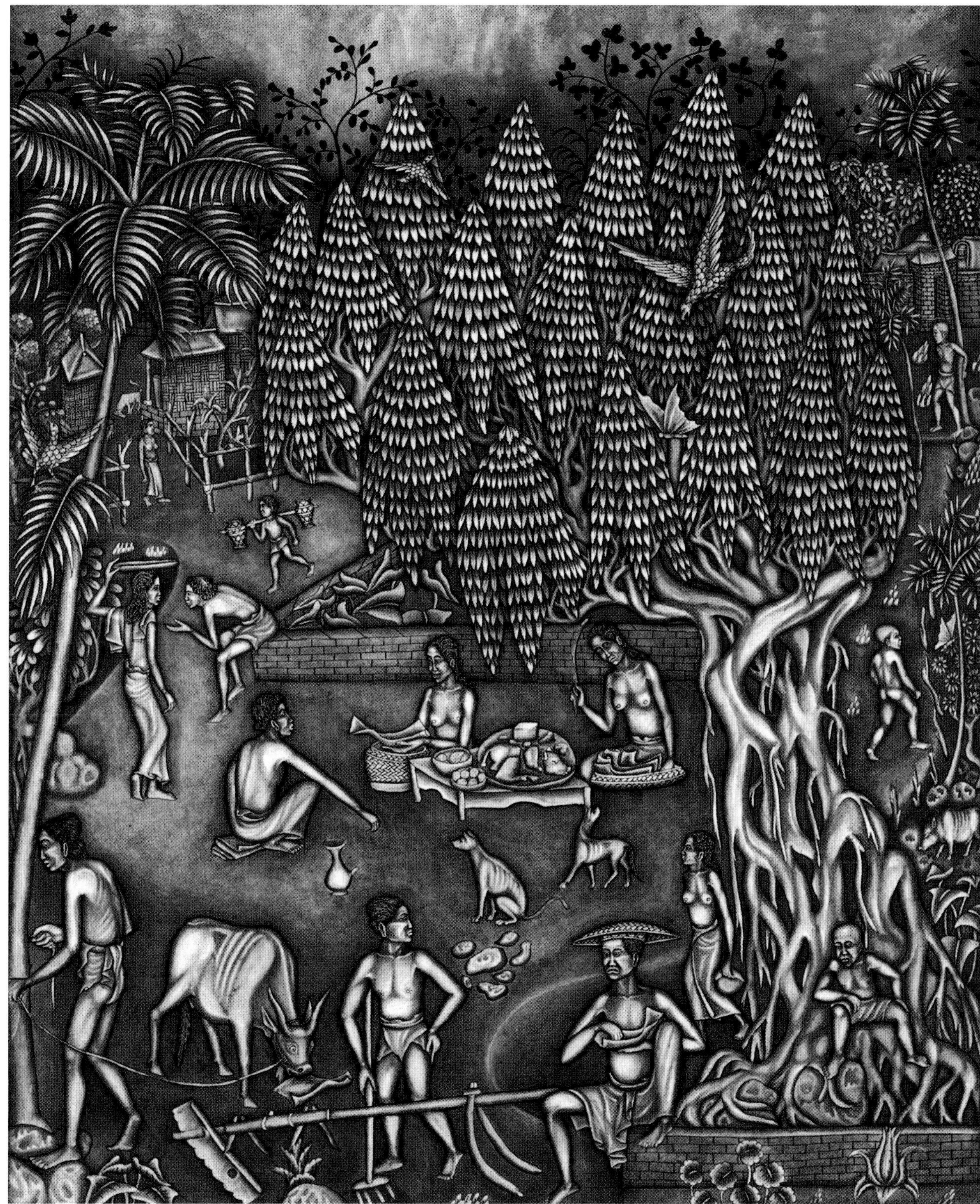

OPPOSITE: *Landscape with Women Bathing in Sacred Spring*
I Ketut Ngéndon

An elaborate temple with a sacred spring is depicted in this picture. Two women are bathing in a fountain set in the wall; one is combing her long hair. A third carries water away. A great holy banyan tree is part of the temple complex. In the distance are houses, rice fields, and another temple. The three-dimensional quality of this picture gives it a more Westernized look than most others. The slightly awkwardly drawn nude woman echoes popular Western photographs and drawings that Ngéndon had probably seen.

ABOVE: *Village Market*
I Tombelos

Under a highly stylized banyan tree of the kind found at the center crossroads of most villages, a woman sells snacks; a man eats food while his plow lies at his feet; and another man is about to untie his cow, which nibbles on the remains of someone's lunch. The trunk and branches of the tree are fairly naturalistic, but the leaves are drawn in a standard abstract design very similar to those in Balinese temple paintings.

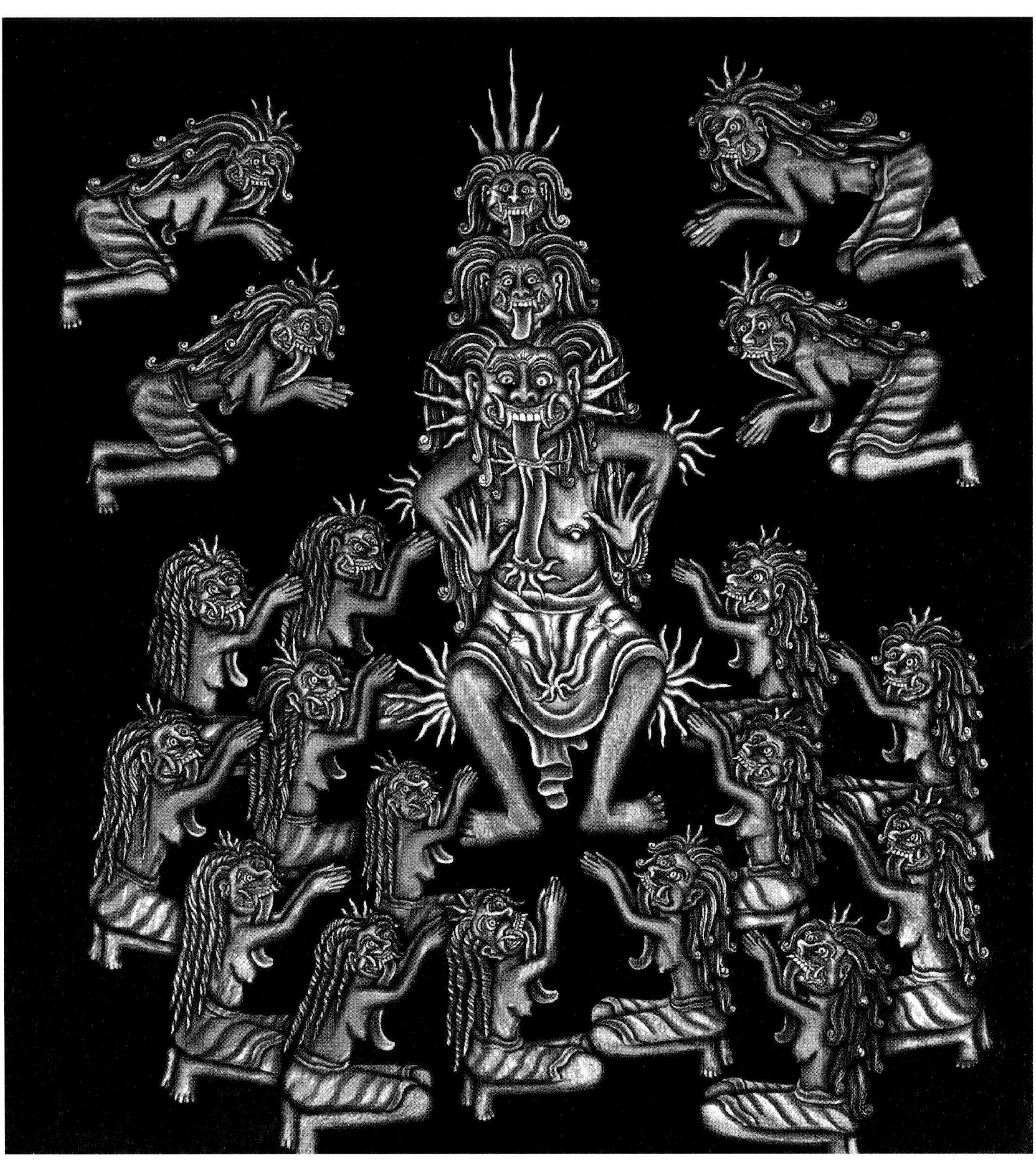

Balinese "Witches"
Ida Bagus Nyoman Tjeta

A common image in Batuan art is what the Balinese call a *rangda*. While the usual Western translation for *rangda* is "witch," the term is misleading and a better translation might be "sorcerer or deity in ferocious form." The *rangda* image is of an old woman with pendulous breasts, popping eyes, fangs, a long tongue, and long fingernails. But femininity is not central to the idea, since a male sorcerer on a violent rampage may take the shape of a *rangda*. (See chapter 4 for further examples and discussion.)

In this picture, the usual *rangda* form has been modified in two ways: she has been given three heads to show her great mystical potency (as in some sorcerers' talismans), but in the spirit of tourist paintings, this *rangda* has rounded breasts. The strong symmetrical composition is also quite untraditional.

Western modes of naturalistic sketching. Further, his view of Bali from afar reflects the distance that the foreigners placed between themselves and Balinese life—looking at its events as disengaged spectators. In his drawing, Ngéndon looks at Bali through the eyes of Bateson and Mead, far out at sea, moving from one exotic culture to another.

Nonetheless, his drawing retains traces of his own culture. For instance, the dramatic gestures of the grieving Balinese are akin to the extravagant formalized motions of Balinese dance-drama. And the details of the leaf forms on the trees themselves betray their other origin in traditional Balinese fabric designs.

Ngéndon's paintings exemplify what might be called the new "naturalistic" style inspired by Western pictorial conventions, and also the trend to portray picturesque Balinese village life. Despite the occasional stiff angularity of his figures, he caught the sentimental, pretty manner that appealed to many travelers, and selected scenes to paint that reflected the focus of the tourists' photographs.

The rest of the painters of Batuan, however, did not fully take up Ngéndon's way of drawing, as a glance through this book shows. This was probably because none of them reached the degree of Westernization that Ngéndon did. He lived for several months in Westerners' houses, which gave him the opportunity to study images in the magazines and books there.

The other painters of Batuan learned through Ngéndon how to give their figures more rounded limbs and relaxed postures, and how to build a scene with a central event set in a background of buildings and trees. While they admired Ngéndon's foreign panache, most of them took their paintings in quite different directions. This was because they understood only partially what was expected of tourist art in this early period of the genre, but also because, given the opportunity, they chose to explore matters of great concern to themselves.

Ngéndon, on the contrary, even attempted to make some realistic portraits of members of his family and pencil sketches of his own rather modern house. When he did so, he is said to have angered Bonnet, who deemed these subjects and styles "unBalinese" and "inauthentic," and rejected them.[14] This paternalistic promotion of "the right kind" of Balinese pictures, those which were acceptable only so long as they were not too Westernized, was a minor version of the more general condescending colonial policy toward the people of the Netherlands East Indies, and, in a sense, of the stance of the tourist industry of the present as well.

A painting by I Tombelos, an apprentice and cousin of Ngéndon, is done in a slightly different manner but also adopts Western pictorial conventions. It shows the central common area of a village, dominated by a huge shady banyan tree, where market women sell snacks to passing plowmen. In Balinese villages there is usually a temple next to such a tree, and during an important temple festival, performances of dance-dramas, and sometimes cockfights, are held in front of it.

Tombelos' drawing is more distinctly "realistic" in its rendering of figures than most others in this collection. In addition, like those of Ngéndon and many of those of Tombelos' other fellow villagers, it has the shape of "a scene" in the Western sense—a group of people set in a place with perspectived buildings and trees as a frame for them. His figures are similar to Ngéndon's (note the woman carrying something on her head at the left) and thus to Western photographs and drawings. But Tombelos made his picture into a decorative design, representing the vegetation not naturalistically but ornamentally, his leaf and flower forms drawn from textile designs of repeated petals in strong patterns.

One of the defining requirements of tourist art, which all the Batuan picture makers followed faithfully, is that it show only a traditional world. Ngéndon's and Tombelos' pictures, like all the paintings from Bali of this period, and indeed like tourist art around the world, strikingly avoid Western objects such as cigarettes, Western shirts, and automobiles, which were in fact, even then, seen everywhere in Bali. A strong taboo against any sign of modernization is evident in these pictures, a taboo that held until the late 1980s.

The works discussed above are examples of the mainstream in Balinese tourist art: landscapes or panoramas busy with typical Balinese activities, particularly the ceremonial spectacles that tourists loved to photograph.

Another type of picture popular with visitors was a standardized "oriental" myth made into a decorative pattern. For example, a painting by Ida Bagus Nyoman Tjeta shows a three-headed demonic being with her minions, who are lesser versions of herself. A third common kind of tourist painting was that of a dancer in costume, standing alone against a white background, such as the two figures from the drama shown on pages 56 and 57. All three painting types can be taken by a foreigner as emblematic of Bali. But most Batuan painters in the 1930s did not make these sorts of pictures.

A Different Kind of Patron

The two European artists Spies and Bonnet, together with the first painters in the Ubud area, had probably established the fundamental route of the new pictures, but the Batuan people took their pictures off on a side road. An important reason for this detour, I believe, was the special relationship the Batuan villagers had with the anthropologists Margaret Mead and Gregory Bateson.

The anthropologists explicitly avoided influencing the painters in any way, since they were searching the pictures through Freudian eyes for unintended projections of unconscious wishes and modes of conception of bodily processes. For this reason, they were careful not to give the people of Batuan any pictures to look at, and they made a list of any direct requests they made in regard to content.

Yet they may have indirectly had important effects on the paintings that were made for them. Ngéndon's "goodbye" painting, for instance, was made expressly for Bateson and Mead, and the image of Bali at the top was put there to tell them something about the people they were leaving. In desiring to please the anthropologists, the people of Batuan must have watched them carefully to see what they wanted.

From the outset of their dealings with the painters of Batuan, the anthropologists refused to buy any pictures that they knew were copies. They thus forced the Batuan people to give up their custom of duplicating pictures that had sold well (at least for those that they brought to Bateson and Mead) and to try out new ideas. Then, too, the anthropologists spoke Balinese, and that may have had even greater effect. Most foreigners (including, I believe, such old-time residents as Spies and the anthropologist Jane Belo) spoke primarily the colonial trade language, Malay.[15] The people of Batuan may have felt that, even though Mead and Bateson were just a different kind of tourist, since they spoke their language they might be able to understand more complex images. Most important of all, Mead and Bateson insisted on having the painters tell them the folktales or myths that some pictures illustrated, and thus stimulated the painters to find other stories than those of the standard tourist art clichés. Given the special circumstances of the anthropologists' presence in Batuan, the picture makers were stimulated to ransack their cultural heritage for ever new sources of images and stories.

Although Mead and Bateson spoke Balinese, these pictures are set in a pictorial language that is not Balinese. In a sense, each drawing is the product of an act of translation into a language that the speaker does not know very well. Like anthropological informants who gradually learn how to answer the questions, implied or direct, of the researcher, these painters were asked to "speak a language" that was not theirs: in this case, making pictorial images within a naturalistic tradition.

As they became more experienced, particularly in the postwar period, the images they made became more standardized or conventionalized. But in the 1930s, the young people of Batuan still did not know this new "language" very well. In consequence, they went far beyond the standard, pretty images that sold well to tourists and turned toward expressing matters of deep concern to themselves. These Batuan works of the 1930s, while rooted in tourist art, are themselves not a pure tourist art but something different.

Two Painters and Their Works

Ngéndon and Togog were among the very first from Batuan to try the new craft, and each in his own way was influential on those who followed. Ngéndon's paintings, as I have said, were closer to the mainstream of tourist art coming out of Ubud. Togog, on the other hand, led by his example in the direction traced in this book.

The two artists were very different from one another in their lives. Togog came from a noble Brahmana clan in the center of Batuan, Ngéndon from a commoner neighborhood on the edge of the village. Ngéndon's house was on the road leading from Denpasar to Ubud where tourists even then often passed, and his mother was a successful market woman, while Togog's home was well off the road and his grandparents and cousins were high priests *(pedanda)*.

Ngéndon learned peddling early from his mother and soon was accompanying an older cousin, Patera, on trips to Ubud and Denpasar to sell tourist woodcarvings, which had been well established as a commercial craft long before the advent of the painting market. Patera made his first picture after urging from Bonnet, and Ngéndon soon followed. Patera and Ngéndon were the ones that Spies contacted when he wanted to bring his foreign guests to Batuan to watch the dances at temple festivals. After Patera died in 1935, Ngéndon became Batuan's impresario, meeting the foreigners when they came, organizing Batuan's dance groups for presentations in the village, and setting up arrangements for performances in Ubud or Denpasar. He helped to create two new tourist dances, a comic one now known as "The Frog Dance," and a

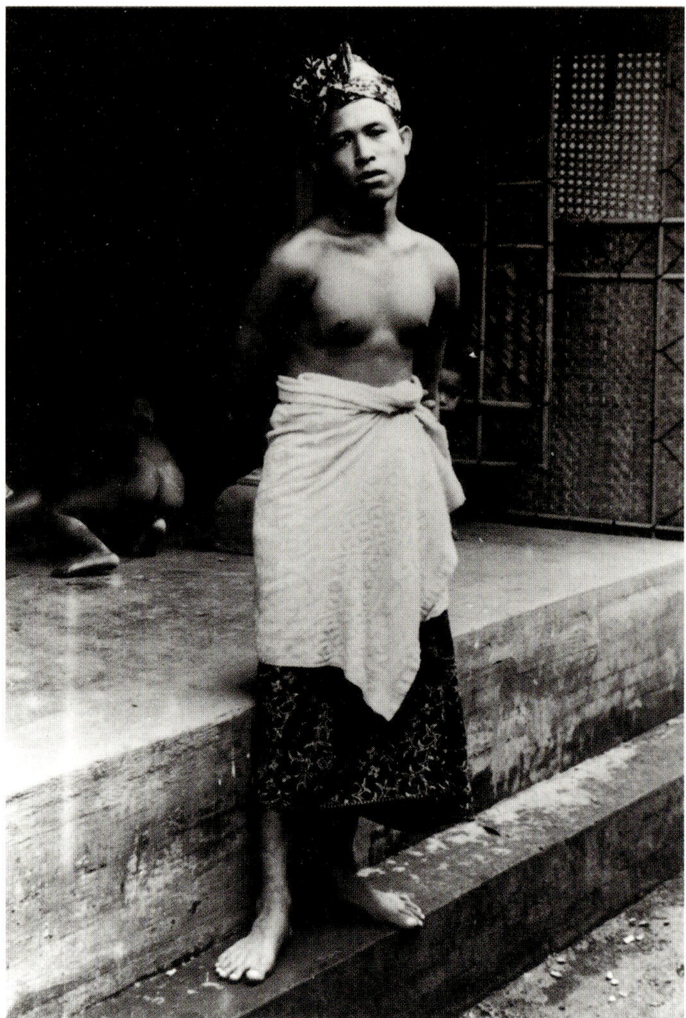

I Ketut Ngéndon
Photograph taken by Gregory Bateson in 1937

more serious one based on a modification of the sacred *rejang*, which is performed by the women and girls of Batuan during the ritually dangerous season from November through March. Ngéndon arranged for new costumes, added a new detail of gold-painted fans, chose the prettiest dancers, and rehearsed them until the dance was elegant and polished.

Ngéndon built a small Western-style house with peaked roof and no walls around its yard, right on the road where Westerners could easily see him and stop to arrange for dance performances, or perhaps to buy carvings and pictures. He persuaded some of his younger friends to make pictures there for the travelers to see.

The link between presenting dance performances to tourists and making carvings and pictures is clear. This association directly affected the content of the pictures that Patera, Ngéndon, and their followers made. Tourist "spectacles," dance performances and rituals were important in their works.

The brutal manner of Ngéndon's death by execution in 1948 tells us something of great importance about his life. During the Japanese occupation in 1942–1945, with its accompanying promotion of anti-Western and nationalistic ideologies, Ngéndon met an artist from Java, the center of political sophistication at the time. He went with him to Jogjakarta in Java, where, according to accounts in the 1980s, he met Sukarno, the leader of Indonesia's revolution. Ngéndon came

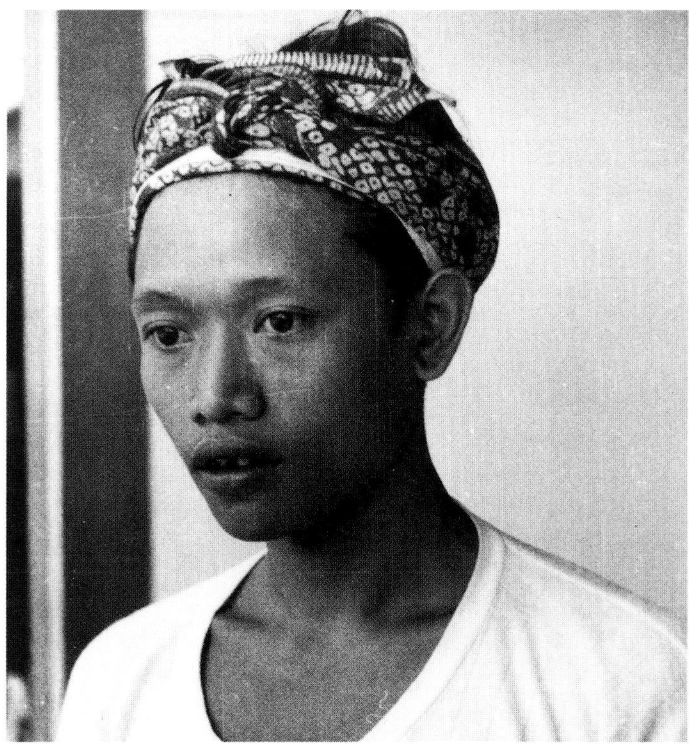

Ida Bagus Madé Togog
Photograph taken by Gregory Bateson in 1937

back with the nationalist message, advocating the expulsion of the colonial power and the establishment of an independent republic of Indonesia. He organized a Batuan cell of the nationalist resistance movement. When the Japanese were vanquished in late 1945, Sukarno and his group proclaimed Indonesian independence and initiated a five-year armed struggle against the returning Dutch to attain it. Ngéndon took a prominent part in that struggle in the Batuan region.

During the period between 1947 and late 1949, the Republic of Indonesia had been pushed back to the area around Jogjakarta, while the Dutch had re-established themselves elsewhere in their former colony, including Bali. The nationalist movement in Bali continued to oppose the Dutch puppet government established in Gianyar, headed by a former king. But most of the people of Batuan remained loyal to the Gianyar royal house and opposed nationalism. Ngéndon helped his little rebel group set up literacy schools and conduct information campaigns (that true freedom could be gained through Western education was a central tenet of the nationalists), until the Dutch military took forceful action against the movement. He then joined the armed guerrilla forces. The leaders of Batuan were not sympathetic to the nationalist cause, and Ngéndon went into hiding, taking with him ten or fifteen Batuan people (including two painters, Djatasoera and Tjeta). Ultimately the greatly superior Dutch army smashed them. Ngéndon was captured by the Gianyar police, brought to the strongly anticolonial village of Sukawati just south of Batuan to be publicly beaten as a lesson to all. Ngéndon was then taken to his neighborhood's graveyard in Batuan, where he was killed with a shot in the forehead. His family were falsely told he had been shot while trying to escape. They were forced to bury him surreptitiously, and it was not until after the victory of the Republic of Indonesia in 1950, and complete independence from the Dutch, that Ngéndon's cremation was permitted by the local community.[16]

In the 1980s, I spoke with people who had known Ngéndon in the 1940s; they told me that Ngéndon had a clear idea of the nationalistic issues of the day. He attacked not only the legitimacy of the colonial presence but also the inequities of the caste system, and he even criticized some traditional religious practices, such as the use of coins in offerings.

In the late 1930s when Bateson and Mead knew Ngéndon, he may not yet have reached a developed nationalist position. Yet he spent a good deal of time among Westerners and must already have had a sense of dissatisfaction.

All of this leads me to suggest that while Ngéndon used pictures and dance performances to make money, this was not his primary motive. It was Western modernity and Western forms of power that fascinated him. All the evidence we have indicates that Ngéndon felt an increasing resentment at being prevented from sharing in the advantages of Western life and at the colonial patterns of domination and appropriation of Balinese talents for outsiders' pleasures.

Togog, in contrast to Ngéndon, appears to have been profoundly unconcerned about Western expectations of his paintings. He never showed any interest in Western matters. He did not go to school, nor did he ever learn to speak more than a few phrases of Malay. As a trained ritual specialist from a priest's family with many spiritual clients, Togog was well acquainted with Balinese literature and oral lore. While Ngéndon's pictures were primarily about the surface aspects of Balinese life as might be viewed by an outsider, almost all of Togog's pictures concern religious and mythical subjects, with an insider's concern for strange magical events that he recounted or depicted in precise detail. Even his earliest drawings reveal a deep knowledge of his own culture.

Ngéndon's paintings were directly indebted to those of the Westerners and of the Westernized Ubud picture makers, but Togog's pictures often shifted away from naturalistic or "pretty" styles. Togog's strength in picture making was neither draftsmanship nor design but narrative. Through the depiction of story episodes he could hint at the depths and complexities of communal, religious, and perhaps even personal concerns.

Although he was close to eighty years old when I came to know him, Togog was still painting. He was always affable and obliging and at the same time dignified, as befitted his station as the oldest member of a very important Brahmana priestly house with many ritual clients, both commoner and noble. In the company of strangers he was usually reserved and silent, but when among friends of his own age he loosened up, laughingly telling stories about events in his past life, even breaking into song at times. Togog's forty-year-old son, Ida Bagus Putu Gedé, also a very fine painter, often joined us in ethnological discussions, and it became immediately clear that compared to his son, Togog was old-fashioned both in his speech and his ways. His tales to me about his youth showed him to have been something of a wanderer from home (as many boys and young men of Bali often are) and a gambler. He seems to have kept a distance from the disturbing political events of the postwar world of Batuan. During the time that I knew him, as well as in the period of Mead and

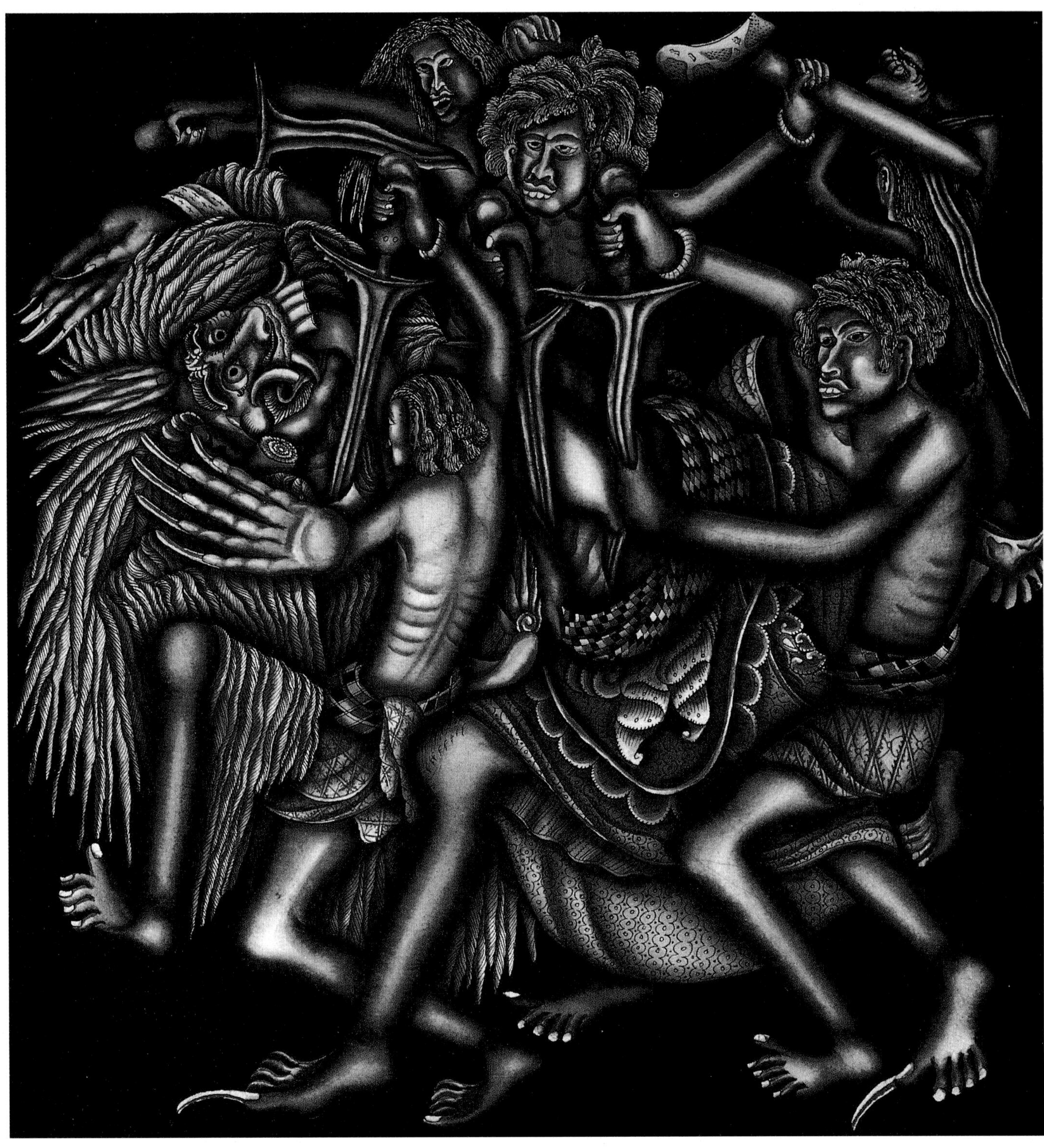

Attack on Calon Arang, the Queen of the Sorcerers
Ida Bagus Madé Togog

Seen in this picture is a climactic moment in a village ritual in which a spirit being has entered the *rangda* mask that portrays the mythical queen Calon Arang and, through it, the dancer wearing the mask. She utters fierce threats against the health and well-being of the village until the men come to attack her with sharp daggers. They are themselves possessed by other, benevolent, spirit beings.

At the moment portrayed, the villagers seem about to vanquish the demon, but she whirls around, and with a fierce glance and a wave of her magical cloth, stops them and makes them turn their knives on themselves, pressing the sharp points into their own breasts. The knives are sharp but no villagers are hurt if the benevolent beings protect them. If blood is drawn, the Balinese say that the deities and demons were not actually present, and the ritual was a failure.

Bateson's collaboration with Togog, he worked every day on new paintings. Making pictures, telling stories, chanting songs, and carrying out ritual activities seemed to be the wellsprings of his life.

It is likely that in Togog's early years he had expected to become a priest. All the women of his family—his aunt, mother, and later, wife—were ritual specialists *(tukang banten)*, whose daily work was the preparation of complex offerings and the supervision of ritual preparations for commoner clients. His wife was the daughter of a high priest as well. Ritual specialists and priests were always compensated for their work, but mainly in foodstuffs and clothing, and this was the basis of their subsistence. Togog's earliest memories were of month-long stays in a noble court with a Batuan great-aunt who had gone there to work on cremation preparations. As a young man he was already experienced in making the more elaborate kinds of offerings and in carrying out the rituals needed for burial or cremation, tooth filing, and laying out new houseyards and building houses within them. For many years he was the chief attendant and assistant of a high priest who was his cousin. When he married a divorced woman, just before he took up drawing, he no longer had the necessary purity to become a priest. But he spent the remainder of his life as an active ritual specialist.

When Togog spoke with me, he was much more interested in and proud of his knowledge of classical literature than he was in his craft as a picture maker. He was an enthusiastic singer of hymnlike poems *(kekawin* and *kidung)*. These classical songs, in a sacred literary language called *Kawi* by the Balinese, usually tell stories of legendary heroes and holy men, animals that behave like humans, and gods and demons. The anecdotes of his early life that Togog told most often were about the times when he learned new songs and new stories.

Togog told me how, when still only a small boy, he was so fascinated by the tales told him by an old woman who lived nearby that he would secretly climb his grandfather's coconut trees to steal coconuts to give her in return for an evening of storytelling. All her fabulous plots and characters found their way into Togog's paintings, together with stories drawn from the *kidung* and *kekawin*, and from the dance-dramas of *arja* and *gambuh*.

Togog made pictures of all kinds, even the sorts of scenes of "daily life" that Ngéndon and Tombelos did. But none of his works have Ngéndon's strong naturalistic vision. Instead of showing what Bali looks like, Togog created images of what Bali is about.

One of Togog's early paintings shows how his work contrasts with that of Ngéndon. The picture is a representation of a quite common but spectacular ritual dance-drama, one that was very popular with tourists, called by Balinese the Calon Arang after the name of the evil queen who is its central character. Queen Calon Arang has the mystical potency to transform herself into a malevolent demon who is spiritual leader of all the sorcerers (male as well as female) of every village. The performance starts as a comic play about long-ago personages but rapidly becomes a ritual encounter among a crowd of actual spiritual beings struggling over the well-being of the village.

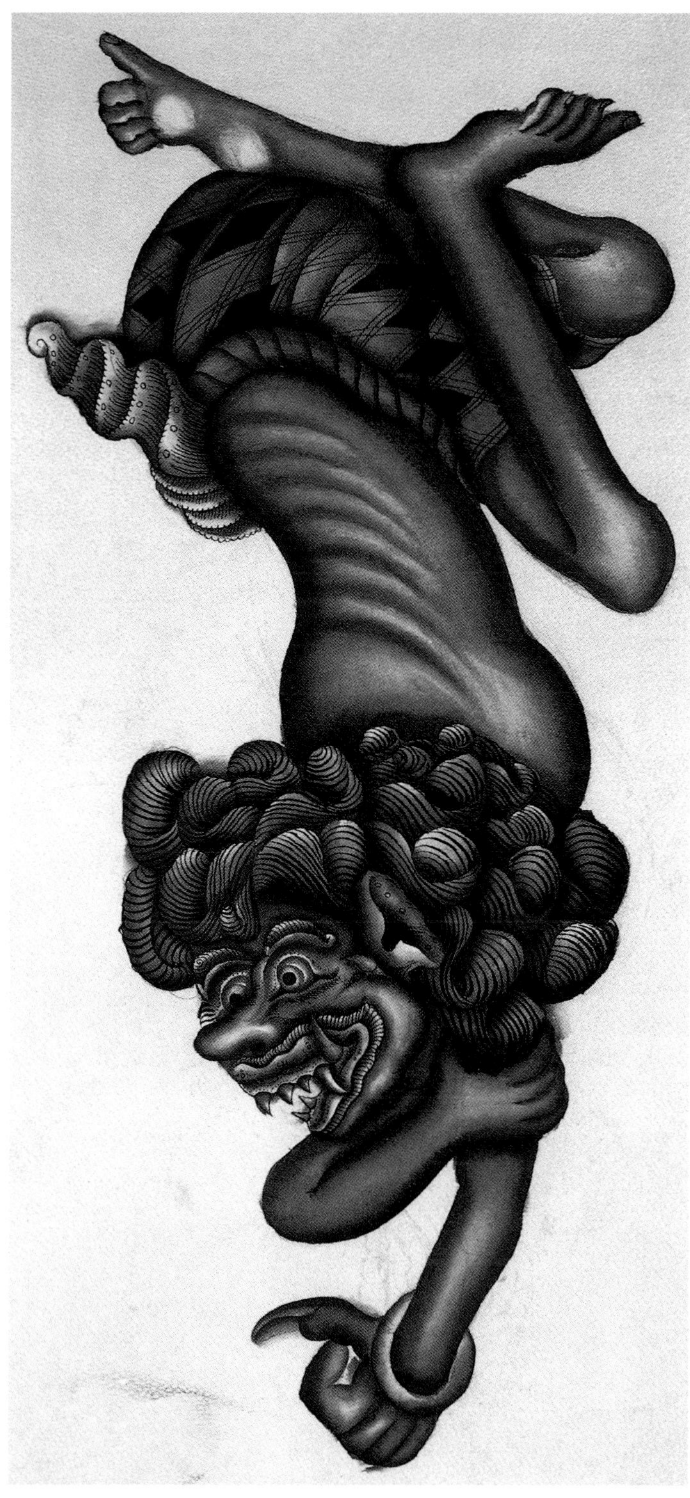

Sorcerer's Talismanic Image
Ida Bagus Madé Togog

Here, a demon hurls itself through the air head down and attacks its victim with its long thumbnail. Togog identified it as a *buta sungsang* or "upside-down demon." To put one's head lower than the rest of one's body is to pollute the sacred soul-stuff that lives in the head and risk unleashing a powerful destructive force. This being might be the familiar spirit of a human sorcerer, dealing out death at his orders, or he might be the sorcerer himself in demonic form. Diagrams depicting this demon can be found in small handbooks used by both sorcerers and healers.

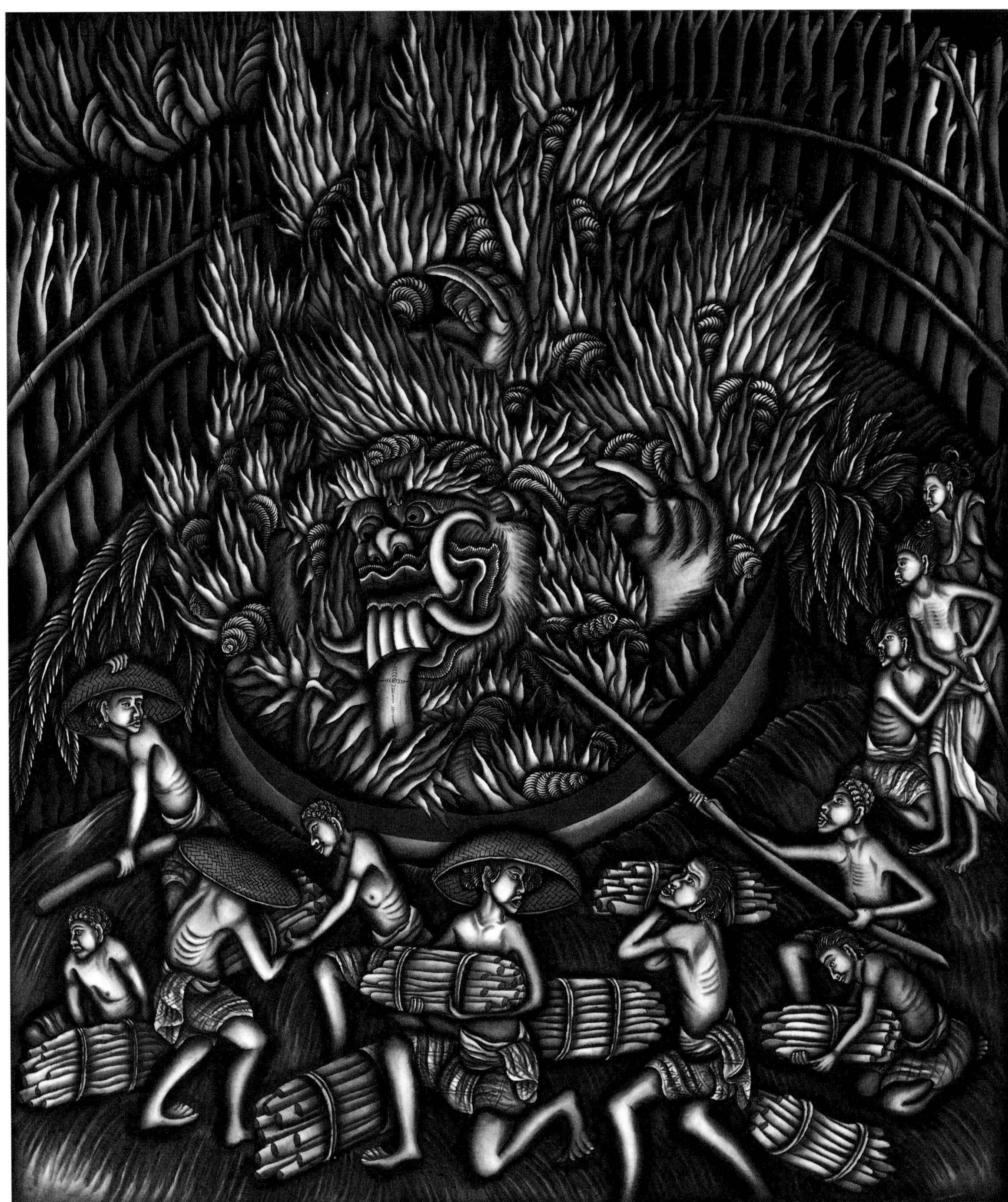

In the play, masks of unusual mystical power are worn, which then are entered by malevolent or benevolent spirit beings. Other people, not masked, soon are also possessed, and a chaotic battle ensues.[17]

Certain villages are renowned for the violence of their members' behavior when possessed. Tourists are regularly taken to ceremonies in these villages. In fact, in the mid-1930s two villages worked up special versions for tourists, which they put on during the daytime so that the foreigners could make photographs. One of these tourist performances was filmed by Mead and Bateson, and they made their analysis of the symbolism of the ceremony a central part of their book *Balinese Character.*[18]

In Togog's own village of Batuan, this violent ritual of possessed stabbing of one's self is not performed. In fact people rarely go into trance there. Togog told Bateson, in regard to his picture, that he had recently gone to watch the ritual in a village some distance away. As a spectator of such a ritual performed by "other people," Togog may have seen it through the eyes of a tourist, and perhaps he chose the subject with an idea that it would please the foreigners who had also gone to see the performance. At the same time, Togog was expressing in his drawing an intense personal interest in what Westerners might call the "occult," a concern that shows up in many of his paintings.

In the picture of the men attempting to stab the sorcerer-queen, Togog has caught a moment of dark, violent combat. Another early drawing by Togog shows a terrifying demon one might meet on a dark night, who flies through the air, head down and feet in the air, to stab victims with a sharp thumbnail. This picture draws on common Balinese knowledge of the sorts of evil spirits that inhabit graveyards, crossroads, heavily wooded areas, and rivers, or who are the forms that malevolent human beings might take when, werewolf-like, they transform themselves into various kinds of death-dealing monsters to bring disaster to their fellow villagers.

A last example, also by Togog, the painting of *The Story of the Demon Who Pretended to Be a Priest*, plays on the profound ambivalence that Balinese have toward those who learn the lores of healing and priestly ritual. Because the mystical power that priests and healers employ is the same as that of sorcerers, and is itself morally neutral, it is difficult to tell whether someone is using his powers for good or evil. In the story of the false priest, even the priest's wife cannot tell which being is the good priest and which the false one.

As a man who deeply studied the classical religious poetry and ritual manuals, Togog was particularly sensitive to the moral dilemmas raised by the fact that magical learning may be used for both good and evil purposes, and that a priest's inner intent may not be outwardly apparent. The theme of this story—the contest for mystical mastery, first between the demon and the priestly couple, and then between a commoner and the demon—is one of his favorites. The commoner hero learned his potent solution to the priests' dilemma from a bird. A Balinese would interpret this bird to be a messenger of a deity, who came to bestow on the commoner extraordinary magical powers. The theme of contest for mystical mastery also underlies the two pictures discussed above depicting men attacking Queen Calon Arang and the sorcerer's talismanic image.

In the painting of the demon masquerading as a priest, Togog used the new naturalism to depict the figures gathering firewood and the great fire itself. Through showing the villagers as ordinary human beings, he was able to domesticate a rather frightening tale, bringing it down from the remote heights of myth to the terrifying proximity of the everyday. As with Ngéndon, but in a different way, Togog made pictures that take from the West as well as from Bali.

The relationship of Togog's paintings to those of others in Batuan is very complex. In subtle ways, Togog sometimes took precedence as the innovator or guide, but nearly as often he was stimulated by the work of others. About a dozen people began to make pictures very soon after Togog. Most of them were helped by him at the outset and were close kin who frequented one another's homes. Some made large, complex story pictures almost as early as Togog, but no one attempted to imitate his imposing images of sorcerers and deities, or to illustrate their own dreams. They, too, took their works in directions away from the naturalistic and decorative.

The Batuan painters seldom portrayed worlds of light and harmony and laughter, or the external world of mere appearances. Rather, they grappled with those forces that, for them, are concealed under the surface of things, the real world of dangerous, invisible, supernatural beings and powers. Since in Bali one of the main ways of speaking about such matters is through telling stories, many of the pictures are formulated through narratives drawn from folktales, shadow puppet shows, and the popular dance-dramas. And many pictures went further, portraying sorcerers, demons, and malevolent spirits. If they can be taken as individual statements, these pictures reveal a great deal not only about the inner preoccupations of their makers but also about their fundamental notions of the universe.

OPPOSITE: *The Story of the Demon Who Pretended to Be a Priest*
Ida Bagus Madé Togog

This is the climactic moment in a folktale about a man and wife who both are high Brahmana priests. As Togog told the story to Bateson, the demonic spirit of a tree was offended when the priest hoed too near its roots, and the demon decided to seek revenge. He took the form of the husband, deceived the wife and went to bed with her. When she woke she was lying between two identical men and she couldn't tell the difference between them. She went for help to the king, who offered a reward to anyone who could solve the problem. A magic bird came to a commoner client of the priest and told him what to do. He went to the two husbands and said, "Which of you has the magical power to make yourself small enough to fit into this water jug? The one that fits is the true priest and the other will be burned up." The villagers all gathered firewood for a great fire. Then the priest-husband who was really the malicious spirit jumped inside the water jug and the man quickly threw him, jug and all, into the fire. As he burned up, he was transformed into a malicious spirit again.[19]

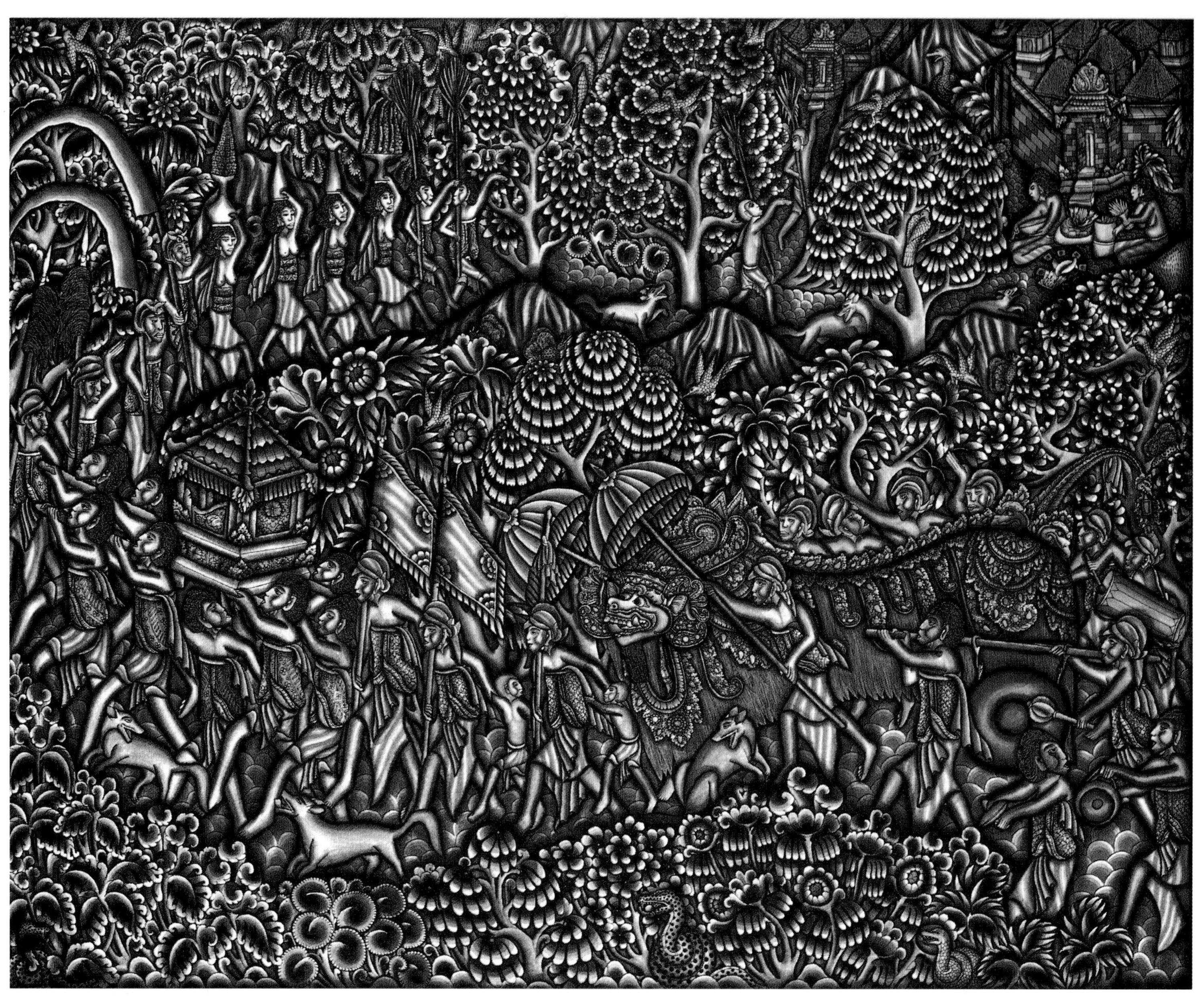

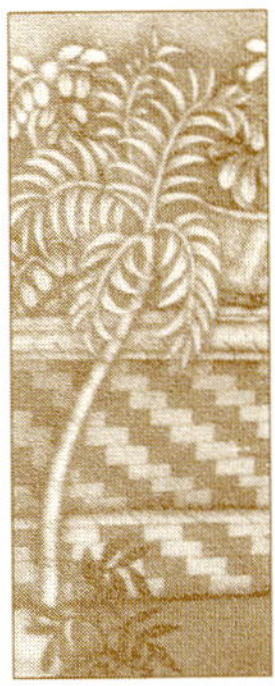

The Everyday World of (Mere) Appearances

The painters of Batuan depicted the "ordinary" life that Spies and Bonnet had urged them to portray as bustling with religious festivals and their accompanying dance-drama performances. Since life for the Balinese is largely taken up with transactions with the unseen world, it is no wonder that their pictures of "everyday life" depict mainly rituals. Even the dance-drama performances are mounted with an audience of invisible beings in mind.[1]

The picture facing, *Procession to a Temple*, shows a grand parade of village deities and their congregation going from one temple to another, or perhaps from a temple to the sea and back. Foreign visitors were frequently taken to see such processions, which form a highly public and spectacular step in most important temple ceremonies.

This picture, like many of the others, results from joining a Western-based naturalistic mode of presentation with conventions that are fundamentally Balinese. It is also a good example of the Balinese taste for copiousness. Here the result is a fabriclike surface with a strong two-dimensional texture. However, the artist modifies that continuous overall pattern by painting a dark shadow behind the back of the dragon (right foreground) and behind the line of bushes and rocks above him to create a layered articulation of foreground and background.

For a Balinese, such a procession is an expression of the whole community's respect for the power of those deities and demons that have given them life and that may aid in protecting and augmenting that life. The rhythmic repetition of legs and arms in this picture creates a feeling of complexly coordinated social activity, a sense, perhaps, of harmony or balance.

Balinese temple rituals bring about a visit into our visible material world of a swarm of spiritual beings who "come down" from the other world to stay awhile among their devotees. Each temple has one or two primary deities, always accompanied by entourages of lesser beings. After the spiritual beings arrive, they are purified and receive new clothing and preliminary offerings (sometimes they are also carried to the sea, as in Keteg's picture). The priest then presents the offerings of each household and those of the community as a whole to these beings, who partake of their essence, then bless them. After the ceremony the family members take their offerings home and by eating them receive some of the blessing through the food. During their stay in this world, the deities transform specially prepared water into holy water, which is then sprinkled over the members of the congregation. This moment, the heart of any temple ceremony, is when the god of the temple bestows, through the water and the food, a sacred gift of life and fertility on the region and onto the members of each household.

The early stages of a temple festival are shown in a picture by Sanoer. Its maker chose a long, narrow format in which to depict a complex assemblage of several components of a ritual festival. In any major ceremony, at the main moments of worship as many as three different orchestras may play at once, within hearing of one another, while a group of older people sings *kidung* hymns, two or more priests chant, and the congregation prays. In this picture there are two orchestras and two dance performances as well as the priest reciting mantras and ringing bells. Such energetic noisiness is another expression of the Balinese value of *ramé*, or copiousness.

Sanoer's picture has no center, since the various episodes are set out in a line. The multiplicity of simultaneous events seems to require such a multifocused composition. Experiencing the performed arts as many simultaneous presentations is in itself decentering.

The picture shows a moment in a temple ceremony, held just outside the great gateway of the temple (on the right of the picture), when offerings and prayers are addressed to the hosts of potentially malevolent spiritual beings of the vicinity.

OPPOSITE: *Procession to a Temple*
I Keteg

This densely packed composition portrays the deities of a local temple being transported on an enclosed palanquin. The deities have been invited to descend from the other world into this world, and while here they temporarily enter small wooden figures. During their visitation these spiritual beings are entertained, feasted, presented with new clothing, and, often, taken to the sea for purification. The festive parade is returning, possibly from the sea, to a temple at upper right, where two women kneel outside the gate, offering food and flowers on the ground before them to welcome the approaching deities. In the accompanying throng are women bearing offerings on their heads, men with lances and banners, a portable gamelan orchestra, and the great dragon, or *barong* (a large sparkling four-legged mask and costume worn by two men), who is a protective demon of the village.

The dark tone of this picture belies the gaiety, sociability, noisiness, and above all the bright colors of such a procession. The dragon figure in actuality is especially bright, with mirrors sewn all over its gold-painted headdress and clothing, which shimmer as it dances with comic steps and syncopated rhythms.

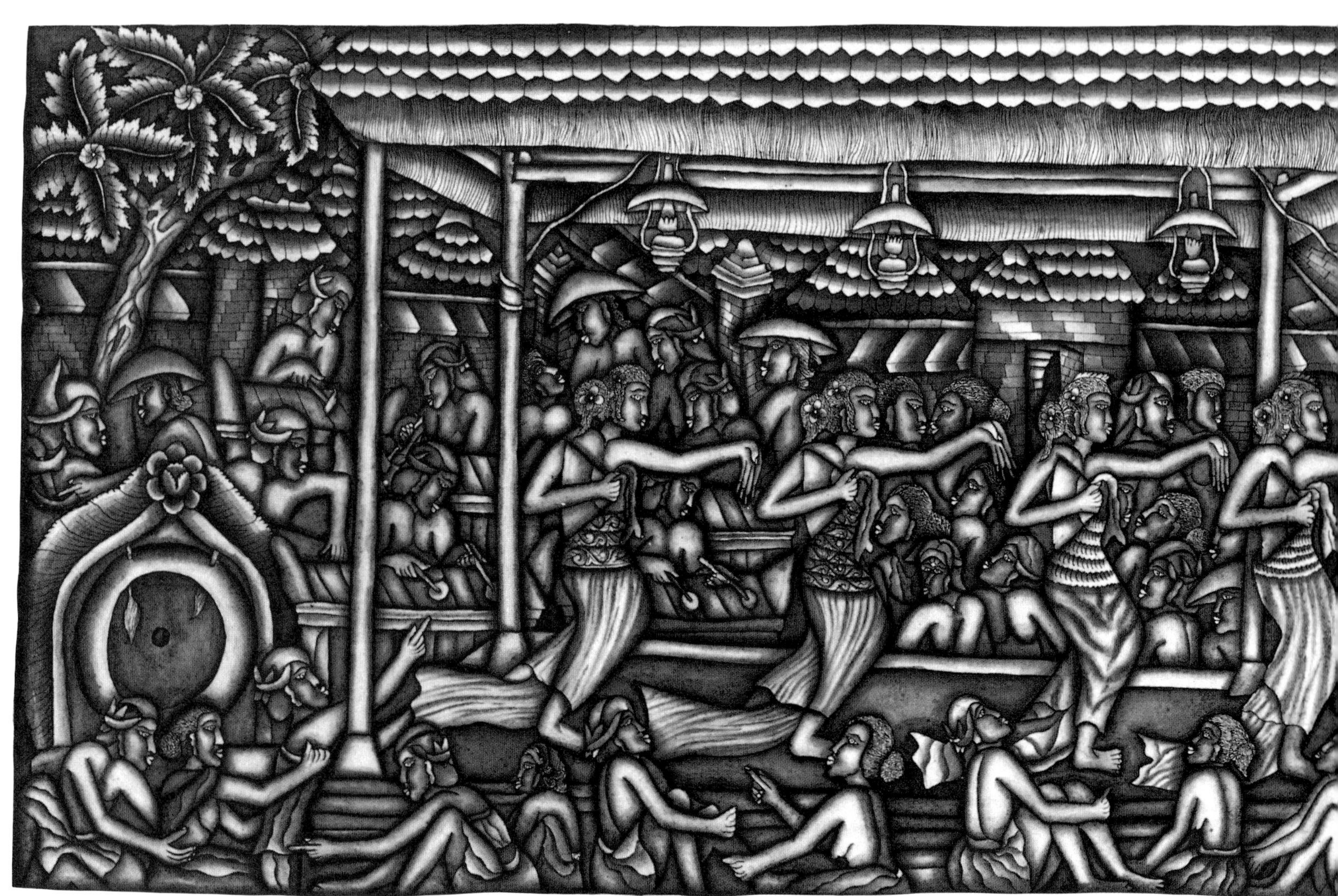

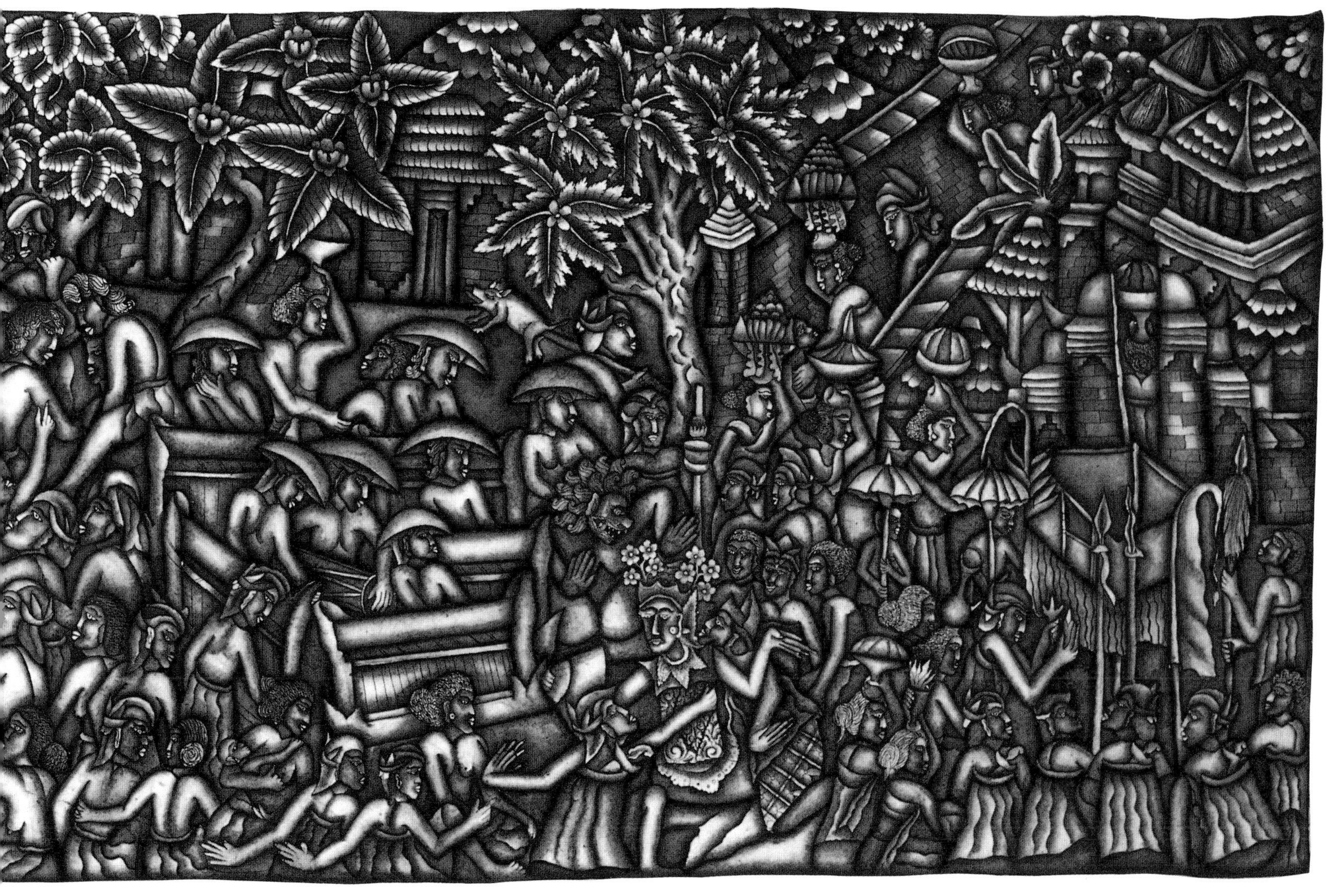

Temple Festival
Ida Bagus Nyoman Sanoer Tampi

A temple festival requires the simultaneous performance of several orchestras and several dance performances along with priestly rituals. At far left is a gamelan orchestra accompanying a sacred dance called *rejang* (performed by the four women with left arms outstretched). To the right is another orchestra and a *jogéd* dance, in which an elaborately dressed dancer invites men from the audience to join her in an improvised duet. The first is a highly sacred dance, done with slow solemnity; the second is relatively secular, erotic, and boisterous, and parodies other dance genres.

On the far right, a commoner priest *(pamangku)* welcomes the deities in front of a high bamboo shrine *(panggung)*, placed just outside the main gate of the temple. Just above the worshipers, dressed in properly respectful clothing, is a line of women bearing household offerings on their heads for consecration and prestation within the temple.

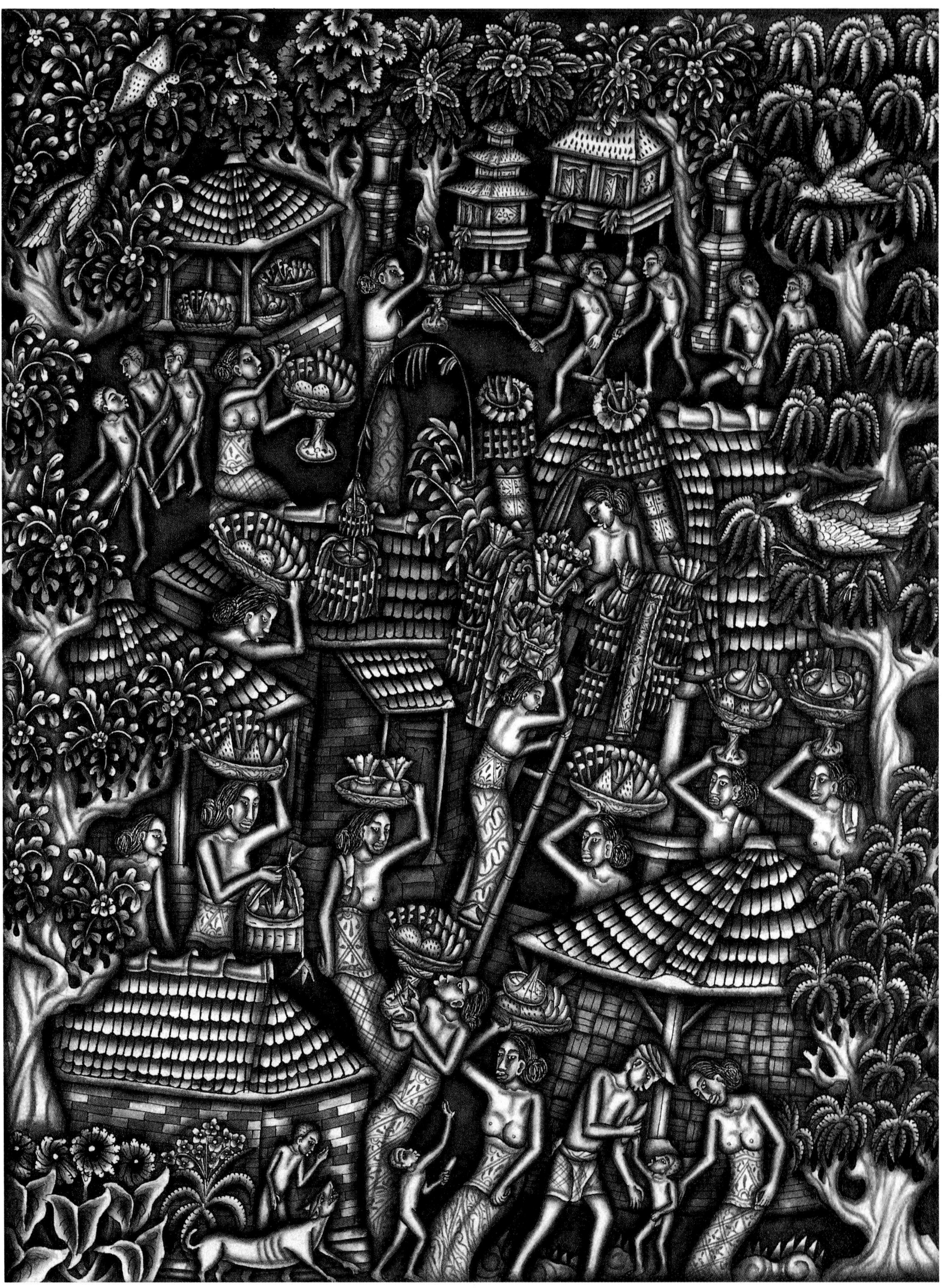

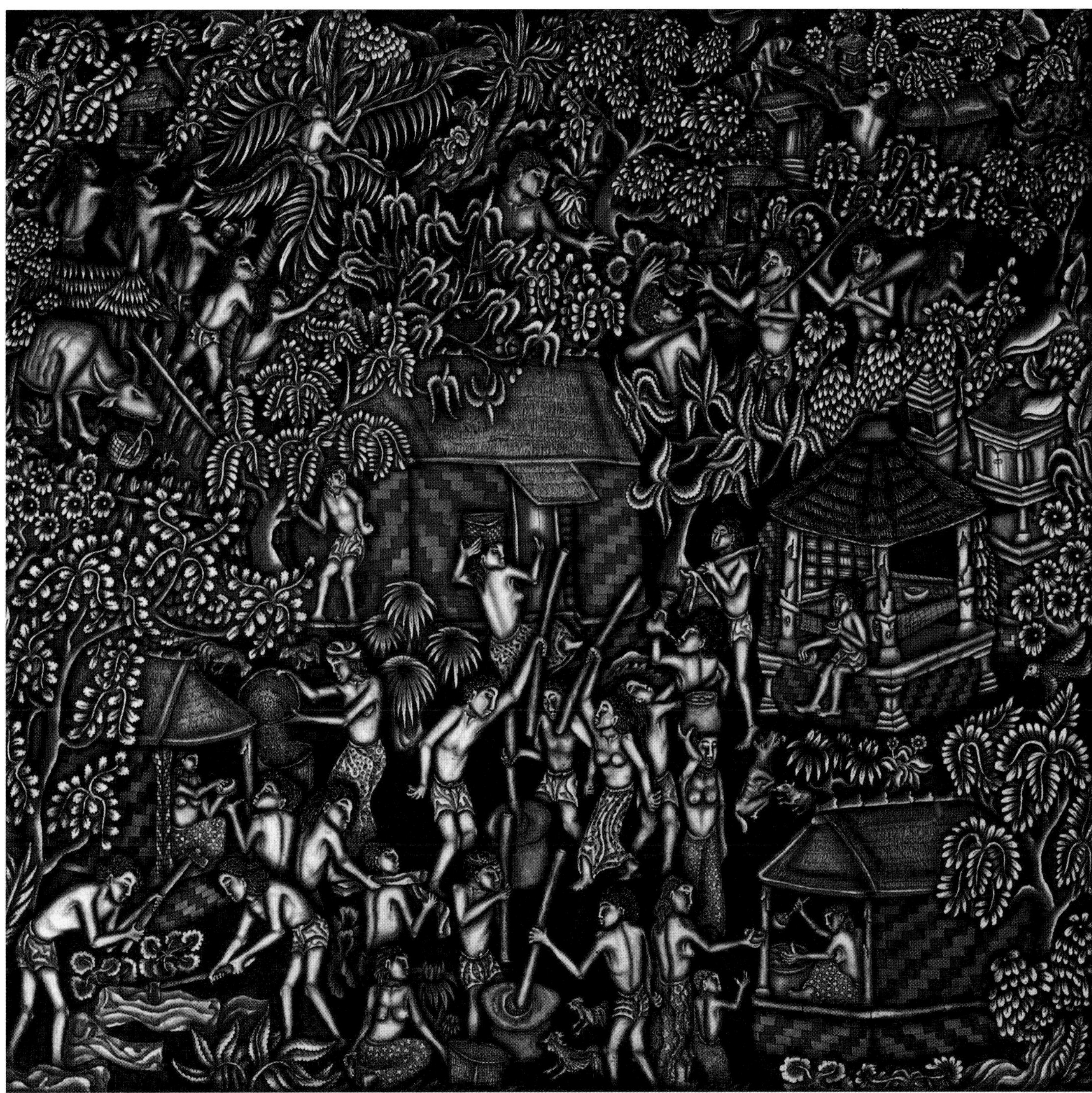

OPPOSITE: *Harvest Ceremony*
Ida Bagus Madé Tibah

In Balinese villages in the 1930s, after the rice was harvested, the bundled stalks were stored within the house yard in a rice shed on stilts, which is higher than the other structures. In this picture the rice shed is center right. A woman inside looks out, receiving an elaborate offering lifted by a woman on a ladder. Around and below the rice shed are the four buildings required in any traditional house yard.

The top sector of the picture, behind the living quarters, is the family temple with its houselike altars, where two women with raised right arms present offerings to the family deities. Other women bring more offerings on their heads, and children play here and there.

ABOVE: *Festival Preparation in Village Household*
Ida Bagus Nyoman Poedja

This scene is of a typical Balinese courtyard, with the standard four main living pavilions facing one another in a square. At the bottom right is the kitchen, where food is being dished up. To the left of and above the kitchen are two pavilions for sleeping. In the center is the fourth, with the closed door, where sacred things are stored and certain people may sleep. At the right, behind the sleeping pavilion, are two small spirit houses. Several people join in chopping wood and pounding rice with long pestles, indicating that a festival is in preparation.

In what appears to be a separate narrative, the upper half of the picture shows two groups of men, one with torches and the other with clubs, about to capture two thieves (upper right) who are taking a package out of a house yard by passing it over the wall next to a locked door.

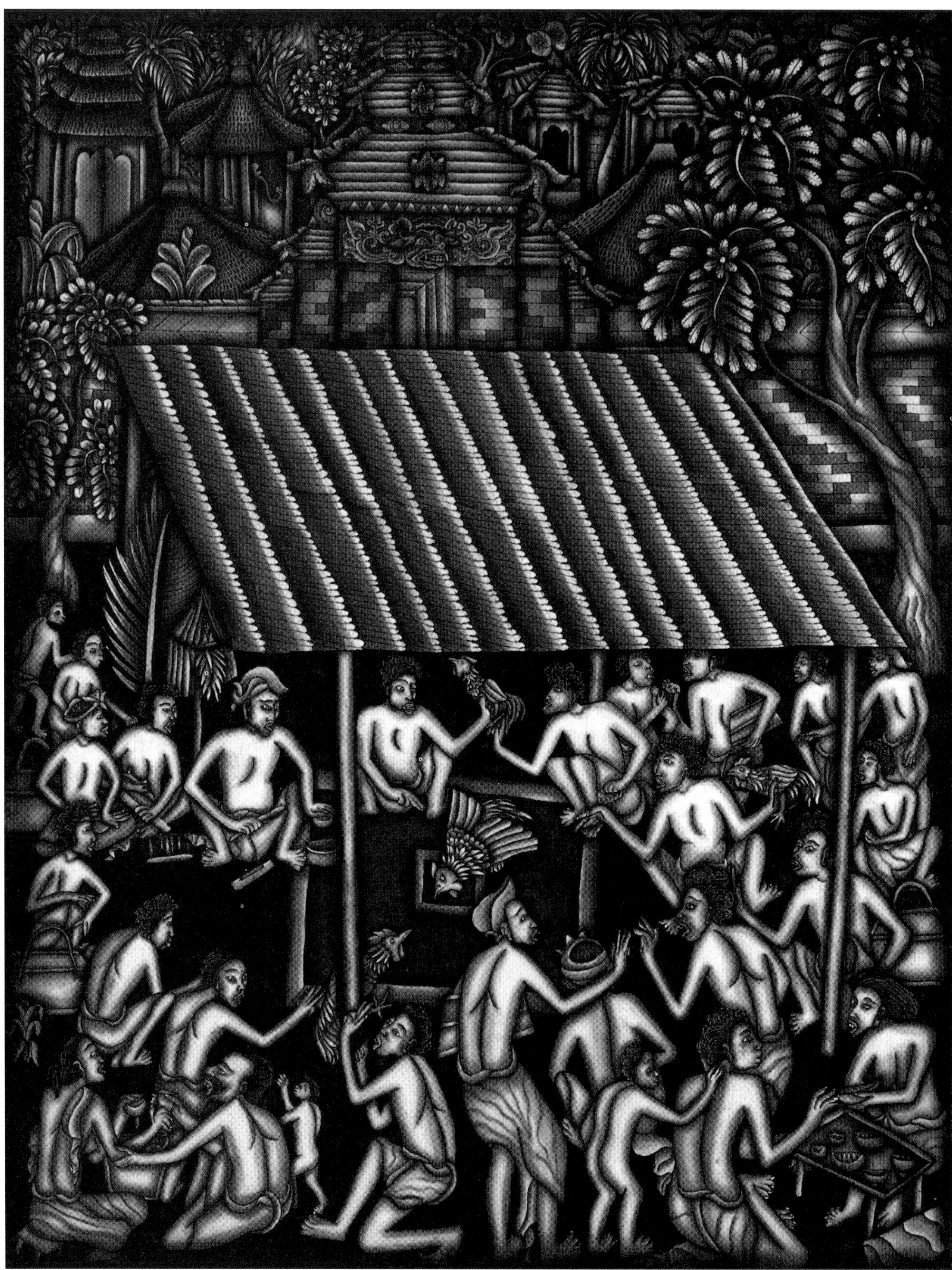

They are requested to return to their proper locations and to permit the ceremony to continue.

This ritual over, the group then goes to the inside of the temple, where special offerings from each household (the tall confections being carried on women's heads) are displayed. Then, when all is ready, the priest or priests, with their mantras and prayers, begin the temple ceremony.

Another picture shows a ritual that is not held within a temple, but rather in the home. *Harvest Ceremony* illustrates a family's rice being brought in and offerings being placed in the shed where the grain is stored. While this picture conveys a peaceful, though busy, atmosphere, its composition is erratic. The whole is coordinated neither through a constant perspectival viewpoint nor through systematic design.

Each picture is a different solution to a technical problem: how to include all the many essential parts of a ritual on one small sheet of paper. Most Balinese ceremonies are intricate combinations of many acts, some of which are simultaneous and some consecutive. Lay Balinese are baffled by their complexity and often need ritual specialists to lead them through the successive steps of preparation and performance. Some of the Batuan picture makers knew these details because they were sons and assistants of ritual specialists, but even for them the task of representing a complete ritual all at once was new and difficult. Sometimes they attempted to draw simultaneous ritual events in a row, as in Sanoer's picture, or they would produce a series of independent pictures, but more often they distributed the various acts of worship over the entire area of a picture.

Whether a ritual is held in a temple, home, or elsewhere, there is always a great deal of festive preparation of foods and other sorts of offerings. A picture by Poedja, *Festival Preparation in a Village Household*, catches the communal flavor of this activity by showing people collecting wood for cooking and pounding the hulls off rice grains. The tourist view of Bali is of a contented paradise, and the picture maker here presents first that peaceful image of people working together, but then introduces a discordant, undercutting note by showing theft and its vigilant interception.

A last example of a ritual scene is *A Cockfight at a Temple*, by I Reneh and Déwa Wayan Kandel Débel. Many tourists were taken to cockfights, in which Balinese enthusiastically bet on which rooster would kill the other. To an outsider, the contest looks like a mere pastime, but the cockfight is necessary in most temple ceremonies, for it produces an offering of fresh blood for the demonic beings in the area.

It is important to note what most strongly tourist-oriented pictures of ceremonies do *not* show, as well as what they typically include. Whether they depict activities inside or outside the temples, they present only the outer look of the movements connected with worship. They do not show, as the pictures in the next chapters do, those who, in the view of all Balinese, are the most important participants: the clouds of invisible beings of various degrees of power, whose many varieties resemble the diversity of the population of Bali itself. These many spiritual beings are present at every ritual, partaking of the food offerings, listening to the mantras and the music, watching the dance-drama performances along with the humans. They also help or hinder the human effort to attract the attention and beneficence of the highest deities. For example, the next picture, by Diding, of the ritual bathing of a corpse shows several evil spirits lurking among the participants.

These spirit beings are invisible and intangible, and their attitudes toward humans unpredictable. They are known by humans primarily through their effects on the prosperity or suffering of their people. Their numbers are incalculable. Each temple is dedicated to specific deities, whom the congregation periodically invites to descend among them to be feted, worshiped, and supplicated for aid. But every invited deity is always accompanied by a huge entourage of lesser gods and demons who must also be feted, placated, and worshiped.

There are also many other kinds of local spiritual beings who inhabit every neighborhood. Some of these spirits have small temples or shrines of their own, while other lesser ones inhabit crossroads. The imagined form of one of these spirits can be found in the picture of a demon in a rice field by Reneh on page 66. During a temple festival, some of these local spirits are also invited to attend and share in the festivities, while others are asked to go away through propitiatory offerings set outside the temple. The highest and most distant deities are also invoked in prayers, but invited to witness the proceedings from afar, as for instance, the god Siva, for whom a tall temporary altar is usually erected for the duration of a temple festival.

To call the spiritual beings who visit the human world during a temple festival "gods" and "demons," as we must when we write in English, seriously falsifies Balinese ideas about them, since it implies that each one is either consistently "benevolent" or "malevolent." Any so-called god or demon of Bali is capable of being both helpful and harmful to people. A deity's beneficent act for one group may hurt another. For instance, when a festival is in progress, a ritual may be performed to prevent rain during the days of the ceremonies. The consequence, however, may be that a rain storm moving toward the locality will simply be diverted toward another community, drenching *their* offerings and *their* performances. A more serious example is that of contagious disease: The demon Ratu Macaling (page 67) brought cholera epidemics every rainy season to most of south Bali. In Batuan in the 1930s a famous healer was said to have made a pact with the demon to pass by Batuan. As a result, Ratu Macaling's destructive entourage went to neighboring villages instead.

OPPOSITE: *A Cockfight at a Temple*
I Reneh and Déwa Wayan Kandel Débel

A cockfight is being held in front of a temple, whose gate is shown as the triangle at top. The placement of the cockfight indicates that it is part of a series of rituals, although for many participants it is primarily an opportunity to compete and gamble. Squares marked on the ground contain the two roosters about to fight. Around the edges people make bets, their extended fingers indicating the odds they want. Several people hold other roosters, awaiting their turn to pit them against one another. At the upper left corner of the square sits the umpire and timekeeper, the man with a head scarf and a small bowl in one hand. The bowl has a hole in it, and the time is measured by how long the bowl takes to sink into the water of the larger basin below it. At bottom left and right women sell snacks.

The demonic look of a being does not necessarily mean that it is malevolent. In Keteg's picture at the beginning of this chapter the great dragon figure, the *barong*, has a huge fierce mouth, fangs, and popping eyes. But for all his ferocious appearance, the *barong* is not at all dangerous, at least not to those who show him the proper respect. In fact, the *barong* is protective of his followers, and many people have personal tales of how a *barong* has come to their rescue, even as far away as Jakarta. However, in the act of protecting his followers, the *barong* can harm other people who might desire to hurt them. There are cases in which lingering illness and death have been ascribed to the action of a *barong* seeking revenge for earlier misdeeds by the suffering person.

Sometimes, as in the example of the death-dealing Ratu Macaling, the element of malevolence is the primary attribute of the being, but even he can be placated with offerings, dances, music, and spells and rendered harmless for a brief time. Other deities, such as those of a village temple, are usually benevolent because of the regular respectful attention paid to them by the villagers. Only in extreme cases, as when a member of the congregation commits a particularly sacrilegious act, is such a god likely to transform momentarily into a wrathful destructive demon.

The capacity of spirit beings not only to change from a well-wishing attitude to destructive anger and back but also to take many different shapes at whim, has important implications for Balinese conceptions of truth. It implies that humans may not always know what form a being will take, nor can they know from the form of a prepared vessel what being may have taken his seat in it. Therefore, an artist who wants to portray such a being can use his own fantasy at will. Normally these beings are formless, and only when they manifest themselves do they take specific shape. Temple congregations provide physical objects (small figurines, even bowls of water) for deities to inhabit during their visitation in the human world. Certain masks, and occasionally people, perform the same function of being a material vessel for the spiritual being.

To speak about this metaphysical volatility, the Balinese make a distinction between what they call *niskala*, or "invisible" and "intangible," and *sakala*, or "visible" and "tangible." The spiritual beings and powers of the cosmos are *niskala*, yet they must take *sakala* forms to be efficacious in the world and to have material effects. Higher deities, when moved to action, take lesser demonic forms, which then may make themselves visible to human beings. To represent the visible world, as do most of the pictures in this chapter, is to show only the minor *sakala* aspect of experience.

Many Balinese today stress that their religion is at base monotheistic, that the greatly varied gods and demons are, in fact, all manifestations of the one God, who sends out avatars as numerous as the rays of the sun. However, no present-day Balinese religious leader has succeeded in establishing doctrinal uniformity on this or other matters. Not only is every locality different from every other in the modes of worship and ways of speaking about it, but different social groups, too, cannot agree. There is, no doubt, a central core of principles to which all Balinese adhere, but no one, Balinese or Westerner, has yet been able to explicate these adequately. This is in part because, as everywhere, people in actuality have quite diverse beliefs. The pervasive inability to make firm generalizations about "Balinese religion" is largely due to the Balinese conviction that the beings and powers that govern their universe take many forms, require many sorts of ritual recognition, and are known to human beings only partially and fitfully. And because, they believe, what counts is what people do, not what they say.

Death and the Unseen

Most of the pictures of rituals made for Bateson and Mead in Batuan went far beyond the clichés of those made directly for tourists. The latter usually portray simplified versions of temple rituals and cremations, depicting only certain standard moments such as the sprinkling of holy water by the priest, or the paradelike carrying of the cremation tower. The Batuan artists, instead, drew many rituals and portions of rituals not usually viewed by foreigners. This showed up particularly in the pictures showing the ceremonies surrounding death and mourning.

Balinese cremation, because of its visual exuberance, which makes it so suitable as spectacle, is often depicted in foreign writings and photograph books. For instance, Gregor Kraus in 1920 climaxed his highly popular book of photographs with a series on cremation, as did Miguel and Rose Covarrubias in their photographs in *Island of Bali*.[2] The royal cremation, with its elaborately carved and painted tower and crowded, riotous rush to the burning ground, has often served as a master emblem for Bali.

Oddly, none of the pictures in the Bateson-Mead Collection shows the burning itself, and only one shows the tower. Perhaps this was because the Batuan picture makers were not content with making images of the vivid and exciting moment of carrying the body to the burning field, but went on to show more intimate (and often ritually more significant) steps in the mortuary sequence.

This sequence may take years to complete, and the cremation is by no means the final step. In this series of rites the soul of the deceased is repeatedly purified of all its material and worldly attachments and is thus freed to be reincarnated in the body of one of its descendants or to join the undifferentiated soul-stuff of the universe. What happens if all the ceremonies are not carried out is illustrated in the picture by Djata of the Bima Suarga tale on page 56, where the souls of those people who have not been cremated hang upside down by their feet from a huge tree. Another belief is that uncremated spirits will hover around the village and cause trouble until ritually freed.

The cremation proper, the burning of the body, enacts a double narrative—first, a story of the passage/metamorphosis/demanifestation of the soul, and second, a story of the nobility and worldly eminence of the deceased and his kin. All steps in death rituals are accompanied by feelings of trouble, uncertainty, and anxiety about whether the survivors are doing the right thing for the deceased, or are exposing themselves to his wrath.

The first step in the entire mortuary sequence, right after death, is the cleansing of the body, both physically and spiritually. It is then elegantly dressed and provided with provisions

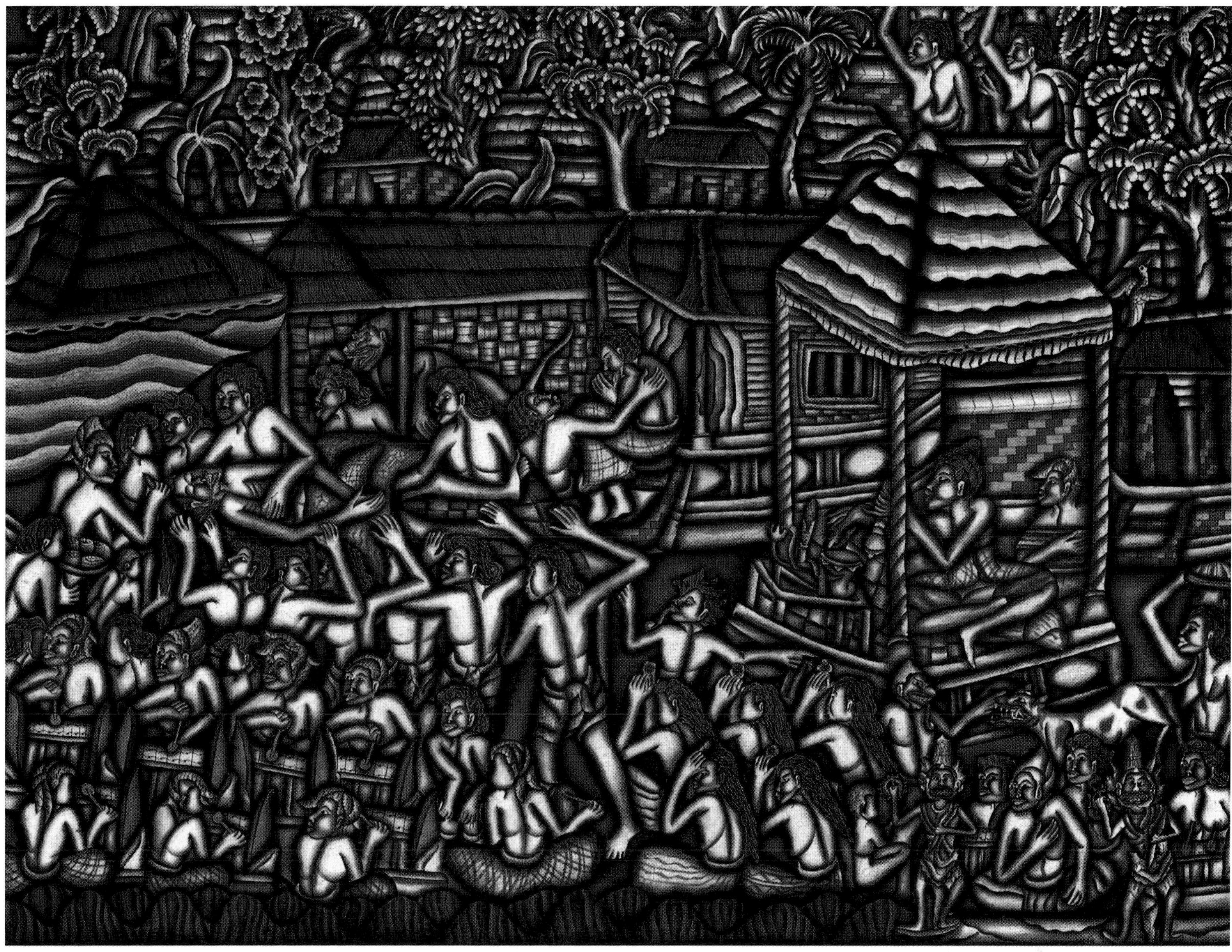

Death Ritual: Bathing the Body and Paying Last Homage to the Deceased
Ida Bagus Ketut Diding

The first step in the complex Balinese funerary sequence, a moment of great domestic intimacy, comes soon after death when the members of the immediate family, led by a Brahmana ritual specialist, ceremonially bathe the body. They sprinkle several kinds of holy water on it, anoint it with perfume, and dress it in new clothing and jewels, preparing their kinsman's soul-substance *(atma)* for a journey away from them. When all is ready, those in the family who are junior to the deceased kneel down and pray to him, an act referred to as *mapamit*, or "taking leave."

Note that among the figures can be discovered some evil spirits, invisible to the people, who are attracted to the dead flesh. The apparent serenity of the funeral, in fact, is revealed to be in considerable danger. One of these figures is near the center of the picture, between the people with their hands on the body and the priest's pavilion. Another is just below the priest. Dogs can see these invisible beings, and one is barking at the evil spirit.

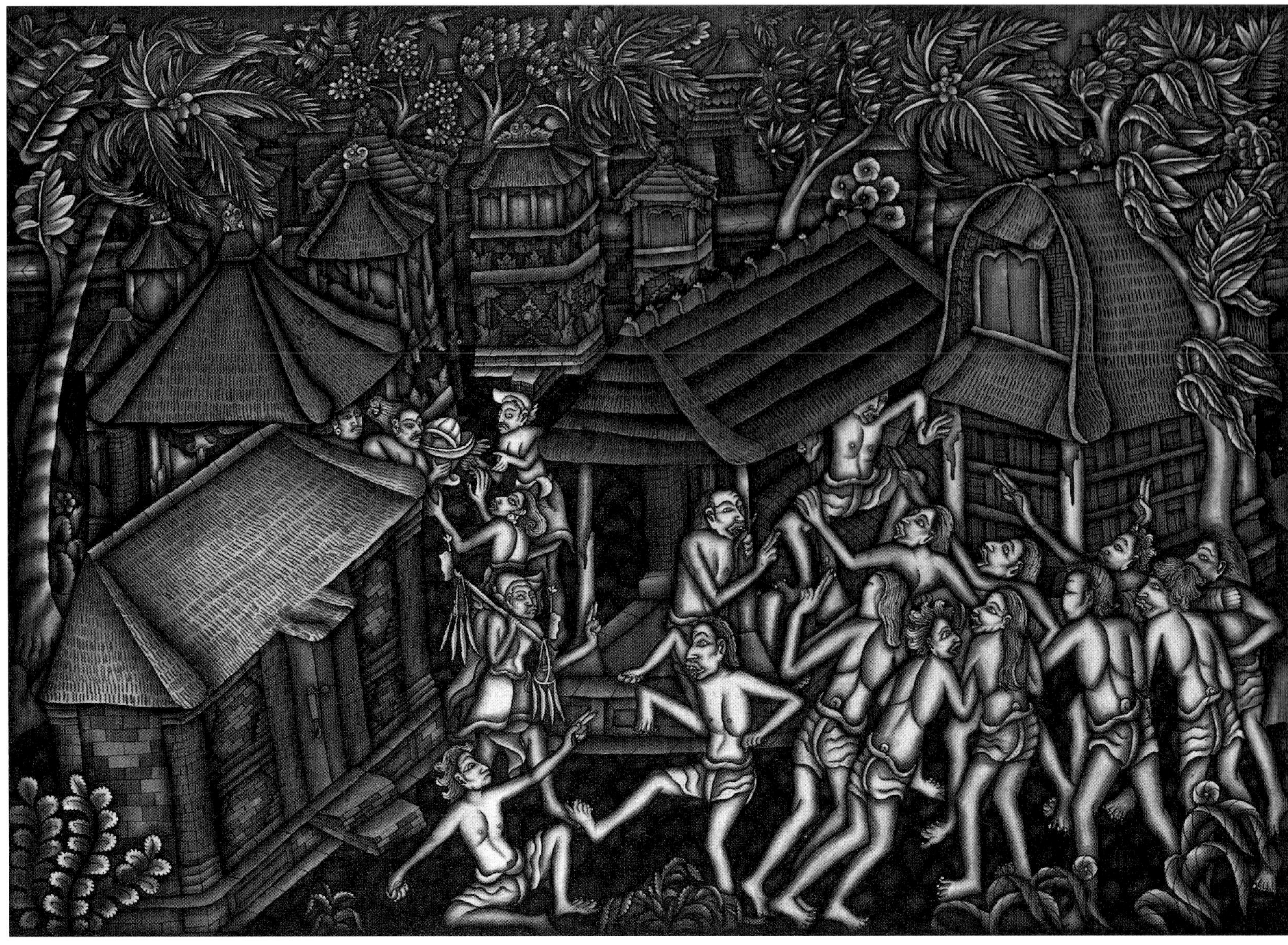

ABOVE: *Cremation: Taking the Body from Its Bed*
I Reneh

Prior to the procession to the graveyard or burning ground, members of the village take the body, which has been ritually purified, clothed, shrouded, and wrapped in grass mats, from the bed at home and place it on either a palanquin or, if this is an important person, a tall decorated tower.

The group of men who will carry the body are gesturing aggressively both against the invisible beings who may want to capture the body and also against each other, with one side maliciously threatening to desecrate the body and the other side protecting it. The picture maker has drawn the trees blowing to maintain the feeling of excitement.

OPPOSITE: *Cremation: The Start of the Procession*
Ida Bagus Madé Djatasoera

This picture shows the moment in the cremation of a high Brahmana priest when the body is placed on a highly decorated carrying tower. The body is the small white bundle near the center of the picture, held by a close relative standing on the tower. The gesturing men are about to pick up the tower by the lattice of bamboo poles and carry it from the village to the burning ground near the graveyard. This is always a moment of high tension because of the vulnerability of the body, and possibly its carriers, to the hungry spirits of open roads and crossroads. Everyone is anxiously yelling, goading each other to daring with accusations of cowardice.

Bateson chose this picture as the focus of his well-known article "Style, Grace, and Information in Primitive Art." It was one of Bateson's favorites, which he sent as a gift to his mother in 1937 and later, after she died, hung on his own wall. The only picture from the collection that he kept, it came to stand for him for the whole collection, and in a certain way, for Bali.

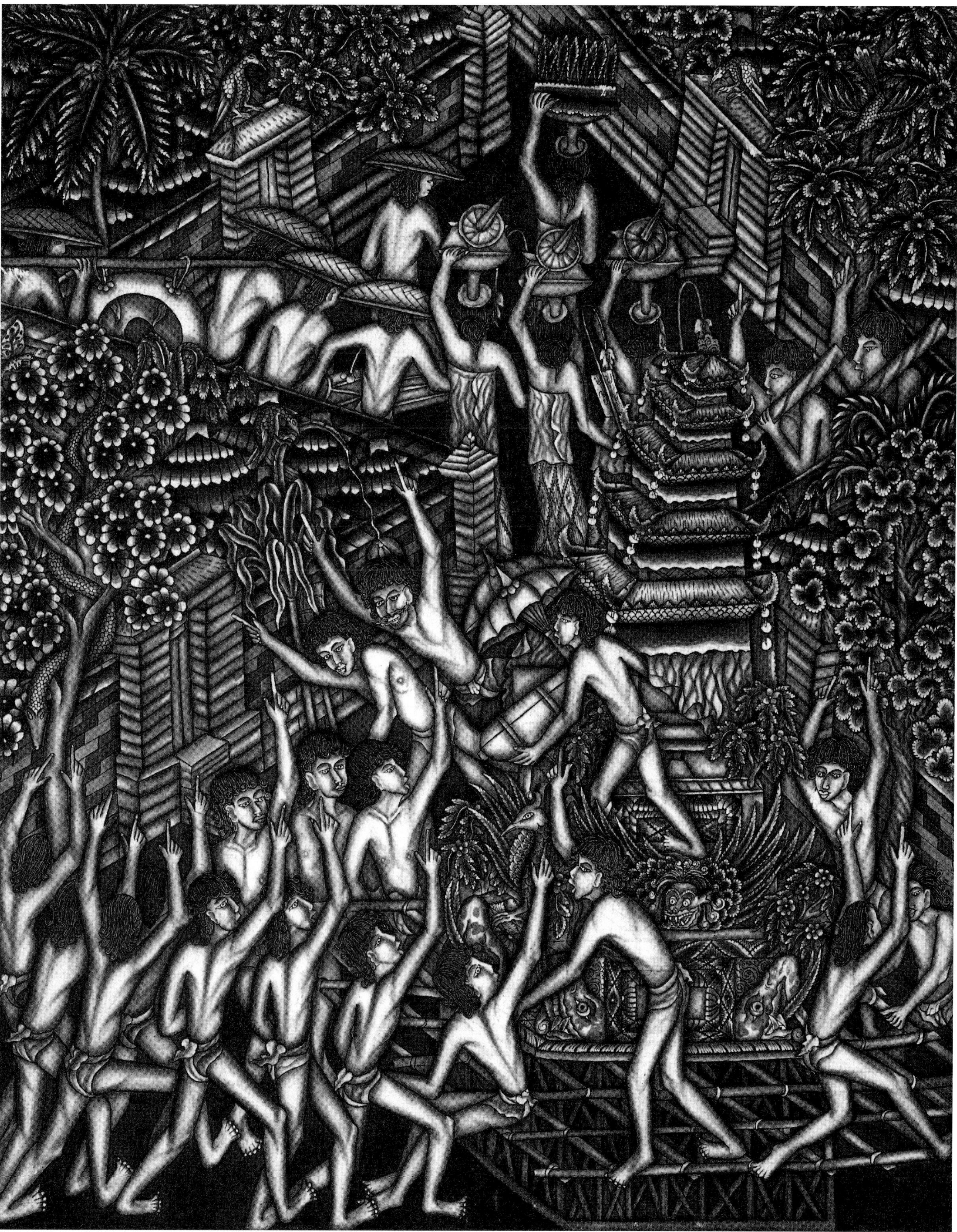

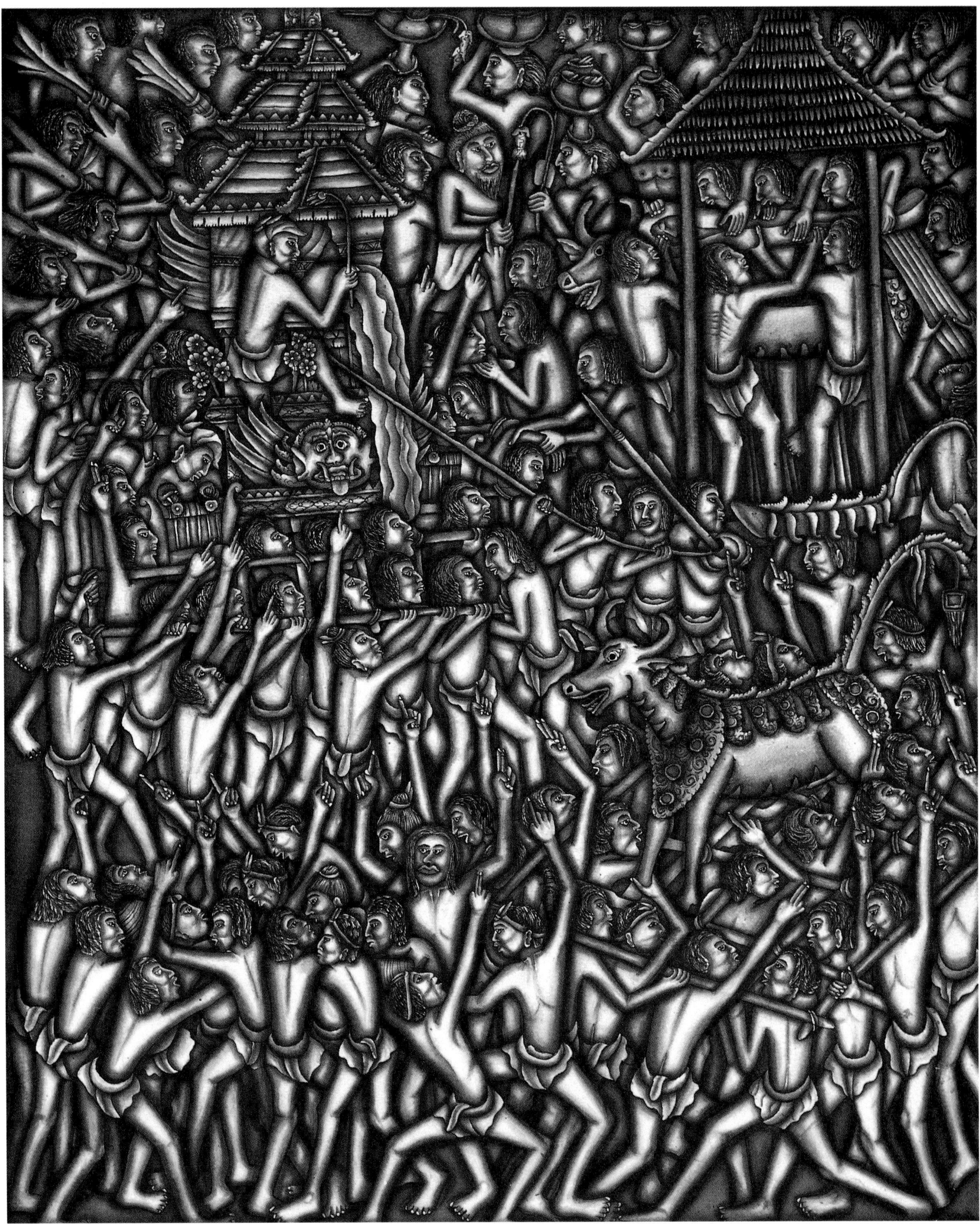

for its journey away. The mourners both bid farewell and offer their respect to the sacred soul-stuff of the deceased. A priest performs a series of ceremonies to consecrate the ritual paraphernalia, again purify the departing soul, consecrate it, and send it on its way.

At this point the body may be buried, to be disinterred years later and cremated, or it may be burned directly. After the burning, the ashes are ritually pulverized by the family members all together, each with a hand on the stone pestle. The powdered ashes are placed in new receptacles and, with equipment for the journey, are taken out to sea. A month or more after the cremation an even more significant ceremony *(nyekah)* is carried out, which again severs the soul from the world and bids it farewell once more. The *nyekah* ritual is a kind of rerun of the cremation, but with symbolic representations of the corpse. The Batuan pictures relating to mortuary rituals show some but not all of these steps.

The picture *Death Ritual: Bathing the Body and Paying Last Homage to the Deceased* shows several moments in the sequence that are in many ways more important personally to Balinese than the flamboyant parade to the cremation. It is at this point that grieving family members perform last acts of tender solicitude in bathing and adorning the body. Usually they surround the body and place their hands on it at the same time. When ready, they perform an act of saying farewell to the personal spirit of the dead person. The reverse side of such solicitude is apprehension about the dead person's irritation or anger, for if these rituals are not carried out correctly and the spirit is not properly released, the hovering spirit of the deceased will cause suffering and illness among his or her descendants until the rituals have been performed.

The picture actually shows two temporally separate steps, the bathing (left) and the subsequent ritual act of homage and farewell (middle). At the right, under a roof, is a high priest, or *pedanda*, who performs a prayer during the bathing ritual. The two figures at the lower right are probably an awkward representation of a shadow play that might be performed at such a ritual, the *wayang lemah*. It is carried out by a shadow master with shadow puppets, but during the daytime with no lamp and no screen. All shadow puppets are in profile, however, and these figures are shown frontally, which may be the picture maker's mistake.

In the picture by Reneh of the moment when the dead body must be taken from its bed and transported for burial or cremation, the attention is on the struggling men of the village as they handle the corpse. The men who carry the body traditionally yell and jump to scare away the lurking evil spirits, and taunt one another to embolden themselves. Their mingled fear and excitement sometimes turns to nasty fighting between factions within the village (as depicted here). While family members try to protect the body, their enemies pull and throw it so as to desecrate it. Such a violent attempt to desecrate the body, called in Balinese *ngarap*, was not unusual and indeed happened in Batuan seven months after this picture was completed, on August 24, 1937, while Bateson and Mead were watching and filming.[3]

Two other pictures, by Djatasoera and Sawa, show the flamboyant carrying of the body high on an elaborately decorated tower to the burning ground. At every crossing of a road, path, or stream, the many men carrying the tower noisily revolve it to confuse and scare away the lurking spirits. When they arrive at the burning ground, the corpse or corpses are placed in large wooden sarcophagi carved into bulls or fishlike figures for the cremation. Another series of rituals is carried out here by a priest.

After the burning, a series of further rituals is conducted, as shown in a second picture by Djatasoera. Members of the family pulverize the remaining pieces of bone into ash, and after another series of rites, the ashes are released at sea. A month, or even years later, a second purification ceremony is held. Usually, this ritual is considered the final one, and the soul is thought finally to be completely severed from its body and its concerns with still-living kin.

The question as to where the soul *(atma)* goes after death and cremation is given a number of contradictory answers. The Balinese do not seem to be troubled by these contradictions, which suggests that they consider the different fates equally possible. Most, however, agree that as long as the body has not been cremated, the person is considered to hover around, watching over his or her surviving kin. If angered, this spirit being may cause illness and death. At every major ceremony, special plates of festival food are brought to the graveyard and placed on each grave by survivors, who may speak briefly with their deceased relative. After the final purification ceremony the spirit may join the formless, anonymous beings termed *leluhur* ("higher ones") who are worshiped in shrines in family temples and in the central village temple, the Pura Désa, where they melt into the village gods. However, these beings still retain one aspect of their prior living identity, the status of their title, for no one of higher title may worship the *leluhur* of lower title.

Another route for the soul after death is reincarnation into the body of a descendant, bringing with it all the burdens of punishment for earlier sins. This is probably the most common occurrence, for many infants are taken to a diviner to discover which forebear has been given new life, and many calamities that befall a person are attributed to punishments for actions taken in an earlier life.

There seems to be a third possible route, as represented in the intricate pictures of *suarga*, the "other world," carved on many temple walls (and in the picture by Djata on page 56). Not only the souls whose descendants were so reprehensible as not to cremate them are doomed to hang head down, but also those who lived immoral lives are tormented in specific ways. For instance, the sexually promiscuous woman is

OPPOSITE: *Cremation: At the Burning Ground*
Ida Bagus Ketut Sawa

Seen here is a later moment in a cremation, when the body on the tower has arrived at the burning ground and is being transferred into a wooden bull-shaped sarcophagus within which it will be burned (upper right). At lower right another bull-shaped vessel for a second cremation at the same time is being maneuvered into place.

In this picture, in contrast to the previous one, the viewpoint is close to the struggling people, and the tower correspondingly is stressed less; as a result, the viewer no longer sees the event as a distant spectacle but as a close participant.

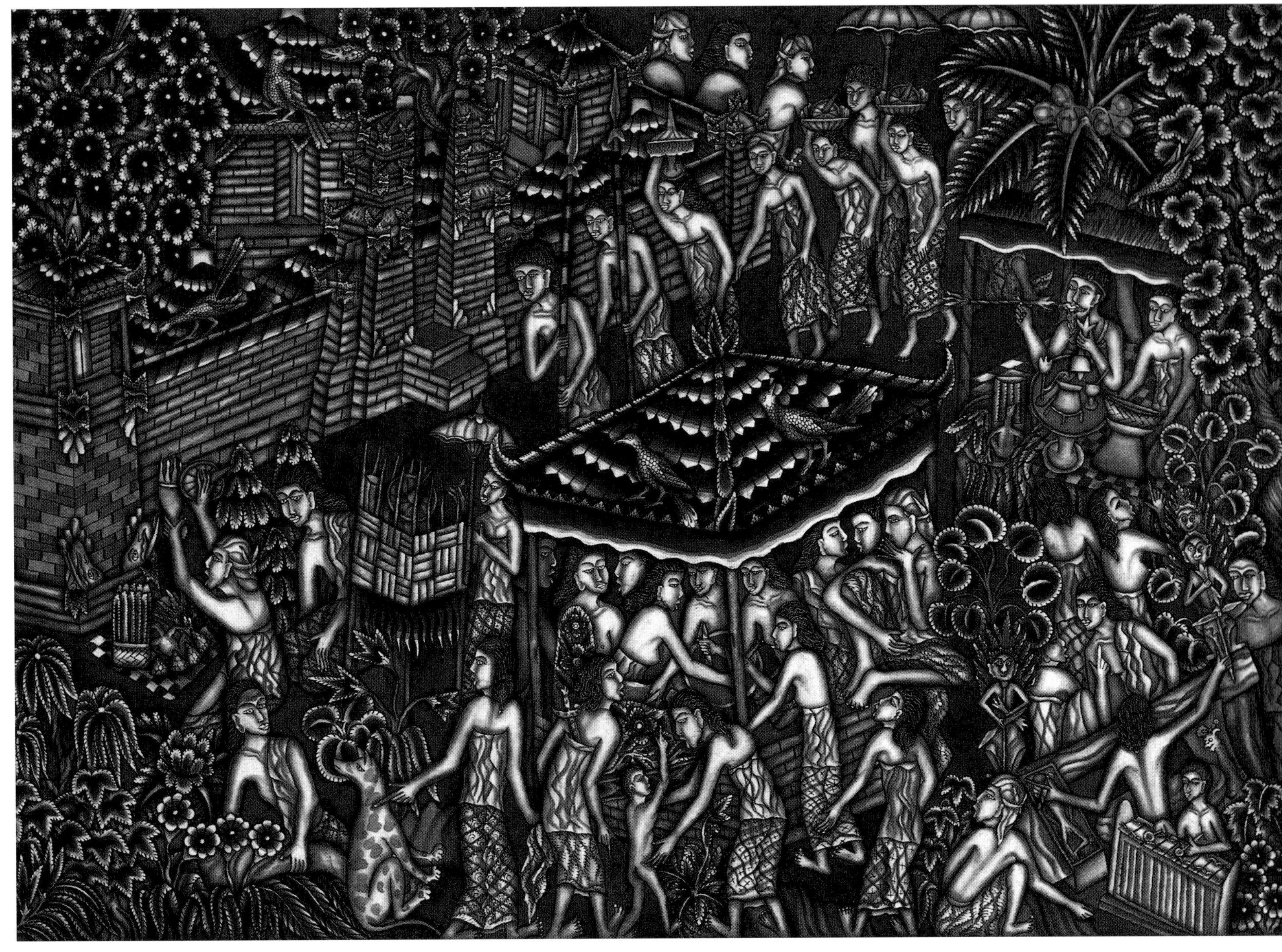

Cremation: Ritual Grinding of the Ashes after the Burning
Ida Bagus Madé Djatasoera

Another moment of familial intimacy in the cremation cycle is depicted here. After the body has been burned, the ashes are gathered together in an earthen bowl, and each member of the immediate family joins in grinding with a mortar and pestle the unburnt remnants of the deceased's bones. Usually several kin at once place their hands on the mortar, in much the same way that all the family members placed their hands on the deceased's body when it was ritually washed, and just as they had visited and touched or fed that person while ill. They can be seen doing this in the center, under the roof. To the right and above is a priest *(pedanda)* praying. At bottom right is a daylight shadow play *(wayang lemah)*, done with no lamp or screen and no audience but the deities. (Compare the picture by Diding on page 33.)

After the ashes are ground to a powder, they are placed in a special receptacle and carried to the main temples in the village, where someone speaking in the name of the deceased takes formal leave of the local gods (lower right). Then the receptacle is taken to a body of water, preferably the sea, and released, following one further ritual of farewell and blessing.

repeatedly raped by wild boars, or the man who cruelly killed birds is pecked at by clouds of them. These unfortunate people may not advance to the characterless status of *leluhur,* nor be reincarnated as one of their descendants after this purgatorial period. The Balinese notion that all living forms go through kaleidoscopic transformations and that we humans can know only fragments of what happens seems to allow them to entertain all possibilities without insisting on logical exclusiveness.

Ritual Dramas

Another kind of "life-in-Bali" picture that Batuan painters made was of dancers and players in performance. While the pictures themselves do not stress the point, these performances are nearly always integral elements in rituals. With their masks, music, and danced gestures, the performances are enhancements of the sacred costumes, music, words, and gestures of the priests and congregation. The dance-dramas provide a visible form for the invisible beings. The performance of a masked dance becomes an actual visitation when a spiritual being enters the mask or the performer and speaks and acts through him.

In the 1930s an extraordinary variety of dance-dramas was produced, many more than today, especially in the fairly affluent Gianyar region. Nearly every night a village troupe somewhere in the vicinity performed. Performers and audiences would travel long distances for these shows. Every one of these genres had slightly different dramatic and dance conventions, and different kinds of music and songs, costumes (some masked, some not), and choreographies. And each had quite different repertoires of stories.[4]

Even the most secular of dances is considered to have ritual and cosmological overtones. One very rowdy erotic courtship dance, the *jogéd,* in which men in the audience take turns dancing provocatively with a woman dancer, has strong sacred components (see pages 26–27). Formally, this erotic courtship dance has no story line, but the plot is the eternal one of seduction and rejection, of playing with the fires of lust and desire. The dance may be staged in places far from temples, but the woman's elaborate headdress is a copy of a sacred headdress of the *sanghyang* dance, which, when worn, invites a spirit to enter the body of the dancer. In the *sanghyang* dance there is also a seduction, but it is carried out between spirit beings. The *jogéd* dance echoes these cosmological and ritual concerns. From a Western perspective, in which secular and sacred are clearly opposites, Balinese performances are confusingly always both, though in differing mixtures.

A picture by Tombelos shows this conflation of secular and sacred in yet another way. It portrays a highly sacred dance, the *rejang,* which was adapted for tourist productions. In Batuan this dance is still performed frequently in the evenings between November and March, dangerous months when the demon Ratu Macaling invades the region, bringing epidemics of cholera, typhus, and other diseases. All the women and young girls of the village participate in propitiating Ratu Macaling and his entourage with their dance. In the 1930s this dance was accompanied by an endless series of cockfights as well. In about 1935 the village created a tourist show from the *rejang,* using only the most beautiful dancers, under the leadership of Ngéndon, who persuaded them to purchase elegant costumes and who brought the foreigners to see it. For a ritual *rejang* see the picture by Sanoer on pages 26–27.

In most of these pictures of performances the players are shown encircled by an audience. Often a large part of the picture is taken up with village homes in the background. The pictorial implication is that a dramatic production is always solidly situated within its community setting. Indeed, most such shows are commissioned by the local group, normally the congregation of a temple, and the musicians are usually local people, and often the actors and dancers as well. The composition of the pictures stresses this close integration of performance and local community.

A few of the pictures evoke the sense of gaiety of these festivals, but most give a more somber impression. In fact, there is always a great deal of excitement and fun at these festivals and performances. While some of the content is serious, every show contains a great deal of sharp satire and riotous slapstick. For all Balinese, and especially for young men such as those who made these pictures, these ritual festivals and dramatic performances are of great importance. The large number of pictures made for Bateson and Mead that were based on dance-drama stories is evidence of the significance of these plays in the lives of their makers.

No matter what the genre, there are always several "clowns," whose function in these plays is much more than maintaining a high level of hilarity. These clowns are storytellers called *penasar,* meaning "he who provides a foundation," and they recount the drama as it unfolds. A *penasar* might play a servant to the prince; or an ugly, greedy older woman (often a mother or mother-in-law); or a coarse younger woman (often the ugly sister who is smuggled into marriage with the prince instead of her lovely princess sister); or a cowardly soldier or officer in the army; or a lazy villager who is tired of making so many offerings. Many of the more elevated characters do not speak and are confined to miming their intentions and feelings. Others express themselves in the classic language of *Kawi* or in elaborate literary Balinese, which most Balinese cannot understand. So the *penasar* speaks for them in everyday Balinese, the language of this world. Through his witty dialogue and numerous asides to the audience, the *penasar* explains the dramatic circumstances of the heroes, describes what has happened offstage, and even what is happening onstage. Within this tightly structured dramatic tradition, the *penasar* provides moments of informality as well as keeping the story going. Through his interpretive interventions he forges the vital link between the content of the plays and the lives of the audience.

Western viewers of these Balinese paintings of performances (and of the actual performances as well) are always struck by the casual way members of the audience come and go during a show, talking and flirting with one another, buying snacks, caring for small children, even taking naps. Some observers (Spies, and following him Mead, Bateson, and Belo, in particular) have stated that Balinese do not pay close attention to the plots and characters of their plays. This, I believe, is quite false, and an important body of evidence is the Bateson-Mead Collection itself, in which major stress is placed on stories by the picture makers.

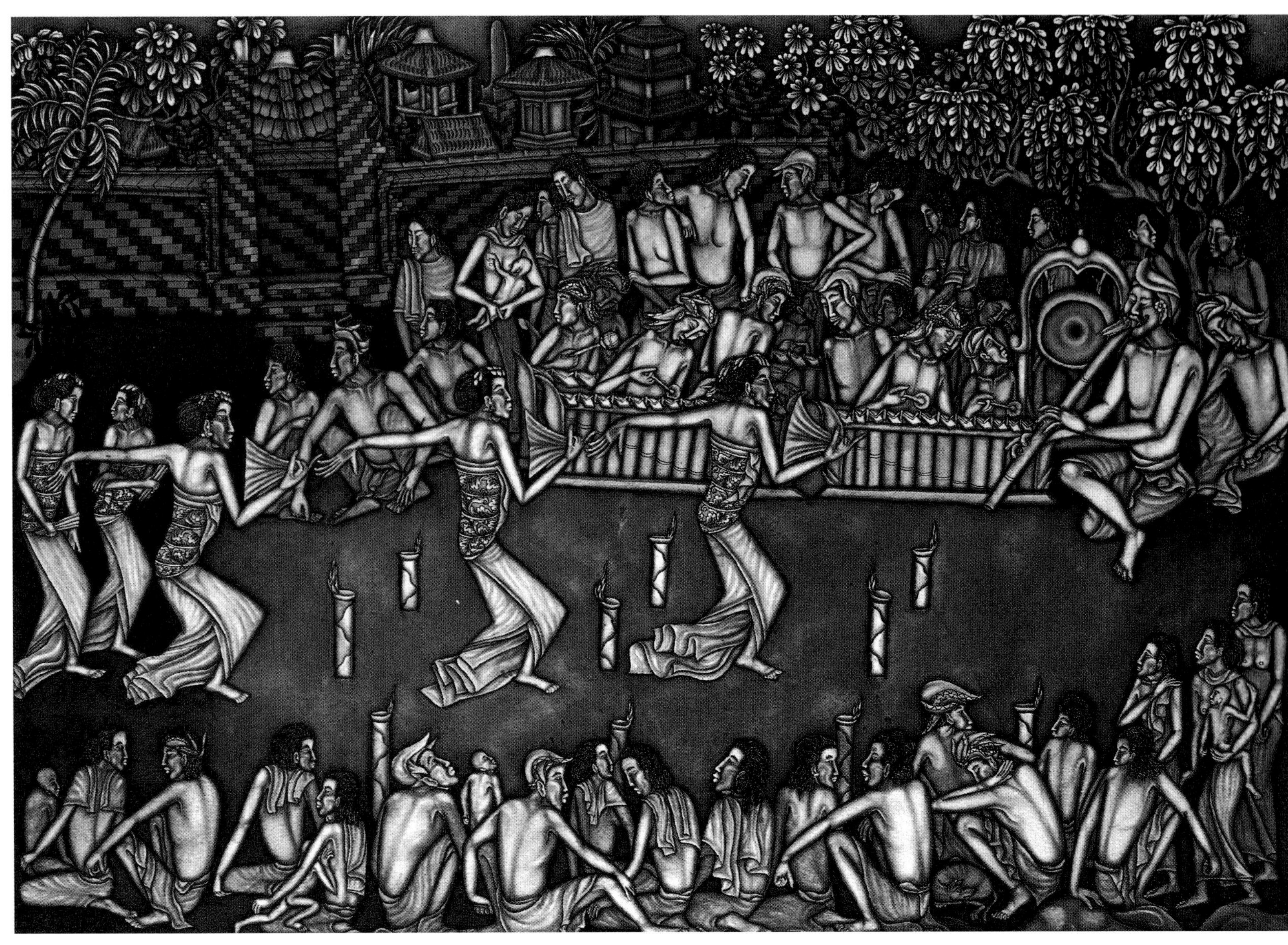

Rejang *Temple Dance*
I Tombelos

The *rejang* is a solemn sacred dance in Batuan, performed by all the women in the village as part of a ritual in front of the village temple, the Pura Désa. The dancers propitiate disease-bearing demons with the slow, sensuous movements of their bodies and extended arms. But depicted here is a tourist version of the *rejang*, marked as a commercial spectacle by the costumes and fans held by the dancers, the careful staging of "traditional" bamboo lamps along the dance area and the head scarfs of the musicians, and by the absence of offerings and other ritual-related objects.

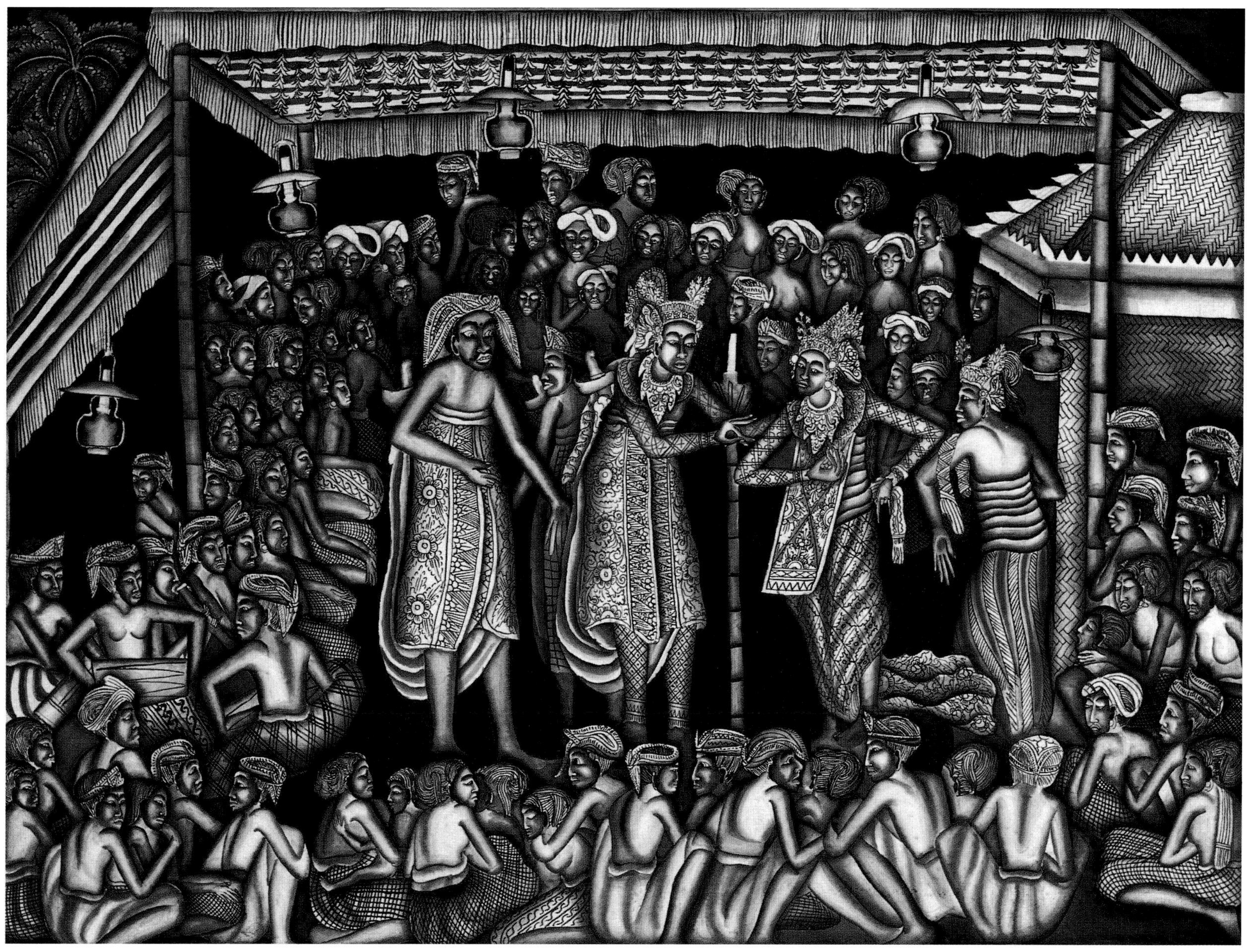

Performance of an Arja *Play*
I Ketut Pateh

The stage for this popular form of drama, a sort of light opera, is a temporary shed of bamboo and plaited palm leaves. Light is provided by kerosene lanterns, one of which is placed on a bamboo stand near the center of the picture. There are five actors in the picture, recognizable by their costumes as standardized *arja* characters: a prince and a princess are in the center, gesturing toward one another. The prince is at the left, with an identifying headdress; a *kris*, or ceremonial dagger, on his back; and an elaborate skirt, which is pulled through his legs and tied behind him. The princess to his left wears a long rectangular apronlike costume. To the left of the prince are two retainers (one barely visible, next to the prince's *kris*), and near the princess is a woman servant. These are the "clowns" *(penasar)* who interpret the story to the audience.

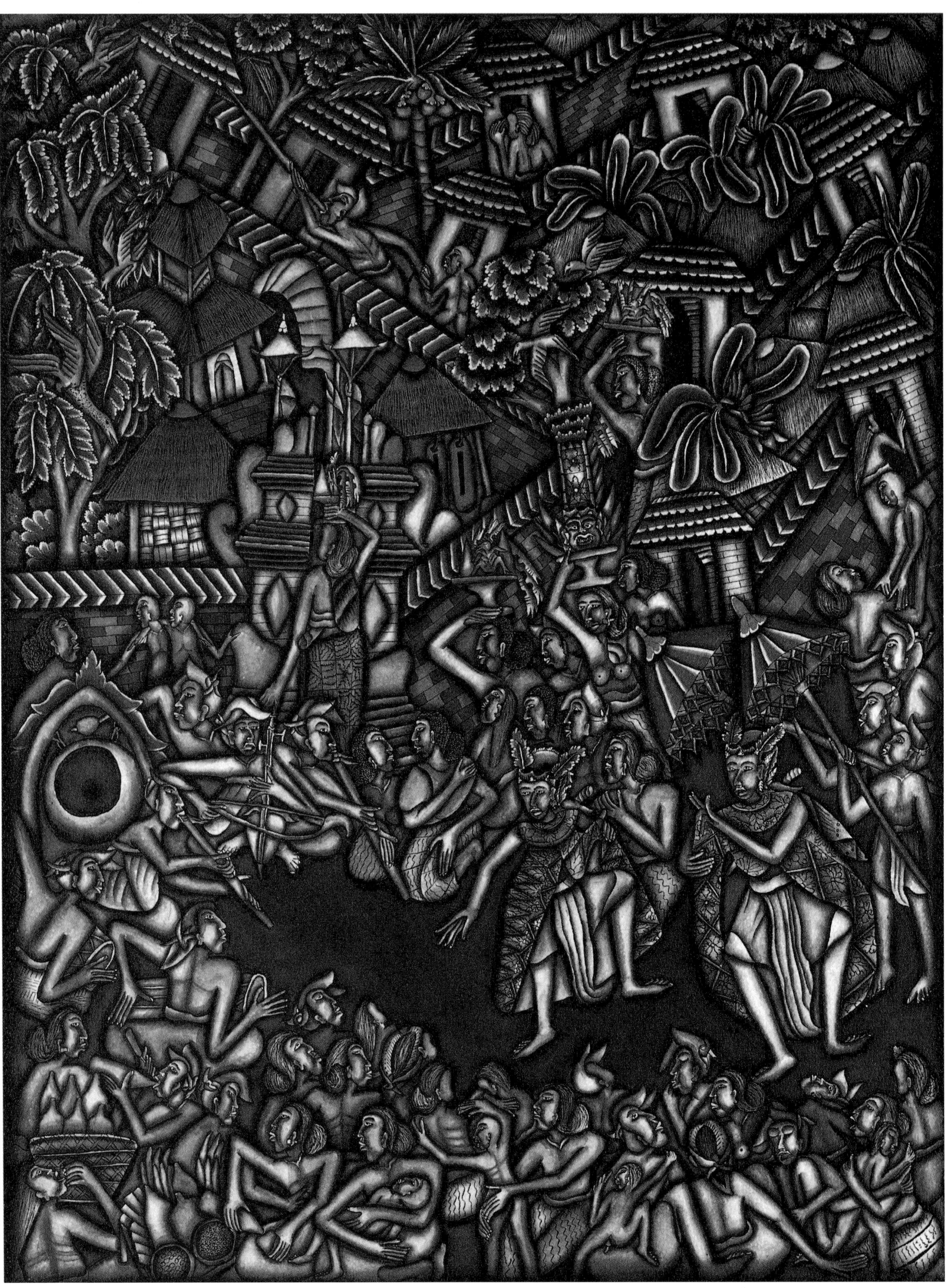

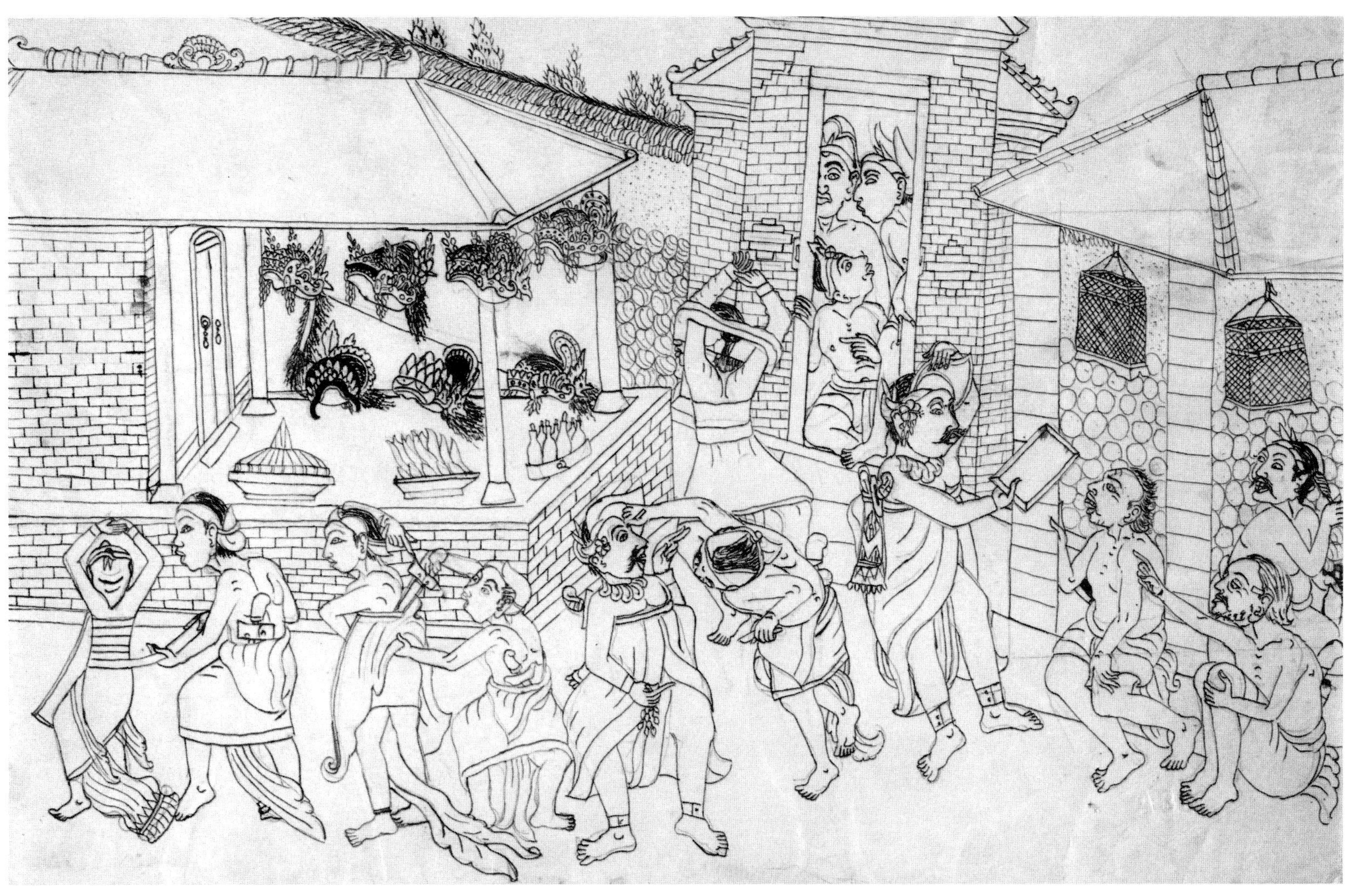

OPPOSITE: *Performance of a* Gambuh *Play*
Ida Bagus Ketut Sawa

The *gambuh* dance-drama form, seen here, is a specialty of Batuan. At middle left is a temple, complete with altars, banners, and ritual parasols. A group of women enters it bearing offerings on their heads. The dancers' costumes are meticulously and accurately drawn, as is the *gambuh* orchestra, which includes three-foot bamboo flutes *(suling)* and a string instrument called a *rebab*. Although there is no indication of what story is being portrayed, the roles shown are probably those of young warriors *(arya)*. The artist, Sawa, who was about twenty years old, often danced the part of an *arya*.

The upper half of this picture is given over to a depiction of village roads and doorways, stressing more than usual the contrast between performance and community. The man holding a child by the hand in the upper center is not concerned with the show at all, but rather is engaged in a common sport, hunting birds with a blowpipe.

ABOVE: *Costuming Up before a Dance-Drama Performance*
Désak Putu Lambon

Backstage before a *gambuh* dance performance, the men and boys are putting on their costumes. Headdresses hang from the eaves or rest on the floor of a high pavilion, a *gedong*, where they may be stored between shows. The figure on the left, smaller than the others, is being dressed in women's clothing, although his head scarf identifies him as a man. In the *gambuh* at that time, men performed women's parts. The dancer in the center is being helped with his face makeup. On the right, two older people, seated, speak with the man playing the *penasar* role, who checks his headdress in a mirror.

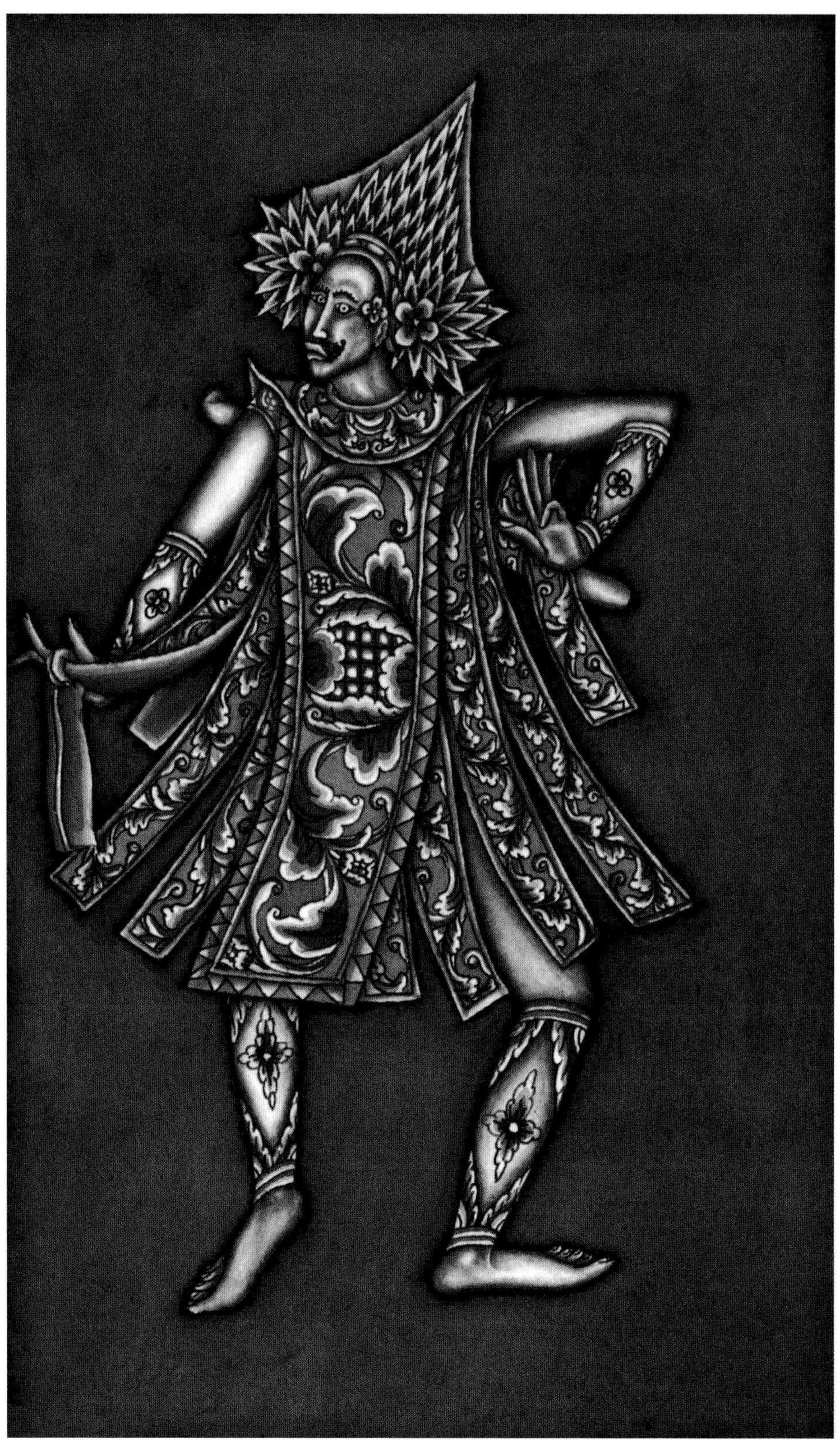

Two Players from a Baris Melampahan
I Tombelos, with I Taweng

ABOVE AND OPPOSITE: Above is a *baris* dancer whose costume of long decorated strips of cloth and pointed headdress shows him to be a noble hero-warrior. Opposite is a *penasar*, or servant follower of the warrior. The *baris* never speaks but mimes his lines, which then are spoken for him by the *penasar.* In addition to being spokesman and interpreter, the *penasar* is also a clever clown. These two personages appear in the next picture, which shows a *baris melampahan* performance.

The format of these two pictures, in which a single figure is set against a plain background, was more commonly followed by the Ubud picture makers than the Batuan artists. A single figure against a plain background was easier to produce than the larger compositions. Many people made both kinds of pictures, inserting the images first worked out in the easier small mode into the more complex larger picture.

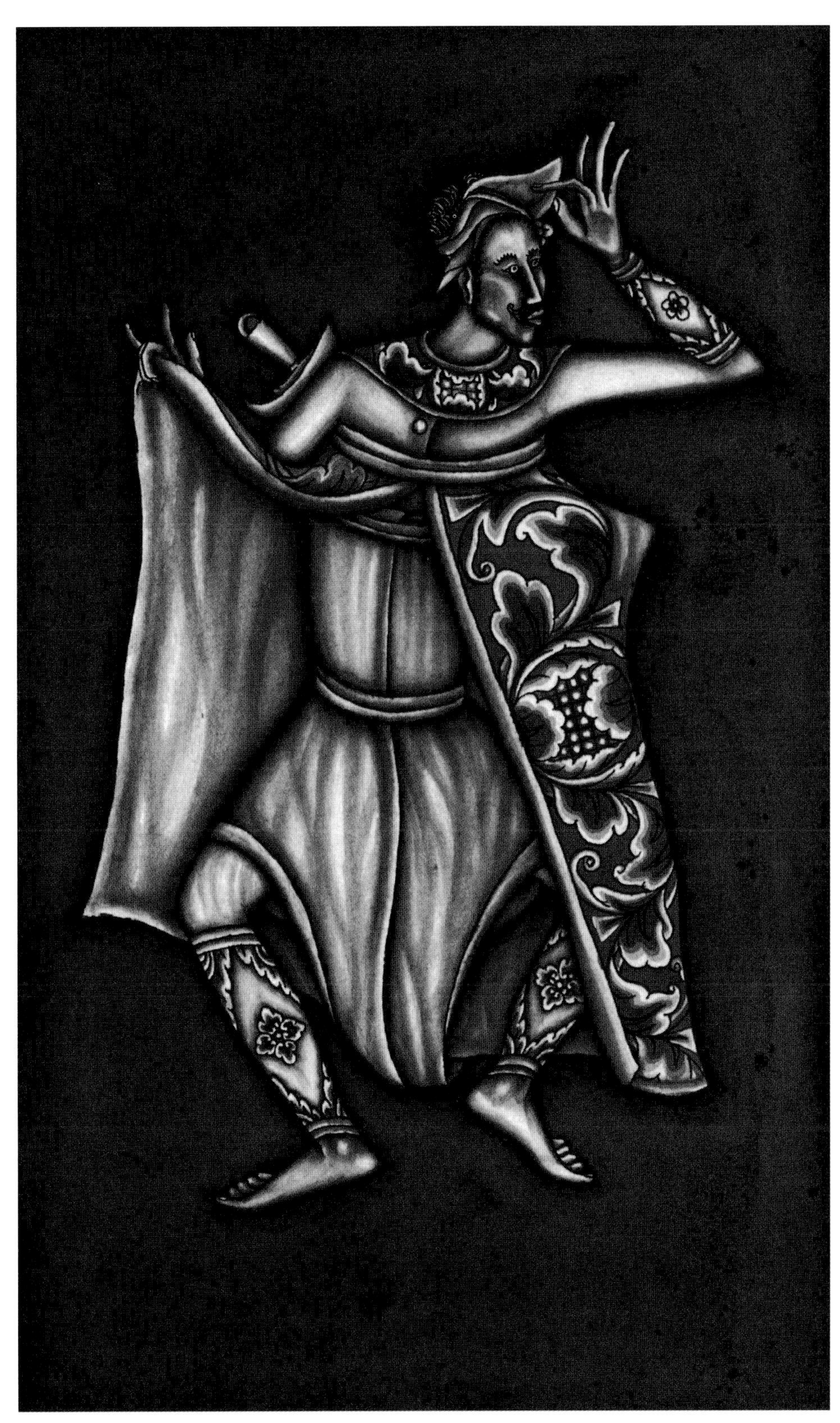

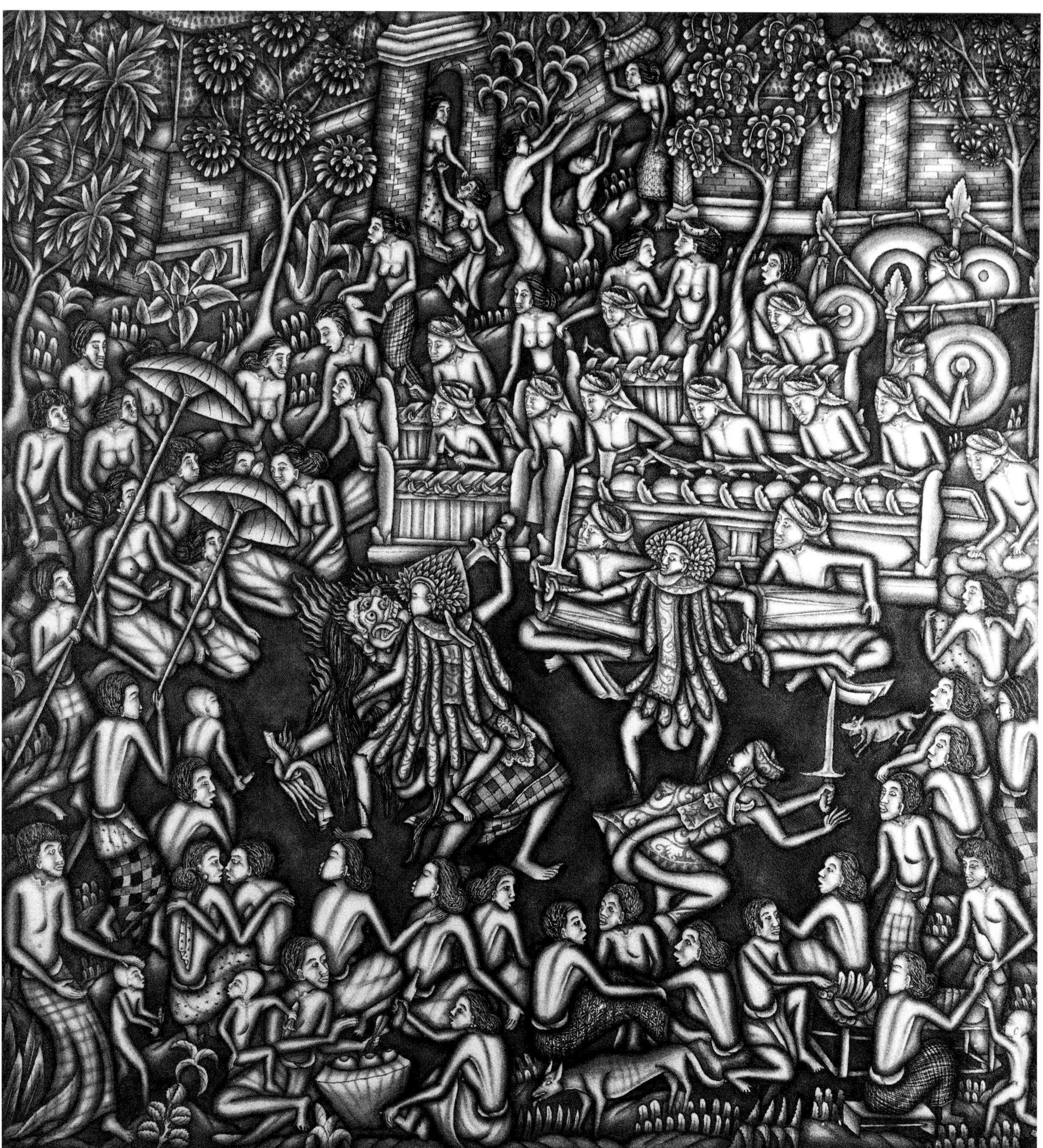

The most popular of all the dramatic forms that could be seen almost nightly in the southern heartland of Bali in the 1930s were the *arja* plays—rich mixtures of popular songs and formal dances, comic and dramatic dialogues, and slapstick farce, all pulled together in stories relating magical triumphs over disastrous troubles. These plays drew large crowds of all ages. The stories of the *arja* repertoire were constantly being renewed, borrowed from almost any available source. They came from old folktales, from stories told in other parts of the archipelago such as the Amad cycle, of Muslim origin, and even from Chinese theater. The songs of the *arja*, in everyday Balinese, were continually created. They evoked personalities and situations of love and combat and often could be heard in fields and kitchens.

Arja was frequently staged in Batuan, and many Batuan people were members of a troupe centered in the village of Sukawati to the south. During one period Ngéndon was the general manager of an *arja* group in Batuan for which he arranged bookings and new costumes and also played in its gamelan orchestra. It is no surprise that *arja* stories provided material for many of the Batuan pictures.

The *gambuh*, shown in Sawa's picture and in Lambon's (page 43), is a courtly dance-drama in which the main characters, princes and princesses from a long-ago feudal time in Java, give stories mainly from a cycle concerning the legendary Prince Panji and his adventures in search of a long-lost love. There were in the 1930s only a few *gambuh* troupes on the island, and one of the best was in Batuan. Today, it is a sacred dance, performed in front of Batuan's village temple, the Pura Désa, during major ceremonies, although it is permissible to stage it at secular times and places. The Batuan troupe often performed at the Gianyar royal court and at other village temple festivals. Walter Spies did an extended study of the Batuan *gambuh* repertoire, and Colin McPhee of its music. Both frequently arranged for special performances for themselves and their guests.[5] The people of Batuan consider today (and no doubt did in the colonial period) that the *gambuh* stands for themselves and their village, especially in relation to foreigners. In a lesser way, the nontouristic original *rejang* dance in their eyes is also strongly emblematic of Batuan.

One dance-drama genre that has disappeared in its original form but was very popular in the 1930s is the *baris melampahan*. In it all the male heroes wear the same costume, that of a warrior, or *baris*. (In contemporary Bali, the dance of the *baris* is simply a virtuoso solo dance performed before a dramatic show, often by a small boy or youth of slight build.) *Melampahan* means "telling a story." In this drama, however, the warriors did not speak; their lines were spoken for them by *penasar* clowns. The stories are said to have been taken from the Ramayana or Mahabharata cycles, epic poems of Indic origin, and the music was provided by a full *gamelan gong*, the larger form of the Balinese orchestra.

In his picture of a *baris melampahan*, the artist Djata shows a specific performance rather than a generic one, as is usual in these pictures. Djata said it was the story of "Radén Laksmana," and the details he gave correspond exactly to an account by Walter Spies and Beryl de Zoete of a showing in the village of Tegaltamu, near Batuan.[6] The similarities between their circumstantial description and this picture are striking, from the postures of the dancers, to the components of the orchestra, to the story itself. The painter not only has depicted the ethnographic detail of the play but has given us the specific Tegaltamu version of it.[7]

Note the *rangda* figure in the play struggling with the two warriors, an example of the use of type characters in these plays. The *rangda* mask and costume were normally used in the Calon Arang performance of that village, but could easily be borrowed to show the fierce combative transformation of the demon in the story. Dramatic performances, since they are part of rituals, are settings for intercourse between human and invisible beings. As such they are also the medium for visualizing these interchanges.

These pictures of various kinds of dance-drama performances show how elaborate the costumes were and, to some extent, how formal the dance movements. However, when the picture makers of Batuan began to portray the fabulous stories told through these performances, they exploited the new Western pictorial conventions of naturalism to ground their fabulous tales in down-to-earth images of ordinary clothing and gestures. They were able to suggest in a new way the notion that is understood but not explicit in their traditional arts: that their daily activities are shot through with issues of mystical mastery.

OPPOSITE: *Play Performance of a* Baris Melampahan: *The Story of Radén Laksmana*
I Madé Djata, with the help of Ida Bagus Putu Sentoelan and Déwa Kompiang Pasek

The *baris melampahan* is a now-forgotten kind of dance-drama in which all the heroes wore the same elaborate costume, that of a warrior. The painter Djata told Bateson that this picture depicts the story of Radén Laksmana, the brother of King Rama of the Ramayana cycle. Laksmana is killing a demon who is dressed in the mask and clothing used in other plays to depict an evil widowed "witch" *(rangda)*. This figure, however, is not a witch but a figure in the Ramayana, a demon named Surpanaka. The ugly sister of the demon king Rawana, Surpanaka fell in love with Prince Laksmana, but was rejected by him. Here, in a rage she has just transformed herself into a *rangda* to try to kill Prince Laksmana and his brother, King Rama, only to be vanquished by the two. The crouching figure is the *penasar*, playing the servant of the two brothers.

It is common in Bali for masks to be switched from role to role according to need. The *rangda* mask is used in many different genres whenever a being of great supernatural force must appear angry, powerful, and destructive.

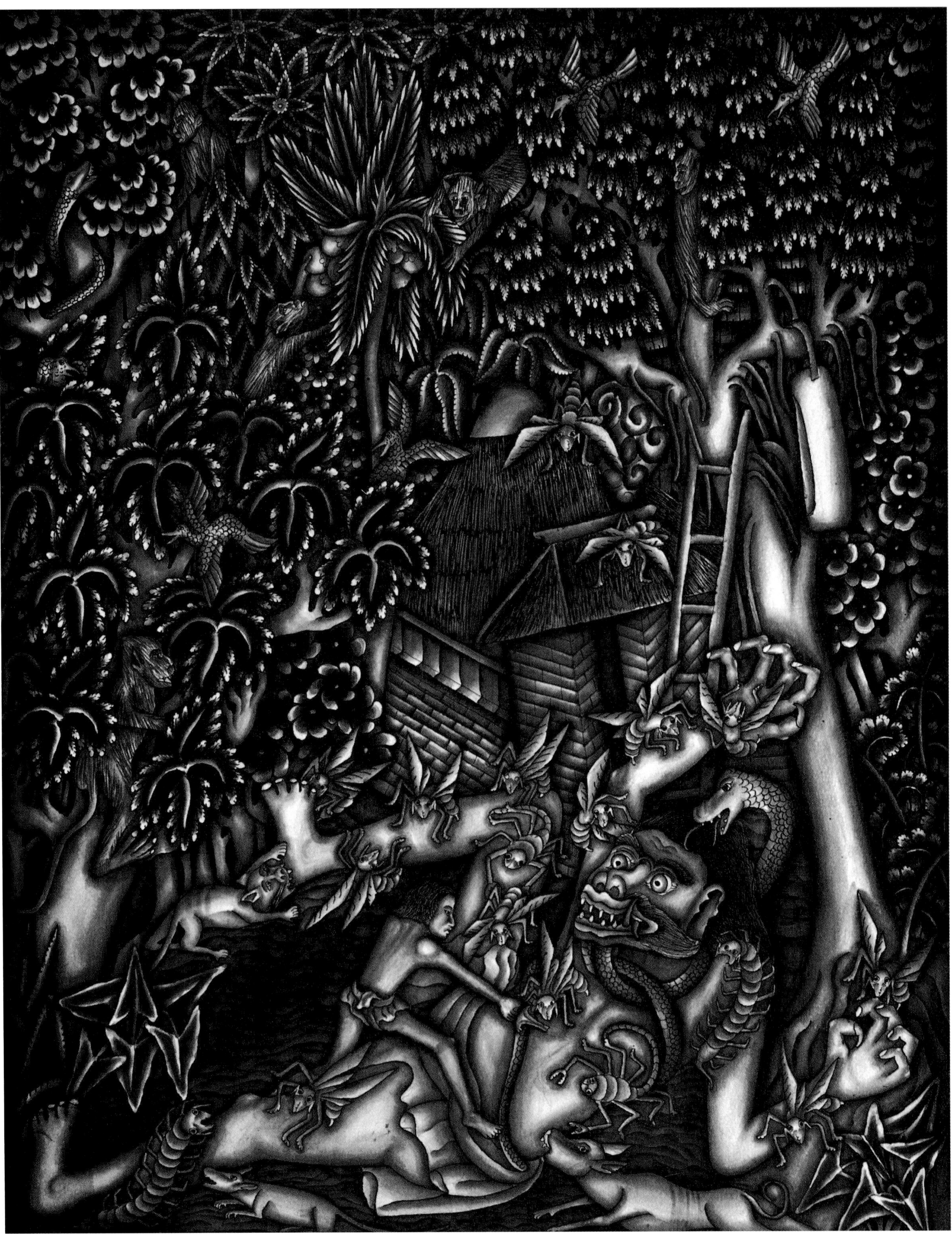

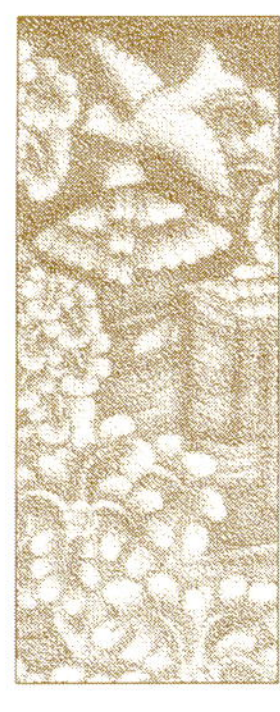

Chapter 3

The Magical Story World

A Portfolio of Storytelling Pictures

The picture makers of Batuan took the tales they illustrated not only from their vital dramatic tradition but also from an equally pervasive source, oral storytelling. In intimate family settings, at night—often in the dark, since at that time lighting by candle and kerosene was prohibitively expensive—older people told youngsters tales they themselves had heard in childhood, or they retold the plots from dance-dramas they had seen. None of the formal constraints of the public performances were at work, and the tellers used a directness and a realism of gesture and dialogue that are more circumscribed in the staged genres.[1] These oral performances were closer in spirit to the new kind of pictures that the picture makers were making, since they were in the colloquial language and used images from everyday life.[2]

Here follows a selection of the story-pictures. The texts are, unless otherwise noted, fairly direct translations of the words of the painters themselves as dictated to Bateson or his assistant, Kalér.[3] Each picture and text is followed by my comments, pointing out at times the relation of the picture to the theme that I will take up in chapters 4 and 5, the preoccupation with the mystical power that some call *sakti*.[4]

The Tale of Little Képét

The King of Daha had two children, a boy and a girl. But the boy was as tiny and thin as a lizard. He called together all the priests in the Kingdom and asked their advice.

They told him to banish the boy into the forest. So he was abandoned there in a box. Along came an old woman who lived in the forest. She had no children and her name was Men Bekung (Infertile Woman). She was gathering leaves and grasses for her cow. She found the box and she opened it and found the child, as tiny and thin as a lizard.

She took him home with her and gave him rice to eat. She gave him soft cakes made of rice flour, as you would a baby. She called him Képét. He grew a little fatter and then she had to leave him at home when she went out to gather fodder again.

The story goes that when she was out, an ogre *(raksasa)* came to her house and asked, "Képét, Képét! Where is your mother, Képét?"

Képét ran and hid inside a rice mortar. The ogre couldn't find him, and while standing right over the rice mortar, scratched and scratched himself, found a louse and squashed it. Képét laughed at this, down inside the rice mortar, and the ogre heard him and said, "Here you are, Képét! Come with me to my father's house. He'll give you rice. He'll give you meat." Képét didn't dare say no, so the ogre put him in a box and took him home to eat him.

Now I'll tell you about Men Bekung. When she came home, she asked her cat and her mouse and her puppy: "Cat, Mouse, Puppy! Where's Képét?"

"He was taken away by an ogre!"

"Go and find him and I'll give you something nice to eat!"

So they went and found him in the ogre's house, but he was down inside the box. Mouse said, "Oh! How can we get him out of that box, Cat?"

"Don't worry. You chew a hole in the box and I'll sing while you do it!" So Cat sang, "*Tut-a-tut, nyéng! Kerepet-kerepet.*" [This is a kind of vocalizing of the sounds of gamelan music, and the painter told Bateson that *kerepet* was the sound of the mouse gnawing on the wood.]

When the ogre heard Cat's song, he liked it and he danced to it. Finally Mouse made a hole big enough to escape through, and Mouse brought Képét home again.

When the ogre opened the box, Képét was no longer there. "Hey!" he said, "Képét's escaped out the side. I'll go after him!"

When Men Bekung saw Képét again she said to Cat and Mouse, "Now that you've brought Képét home, I'll give you your reward. And I'll guard him here in my house. I'll let the ogre eat me instead of him."

So when the ogre arrived, she said, "Well! Hello, Mr. Ogre! You can eat me up, but not Képét!" So the ogre sharpened his fangs and ate her up. And he went home and went to sleep.

Now I'll tell you what Képét did. He called to the cat and the mouse, "Cat! Mouse! Come on, let's go look for Mother!" On the way they met Scorpion, who asked, "Képét, where are you going?"

"I'm going to the ogre's house."

"I'll go with you!"

"Come along if you want to then."

And then they met Centipede, and said the same things. And then they met Wasp and Snake, and they came too.

OPPOSITE: *The Tale of Little Képét*
Ida Bagus Ketut Sawa

So when they got there, Centipede hid under the pillow, and Scorpion by his feet. Wasp hid in the signal drum. Snake hid in the doorway.

When the ogre came home and lay down to sleep, Centipede bit him, and he woke up and felt around for his matches, and then Scorpion bit him. So then the ogre went to beat on the signal drum to call his friends to help him, and then Wasp bit him. And then he fell down, and Képét stabbed him to death.

Then Képét went into the ogre's house and took it for his own home. How much wealth the ogre had in gold and in coins! Képét took it all, and he was very happy. And because he was now so rich, many people came to be his servants and followers.

Well, there was a cockfight at the palace of the King of Kuripan, and Képét went to compete. He entered a rooster in many fights and he never lost. Even the King of Kuripan lost to him. Because he had not yet lost a bout, he was not allowed to leave.

The King said, in rough words, "Hey! You! Képét! Who's your father? Tell me the truth! You can't be a commoner!" [True aristocrats can't lose in cockfights, because their *sakti* is too great.]

So then Képét acknowledged who he really was: "Well, I'm the son of the King of Daha. He had two children, and he banished me to the forest. I was brought up by Men Bekung. There, at Men Bekung's place, I was called Képét. But in truth I am from the Kingdom of Daha."

"Well! If that's so, you're my nephew. Where do you live now?"

"I live in the forest," Képét answered respectfully.

"I can't permit you to live any longer in the forest. Come with me, we'll go to Daha." So they went there, accompanied by a throng of people.

The King of Kuripan said to the King of Daha, "Respected father, this is your own true son, who was banished to the forest long ago!"

The King of Daha answered, "Bah! I don't have such a son!"

Képét said, "Here is a proof that I should call you 'father.'" [This proof is not described. Usually these tokens are rings, but it might be a dagger.]

"Well!" said the King of Daha, astonished. "Yes indeed you are my son. From now on, you will have the Kingdom of Daha. Now you will no longer be called Képét. Your name now is Serijing Melayu."

Sawa's picture centers attention on the killing of the ogre, that is, on the little man's moment of triumph. His attention to the details of the small stinging beasts who are Képét's helpers, and on the claws and grotesque face of the monster, makes it difficult to discern little Képét lunging his dagger into the monster's belly. The object hanging from the tree is the wooden signal drum that every community has for calling people together.

Little Képét, as the son of a great king, has inherited a great deal of *sakti*, and it is this that draws to him the loyalty of the animals of the forest and that gives him the ability to kill the ogre. The dagger with which he kills him is probably magical.

The story is typical of many Balinese tales, telling of a poor and apparently weak person winning over all sorts of obstacles and becoming rich and powerful. This kind of story the Balinese refer to as *gantian*, stories of metamorphosis, or of turning the tables. Many of these stories pivot on the idea that the protagonist is in actuality a prince with hidden *sakti*. The mention of the kings of Daha and Kuripan in the tale of little Képét suggests that this was the plot of a dance-drama, perhaps an *arja*. However, the style of the telling, with its emphasis on dialogue, suggests that it was also a commonly told informal tale.

Képét's tale is about a son's rejection by his father and ultimate regaining of his father's respect, and about the reversal of position of a weak little man over the worldly powers-that-be, but it also concerns the continuity of a royal line. In the Balinese political world, where all authority of this sort is contested, such a story also tells of the establishment of a particular man to the throne. That man, Képét, has proven his mystical mastery (his *sakti*), first over a local strongman (the ogre) and subsequently, through the medium of the cockfight, over all the other potential claimants to the throne. The story is evidence that mystical mastery, courage, wealth, and power go together. The legitimacy of every reigning royal house in Bali over the centuries is supported by tales like that of Képét.[5]

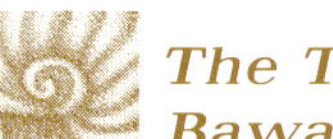

The Tale of the Two Sisters Bawang and Kesuna

The King of Daha had two daughters who were very beautiful, named Kesuna and Bawang. The prettiest one was Kesuna. When their mother went to the market, she told them to stay home and make dinner. But Bawang didn't like to work, and instead wanted to go roaming around to her friends' homes. So Bawang told her younger sister to thresh some rice in a mortar and pestle for their dinner.

"Pound the rice, and after you're finished, I'll winnow it." So Kesuna pounded the rice until it was done, and then asked her sister to winnow it. But again, Bawang didn't want to do the work.

She said, "You do it, and after that's done, I'll cook it." So Kesuna winnowed the rice, and when it was all clean, her older sister told her to cook it.

"Cook it up, and then when you're finished, I'll fry some fish." After the rice was ready, Kesuna, tired out, fell asleep, and Bawang ate all the rice up happily.

When their mother came home from the market, she found Bawang alone, eating, and Kesuna asleep. Bawang told her mother that because Kesuna didn't want to do any work, "I did all the cooking myself." So her mother grew angry, and she beat Kesuna.

Kesuna wept and ran away from home. She came to a temple in the forest and there she cried and felt very sorry for herself. A yellow bird came to her and, because she had actually behaved properly, gave Kesuna some fine clothes and jewels.

Then Kesuna went home again, dressed in her new finery. On the way she met her older sister, Bawang. Bawang

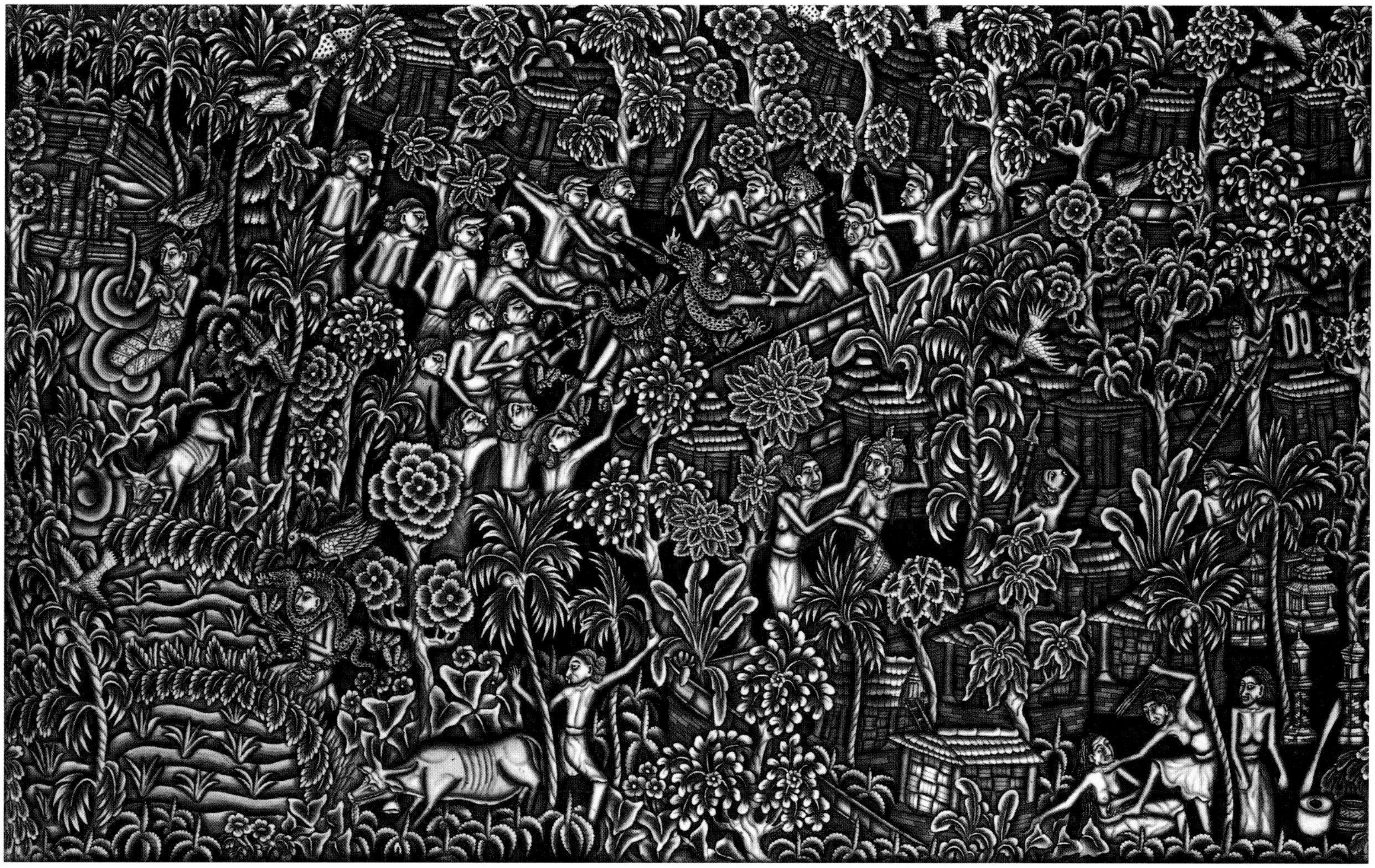

The Tale of the Two Sisters Bawang and Kesuna
Ida Bagus Madé Tibah

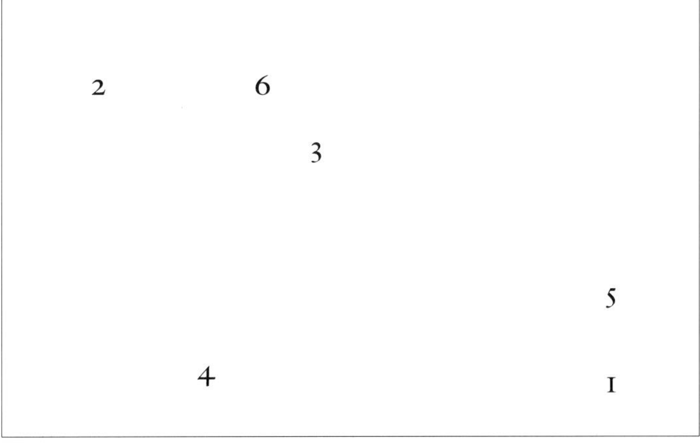

1. The selfish sister, Bawang, persuades her good younger sister, Kesuna, to prepare the day's dinner. When their mother arrives home from the market, she says that Kesuna has done none of the work. The mother beats Kesuna.

2. Kesuna goes to a forest temple where she prays, and a bird gives her jewelry and new clothing.

3. Returning home, Kesuna meets her lazy sister, who demands the clothing.

4. The bird gives Bawang clothes of snakes, caterpillars, and leeches.

5. A farmer sees Bawang in trouble and beats on the signal drum to call the villagers to help.

6. The villagers try to free Bawang of the insects and snakes covering her.

wanted to have some fine clothes, too. She asked Kesuna for hers, but she wouldn't give her any. Bawang was angry at her. So she went by herself and asked the bird for some fine clothes. And the bird gave her, instead, clothes made of snakes and caterpillars and leeches. The reason he gave her those was that her behavior had been bad.

When the village people saw Bawang wearing those terrible clothes, they tried to pull them off her.

The events in this tale are distributed in various places over the paper in an apparently random way (see diagram). While the viewer's attention is drawn first to what is going on in the upper middle part of the picture, this central event turns out to be the last scene in the story. This mode of composition can also be found on large traditional temple hangings. In this picture, as in that about little Képét, the painter has chosen to stress the moment of triumph of the good sister, the punishment of her tormentor.

Despite the claim at the outset that the two sisters are the daughters of the King of Daha, a legendary kingdom where many of these stories take place, their names, Bawang (Red Onion) and Kesuna (Garlic) are the sort of homely, rough names that peasants give their children. The tasks of cooking—threshing and winnowing the rice, steaming it, frying the fish—are the daily chores of every peasant household, and the drawing catches that ordinary quality. Going to a temple to pray for a blessing is just as commonplace. In any case, such magical occurrences can happen to anyone. The miraculous clothing could have been found somewhere and a painful attack by insects and leeches is not incredible. The help given to the suffering bad sister by members of the village is, again, just what anyone would do, not only out of compassion, but also out of fear, for such an unleashing of magical misfortune is potentially dangerous to all.

This picture emphasizes the ordinariness of mystical mastery in a dangerous world of competing powers. Its locus, as with most of these tales (and their illustrations), is the world of human beings, of villagers and family members, whose access to *sakti* is small but significant.

The Story of Amad and Mohammed Killing the Men in Iron Armor

The father of Amad and Mohammed was meditating in the forest, praying for the well-being of his sons back at home. That's how it happened that Amad and Mohammed were able to buy a little multicolored magic dove. [This is a bird of great *sakti*.] And then the news went around that they had a little magic dove.

The old King of Besah heard that Amad had a multicolored turtledove. He wanted to have it. If he could eat it, he would be the ruler of Mesir. So he bought some magic, the King did, from a *pedanda*. The magic flew at Amad's mother so as to get the dove. So after the magic hit Amad's mother the King sent his servant to Amad's mother and told her that he wanted the dove. Amad and his younger brother Mohammed were at school in the priest's home.

The servant went back and told the King that the dove was there but that it had already been cooked, and that Amad and Mohammed were not home. So the King said, "Just go and get it! Right now! Bring it home on your head!"

So the servant went to get the dove, but before he got there it had already been taken away by Amad and Mohammed. Their own servant had realized that he should go and look for Amad and Mohammed in the priest's house and tell them to come home, that the King was going to take their magic dove.

So then Amad and Mohammed went home and grabbed the dove which was roasting over the coals, and they ran away with it, eating it at the same time. The younger brother ate the head and the innards, and the older brother ate the body.

So then the King's servant told him, "The boys have taken the dove, Oh King." So he ordered the servant to follow them and to kill them. So then a hundred soldiers ran after them too. The soldiers were called "the Iron Men" because they were dressed in iron clothing.

They ran after Amad. In the forest Amad and Mohammed found their father, the holy man, meditating. The man of *sakti* told them, "Fight them! Here are two *kris*, one for each of you, use them to stab the Iron Men."

So they fought against them and they killed many of the Iron Men, and the rest ran away.

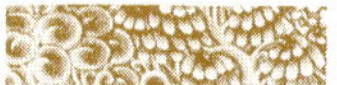

As can be guessed from the names of the protagonists, this story comes originally from the Middle East, probably brought to Bali by Muslim Javanese or Bugis in the nineteenth century. These "Amad-Mohammed" stories form a lengthy cycle and are often performed in dance-dramas.

The picture shows an episode when the hero brothers confront and defeat the army of soldiers in armor. Their victory is possible because of the magical powers of their dove and of the magic daggers bestowed on them by their holy-man father.

In the foreground the two brothers are standing in front of their father's cave. One has received a *kris*, and the other is about to take his. The father, in cross-legged position, is partially obscured behind the middle tree. He is overgrown with leaves because he has not moved from his position for years. It is unclear whether the artist intentionally hid the meditating hermit behind a tree, or whether this is a compositional accident. In the center of the picture the two brothers are killing the soldiers. Since Togog had never seen armor, he had to imagine it. He gave the soldiers short bolero jackets, apparently following the prevalent Balinese notion that the iron substance itself provides magical, not physical, protection.

A pervasive theme, present in most of the pictures, is the contrast between the forest and the village, between areas of danger and those of security. This opposition is played up in

OPPOSITE: *The Story of Amad and Mohammed Killing the Men in Iron Armor*
Ida Bagus Madé Togog

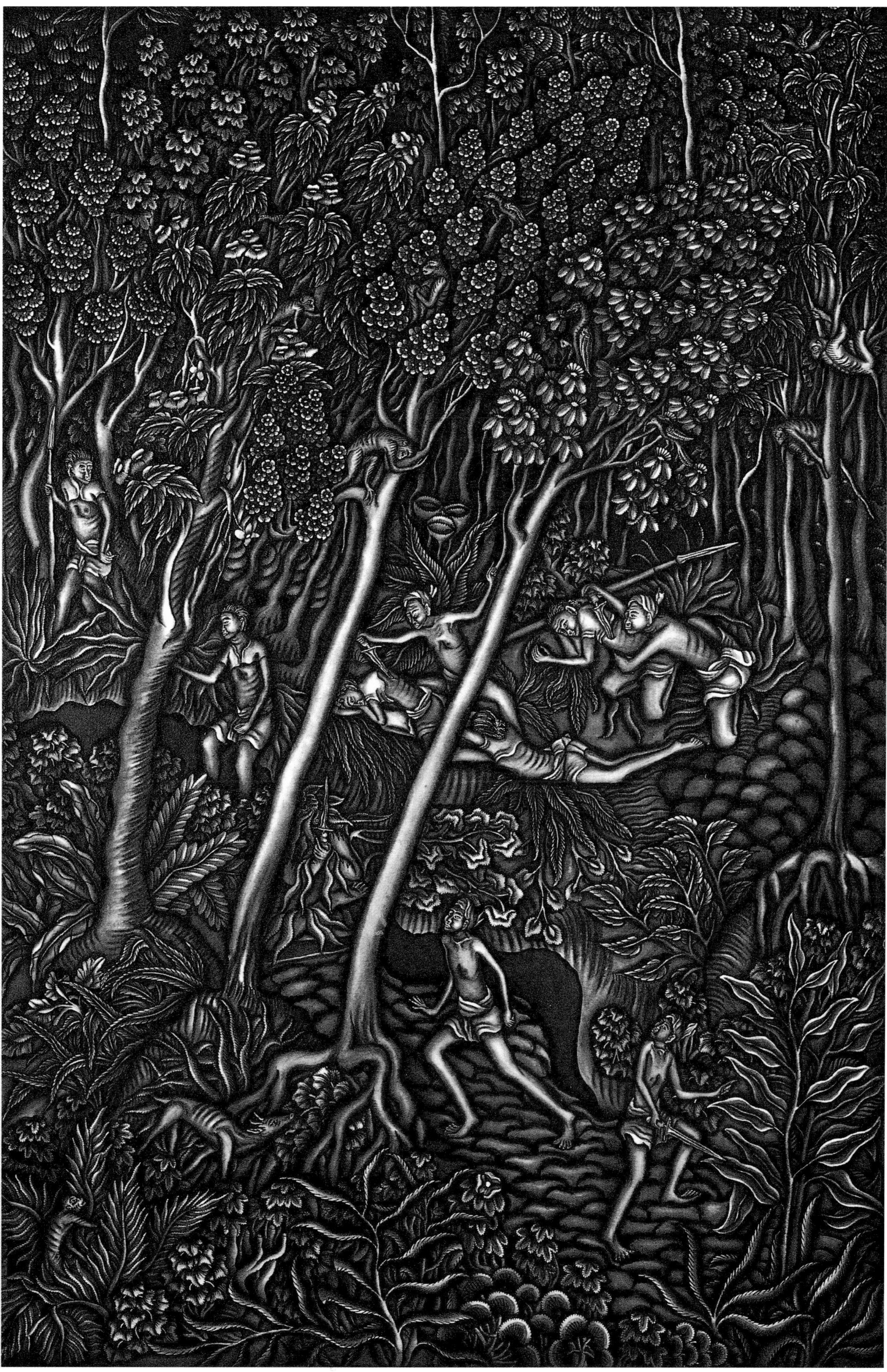

many of the stories on which the pictures are based. The plots of traditional shadow plays always take the viewer alternately into forest and civilization. The forest is where battles are fought and where the hero goes to meditate, make contact with the unseen forces, concentrate them within himself, and then turn to the battle. The civilized world of the village, the royal court, the temple, and the home is the setting for most dialogues.

In everyday life in Bali, any "wild" spot such as an overgrowth of bushes around a ravine or small watercourse, or a graveyard, is known to be inhabited by dangerous spirit beings. It has been centuries since most of the major forests, except in the mountains, were cut down. They have been turned into houseland, riceland, or cultivated tree gardens. But in stories the jungle remains a powerful image of uncontrolled violence.

Village areas are cultivated spaces, and rituals are almost all oriented to clearing them of evil demons, which are sent back into the forest and sea areas, the regions where human beings have no control. However, gods, too, come from these dangerous regions—the mountaintop, the volcano, is the abode of the highest deities—and the rituals involve bringing them and their beneficent influence into the village. The contrast remains—the interior of the village versus its exterior, controlled peace and prosperity versus turbulence and uncontrollable power.

Almost all the stories related in regard to these pictures, and almost all the stories of the shadow play and other dramas, turn on this contrast. The heroes and heroines are exiled to the jungle, or go there on their way from kingdom to kingdom, or go there to meditate and pray for useful *sakti*.

Many of the pictures depict the jungle, and many others show villages surrounded by tangles of foliage. When these leaves and tree trunks are closely studied, however, it becomes clear that the wilderness has been domesticated into flowering bushes and friendly coconut trees.

The Battle between Grantang and the Ogre Benaroe

(from an account by Beryl de Zoete and Walter Spies)[6]

Cupak, the elder, was ugly in shape and character; a lazy but cunning youth who tried to get the credit while the beautiful and delicate son, Grantang, did the work. When they went to the fields Cupak spent his time in snaring birds or in idle talk; but when they returned home with cows and plough it was he who arrived first, all splashed with mud, while Grantang, who had really done all the ploughing, came fresh and charming from bathing in the stream. Cupak boasted that it was he who had done the work, and it was he who got all the tidbits, while Grantang was scolded for his laziness and beaten.

In the Kingdom of Daha, the King had called together all the dignitaries of his kingdom to consult about the rescue of his daughter, Mustikan Ing Daha, who had been stolen away by the ogre, Detya Manarung. The King swore that whoever killed the ogre and rescued his daughter should marry her and become heir to the throne. Cupak at once vowed that he would kill the ogre, boasting that ogres were to him no more than flying ants which he crushed between his fingers. It was in vain that Grantang tried to hold him back; he had to go too, and after a great feast they set forth.

After a number of adventures, at last they came to the ogre's palace, set in a lovely valley and enclosed by high walls. And they heard the princess weeping and the ogre consoling her with the softest words he knew.

They climbed a great tamarind tree and looked down into the garden, and Cupak trembling with fright said to Grantang, "I had better challenge him from up here while you go down and fight, for your voice is so weak that he will never hear it. But tie me fast before you go."

So Grantang climbed down and put the ogre to sleep with a spell; and the princess fell at his feet, for he was so beautiful that she thought he was a god.

But when Cupak heard her promise to marry Grantang if he would save her, he shouted furiously from the tree: "Bring her up here. I am the elder and she belongs to me by right." And Grantang did so.

The princess told him that the ogre could only be killed if he were wounded in the mouth, so Grantang shot an arrow into the mouth of the monster, who had woken up and was shouting up into the tree, and killed him.

Then Cupak ventured down and struck him again with the arrow and said, "Now he is really dead, and it was I who killed him."

Cupak convinces the King that he is the rescuer and wins the princess. But in the cycle of stories, after a long series of other adventures, Grantang finally wins the girl, and Cupak is banished from the country. This version is excerpted from the longer tale recorded by Walter Spies, who worked between 1931 and 1936 with Beryl de Zoete on the book *Dance and Drama in Bali*. He appears to have taken down his stories verbatim from various Balinese storytellers. This version was very likely heard by the painter Sasak.

Oddly, Bateson did not ask Sasak for the story of Grantang and Cupak, and although five other people also illustrated it, none of them provided the story either. It is likely that they were afraid to recite this particular tale because there is a taboo in Batuan on the performance of the story within the village boundaries. It is said that the last time it was performed, a great tree toppled onto the audience and killed many people. The story of Grantang and Cupak is performed in many genres of drama: *gambuh*, *arja*, shadow play, and also probably a masked version.[7]

This story, like that of Képét, has the form of the revelation of mystical mastery in an apparently weak person. And, similarly, the presence of *sakti* is accompanied by great physical courage and beauty. Here it is a younger brother who wins the hand of the girl, and through her the throne, over his older brother. In the course of actual dynastic history in Bali in the eighteenth and nineteenth centuries, many younger brothers did the same.

OPPOSITE: *The Battle between Grantang and the Ogre Benaroe*
Ida Bagus Nyoman Sasak

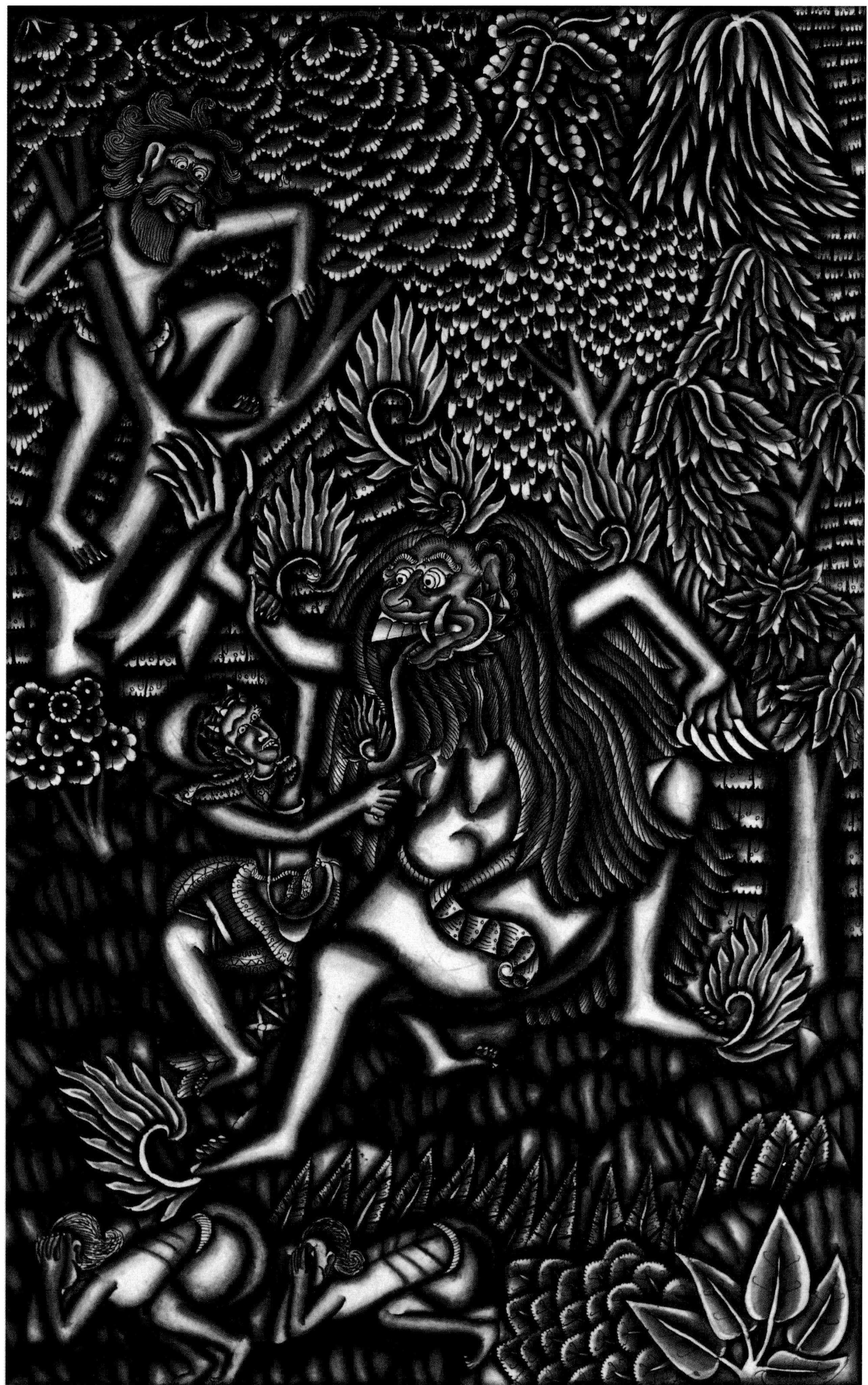

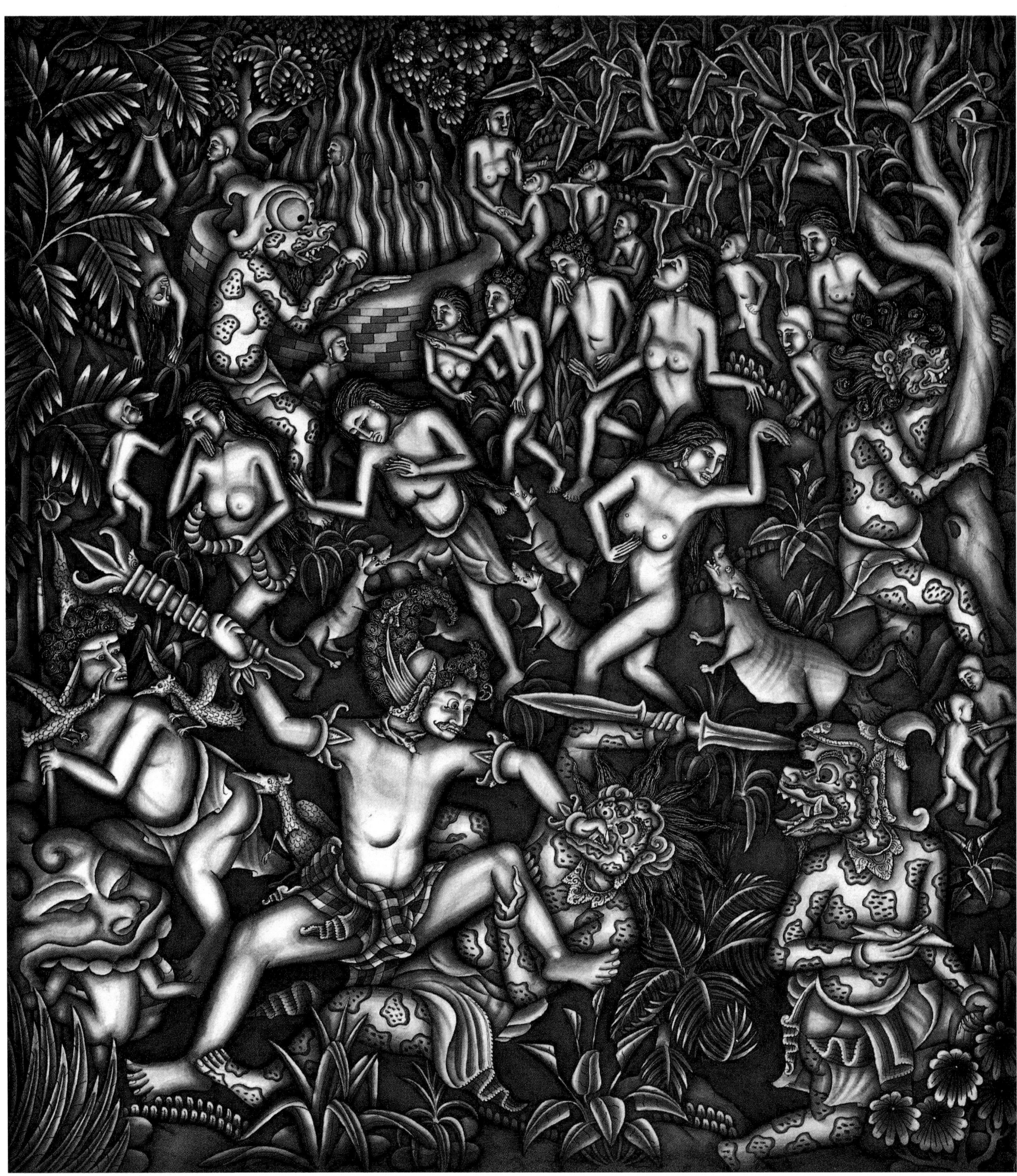

The Mythic Hero Bima Battling the Guardians of the Other World

The story of the hero Bima tells how he braved the terrors of hell to find and release the spirits of his father and mother. To do this he had to confront the demonic guardians of hell, pictured here as the spotted figures with tusks and bulging eyes. When Bima set forth on his mission, his four brothers and the wife they had in common all jumped within his body to add to his *sakti*. When he met the demons, Bima asked for the release of the souls of his father and mother. They refused, and he fought them. He dumped over the pot of boiling oil (at the top of the picture), but his mother and father were stuck on the bottom because the crime of Bima's father had been so great. Out hunting, he had accidentally killed a Brahmana priest disguised as a deer. After further trials, the valiant Bima was finally permitted by the god Siva to rescue his parents' souls.[8]

The Bima Suarga story was a frequent subject of the pictures made in the standard tourist painting tradition, perhaps because it provides opportunities to portray nude women in erotic positions. The tale is told in shadow plays, in carvings on the temple of the graveyard *(pura dalem)*, and in traditional temple paintings. It was the subject of the pictures on the ceiling of the Hall of Justice (the Kerta Ghosa) in Klungkung, made by painters from the nearby village of Kamasan in the early 1930s. Djata and a group of his friends from Batuan had been to see the paintings.[9]

In Djata's picture, according to the brief explanation he gave Bateson, Bima is battling the Demon Guardian of Hell, Jogormanik, for permission to free his mother and father. To the right is the demon Suratma, who keeps the records of the sins and appropriate punishments of people, shown with the writing implement in his right hand. Two other lesser demons are in the background.

At the left is a man being attacked by birds, as punishment for excessive bird killing with a blowpipe. Above him is a woman whose breast is being suckled by a huge leech, as punishment for neglecting her children or aborting one, and another woman is being raped by a boar. To her right is a woman whose skirt is being torn off by dogs in punishment for not weaving. The demon at center right is shaking a tree with leaves of daggers that fall and stab the humans below it. (This image shows up in Togog's dream on page 90.) In the upper left is a cauldron of boiling oil where Bima's mother and father are said to be suffering. At the far upper left is a man hanging head down by his feet, which is said to happen to those whose descendants have not yet performed the releasing rituals of cremation.

Often, each of these images of suffering people is drawn separately. Djata had made a set of small drawings with single figures several months before producing this composite scene. Djata was also familiar with shadow puppet forms, from which he drew the images of the demons.

OPPOSITE: *The Mythic Hero Bima Battling the Guardians of the Other World*
I Madé Djata

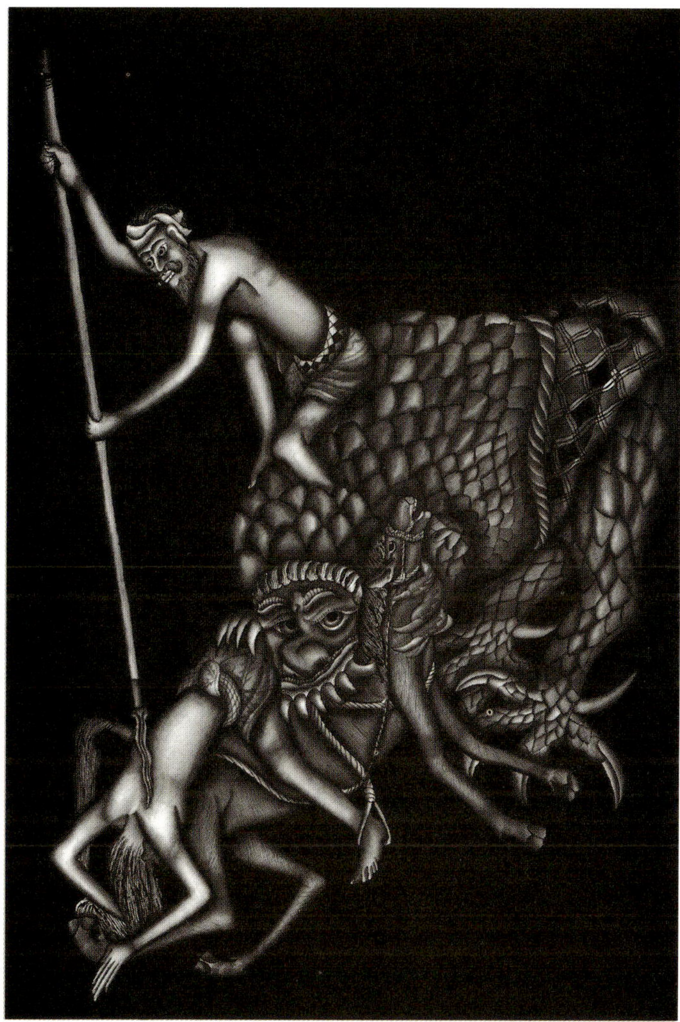

The Victory of King Rangga Lawé

There were once two powerful Kings whose realms lay side by side. They were both masters of *sakti*. When one King, Gajah Druma, fell ill and died, his young son, Anak Agung Anom, took his place. Inexperienced, and weak in *sakti*, the son foolishly ordered his father's four fierce prime ministers to leave their forts at the corners of the realm and come to him, not knowing or ignoring the fact that the four had sworn to the deceased King that they would never abandon their guard posts. Torn by loyalties to both the father and his son, the four prime ministers, in response, cut off their own heads and sent them to the new young King, leaving their bodies on guard. As a result the kingdom was deprived of its guardians and its potency.

The other King, Rangga Lawé, learning of this sudden loss in *sakti* of his enemy, sent his troops to attack him. His own *sakti* was very great and he magically created a battalion of fierce monsters for his soldiers to ride upon. They swept down on the weakened kingdom and destroyed it and its army.

ABOVE: *The Victory of King Rangga Lawé: A Warrior Mounted on a Powerful Magical Beast Makes a Kill*
Ida Bagus Madé Togog
From a set of 8 pictures

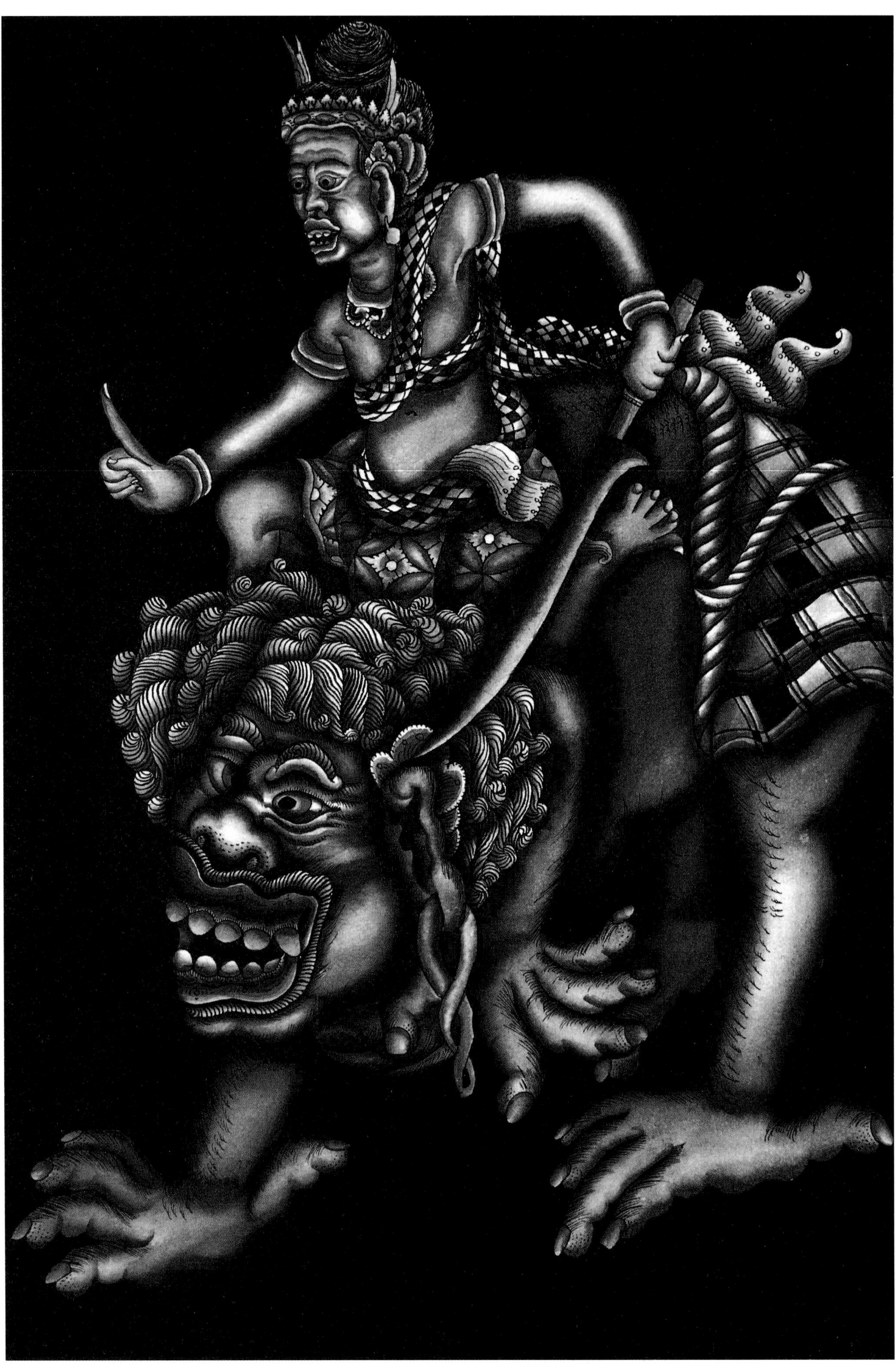

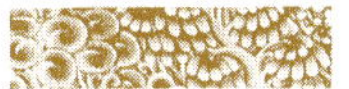

As with other story-pictures, these drawings by Togog show the moment of triumph, in this case between two warring kings. In dance-dramas and shadow plays, the performers select particular events from lengthy tales to enact on the stage. In the dramas, conventionally, the moment of triumph after a great struggle is the high point of the show. The audience usually takes it as a signal that the play is over, and most leave, even before any quickly sketched closing scene. All of this suggests that the combat and the victory are the essential heart of the stories, toward which and from which all else flows.

In this story of warring kings, the issue is the relative superiority of *sakti*. It is notable that the one who wins does so not so much because of the greatness of his own potency, but because the other king has lost his inherited *sakti*.

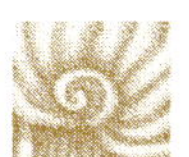

The Story of the Great Sorcerer Basur

(after the story told by the painter with the help of Ida Bagus Poeting)

This is the story of Basur, who asked for the hand of Sukasti as wife for his son, Tigaron. But Sukasti didn't like the way Basur's son looked, and she cried out, "Look he can't even walk straight!" In short she didn't want him [fig. 1].

Sukasti said to Basur, "Why! How could you suggest marriage to *him*? I don't desire him. Look for somebody else to marry him!" That's what she said. She didn't have any desire for him at all.

"I don't like him at all!" she said.

Then Madé Tanu arrived and Sukasti told him to go and bring back his son Madé Tarita, because she wanted to marry him, instead. So then Madé Tarita took Sukasti home and married her.

When Basur returned home, he told his son, Tigaron, that he had had no luck, that he could not have the girl [fig. 2].

Tigaron said to his father: "Father, I was trying to coax the girl to love me, but I couldn't get anywhere. What's your advice? How can I heal my body so that she will want me? If she doesn't want me, I might as well die."

Basur became angry. "Well, son, I'm very ashamed and angry. You stay here and I'll go look for her."

First Basur built an altar with one leg and he took it to the Pura Dalem, the temple next to the village graveyard. There he made an offering to the god Betari Giri Putri.

"I beg from you a blessing," he said, standing on one foot. He concentrated his thoughts on the goddess of the Pura Dalem, asking her to appear. I need not say more; the Goddess Durga appeared. He was granted his wish.

"Hey! You Basur!" said the Goddess Durga. "I, your mother, will grant your wish!"

"Thank you, Most Noble Goddess. I humbly accept your blessing, O Goddess."

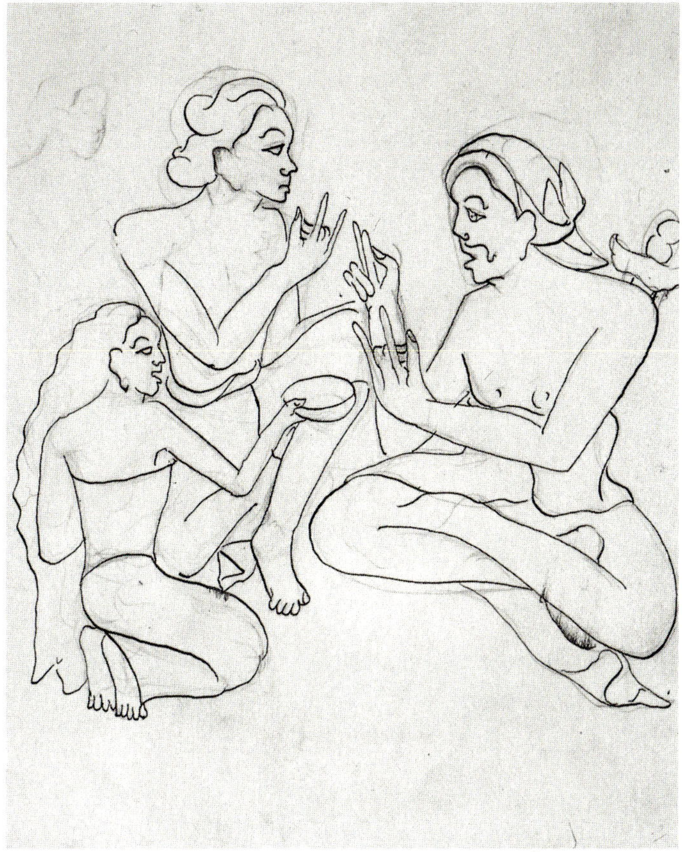

1. Sukasti, her father, and her preferred suitor, Madé Tarita.

He was granted it, and then he used the altar with one leg, and he muttered the spell and he became Rangda, carrying her scarf and a broken earthenware pot marked with a cross of white lime, and then he went to the home of Sukasti [figs. 3–6]. He climbed up in a tree to the northeast, and he could look down on her from there. He made Sukasti fall sick.

Sukasti lost consciousness. Her father and mother wept, just wept, the two of them. They cried out over and over, "Oh God, Ratu Betara, bring my child back to life, make her well again, I humbly give you offerings." But she was still not well [fig. 5].

Her mother said, "Father of my child, what shall we do about our child, she still is unconscious. Where can we go for help? Should we look for a healer *(balian)*?"

No need to say more. Sukasti's father then left the house and went to look for a healer. He went there to the house of the *balian*, and he called out his name.

"Who's calling me? Come in!" And when he came into the courtyard, "Well, come on up here!"

Sukasti's father went up on the pavilion. "What's wrong?" asked the healer. "You haven't been to see me for a long time."

"Well, what brings me to you is this, Grandfather Balian. I want some medicine for my child. She is sick. When she is well again, I'll give you whatever you ask for, Grandfather Balian."

OPPOSITE: *The Victory of King Rangga Lawé: King Rangga Lawé Attacking, Riding on a Magical Monster*
Ida Bagus Madé Togog
From a set of 8 pictures

ABOVE AND OVERLEAVES: *The Story of the Great Sorcerer Basur*
Ida Bagus Putu Blatjok
A set of 6 pictures

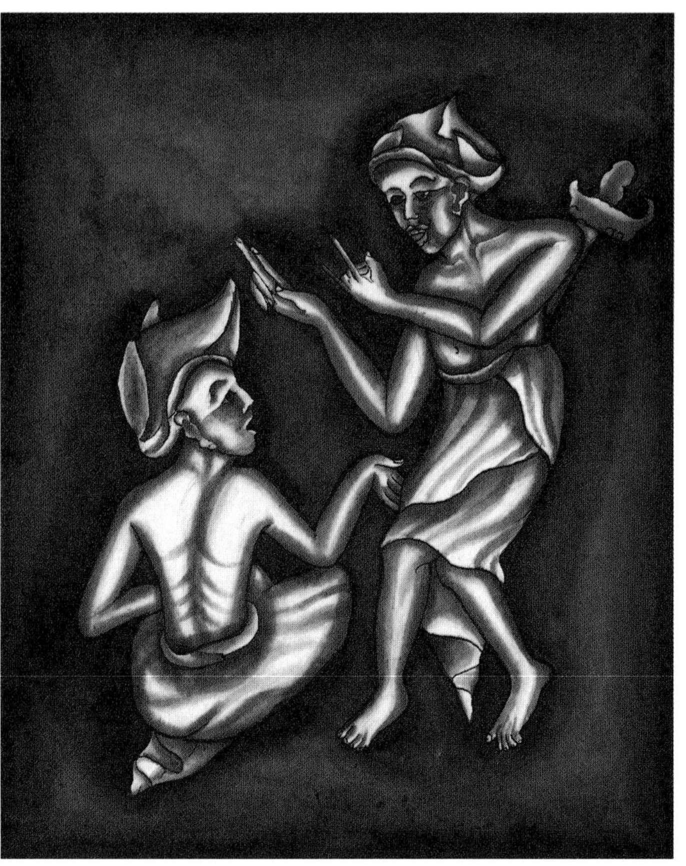

2. The rejected suitor, Tigaron, and his father, Basur.

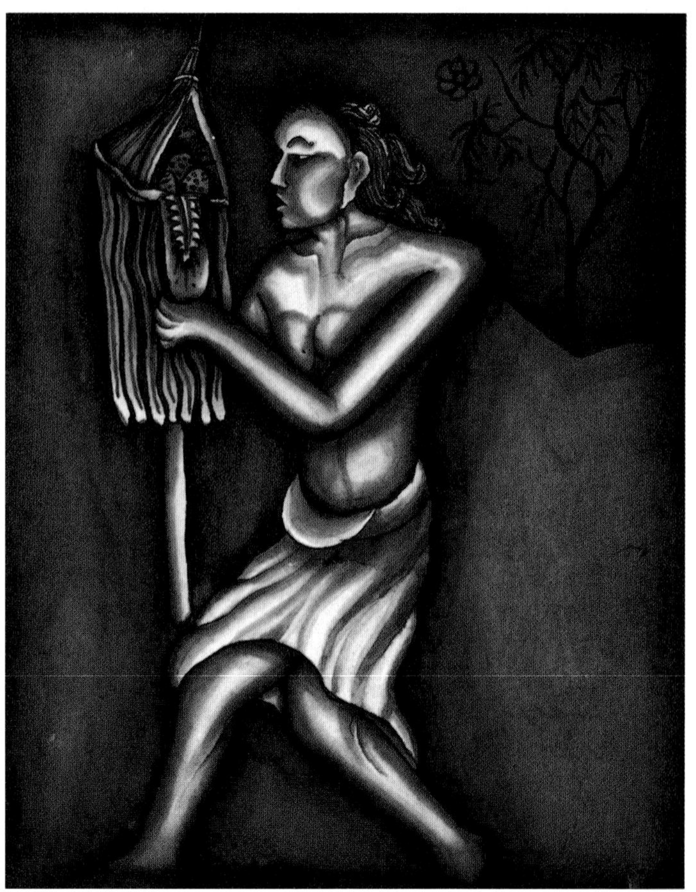

3. Basur sets up the altar before which he will transform himself.

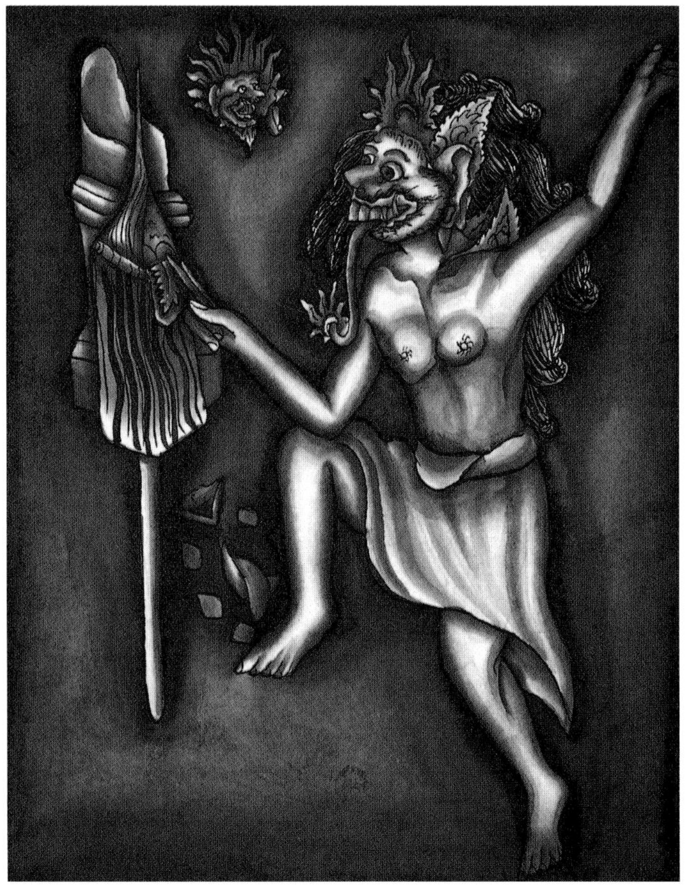

4. Basur has transformed himself into a fierce demon.

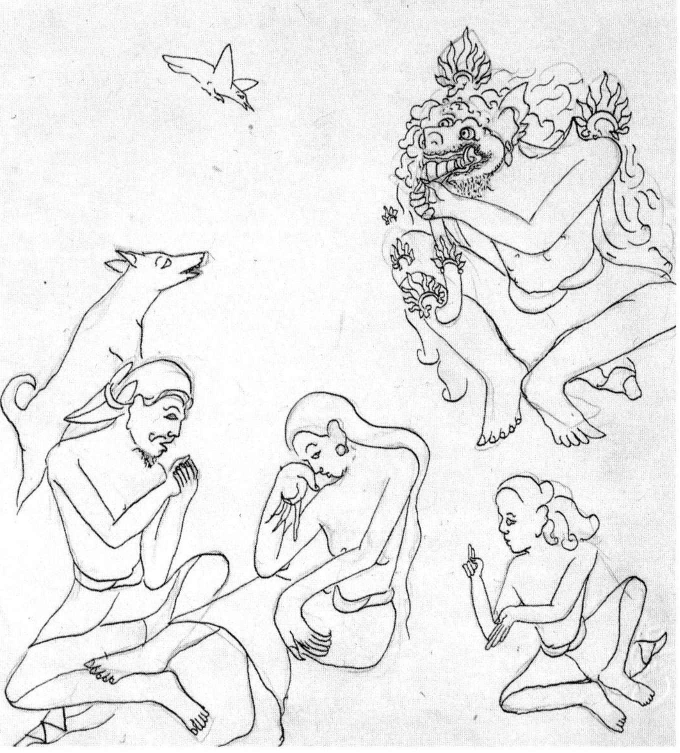

5. The healer says a mantra over suffering Sukasti, while the sorcerer looms above. Only the dog can see him.

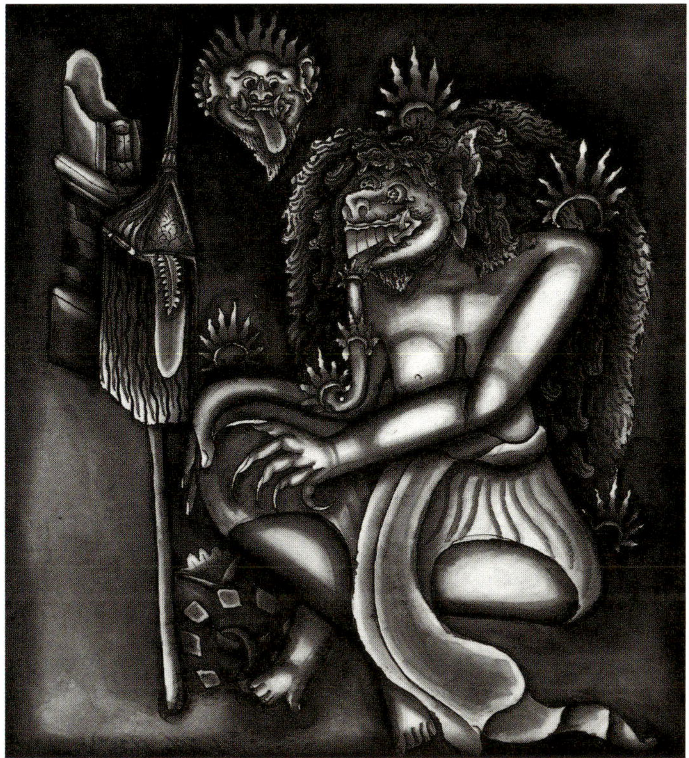

6. The sorcerer in his most potent form.

"Well if that's what you want, I won't wait here any longer." And he took his bag for betel-nut materials and his staff and went on the road to the home of Sukasti. No need to tell any more, he soon arrived there. He walked around and around in the courtyard.

"Oh," the father said, "Grandfather Balian, look how my little one is, completely unconscious!"

"Never mind, that's the way she is."

"But how can I not mind? She's dying, my little one. Isn't she in danger?"

"No, here's how to make the medicine. Take the bark off a *kélor* tree as high as you can reach. Make a vegetable dish out of it with garlic—heat it up—spray it from your mouth onto her forehead and her face on down to the base of her back. Then look for some rubbish and ashes and make a dish of them with garlic, heat it up—grind it up until it is a paste, add vinegar—then put this salve all over her body. When you are finished, leave her alone, let her sleep. Your little one will want to sleep."

When they had done all that, she was sick no more, she got well very fast.

And then the *balian* said: "There was a sorcerer *(léyak)* here in your temple. There he is, standing by the *jaka* tree. Didn't you see him?" The sorcerer came down, and he questioned him. It was Basur.

Basur said: "Oh, don't hurt me, Grandfather Balian! I beg to stay alive, Grandfather Balian. What do you want from me? Do you want money? Gold? Silver?"

"No. Why would I want that sort of profit? I am alone. I have enough. You, how can you think of doing what you were doing? If you had been successful and you killed your niece, wouldn't you sorrow? Now stop doing these things. You must still take care of your child. Look for another woman for your son."

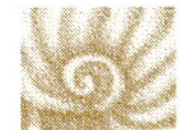

This set of drawings is clumsier than most illustrated here, perhaps because the artist was very young and just learning the techniques. Their crudeness is also due to their unfinished state. Mead and Bateson purchased these pictures even though they were not yet complete, perhaps because they wanted examples of work in progress.

The story and the pictures show a familiar kind of quarrel among kinsmen. The sorcerer Basur turns out to be the uncle of the girl he wants for his son. (Marriage between cousins is a common arrangement in Bali, as is the turmoil that emerges when the match is unacceptable.) When Sukasti falls ill, the family does what any Balinese would do. They go to a healer, a *balian*, who prescribes a medicine that they must themselves put together. The *balian* points out Basur as the evildoer, whom he accuses of practicing sorcery. The conflict dramatized is the opposition between the two sorcerers, a subject that will be discussed further in the next chapter.

Note that when Basur engages in sorcery, he takes the terrible form of a *rangda*. When this story is enacted in dance-drama, this same *rangda* mask is used to show the sorcerer in his fierce and potent moments.

The Story of the Prince Who Was Born as a Water Buffalo

In the Palace of Jenggala there was no heir to the kingdom. So the King and the Queen did *tapa* [meditating, fasting, and going without sleep] in the temple, the Pura Dalem, praying for the fulfillment of their wish for a child.

And the goddess of the temple came down and said, "Well then! My little ones, King of Jenggala and wife, I, your mother, will bestow on you an heir, but you must be steadfast and calm. Now when you go home from here, whatever you see on the way, do not speak and do not be startled. Or it won't happen."

So, just as they were coming out of the temple, just on the outside of the temple, they met a water buffalo.

"Oh!" cried out the wife. "There's a water buffalo!"

"What are you doing?" the King said to her. "You're not being steadfast and calm!"

His wife said, "Oh, now I've made a mistake! [by jumping about]. But whatever is born to me, I will raise as my child."

So after a while she became pregnant, and then after three years of pregnancy she gave birth to a water buffalo. All of the King's lords came to the palace to see the water buffalo baby his wife had produced. So many people came into the King's presence that the water buffalo said, "Mother, Father, since I have the form of a water buffalo, it would not be right for me to reign here. So, I am going to take leave of you. I don't know where I will go. But you, Mother and Father, stay here in the palace and pray for me."

So then he took leave of them, and he fled to the forest, together with many soldiers. Why shouldn't the soldiers come with him?

The story goes that when he came to the center of the forest he found a small temple there. The water buffalo rolled around on the ground, crying pitifully. The deity of

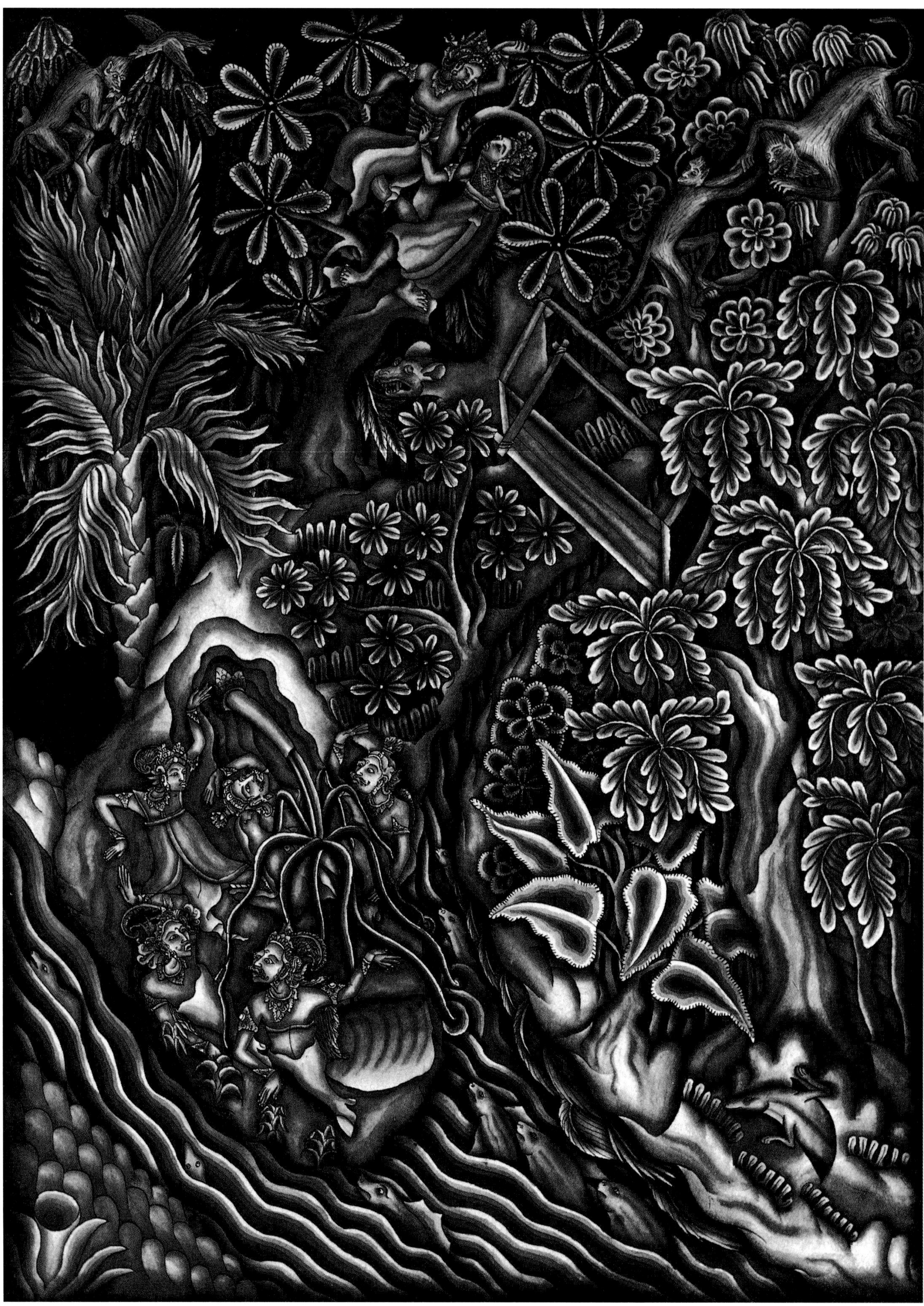

the temple in the middle of the forest came out and asked, "Why are you, my little one, crying here so pitifully? It makes the soles of my feet hot to hear your voice. It made me, your father, want to come out and see you."

And the water buffalo answered very respectfully, "Well, my mother gave birth to me in the form of a water buffalo. I am to reign in the Kingdom of Jenggala, but because I am in the form of a water buffalo, I did not want to follow my father's commands [to reign]. So I left and I came here to come before you, Oh Lord God."

"Well! My little one, what you want is to become a human being! This can be done! Go now to the sacred spring of Surenadi."

So the water buffalo went there, and he saw it was at the bottom of a deep ravine. He wanted to climb down to it, but he couldn't. What could he do? So he threw himself straight down to the spring. When he landed he rolled, and his head and his arms and his legs were broken off. And out of the head was born Panji. And from the rest were born his younger brothers: Punta, Jeruda, Kebo Perekasta, and Widésaka.

So then Panji climbed out of there. Because he was the oldest, he was able to climb up, but his younger brothers weren't able to.

"Older brother, what should we do, we can't climb up there. Pull us up!"

"I can't pull you up, no matter how I try. Younger brothers, just stay here."

So Panji went to the Kingdom of Jenggala. On the way he came to the Forest of Temunggung, and there he saw a *kastuba* tree from which hung a fruit which was a human being. There was a white tiger waiting at the foot of that tree. So he went to the tree to get that fruit, and he was seized by the tiger. Panji stabbed the tiger and killed it. And then he climbed the tree and got her. It was a princess named Ayu Kastuba Berit [whom he later married].

The costumes and postures of the five figures in the foreground are those of *gambuh* dancers, with the hero dressed as Panji, the princely protagonist of *gambuh* dance-dramas. The artist Dadoeg would have been familiar with such details because he was a fine musician and dancer as well as a painter. The story is one performed in both *arja* and *gambuh*.

This picture centers on a moment in a long story of bodily transformation and rebirth. The episode at the top of the picture shows another moment of mystical metamorphosis, which occurs later in the story when the top branch of the magic tree turns into a beautiful princess.[10]

The holy spring is shown in an everyday form of a bamboo pipe shoved into the damp wall of the ravine to tap the underground waters. The fishes and lizards of the river are watching this apparition. The boxlike form in the center is a bamboo bridge over the ravine.

The picture shows a strong sense of overall composition, with a movement of the whole from the bottom right, swerving up through the central spring scene, and going back up to the top right. The stances of the man and woman in the tree are mimicked by a pair of monkeys. The highly patterned foliage is mostly floral.

This picture can be interpreted according to Balinese mystical beliefs. When the water-buffalo prince found the spring, it was deep at the bottom of a steep ravine, and he was forced to throw himself down into it. The fall broke his body into five parts, he himself came from the head, and four "younger brothers" came from the four legs. At birth every person is accompanied by four spiritual "younger brothers," the *kanda mpat*, in the material form of the placenta, amniotic fluid, natal cord, and blood. Buried in the house yard at birth and regularly given offerings, these spiritual beings can cause and cure illness in their older sibling. Their nature and the mystical lore for communicating with them are the subject of many secret texts. One view of the *sakti* of a healer or sorcerer is that it derives from his ability to control his own *kanda mpat* and through them to deal with those of the ill person.

It is likely that some hearers of this story, and some viewers of the drama, would make these associations and place them foremost in their experience of it, while others would focus on other elements in the story, such as the drama of the transformation itself from an ugly animal into a handsome prince.

OPPOSITE: *The Story of the Prince Who Was Born as a Water Buffalo*
Déwa Nyoman Dadoeg Kajoean

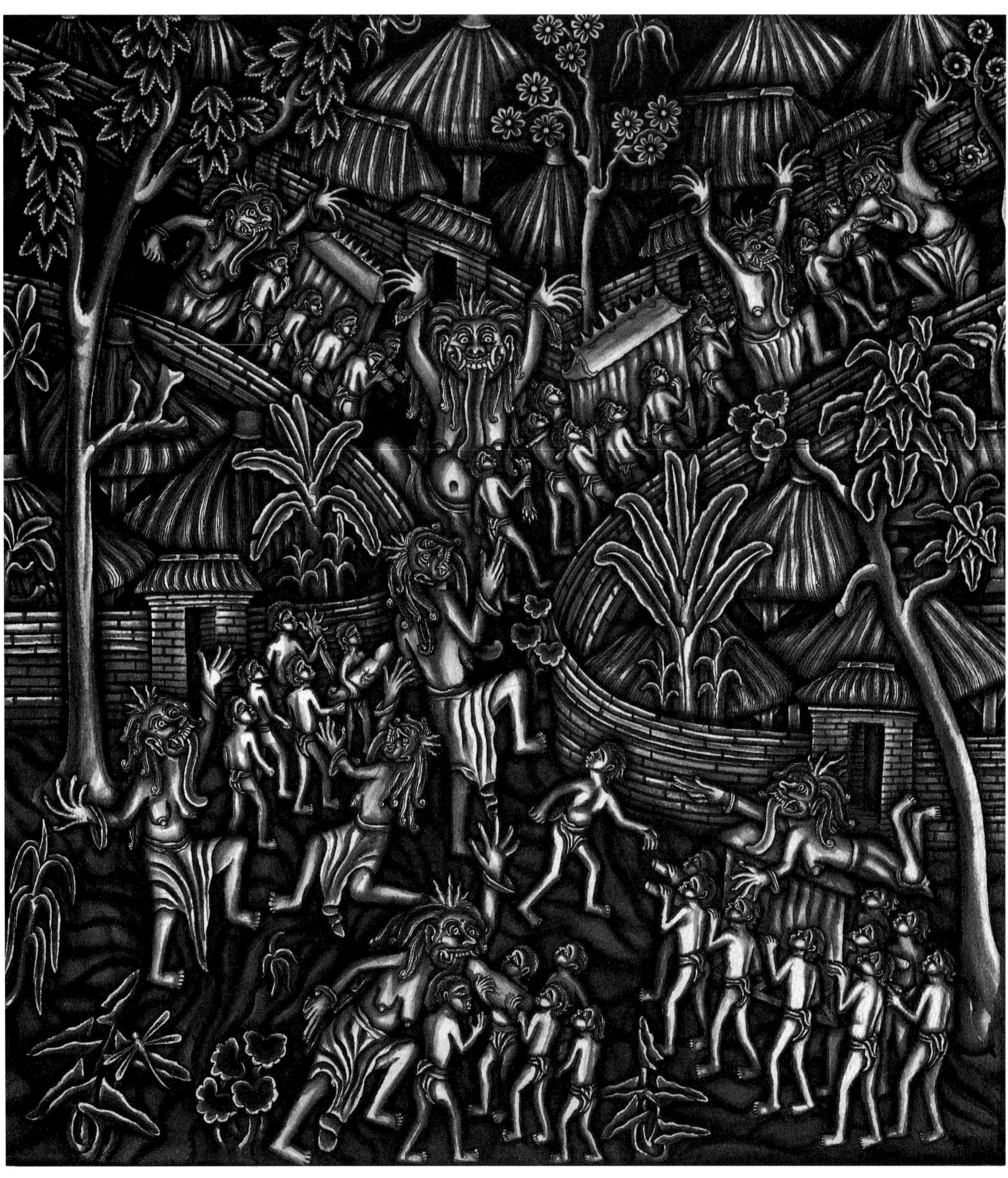

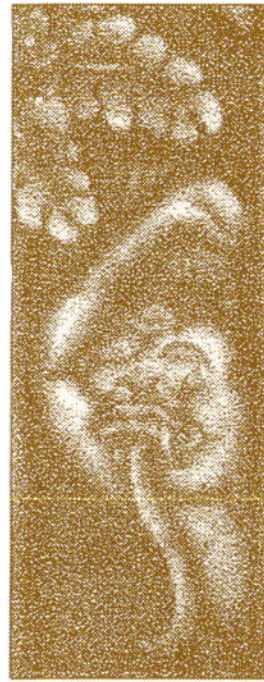

Chapter 4

The Real World of Dangerous Powers

The line between story worlds and the real world is never clear in Bali. Actual encounters with demons and sorcerers, miraculous cures, strange deaths, and mysterious visions in the night are the stuff of daily hushed conversations, as are unexpected prosperity and sudden poverty. Any disaster or sudden good fortune immediately becomes food for speculation about its cause. A chronic, wasting lung disease is thought to be the work of mean-hearted neighbors helped by sorcerers who pretend to be kindly healers. An unusually rich harvest might be explained by the prior discovery of a ring in a rice field, placed there perhaps by a benevolent spirit. The sorts of tales of the previous chapter are of a piece with those of everyday life. The Western notion of "fairy tales" as merely delightful or scary fictions about never-never lands where the impossible can happen would be very strange to most Balinese.

Any terrible happening is attributed to an intentional act of malevolence or rage on the part of some being—human or nonhuman. To find out the cause of such an event, one goes to a diviner/healer *(balian)* or priest *(pamangku* or *pedanda).* Their methods of discovery vary from allowing the spirit to speak through them as spirit mediums to consultation of books of the occult. These diviners give oracular diagnoses whose ambiguousness allows the sufferers to match them to their own suspicions.[1] In cases of serious trouble it is common to visit several diviners, searching for one that satisfies. A particular diagnosis usually implies a particular therapy. Curing strategies include eating an herbal concoction containing magical ingredients, carrying a specially made talisman, putting offerings in certain places at certain times, or carrying out a major ritual, such as a cremation for a neglected dead kinsman. Any of these actions may be understood either as protection or as counterattack.

Afflicting Beings

Balinese accounts of the causes of afflictions are diverse. One is the suspicion that the victim has had a chance encounter with a spiritual being who reacts in fury when his space is violated. For instance, the demons who live in rivers, streams, large trees, and especially crossroads lie in wait for an unfortunate person who accidentally steps too near them. Demons of this sort in the immediate vicinity are daily given propitiatory offerings. Sometimes called *tonya* or *detia,* they rarely cause trouble unless aggrieved, irritated, or crossed. A *tonya* can be capriciously malicious, however, or might be the servitor of a sorcerer, always ready to inflict harm at his bidding. The *tonya* in *The Story of the Demon Who Pretended to Be a Priest* by Togog, on page 22, becomes infuriated when the priest hacks with his hoe too near its tree. Another *tonya* is depicted in a picture by I Reneh (page 66).

The spirit-king Ratu Gedé Macaling, another dangerous demon of this sort in the Batuan area, invades Bali every year, spreading plague and cholera before him. Ratu Macaling tales are found in most of south Bali, but the Batuan people are especially afraid of him and perform a special propitiatory sacred dance, the *rejang,* for months on end to keep him away (pages 26–27). Many people of Batuan have seen the lights of Ratu Macaling and his followers coming up the streams in search of victims.

A vivid depiction of this anxious sense of hovering dangers can be seen in a rather crude picture of cricket hunting by a boy of about twelve years, Ida Bagus Madé Bala, on page 68. In the 1930s cricket fighting was a favorite amusement in which the insects were provoked into attacking one another, and bets were placed on the outcome. Bala's pictured demons take the form of those employed by a sorcerer to do his evil will (see the examples on page 86). He had made a set of sorcerers' talismanic drawings for Bateson and Mead's research, copied from priests' handbooks owned by his father, a *pedanda.*

In Bala's picture the expression on the boy's face is not fear but determined courage. This response of bravery to suspected threat is common in the Batuan pictures. For example, see the postures of the men attacking the demon in the picture by Reneh.

Another dangerous power frequently mentioned by diviners is the god of a local temple who may have been enraged by the ritual carelessness of its congregation. The prescribed therapy in such a case is an extra round of offerings at the next calendrical temple festival, or the provision of something special for the god, such as a richly decorated parasol.

OPPOSITE: *Epidemic*
Ida Bagus Nyoman Tjeta

In a time of cholera, villagers are taking the dead to the graveyard. As in normal times, they carry the bodies of adults in roofed palanquins and those of children wrapped in cloths and plaited reed mats. They cannot see the ferocious beings who have caused these deaths, dancing in bestial glee around them and waiting for a chance to seize and eat the corpses.

This picture, identified by the artist as "Calon Arang," depicts a legendary epidemic inflicted through the curse of the evil sorcerer Queen Calon Arang and carried out by her followers.

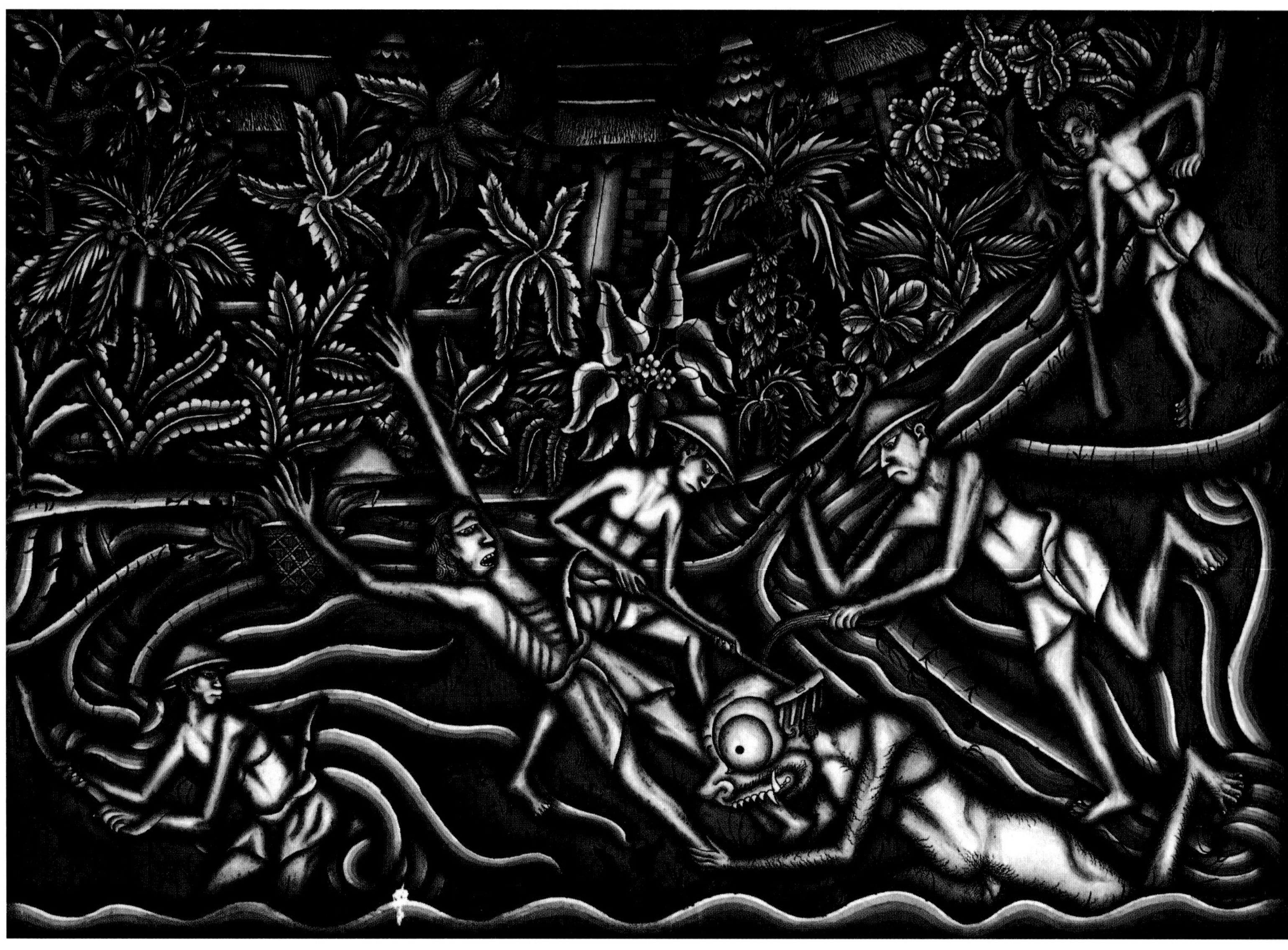

ABOVE: *A Fight with a Demon in the Rice Fields*
I Reneh

Spirits or demons inhabit most large trees, watercourses, and great rocks. If not properly propitiated, they may take affront at humans in their vicinity. In this picture such a demon has made himself visible and is attacking a man, whose companions beat it with farming implements. The demon's head is copied from a shadow puppet named Buta Togtogsil, but its body is naturalistically drawn. Hairiness is a sign of demonic coarseness.

OPPOSITE: *The Demon Ratu Macaling Brings Disease and Disaster Every Year in the Rainy Season*
Ida Bagus Ketut Siring

Pictured here is Ratu Macaling, a powerful demonic being whose name is spoken only in hushed tones. He is thought to live on the island of Nusa Penida, off the south coast of Bali, and to rampage up the streams from November through March, spreading illness and death. In Batuan, during those perilous months the women of the village take turns in a sacred dance *(rejang)* nearly every evening in front of the village temple and make offerings and prayers intended to placate and deter Ratu Macaling.

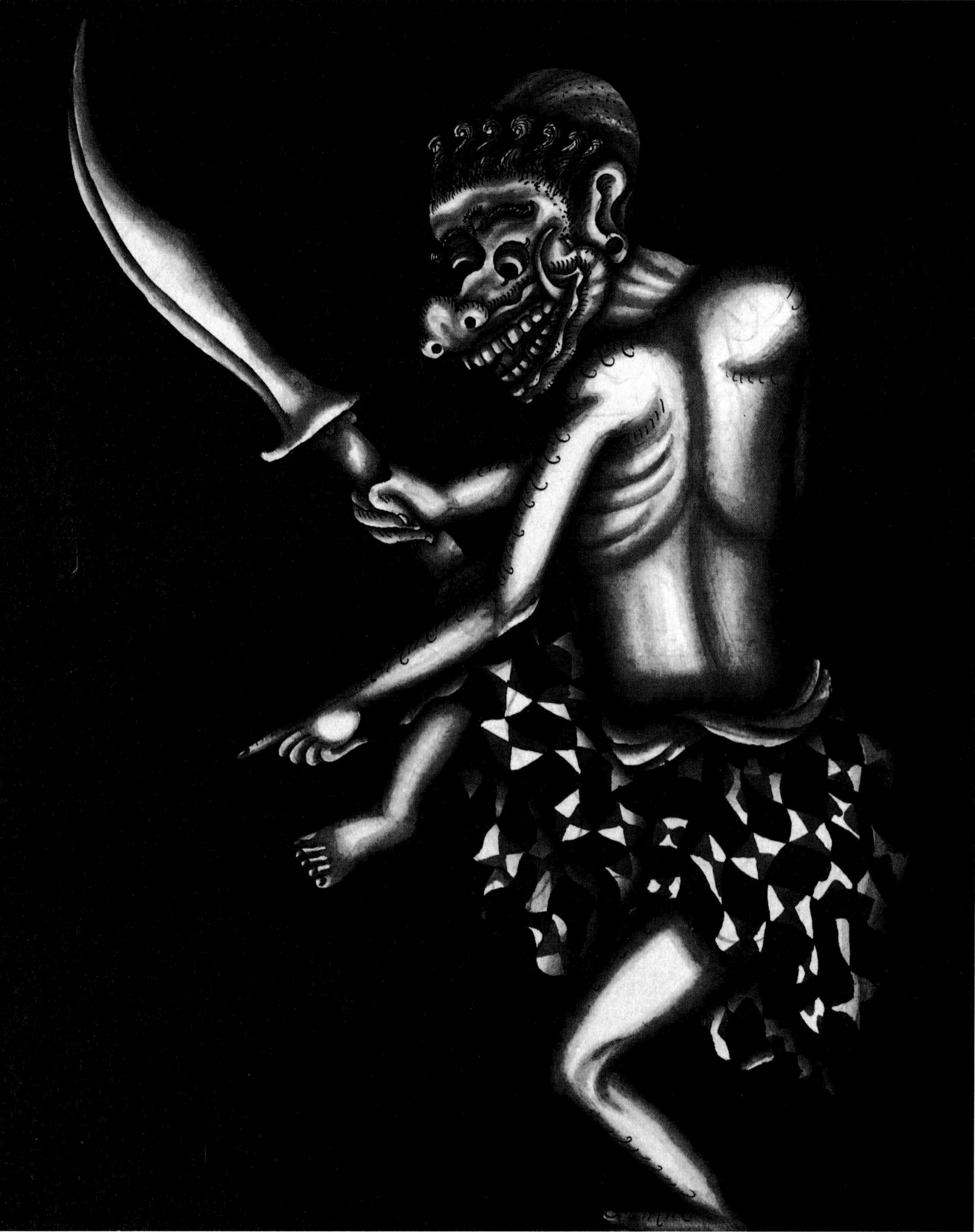

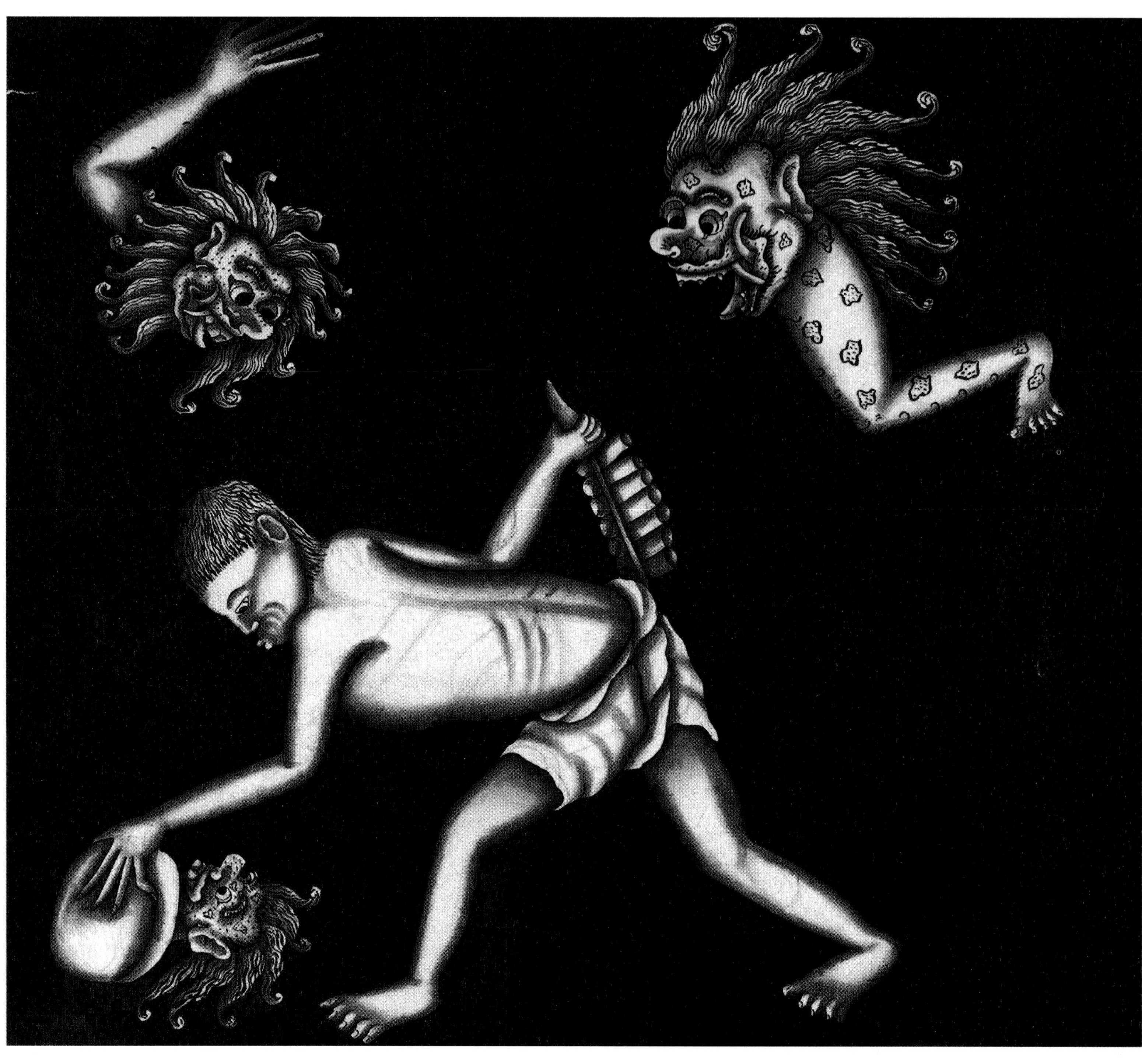

Looking for Crickets under a Stone at Night and Uncovering a Demon
Ida Bagus Madé Bala

This small drawing shows a boy searching at night for crickets, which are made to fight one another in a popular gambling game. The boy holds a set of small bamboo cages for the insects. Crickets are easier to find at night, but one must brave the dangers of lurking ghosts and malevolent spirits. The ones in this picture are similar to those drawn by sorcerers or healers in their talismans.

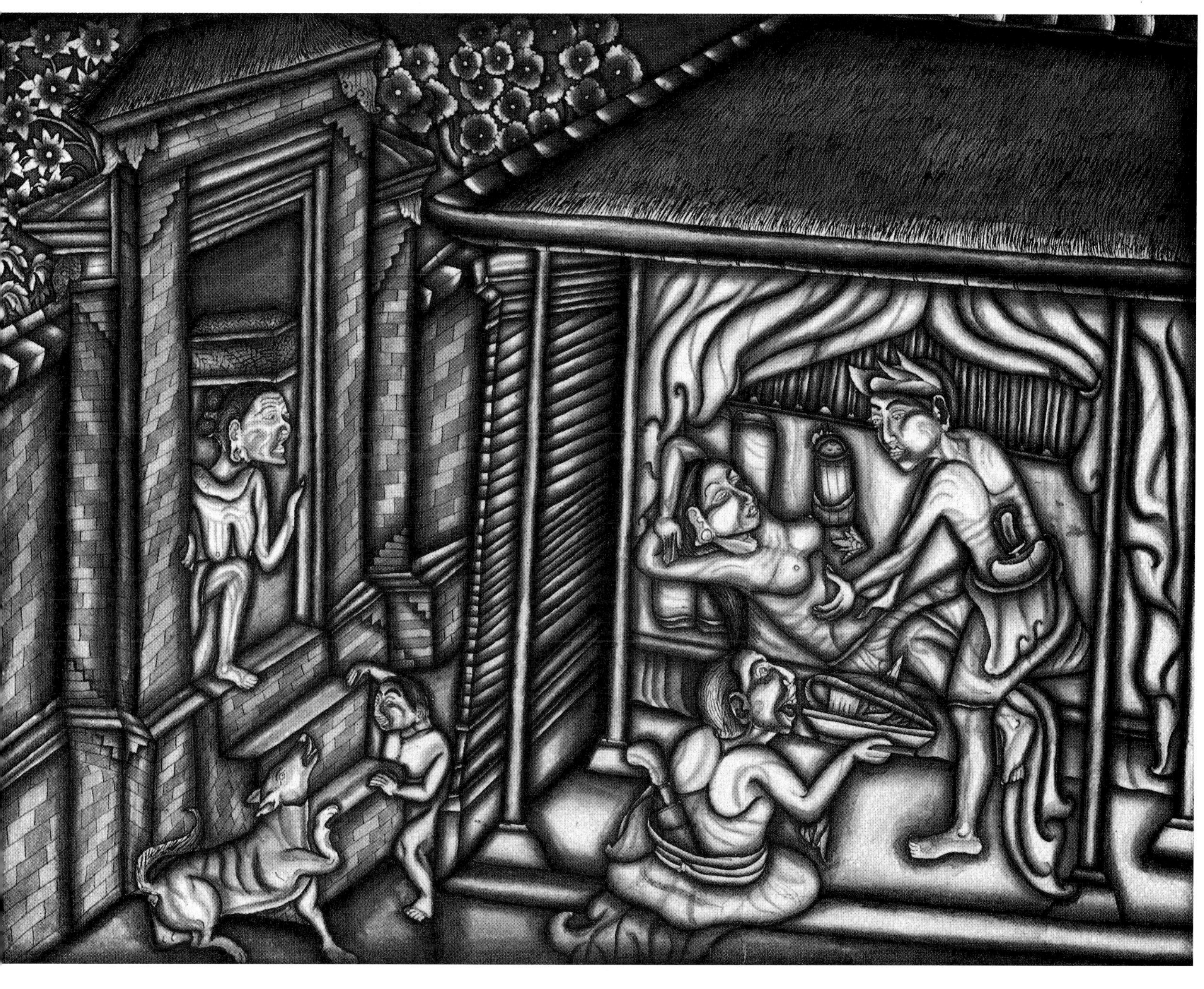

Birth
Désak Putu Lambon

A woman in labor is shown with a healer, a *balian*, massaging her stomach and someone, probably the husband, holding up offerings for the healer to present to the spirits. The lower man has a dagger, or *kris*, in his sash, as does the healer, indicating high seriousness and high status.

Peering in through the doorway into the courtyard is an elderly woman. Although she might be a relative bringing a basket of provisions, she more likely represents someone with malevolent intent. Perhaps she herself is a sorcerer, or perhaps she has obtained dangerous sorcerers' materials to place near the woman in childbirth.

One's own immediate relatives are the most frequently mentioned suspects in affliction. These include the recently dead who have not yet been freed from ties to the material world through cremation. These shades may be angry at their living descendants for their neglect; they may be taking revenge against those who have caused their death; or they may be merely lonely in the other world and trying to draw their loved ones into it with them. Since cremations can be delayed, often for decades, for lack of funds, every family has several of these unhappy relatives hovering around.

Just as worrisome are one's own living kin and neighbors. A person's troubles could be caused by her own brother or sister—or, very frequently, by an in-law—who, resentful over an inheritance settlement or even over the irritations of sharing a common home, has turned to sorcery in hopes of gain. It may be a more distant kinsman, caught in the continuation of a parental feud, who is causing the illness; or it may be caused by the woman next door who believes that the victim has used sorcery to kill her pigs.

To inflict disaster on a hated one, help can be had from a *balian* or other person reputed to have the mastery of sorcery. The most common technique is the use of poisonous substances (either materially or mystically poisonous), which are put in the food or in corners of the sleeping room of the victim.

Direct evidence of malicious use of sorcery is hard to come by, since no one admits to having done such an evil act, and victims themselves are reluctant to speak openly about their suspicions. Merely talking aloud about these fears may bring about violent counteractions.[2] "Speaking of the devil" is always dangerous. However, one hears secondhand stories about sorcery all the time.[3] Some of them are about love magic: a woman is said to be drawn into adultery through the spells of a neighbor, and her husband undertakes to make her seducer impotent, justifying his attack as a defensive counterattack. Other stories center attention on envy—of the good fortune of a prominent trader or the success of a government official. Disputes among brothers about the division of inherited land often generate suspicions of such magical foul play. Sometimes a dispute may go on for years, each side considering that it is only engaged in defense against the other's attacks. Most people when speaking openly about sorcery stress that the only morally justifiable reaction is to set up a mystical wall around oneself and one's family to defend against any unidentified attackers.

Every *balian* is suspected of trafficking in malevolent sorcery, either for himself, or more commonly, on behalf of his clients, though all deny it. The kind of knowledge/potency needed for defense is the same as that required for attack. In the case of a serious illness the final cure is to make the attacker desist or to eliminate him or her entirely.

Léyak: Local Sorcerers

In many villages, there are certain people who are suspected of obsessive wholesale slaughter. These villagers, who may be either men or women, are said to have gained the magical power to change their bodily form and roam about at night in search of prey. Called *léyak*, a term that has been vaguely translated into English as "witch" but is more properly rendered as "sorcerer," these persons inflict suffering only on people they know well. *Léyak* are sometimes said to have a burning desire to eat the flesh of their victims, especially that of fetuses, newborn babies, and small children. Miscarriages, stillbirths, and infant deaths (until recently very common) are routinely attributed to *léyak*.

Déwa Ketut Baroe, in his picture of two *léyak* eating newborn infants, has taken as their model the *rangda* mask used in many dance-dramas—a malevolent woman with large pendulous dugs, long snakelike hair, fangs, and bulging eyes—but this is by no means the only form they are thought to take.

Léyak are considered to have gained their power with the help of a sorcerer and through special secret rituals in the graveyard where the beings who are the sources of *sakti* are to be found. The set of pictures by Ida Bagus Nyoman Tjeta on pages 72–73 provides a how-to diagram for acquiring the ability to harm others, as evidenced by the transformation into a beastlike *léyak*. The painter's own explanatory comments reveal how similar this ritual is to those of sorcerers. Compare these pictures by Tjeta with those by Blatjok on pages 59–61 giving the often dramatized tale of the great sorcerer Basur.

A *léyak*'s steps to infuse herself with power also closely resemble the rites carried out nearly every day in family and communal temples. In fact, the first two drawings could be taken as depicting an ordinary woman praying to the deities for the well-being of her family, except for two telling details, the single post on the altar and the live chick under her foot. Instead of the usual four supporting posts, the altar's single leg signifies that the offering is being made for purposes of sorcery. Just as in normal worship, she is making offerings to spiritual beings up on a high platform and to others on the ground. However, in ordinary worship, only a sliver of meat is needed, not a whole chicken, and in any case, when chicks or chickens are used, they are not stamped to death.

The second drawing shows the woman in a conventional position of worship, and the term the painter himself used for this position, *mebakti*, signifies prayers addressed to the higher beings.

The last four pictures in the set portray some of the forms that a *léyak* can take. In the last one, the painter shows and states that a powerful *léyak* becomes "Rangda, the most *sakti* of all." I will return to this identification of the *léyak* with the *rangda* below.

Léyak are thought of as working their evil alone, with the sole help of a healer as mentor or guru. They are also sometimes thought of as a community with nonhuman sources of power, the spirits and deities of the graveyard and its adjacent temple, the Pura Dalem.

OPPOSITE: *Sorcerers* (léyak) *Eating Stillborn Babies*
Déwa Ketut Baroe

In this graphic image of two so-called witches eating babies, one has pulled out the intestines and offers them to a dog. In another story, the *léyak* feed the intestines of a baby to a scavenging crow. The fire coming from the heads of the two *léyak* is a sign of their mystical powers. The claws on their feet, which are drawn just like the dog's claws, show their animal affinities.

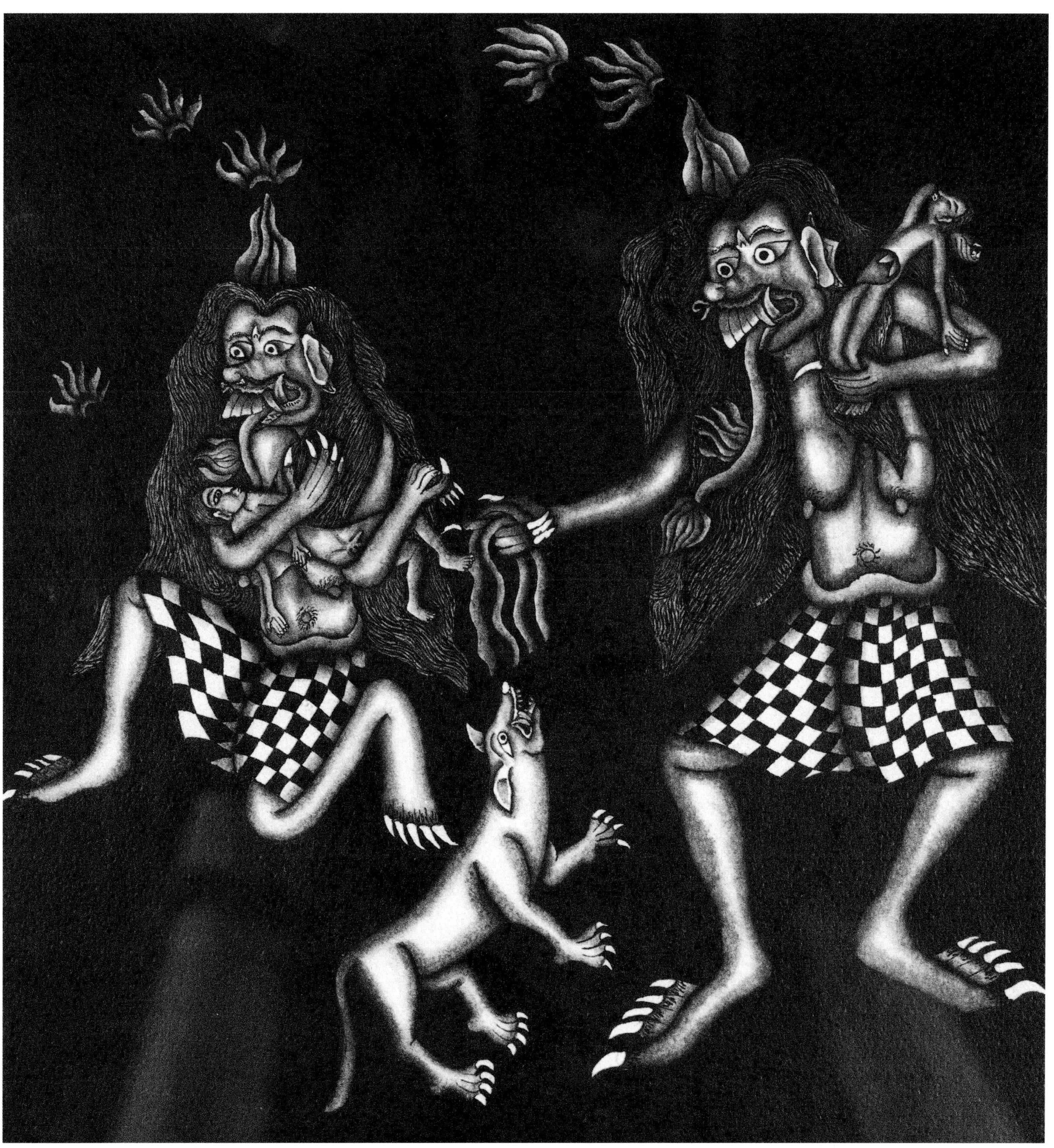

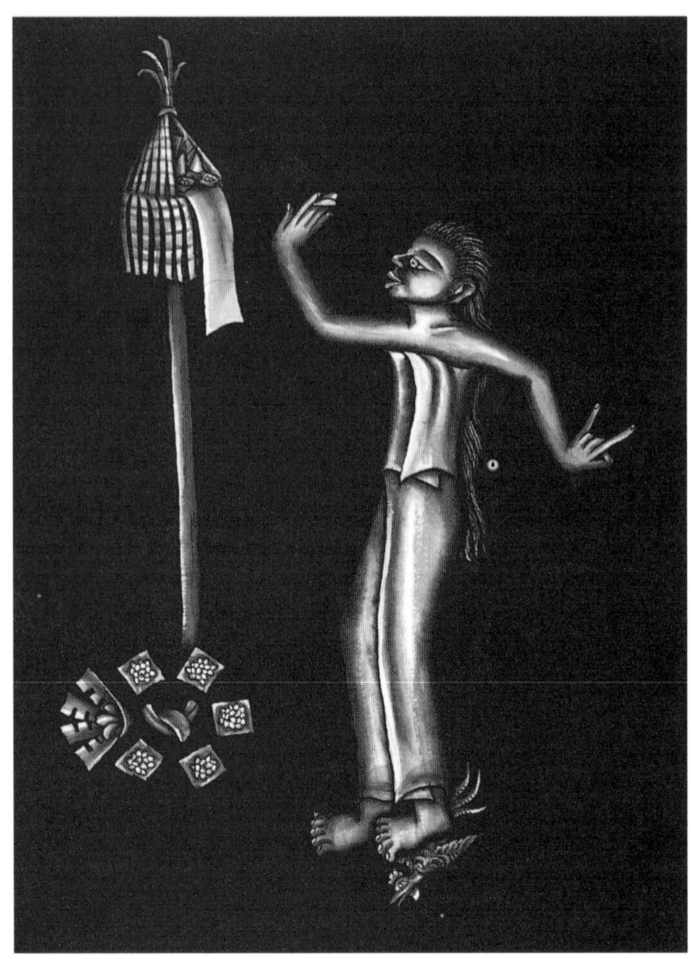

1. Here [a woman] has just set up the one-legged altar.

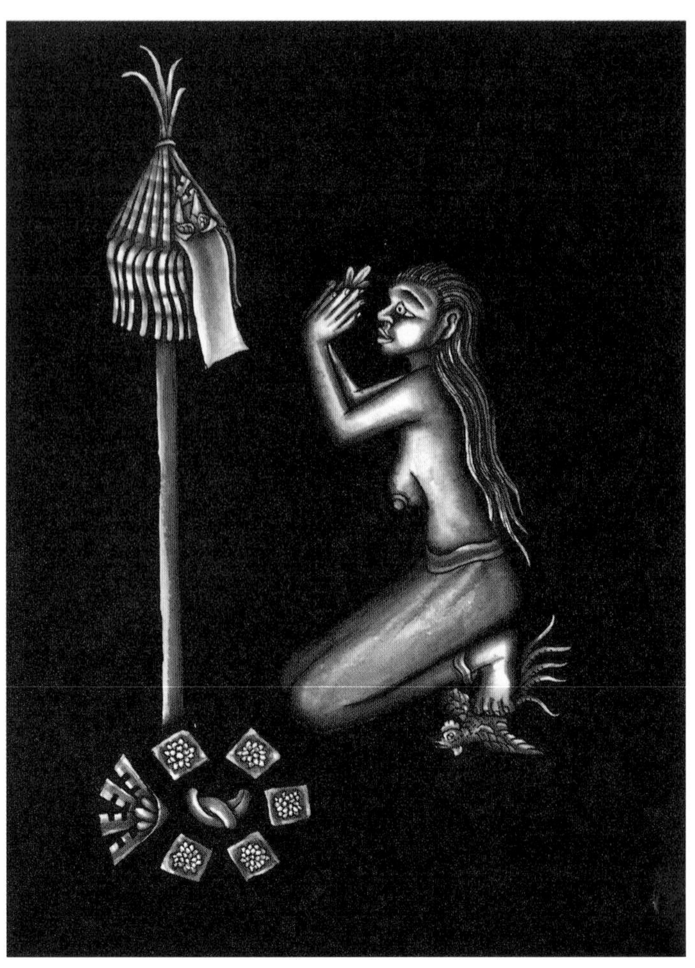

2. She prays *(mebakti).*

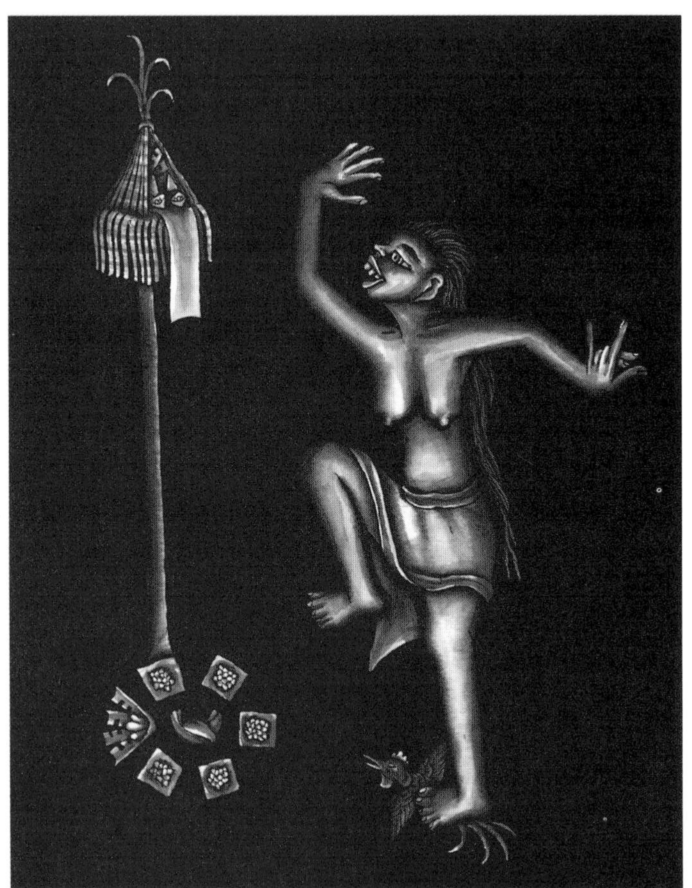

3. She dances in big leaps.

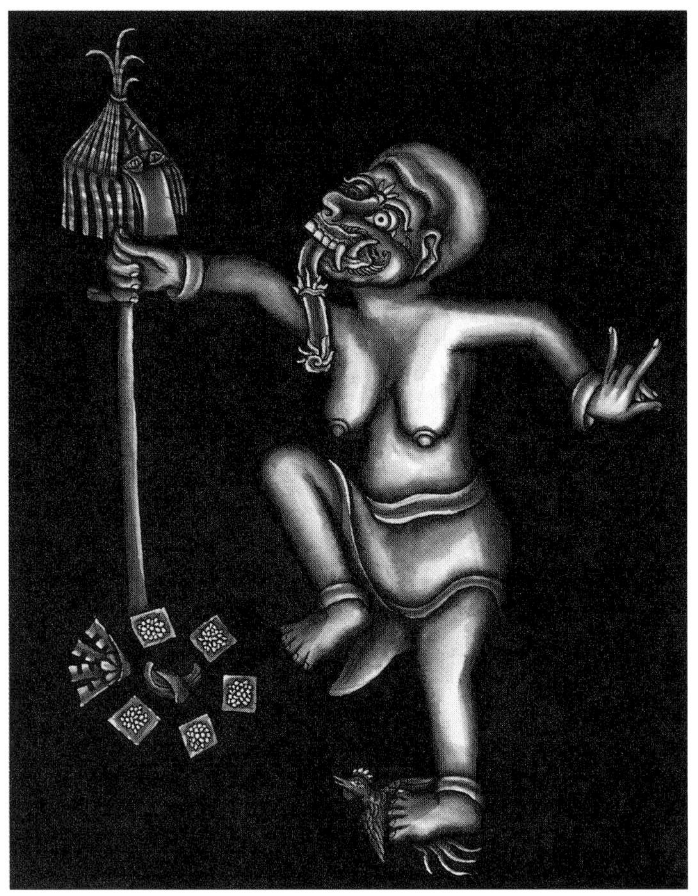

4. She has become a bald-headed *léyak*.

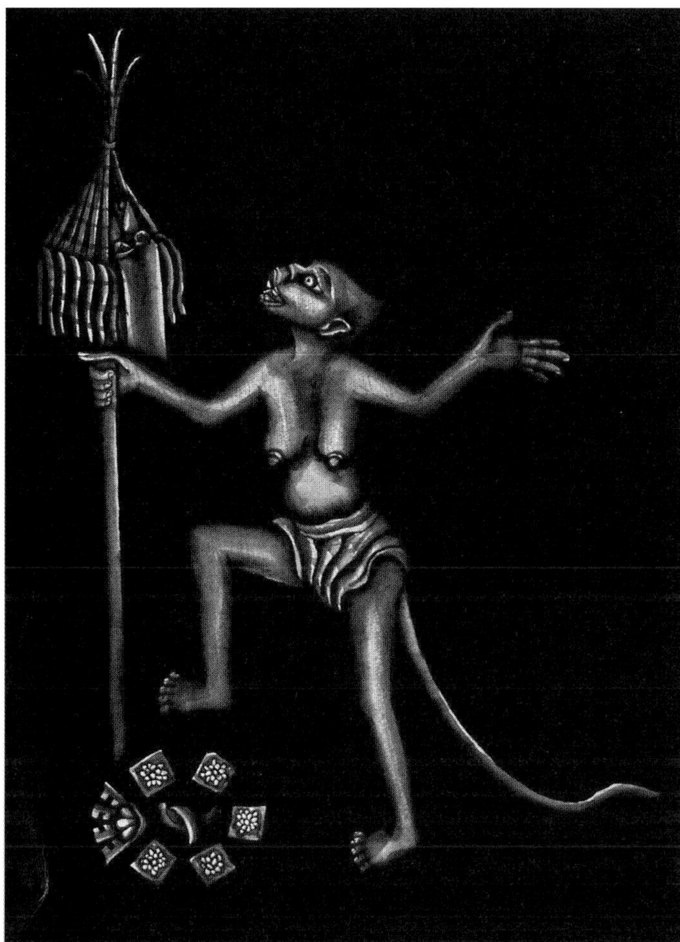

5. She has become a monkey *léyak.*

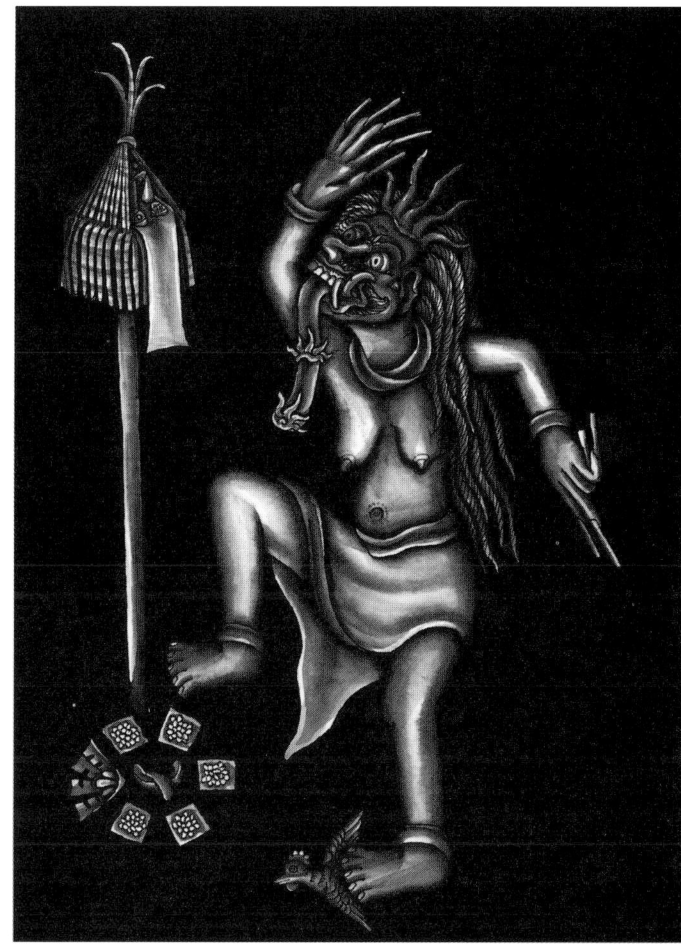

6. She has become Rangda, the most *sakti* of all.

Djata's picture, *A Meeting of Léyak* (page 74), presents the view of *léyak* as a community. The *léyak* meeting portrayed is a point-for-point inversion of a common village ritual. The words Djata used when speaking with Bateson about the elements in his picture present the *léyak* meeting as almost identical to that of a regular village *(banjar)*. A *banjar* is the smallest kind of organized community in Bali. Usually translated as "hamlet," "ward," or "neighborhood," a *banjar* is an organization for carrying out certain community rituals.[4] In the region around Batuan, every *banjar* has its own temple, or at least a special altar, where its god is given a festival once a year. Every month a lesser ritual is held, which requires all *banjar* members to come together, worship, and discuss the practical details of ritual arrangements.

The *léyak* in Djata's picture are doing exactly the same things that *banjar* members do at their meetings. One keeps a record, etched with a knife on palm-leaf strips, of the members' attendance and donation of dues and of their fines if they fail in these duties. This is the seated demon at bottom center holding two palm-leaf pages. At such periodic ceremonies, everyone also brings offerings of food, which are proffered to the god of the *banjar* who partakes of the "essence" of the offering and then returns the leftovers, blessed, for the worshipers to take home. In the picture the *léyak* are bringing offerings of meals made from human babies' flesh. A corpse of a baby hangs by its umbilical cord from the eave of the pavilion (where one might hang a newly killed chicken before cooking it). Another cooked infant is served on a dish carried on a *léyak*'s head and is given to a demon in a priest's turban, who performs the ritual offering. A third small body is in the hands of a *léyak* at bottom. At top center a person holds the arm of a child, which he perhaps has just found.

The purpose of such a ritual, as with those of all temples, is to obtain from the deity a gift of divine energy *(sakti)* with which to protect oneself and one's community against attack from other spiritual beings.

Djata's picture shows an ordinary village that includes *léyak* among its members; the leader of the local *léyak* is the wife of a village headman. This tale echoes the many accounts about acts of evil destructiveness on the part of known neighbors and family members who are revealed to have caused the suffering and death of their fellows. These personal stories often also recount how certain human beings, usually healers, have bravely but sometimes only temporarily vanquished them.

The story that Djata told Bateson may have been the substance of a ritual drama, of the sort discussed below. His statement that the two protagonists transformed themselves into beings commonly represented by the *barong* and *rangda* masks

A Sorcerer (léyak) *Transforms Herself*
Ida Bagus Nyoman Tjeta

OPPOSITE AND ABOVE: The first three pictures in this set show the steps that a woman can take in order to transform herself into various *léyak*. The next three pictures show some of the forms she can take. The captions are Tjeta's.

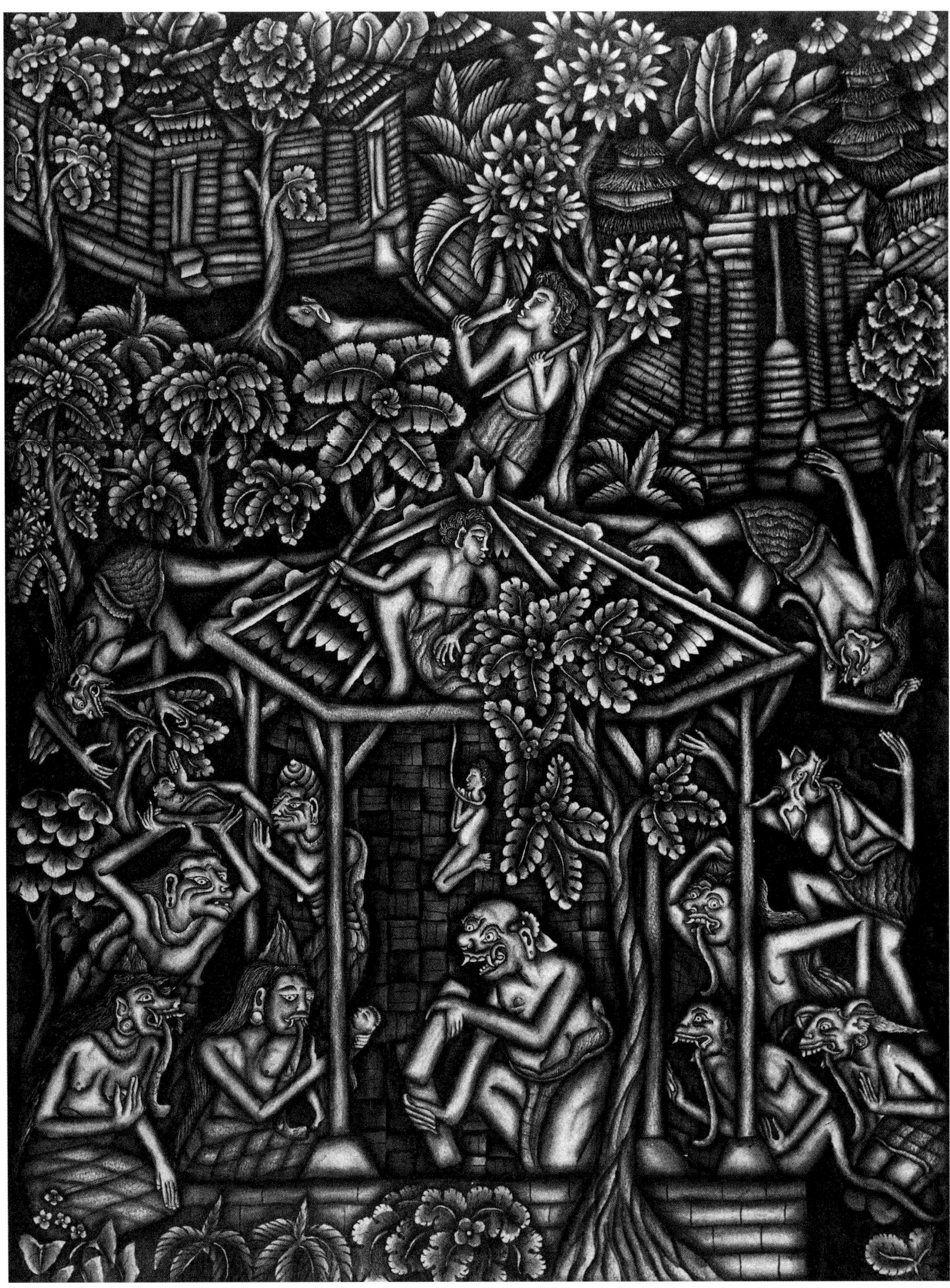

strongly suggests that presentation of the tale may have been part of a regularly performed ceremony, perhaps by a *banjar* community. The story, with its inversion of a *banjar* ritual meeting, explores the ambivalence of the god of the *banjar* itself. It even brings into question the consistency of the deities' benevolence, since both the community of *léyak* and the regular village community may be praying to the same spiritual beings. It is also a statement of the strength of the *banjar* congregation and its god against the strength of the *léyak*.[5]

The Evil Sorcerer-Queen Calon Arang

The great Balinese epic of Calon Arang (see pages 76, 78, and 79) knits together many ideas about afflicting beings and controlling sorcerers. Calon Arang, a legendary widowed queen, uses her powers of sorcery to spread devastation over a neighboring kingdom until she is confronted and defeated by a holy man of great *sakti*, Empu Bharada. He kills her with his superior sorcery, but then relents and brings her back to life.[6]

The Calon Arang story is no mere fairy tale but rather the backbone of a ritual drama, performed with great spiritual danger to everyone. Its plot turns on the practice of sorcery, and its dramatic presentations enact a serious and real continuing battle against the misuse of sorcery within the surrounding village. Indirect allusions to specific local sorcerers may be uttered by the performers, who themselves must have *sakti* in order to protect themselves from the angry counterattacks of any local practitioners of the evil art. Dangerous forces are released and then propitiated by the play and ritual.

The wicked queen's saga is told in diverse media and in many versions, each of which may involve different characters and stress different episodes. At the time that these pictures were made, it was staged not only as a masked play but also as a shadow puppet show. In one nearby village, the story was sung while young girl dancers in trance mimed the action.[7] No matter what the genre, the main performers are always protected by extensive personal ritual, which purifies and strengthens them. In the course of the play, some may be possessed by spiritual beings of various sorts. The picture by Togog (page 20) of entranced men of the village attacking Calon Arang (in her incarnation as *rangda*) with their sharp daggers shows the physically dangerous confrontation that can occur.

The story is about the widowed queen of the land of Dirah, who is feared by all because of her powers of sorcery. (In some versions, she is a widow because she killed her husband by a magical gesture of her hand.) She has a beautiful daughter, whom no one will marry because of their fear of her mother's malevolent spiritual potency. When the queen offers her daughter to the son of the neighboring king, Erlangga of Daha, and he refuses her, she flies into a towering rage. She goes with her disciples to the graveyard and pays homage to the spirits who dwell there and to the goddess Durga in the adjacent temple, the Pura Dalem, and asks for the use of their powers to destroy Erlangga's land. These bestowed on her, she and her followers transform themselves into demonic forms and go to the crossroads of the realm at midnight and dance to the sound of a great gamelan. A plague breaks out and many people, both high and low, are killed.

The scene at the crossroads is depicted in the picture by Tjeta at the head of this chapter. It shows the people carrying their dead to the graveyard, surrounded by the exulting queen and her followers. At the height of their raging attacks, they take the *rangda* form—that of a huge woman with popping eyes, matted hair, flames coming from her head, a cackling scream, and a violent brutal dance. In performance, a *rangda* mask is used for the queen when she is practicing sorcery; so also in these pictures. In Tjeta's picture, these ferocious beings are apparently invisible to the villagers, but some of them seem to register fear in their upturned faces.

The nature of Calon Arang's devastating attack, which spreads not only illness but moral corruption as well, is further elaborated in a picture by Ida Bagus Ketut Diding. Calon Arang's curse has brought out greedy thieves, who are seen stripping a coconut tree (top right) and robbing a rice barn (bottom right).

Another kind of destruction—attacks on livestock and other sources of livelihood—is seen in a picture by Togog, which shows a cow attacked by a demon, and a fisherman pulling a monstrous demonic crayfish out of the water.

In the ritual drama of Calon Arang, usually only one or two of all the possible episodes are performed. First might come a series of darkly comic skits about the villagers' suffering during the epidemic unleashed by Calon Arang, followed by one or two attempts to vanquish her. For instance, an enacted episode might be about the powerful king Erlangga sending his prime minister to fight Calon Arang, who when she sees him, burns him up alive by pointing her finger at him.

Another popular episode concerns the discovery of the source of Calon Arang's *sakti*, her manuscript, or *lontar*. In this episode, the king asks for help from his most powerful and mystically learned sorcerer, Empu Bharada, who sends his son to woo and marry Calon Arang's daughter with the intent of discovering and defusing the sorcerer-queen's *sakti*. He finds out that her *sakti* is in the *lontar* itself and in her knowledge of it. The son steals the *lontar* and brings it home to his father, who then masters the learning in the manuscript and sets forth to confront Calon Arang.

The next episode is depicted on page 79 by Djata, which shows the moment when Calon Arang appears to prove that

OPPOSITE: *A Meeting of Léyak*
I Madé Djata

The painter Djata told Bateson the story of how, in a certain village, many infants were dying soon after birth. The village headman, who himself had lost many children, was angered and decided to do something. It was well known that many of the villagers were *léyak*, and that they met to feast on the flesh of newly born babies every fifteen days, on the mystically dangerous day of Kajeng Kliwon. (On Kajeng Kliwon, all Balinese households set out offerings in their house yards and at all crossroads, and in places such as watercourses and clumps of trees, where potentially dangerous beings live.)

The headman hid on the roof of the village meeting-pavilion during their feast. Through his own great powers he was able to see these normally invisible demons, and he recognized his own wife as the head of the *léyak*. He listened and learned their spells, and then attacked them with their own magic. For the attack, said the painter, the headman transformed himself into Banaspati Raja (a name for the *barong* mask) and his wife took the form of Rangda ing Dirah (represented by the *rangda* mask).

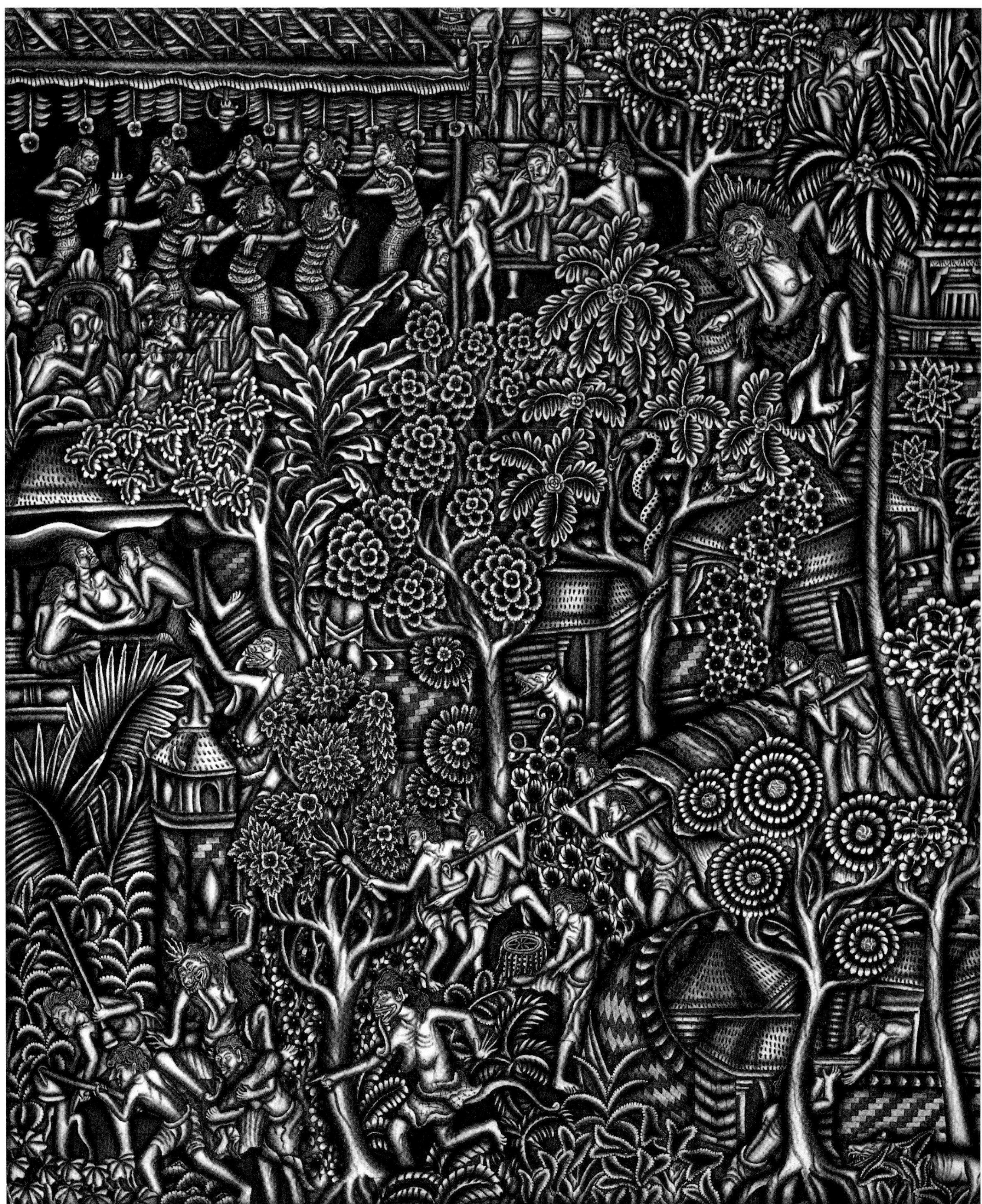

Empu Bharada is the weaker one, when she triumphantly fires up a tree. But right after Calon Arang has turned the tree to ashes, the holy sorcerer turns to her and demands, "You can destroy, but can you bring life back?" She tries but fails, and then he, with a wave of his hand and a spell, restores the tree to moist, green vigor. He then kills Calon Arang, although he later brings her back to life.[8] In some versions she comes to life again from her own power.

The central image of the picture is the burning banyan tree, the leaves of which are the symbol of life in many rituals. The great holy man is proved by the test to be more powerful than Calon Arang. The power to kill and consume a person has opposed the power to give life and has been shown to be the weaker. But the holy man's victory is only temporary, and the battle continues.

The reason that Empu Bharada cannot really kill Calon Arang has less to do with the narrative than with its place in the ritual in which it is embedded, which we will come to directly. What is at stake in the duel between Calon Arang and Empu Bharada is the power to give life as well as to take it away. Life, fertility, and abundance are the goals of every Balinese temple ceremony. The Calon Arang story is employed as a narrative allegory in only some of these ceremonies, but when and how it is used is revealing.

The Calon Arang drama is rarely performed at funerals or cremations, but is seen at some villages' annual temple festival, the Pura Dalem. The play is put on late at night in an open area in front of the temple that lies near the graveyard. The performance is preceded by the usual series of temple rites (described in chapter 2) and forms part of the closing sequence. In the presentation, Calon Arang is first portrayed (by a man) as an elderly woman with a long staff, dressed more like a villager than a queen. Later, when she in demonic fury is about to demonstrate her great powers of *sakti*, the actor dashes into the temple (or into a special small cabin built high on the northern edge of the dance ground), and his place is taken by another man who emerges in the mask and costume of a *rangda*. It is as a *rangda* that Calon Arang does battle with the various emissaries of King Erlangga, including Empu Bharada.

The emissary comes dressed as a royal personage, a prime minister or general, carrying a sharp dagger. Often, he comes as a holy man. If this emissary appears to fail, a group of his soldiers is sometimes brought on, each carrying a dagger with which he attempts to stab the *rangda*, as in Togog's picture, on page 20. Sometimes members of the audience grab daggers and join in the attack. As their combat against the *rangda* heightens, she turns toward them and by gesturing with her white cloth makes their hands turn their daggers against their own chests. They push them in, their arm muscles bulging with exertion, but the sharp point of the dagger cannot cut their flesh. It is as if an attacking being inhabits their hands and arms, while a protective spirit is in their chests—both are equally strong. In some villages, a *barong* mask, a two-person, Chinese-dragon-like demon made of wood and gilded leather and mirrors, replaces the unmasked actor for the final transformation of Empu Bharada, who in this guise enacts his last confrontation with Calon Arang.[9]

The *barong* mask and the *rangda* mask do not necessarily appear together. Bateson and Mead gave the impression that the two personages are forever in opposition.[10] Both masks appear in plays of their own, and both are used to stand for a variety of different spiritual beings. A sense of the meaning of the *barong* can be gained from a picture by Blatjok of cremation preparations, which shows *léyak* hovering around the dead body and the carved sarcophagi being readied for the burning. A *barong* stands half hidden behind the pavilion where the body lies, as though the painter intended to show that he was invisible. In some villages the mask and costume of the *barong* are kept in a lesser temple and brought out to parade around the village on important ceremonial days. Each *barong* mask is considered to be the vehicle of a special protector of that village and is given a personal name.

In performances the wearers of the *rangda* and *barong* masks, as well as those who carry the daggers, are often possessed by spiritual beings, losing awareness of their own acts as they go into furious paroxysms of attack and defense. These possessing beings are thought of as local spirits or members of the large entourages of lesser beings accompanying the *rangda* and the *barong*.

The line between "dramatic play" and "life" has been violently erased. The man who plays the *rangda* may or may not be in trance, as is also the case with his attackers, but all are now in great spiritual as well as physical danger. The daggers can actually inflict serious wounds, but more important, if anything goes wrong in the ritual, some of the participants could go mad, or serious illness could ensue.

Any notions that Calon Arang is just a story are dispelled on recognizing that a performance of the play is a practical act of attack and defense in a world teeming with swarms of invisible beings. These beings, who inhabit the earth along with humans, are willful, irritable, and easy to anger, but also can be persuaded to turn benevolent and bless the people near them. By providing vehicles for the material manifestation of these beings in Balinese rituals, the masks and play bring the spiritual beings into contact with humans, where they can be flattered, told about the situation, propitiated, bargained with, entertained, and even threatened.

Enacting a narrative such as Calon Arang is a means for communicating with these beings, and one of the main channels are the masks themselves, for masks can be, in Bali, much more than mere costumes. They themselves can be the vessels

OPPOSITE: *The Sorcerer Queen Takes* Rangda *Form and Causes Death and Moral Dissoluteness*
Ida Bagus Ketut Diding

The queen in her rage at the king of Daha invades his kingdom and spreads death, destruction, and moral dissoluteness everywhere. She has taken on her demonic *rangda* form, and is shown with a fiery halo (top right) flying above the devastation. Her minions, *léyak* who crave human flesh to eat, hover hungrily about a woman in childbirth (left) and around a body being taken to the graveyard (center). Emboldened by the pervasive evil, thieves raid homes and steal rice and coconuts (top and bottom right). Only two people, in the lower center, can see the ferocious beings causing all this havoc.

At the top of the picture, in front of a temple gate, a propitiatory ritual dance, the *rejang*, is being performed; a peddler sells palm wine and food to the audience; and a mother with two children watches the performance.

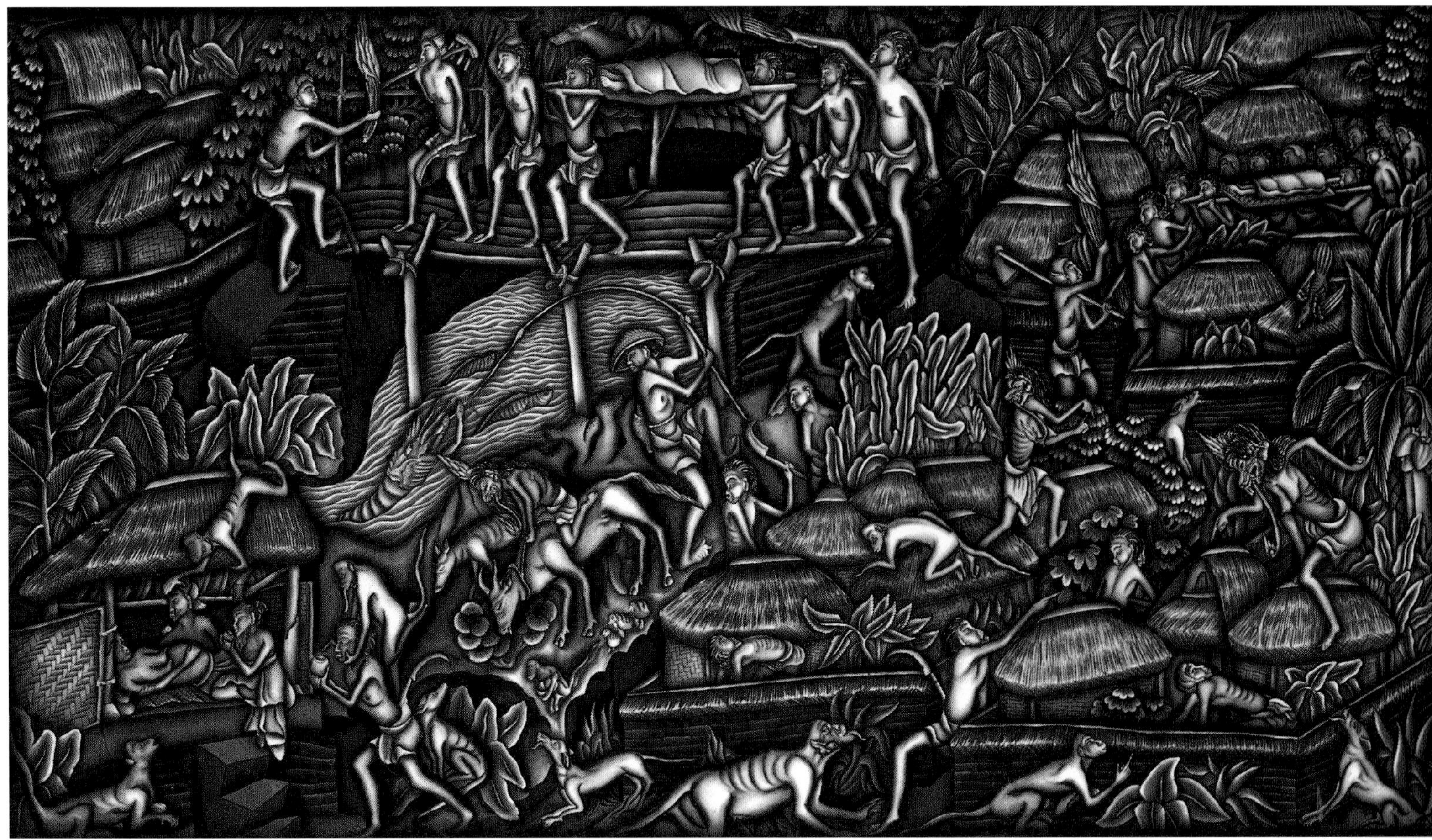

ABOVE: *Calon Arang Story*
Ida Bagus Madé Togog

Togog depicts here the great devastation inflicted on the country by the evil sorcerer-queen Calon Arang. Assorted scenes of misery are scattered over the picture—at top, two bodies wrapped in mats are being carried to the graveyard on simple litters preceded by torches; at center, a man pulls a great crayfish on the end of a fishline out of the water; at bottom left, a woman in childbirth is tended by a healer *(balian)*, and a man with a *léyak* (an evil sorcerer in demonic form) riding on his shoulders brings her holy water. There are *léyak* all around, and at right a *rangda*-like *léyak* stands threateningly astride a rooftop.

OPPOSITE: *"You Can Destroy but Can You Bring Life Back?"*
I Madé Djata, with Ida Bagus Putu Sentoelan

In the Calon Arang ritual drama, the king's most powerful sorcerer, Empu Bharada, challenges Queen Calon Arang to prove that her power *(sakti)* is greater than his. She dances with rage and then says, "I'm going to kill you, holy Bharada, just like I can kill this great banyan tree." She has only to look at the tree and it bursts into flames.

The flames in the center of the picture represent the blazing tree. The sorcerer is portrayed as a high Brahmana priest, recognizable by his cane, long hair twisted into a topknot, and assistant carrying his magical paraphernalia. Calon Arang is pictured in her *rangda* form, the fire coming from the top of her head indicating her *sakti*. At top left one of her followers dances. At bottom right another follower prepares to transform herself into demonic shape. (Compare this image to Tjeta's on page 72.)

The temple in upper right, before which the ritual play is performed, stands for the well-being of the local community as well as the source of Calon Arang's power.

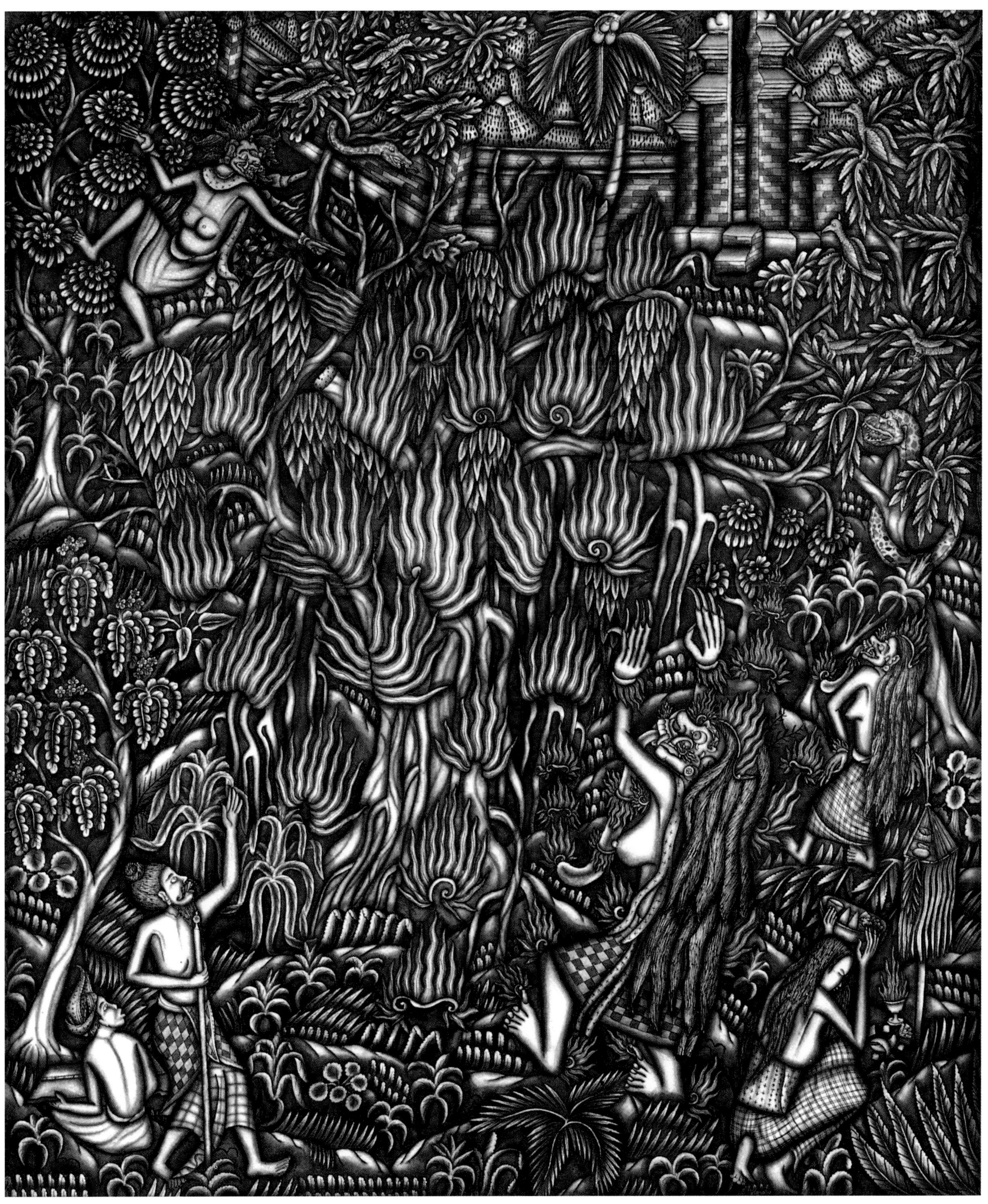

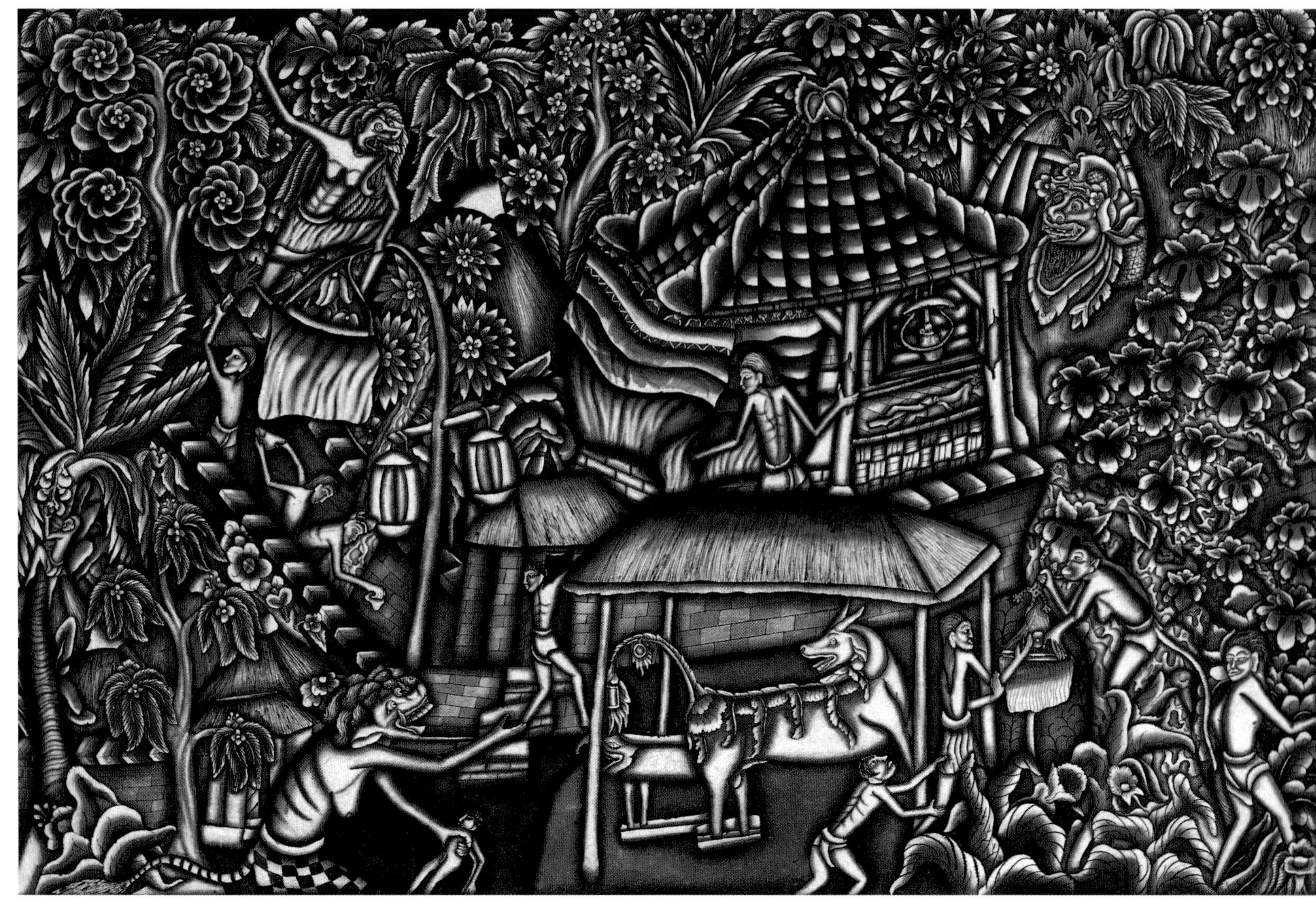

Cremation Preparations Observed by Sorcerers (léyak)
Ida Bagus Putu Blatjok

In this picture a dead body lies in a pavilion hung with curtains. Two carved wooden sarcophagi within which the body will be burned stand in the center foreground. The conventional symbolic objects (a lamp and a tall banner) are set up outside the house yard where a cremation is being prepared. All around are invisible *léyak*. One in the lower left holds a baby in her hand, while another on the right stands next to the one-legged altar that enabled her to turn into a monkey with a long tail. A man at left is carrying a torch, indicating that it is nighttime.

On the upper right, coming from behind the pavilion is a *barong*. Also invisible to humans, it has the head of a demon and is dressed in an elaborate headdress and neckpiece.

for the manifestation of spiritual beings. In fact, when possession occurs in the Calon Arang play, it is never clear whether the mask or its wearer is entered, and the distinction between them disappears.

When not in performance, the *rangda* and *barong* masks are kept respectfully on high altars within temples. Much of the time these masks are not used in performance but instead seated as honored guests on an altar or in a nearby pavilion during a ritual. Each mask of this sort is then treated as a personage, with a personal name, titles, genealogy, and a network of relatives among other such masks of the region. They are talked about as "young" (newer masks whose paint is bright and wood is firm) and "elderly" (older, shabby, and tattered ones). They are also spoken of as having strong and weak *sakti* (although not in this bald way of speaking, but indirectly through allusions) because this quality can swell or diminish. It can be augmented by performing special rituals *(pasupati)*, or allowed through neglect to dwindle into impotency.

At certain other times of the year the masks are put on and paraded around the village, stopping in each doorway to give a blessing, or taken to the sea for purification, as in the picture by Keteg on page 24. In fact, putting on a play using these masks can be seen as only an intensification of this visiting pattern, since it is sometimes spoken of as a chance to allow the mask to "speak out" *(mapajar)* and to "dance" *(masolah)*.[11] It is very likely that the first dramatization of the Calon Arang story, which probably took place around the turn of the century in a village not far from Batuan, was in response to a desire to allow a *rangda* mask to "speak out" and "dance."[12] *Barong* masks also are periodically brought out to dance but not to speak in a different sort of play.[13]

"Speaking out" takes on a terrifying and puzzling meaning when, as often happens at the close of a Calon Arang performance, the *rangda* runs from the lighted performance area into the darkness and shouts hoarsely into the silence. She has just been killed and brought back to life, and the audience is moving to go home when she and a small number of villagers guarding her run to the nearby graveyard. Her challenge may differ from player to player, but the gist of it is, "All you *léyak* come on! Attack me all together! ME! Attack ME!"[14] She does this for only a few moments, then, apparently satisfied that she has thoroughly frightened them away, turns back and reenters the temple, where the priests with incense and holy water remove the *rangda* mask and costume and replace it on the high altar where it is kept until the ceremony comes round again in a year or so.

The meaning of the *rangda*'s shouted challenge to the *léyak* of the neighborhood is profoundly ambiguous. Some Balinese say that she is calling to the *léyak* of the neighborhood to rally and help her in defeating the emissary of King Erlangga. However, other accounts have it that "Rangda" has now fused with Betari Durga, the goddess of the Pura Dalem and protector of the congregation, and is now doing battle not with but *against* all the *léyak* of the vicinity.[15]

This is a central metaphysical paradox in Balinese thought: the *léyak* and sorcerers have received their powers from the great spiritual being of the temple, powers with which they wreak violent affliction on their fellow villagers, yet this being *also* is the protector and life giver of the village. It is to this being that infertile couples go in hope of conception, and the very ill in hope of a cure. In the *rangda*'s sudden turn against the *léyak* themselves, she is acting out that contradiction.

Her switch-about relates to the paradoxical links among sorcery, healing, and *sakti:* the same substances that serve as medicine are also poisons; the same acts that kill also bring life. Destruction and life giving are not exclusive opposites but inclusive complements of one another.

The Calon Arang ritual play is often labeled in Western writings as an "exorcistic" drama. This term, as with others drawn from Christian theology, is misleading. The ritual does not act to expel evil beings from the vicinity, but rather to persuade them to transform themselves from malevolence to benevolence. But the metamorphosis is only temporary, which is why the *rangda* in the play is never killed, but always rises up again.

The deeper underlying philosophical assumption is that the universe and all its contents are made up of one force. This living force, which I have labeled for convenience's sake, *sakti*, takes many forms, from human beings to volcanoes, from small insects to invisible spiritual beings. Such a strong monistic axiom erases all the major distinctions upon which most Western philosophy stands: the contrast between conscious beings and those without consciousness, between matter and spirit, between natural and supernatural, between subject and object, between magic and religion, and between demons and gods. Since all beings are made of the same substance, none can be essentially good or essentially bad, and moral judgments are relative to the circumstances of the actions. Thus "demons" are not necessarily and entirely malevolent and "gods" not wholly benevolent. Rituals are undertaken with the aim of persuading these volatile beings to look kindly on the supplicators.[16]

The English terms "sorcery" and "witchcraft" derive much of their import from the context of the Christian religion, which for so many centuries campaigned against them and relegated them along with "magic" to a separate sphere from religious worship. However, for the Balinese, acts of sorcery are hardly distinguishable from acts of worship, except in intent and consequences. They are all mobilizations of *sakti.*

Within this frame of thought, the serial identifications of *léyak*, *rangda*, and Durga are no longer contradictory, since they are all emanations or transformations of one another.[17] Similarly, the holy man Empu Bharada is successively a high Brahmana priest or *pedanda*, then the fanged *barong*, and perhaps the high god Siva as well. The ritual drama of Calon Arang is sometimes considered to be mainly a means of counteracting the evils of *léyak*, but I believe it to have much broader significance. The story forms an electric node joining the social worlds of sorcerers and unseen beings with those of large and tension-ridden families and Bali's stressful tight-knit villages. It links the experiences of disease and death with royal failure, and well-being with political supremacy. The theme that binds all of these is the magical or spiritual power called *sakti.*[18]

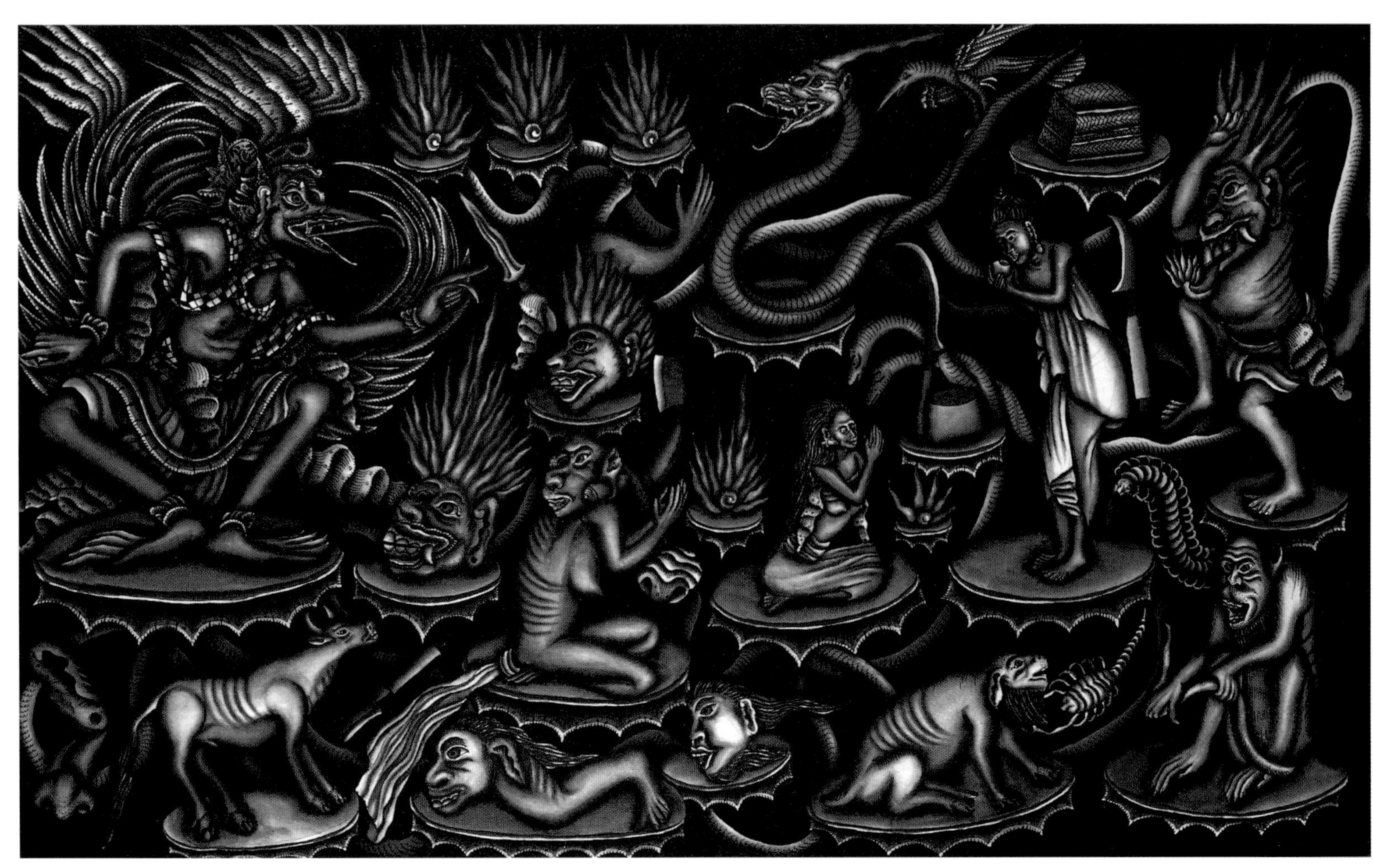

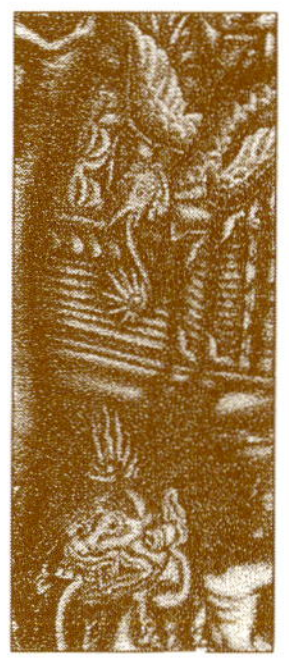

Masters of *Sakti* Powers

In Bali today many people, both men and women, have or are reputed to have the mystical potency of *sakti:* village healers and diviners, shadow play masters, temple priests, and high Brahmana priests. They traffic with the invisible beings of the world with varying degrees of involvement and competence. No one admits publicly to using his or her powers to harm anyone, but everyone understands that the power to heal may require defeating or even destroying an aggressor also armed with *sakti.*

Healers *(balian)* are suspected of practicing sorcery or of purveying the materials needed to their clients. Some boast that they have made people ill with their *sakti* in the past.[1] Diviners are a special sort of *sakti*-master who can diagnose the causes of specific misfortunes.[2] Shadow play masters invoke these powers to entrance their audiences, and the leftover oil from their lamps becomes, through a performance, a miraculous healing fluid. Priests (of both kinds, the commoner *pamangku* and the noble Brahmana *pedanda*) provide protection against the onslaught of sorcerers and of dangerous spirit beings, both through their communal rituals and through dispensing holy water generated at their shrines. Every village has at least a few other people who are thought to have *sakti*, whether self-acknowledged or not. Some are thought to turn themselves into *léyak*, while others in doing their horrible deeds use other forms, as shown in the picture at the head of this chapter. Most *balian* deny "having" *sakti*, but rather see themselves as channels used by potent unseen spirits.

These healers and priests are tamer versions of the masters of *sakti* who appear in stories. As in the tales, over the course of a person's life, *sakti* may mysteriously well up and just as mysteriously dwindle away. The precariousness of the control of *sakti* is recognized by all. In situations of trouble and suffering, concerned people usually go to a number of different *balian*, since they cannot know for sure how potent any particular master is. There is also an issue of fit: each practitioner appears to have greater success with certain afflictions and afflictors than with others. The search is for the *balian* whose *sakti* is most likely to defeat that of the being who is causing their suffering.

Acquiring and Demonstrating *Sakti*

Togog's several illustrations of one of the greatest sorcerers are vivid images of the fierce, fiery qualities that a man of such spiritual potency has. *Sakti*, Togog makes clear, is an ambivalent godly power for both destruction as well as creation. As Togog told the story, the great holy man named Begawan Mercukunda meditated for many years until he finally brought himself face to face with the great god Ida Betara Brahma.

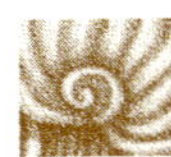

The god said to him, "My child, what is it you wish of me, your father?"

"Pardon me if I am presumptuous, but I would like to have the power to bring well-being to the world and to be able to wreak harm too."

"But that's the power of the gods themselves! Be satisfied with what you have, little one. I'll show you what I can do. Just watch me!"

And then Ida Betara Brahma suddenly transformed himself into a huge demon with three tiers of three heads—nine faces, ten arms, and two feet. Begawan Mercukunda liked that very much.

"Are you impressed?" said Ida Betara Brahma.

"Yes, that is just what I want!" said he, respectfully.

So Ida Betara Brahma gave him the book of many secrets.The *sakti* power of the book entered into his body.

And after that he was able to turn himself into a Garuda bird, but only his head. He could take on many different heads. The *lontar* (book) was named Aji Ugig. Now he could carry out all sorts of sorcery. He knew the

OPPOSITE: *The Mythic Sorcerer Begawan Mercukunda and the Spirits He Can Invoke and Create*
Ida Bagus Madé Togog
From a set of 7 pictures

The holy man Begawan Mercukunda (who might also be called a sorcerer) stands on the right in this picture, dressed in white, with his hair up in the manner of a priest. Meditating, he holds his hands in the *mudra* for invoking spiritual beings and powers. He is holding a cup of holy water. In front of him are some of the fearful beings he has brought into physical manifestation. At the far left is Garuda, one of Mercukunda's metamorphoses. The saucerlike pedestals on which all the figures stand indicate the *sakti* that they embody, as do the three fires along the top. Snakes, scorpions, an arm and hand, a nose, and a bird are intertwined around the beings on saucers. All of these are forms that Mercukunda can take, or, what is essentially the same thing, beings that he can command to do whatever foul or good deed he desires.

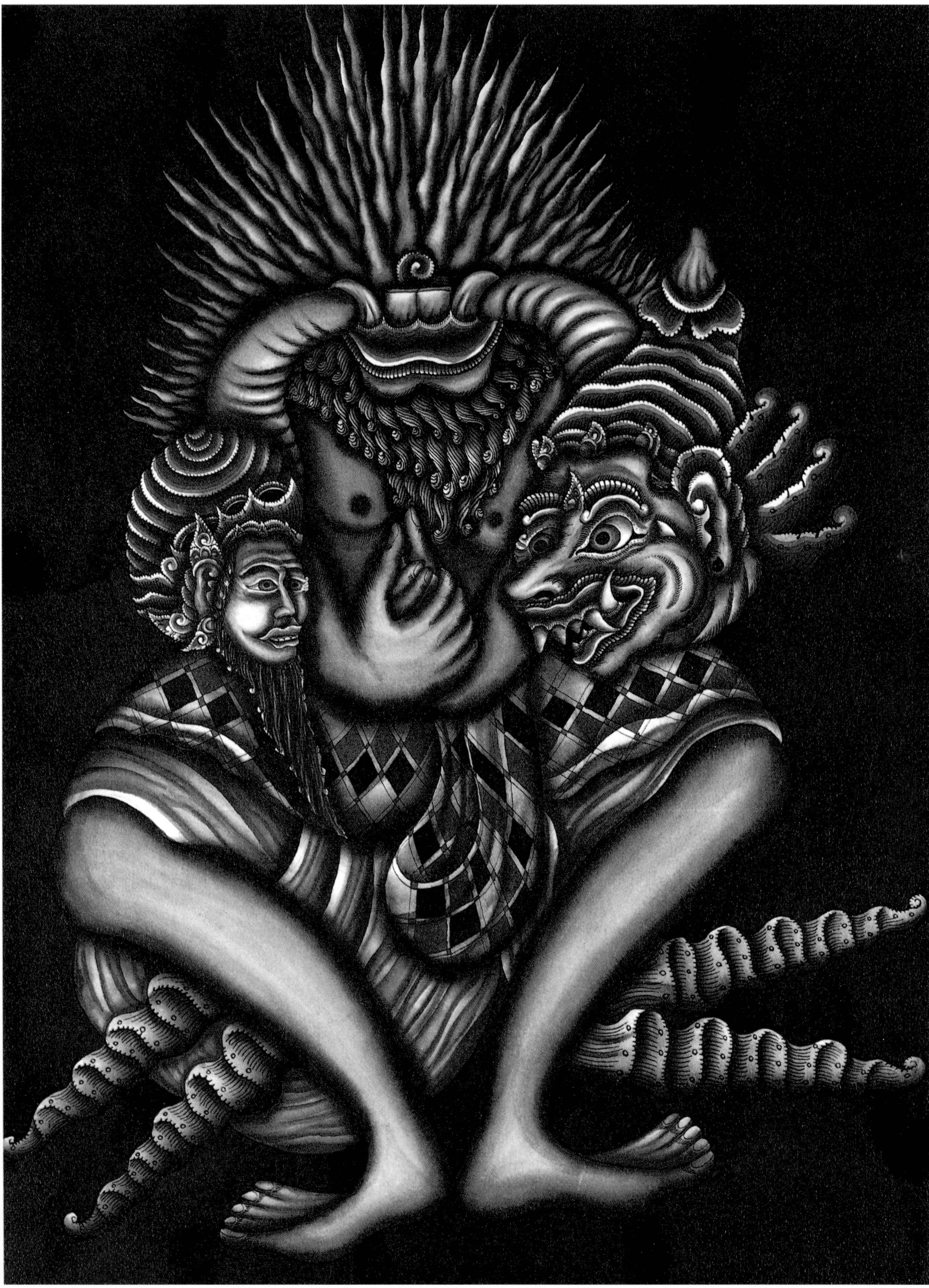

mantra for making people go mad. The *lontar* also told how to put up a magical wall around his house, and how to defend himself.

When Togog illustrated the story of Begawan Mercukunda, he chose not to paint images of the deity Betara Brahma, but rather of the human being who dared to confront him, with whom he may have identified. He could have drawn the deity in his transformed *(pamurtian)* stage, with his piercing eyes and ferocious mouth, multiplied nine times, as other artists have done, but instead he depicted the holy man and the many forms he could take. The pictures he made of the holy man are unusually large and impressive, with deep black backgrounds. He is imagined as a Brahmana Buda, the priestly clan to which Togog belonged.

Sakti, the story shows, is not only the power of the gods but also a human competence. It is the ability to use the powers of spiritual beings and to put them to work for personal goals. When a human being has *sakti* he can partake of the most intense form of intercourse that mortals can have with intangible, unseen beings and powers. But a human has these powers only at the whim of those who give them, who may take them away at any time.

Sakti is also very dangerous to the practitioner. To master it one must have immense inner strength and courage, or its electrical force may turn on one. In Togog's story of Begawan Mercukunda, the would-be sorcerer had to meditate for many years. Balinese meditation, for these purposes, is carried out in places such as forests or graveyards that are teeming with dangerous beings, which must be turned away through sheer willpower. Meditation in Bali is not a serene emptying out but rather an intense focusing of will and energy against external provocation. When Mercukunda finally faces the great god, the god takes his most demoniacal manifestation, but the sage never flinches. In fact, he says he likes it. It is that statement of spiritual steadfastness that convinces the god that Mercukunda is ready.

Begawan Mercukunda gets his *sakti* through a book—but the holy man does not merely read the book, he takes its knowledge/power into himself. Contrary to the ways we speak about such powers in English, *sakti* is neither a possession nor a skill but an attribute. It is bestowed often on people through objects, not only *lontar* books but also rings, stones, iron daggers, and the like. The greatest masters of *sakti* are those who have it as knowledge, while lesser *balian* may have gained their competence not through study, but through a direct gift of an object from the invisible beings. Those who have gained *sakti* through study and training have worked with a teacher, or guru, to whom they become eternally indebted.

Togog's story ends by stating what Mercukunda can now do: transform his head, thereby becoming any kind of being he wants. The demonic beings that Begawan Mercukunda commands resemble closely those drawn by *balian* in the amulets they dispense, which can be found in *lontar* handbooks. A few examples are illustrated by Ida Bagus Nyoman Sanoer Tampi. Togog also depicted a sorcerer's talismanic image (page 21).

Violent combat among masters of *sakti* shows up in several pictures. Conflict has an important place in the system of ideas and images of *sakti*, for only in fighting others can one's *sakti* be tested. Since *sakti* is an attribute that is by nature ephemeral, anyone who has it must constantly demonstrate his powers. The test may be by random malevolent action against people in the vicinity, or, as in the pictures by Diding on page 87 and Rai on page 88, through all-out war among nearly matched masters.

One such war among masters of *sakti* was reported to me by Déwa Ketut Baroe, one of the painters of Batuan, who said he remembered as a child being woken up by his father and brought out to watch the huge bursts of fire that were sweeping across the sky. His father told him it was a battle among *balian*.[3]

In Batuan, in 1988, someone broke into the closed shrine in one of the temples, took the god figures from it, mutilated them, and threw them on the ground in the graveyard. Among the many theories afloat as to who might have done this sacrilegious deed was the belief that it was the magical act of a local sorcerer merely testing his potency. Everyone, however, agreed that the desecrator could not have entered at all if there were not some fundamental spiritual weakness in the members of the temple congregation. The congregation's reaction was not to pursue the thief by legal or mystical means, but rather to embark on extensive costly rituals to demonstrate the reverence that the local people had for the gods of that temple.

When Bateson and Mead asked their Balinese assistant to set down an essay on the meaning of the word *sakti*, he wrote: "The meaning of *sakti* is the ability to prevent anyone from defeating you." He went on to say that this power is hidden in some weak part of the body, such as under the tongue or between the eyebrows, and that if an enemy finds out where the *sakti* is hidden, he can defeat him.[4]

All these examples show that Balinese talk about *sakti* is pervaded with a rhetoric of battle. Their ideas are founded on a view of the world as one of a multitude of beings, human and nonhuman, great and small, in competition for control of one another. This conception seems to be so general and intense that it appears even in the dreams of one of the artists.

A Personal View: Togog's Dreams

There is convincing evidence, independent of the pictures themselves, that the interest in *sakti* on the part of the picture

OPPOSITE: *The Making of a Mythic Sorcerer*
Ida Bagus Madé Togog
From a set of 7 pictures

The sorcerer Begawan Mercukunda, who had great mystical mastery, could take his own head off and replace it with various fierce demonic ones. Here the fire coming out of the shoulders is a conventional symbol of *sakti* power. The head on the left wears a turban of the sort that a high Brahmana priest might wear and represents the sorcerer's normal visage. The head on the right represents him in his fiery efficacious mode. This picture is unusually large for one with a single figure, and consequently has a strong and ominous effect.

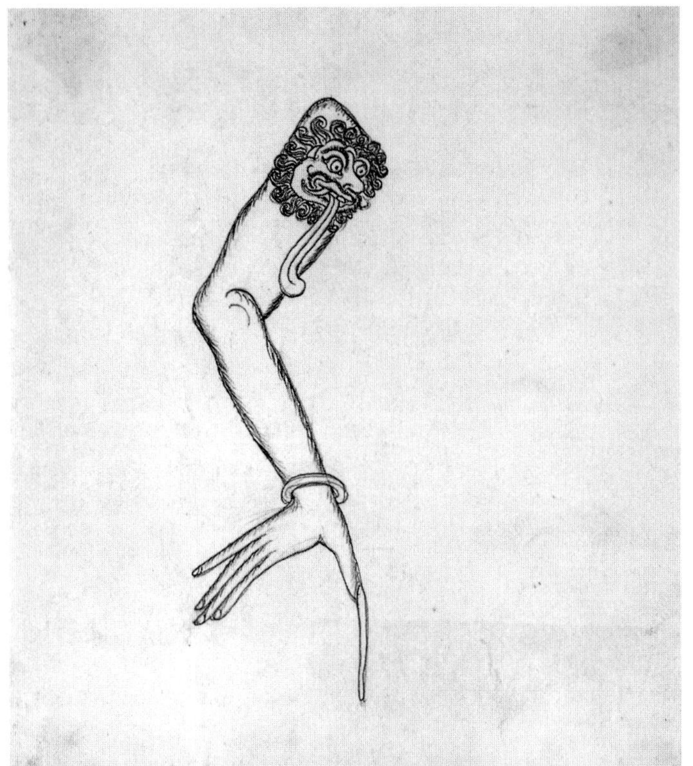

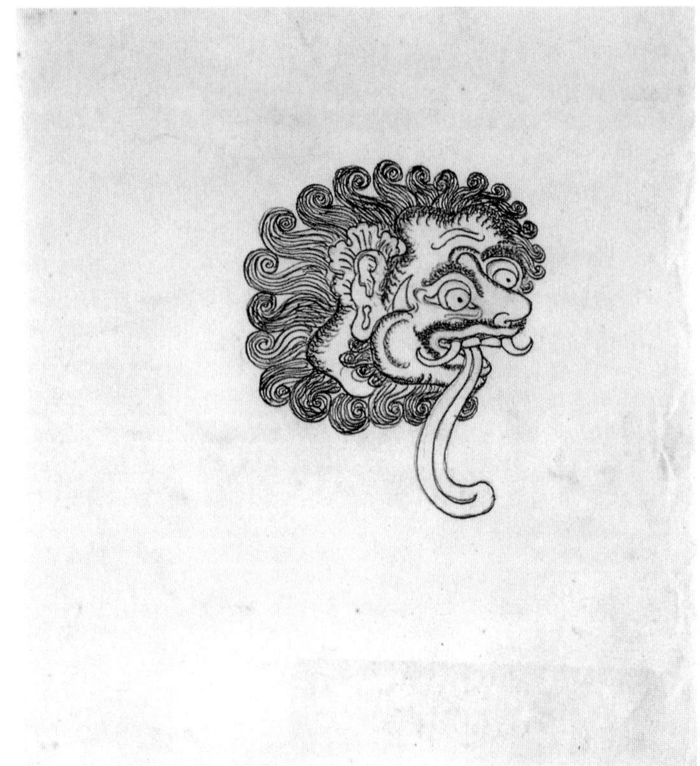

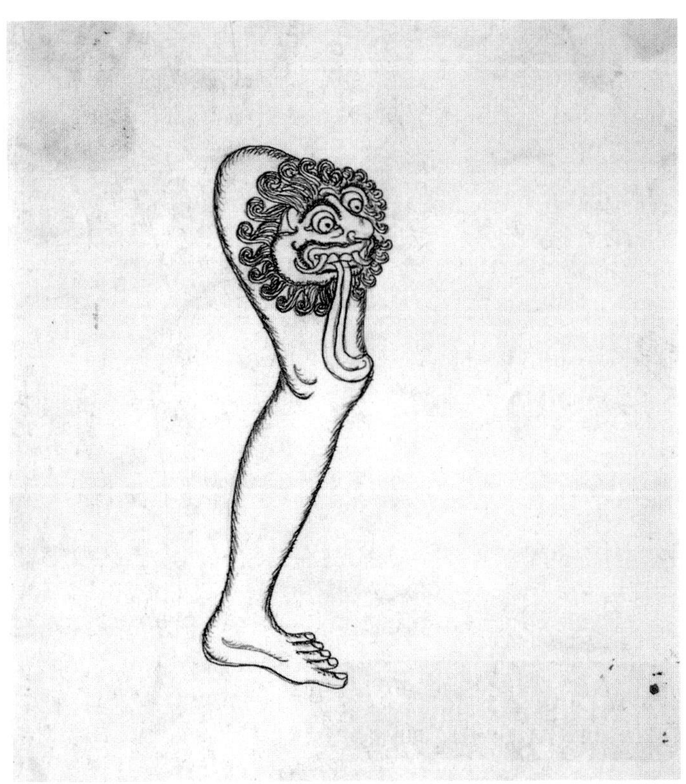

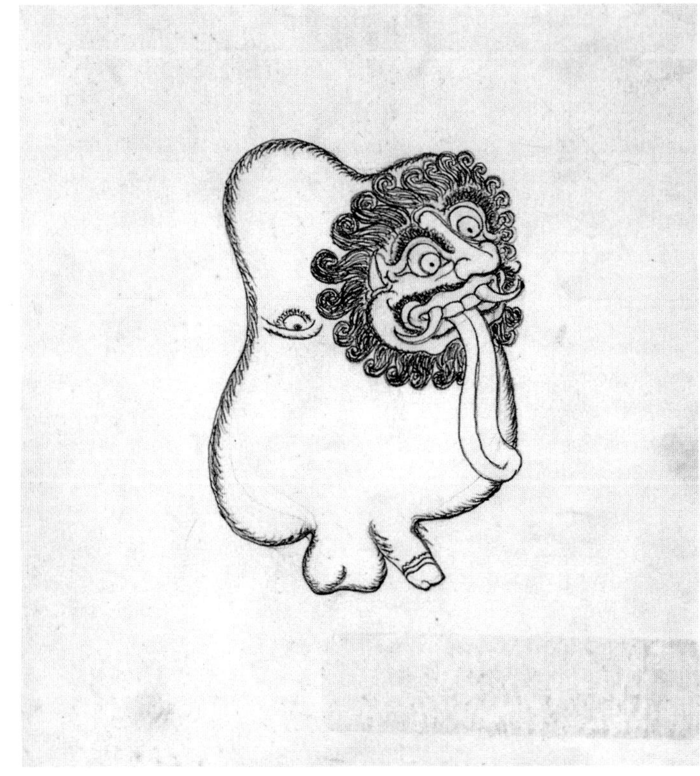

ABOVE: *Sorcerer's Talismanic Images*
Ida Bagus Nyoman Sanoer Tampi

Sanoer's mother and father were Brahmana high priests who owned a large library that included handbooks used by healers. The artist copied for Bateson and Mead a number of the small drawings that are placed in amulets to ward off sorcerers' attacks. These same beings, here animated body parts, are thought to be sent by malevolent sorcerers to attack their victims.

OPPOSITE: *Battle among Sorcerers* (léyak)
Ida Bagus Ketut Diding

Diding told Bateson that this picture shows a battle among *léyak*. Three of the demonic beings are fighting over the body of a baby, which is in an open grave. The *léyak* point two fingers in a gesture of attack, shooting out a magical destructive force. At top left two alarmed people point at the *léyak*, and another watches from the top of a tree. The painter explained that the bird is a crow, which eats carrion, and judging from its fiery tongue, it must be a *léyak* as well.

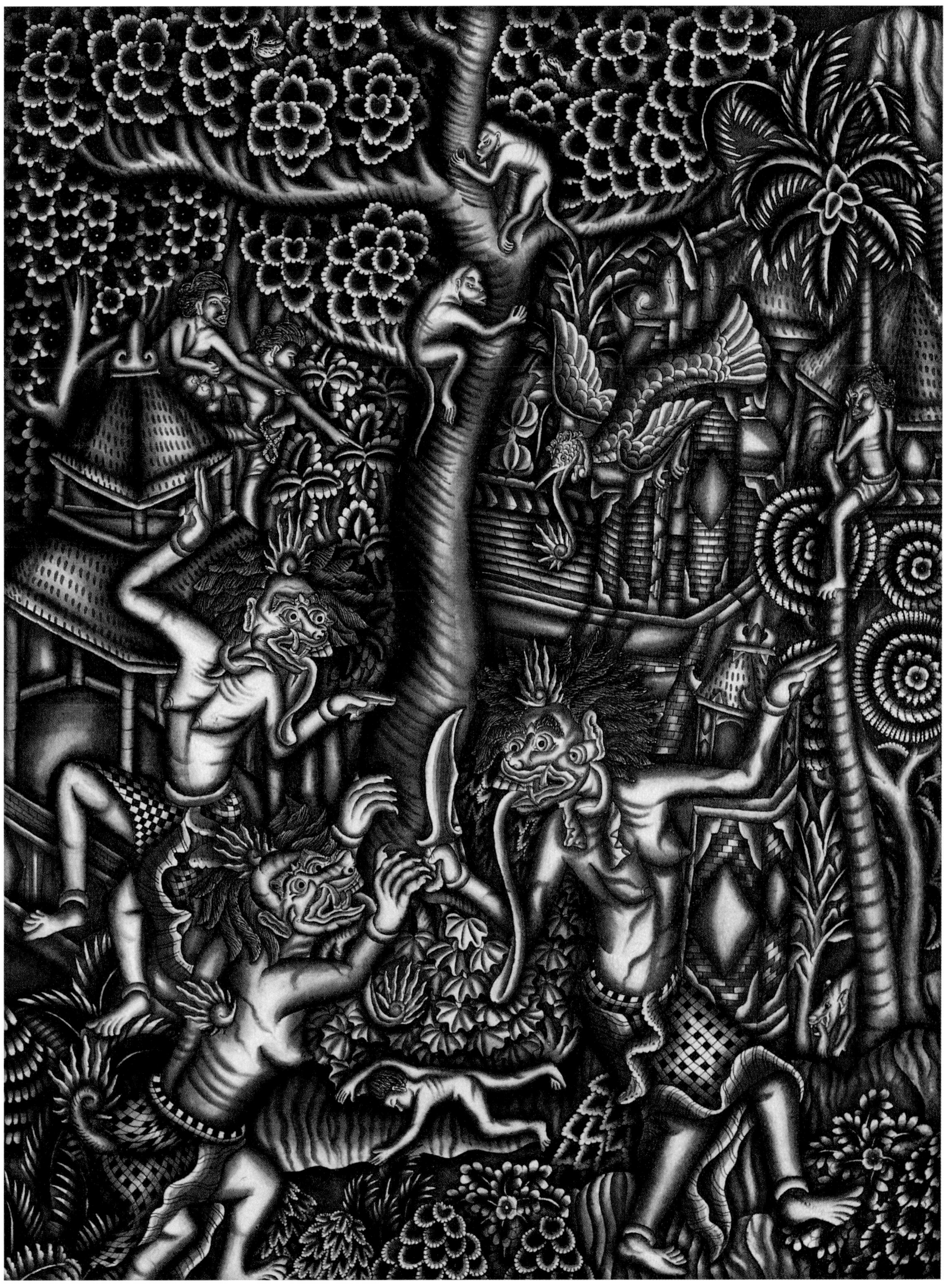

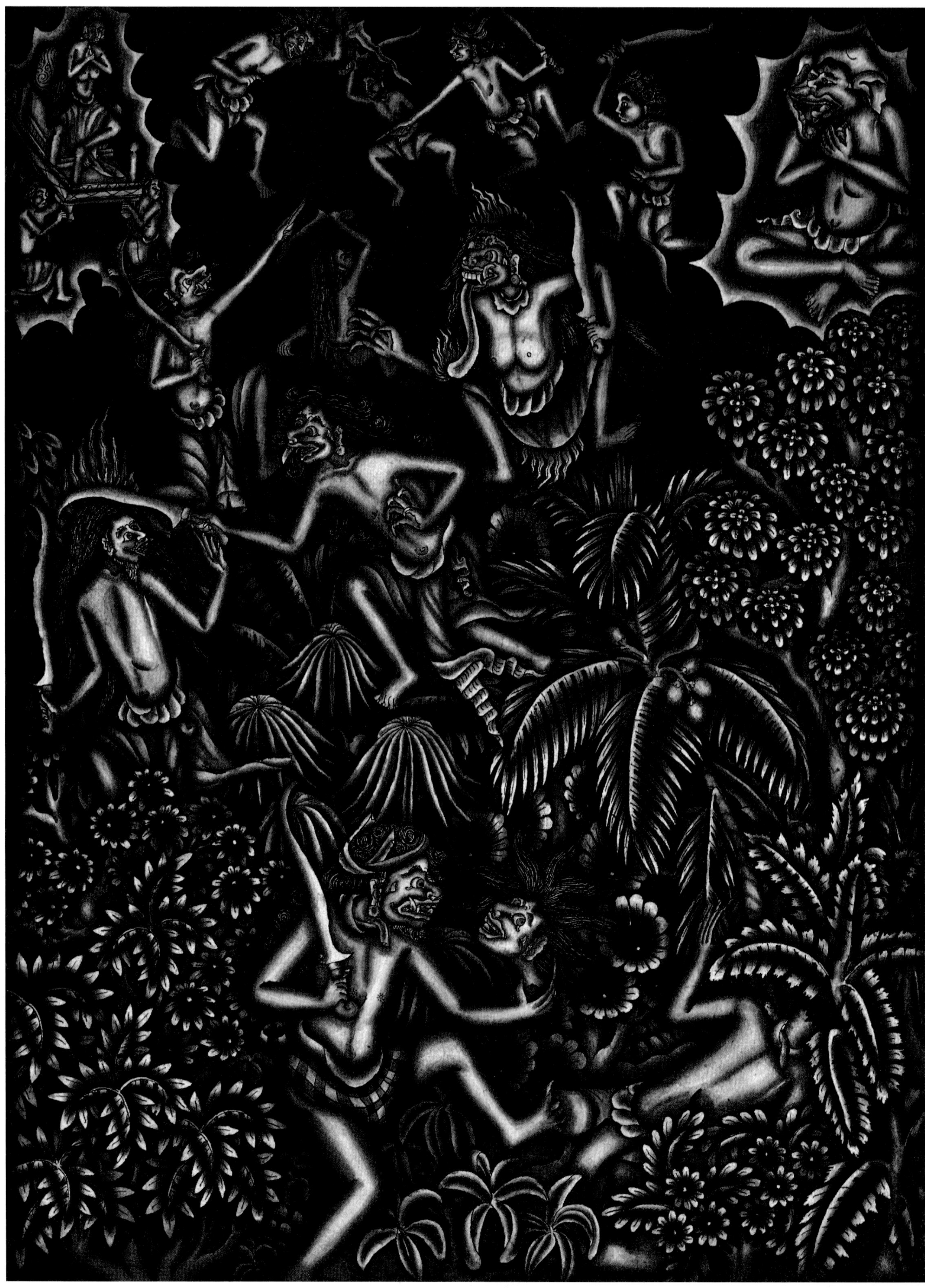

makers was not merely a response to foreign excitement over the exotic ideas of "witchcraft" or "black magic." It is true that many Westerners were titillated by these notions. For instance, Walter Spies played it up in his conversations with his guests, and in a film and a novel made with his collaboration by two of his guests the themes of witchcraft and sorcery were prominent.[5] However, a study of the fifty-seven dreams that Togog related at Mead and Bateson's request shows that he repeatedly dreamt of such matters. The anthropologists had asked him to tell them his dreams in pictures, and he readily began.

For the first three months and occasionally afterward, Togog in his dreams seemed preoccupied with matters of *sakti*, with *léyak*, and other kinds of ghostly demons. I wonder whether they would have been taken by Togog or his fellows as signs of the potential *sakti* of the dreamer himself.[6]

Interpreting dreams, of course, is problematic. While Bateson and Kalér recorded Togog's story of each dream, they did not note down his associations to each dream. Since dream language is one of obfuscation and elision, should we take seriously the dreams' surface alone? If a dream is about events that could have happened in everyday life, I think that, with care, one can read from it something about that life. If a dream is explicitly about sorcery, I believe it tells us something about the everyday understandings of sorcery.

Almost all of Togog's dream texts are coherent stories. Dreams themselves are normally quite chaotic, and what any dreamer reports has already been considerably edited and organized in what Freud called secondary elaboration. In Togog's case, he edited and elaborated his dreams a third time, since he first had to make comprehensible visual images to depict the dream and then, second, had to dictate a text describing the dream. All this secondary and tertiary elaboration must have gone toward preparing an account that was culturally meaningful, first to Togog himself, and then to his investigators. Despite these revisions, the content of Togog's dreams must have been somewhat independent of his conscious concerns to please the anthropologists.

For these reasons, I believe that the manifest contents of the dreams can be taken as evidence of Togog's fascination with sorcery. Further support is provided when the dreams are placed with Togog's other pictures in chronological sequence. While many of his dreams are peaceful, mundane, or about other matters such as sex, the ones about *sakti* parallel the subject matter of his paintings. For instance, during the period that he was painting the violent and magical pictures at the beginning of this chapter, *The Making of a Mythic Sorcerer*, Togog was dreaming of defeating *léyak* and of studying sorcery under the tutelage of a priestlike figure.[7]

There were no established conventions for the drawing of dream images on which Togog could rely. He was forced to look for original solutions. In an interesting externalization of the self, Togog chose to depict himself, the dreamer, as a figure, and Bateson noted on the back of each picture which one he was. The style he used to draw himself and others, in the Western manner with rounded bodies and a suggestion of three-dimensional space around them, seems to "domesticate" even the demonic beings. Many of Togog's earlier pictures had been of single images set against black backgrounds, and he did the dream pictures in this same mode. (See, for example, his picture of men stabbing a *rangda* on page 20.) Their silky dark settings make his figures both forceful and terrifying and give them an air of night and dreaming.

I have no external information about whether Togog actually harbored a desire to become a master of *sakti*. This is a subject no Balinese would talk about directly, for it is both presumptuous to claim such potency and at the same time dangerous, since such a claim might arouse opposition from beings of the unseen world. In the 1980s, when I talked with Togog at length about past events in his life, he sometimes hinted that he had received the gift of *sakti*, but never said so explicitly. Although he was not renowned as a master of *sakti*, one of his sons was.

I give on pages 90–93 a sampling of just four of the dreams about sorcery, dreams with themes of violence, conflict, terror, and the involvement of spiritual beings. Although in some of these dreams Togog runs away from his nightmare demons, in most he turns and fights.[8]

OPPOSITE: *A War among Sorcerers*
Ida Bagus Ketut Rai

According to Rai, this scene depicts a war among sorcerers.[9] While many tales are told of sorcerers vying with one another to show off their superior *sakti*, it is unclear which story this one may be. The artist did not dictate a story to Bateson but he did identify the figures with proper names.

In the upper left corner in a halo is Amtersari, seated on a pavilion in meditating position, who may be a master of *sakti*. In the upper right corner, also in a halo, is Ganesha, a deity. The other demonic figures, Rai said, are humans who have transformed themselves through their control of sorcerers' lore. One at the bottom, with his head off, has been defeated. In the center, the figure with breasts was identified by the maker as Rangda.

Most of the sorcerers have tusks, shaggy hair, and great popping eyes, and they are all armed with swords. The *rangda* figure is one among them, also armed with a sword (unlike her standard appearance, carrying a white cloth, which is a different sort of weapon). Here she is clearly a sorcerer among sorcerers, the only female, but equal to if not stronger than the men.

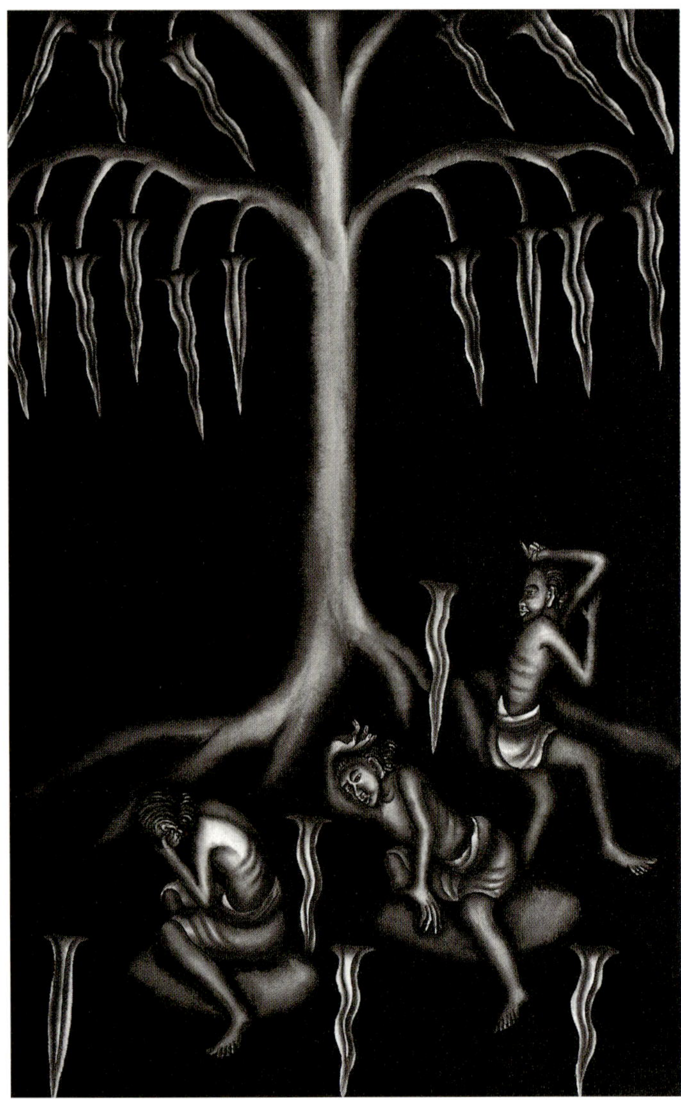
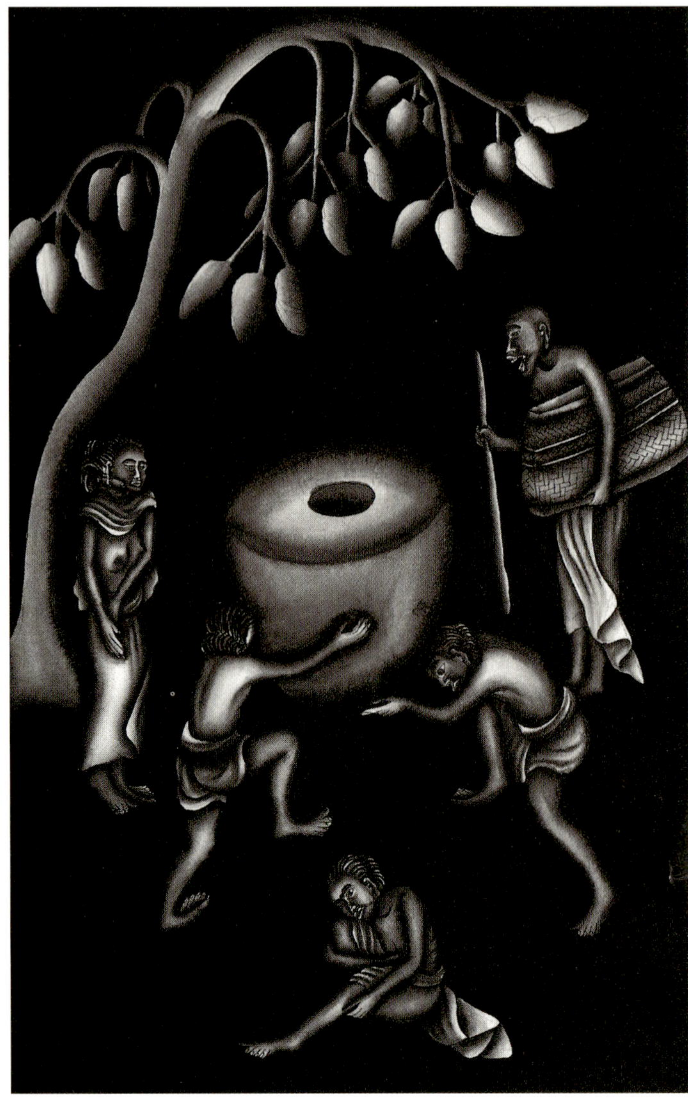

A Dream about a Tree with Dagger Leaves

(dream 6, September 7, 1937)
Ida Bagus Madé Togog

I was walking along a path and there was no one around, and I cried out "Hello! Where is everyone?" Then I saw a tree, a tree with daggers for leaves. And under the tree were some people, three people, and I ran to them and shouted, "Hey! Watch out! You people, hide your heads so that you won't be stabbed by those daggers!" [Left: The dreamer is the man on the right.]

And then I turned and ran away, and after a while I saw a high priest carrying a large flat basket. The old priest said, "Who will carry this stone mortar for me?" And so then I carried it—my legs hurt carrying it—and then I saw a woman under a tree, and I said to myself, "Maybe he'll give that woman to me for carrying the mortar!" [Right: The dreamer is the man at left carrying the mortar.]

The tree with daggers in the first picture is a popular image of one of the punishments of hell (see page 56). This is an interesting example of the evocation of culturally familiar images by a dreamer.

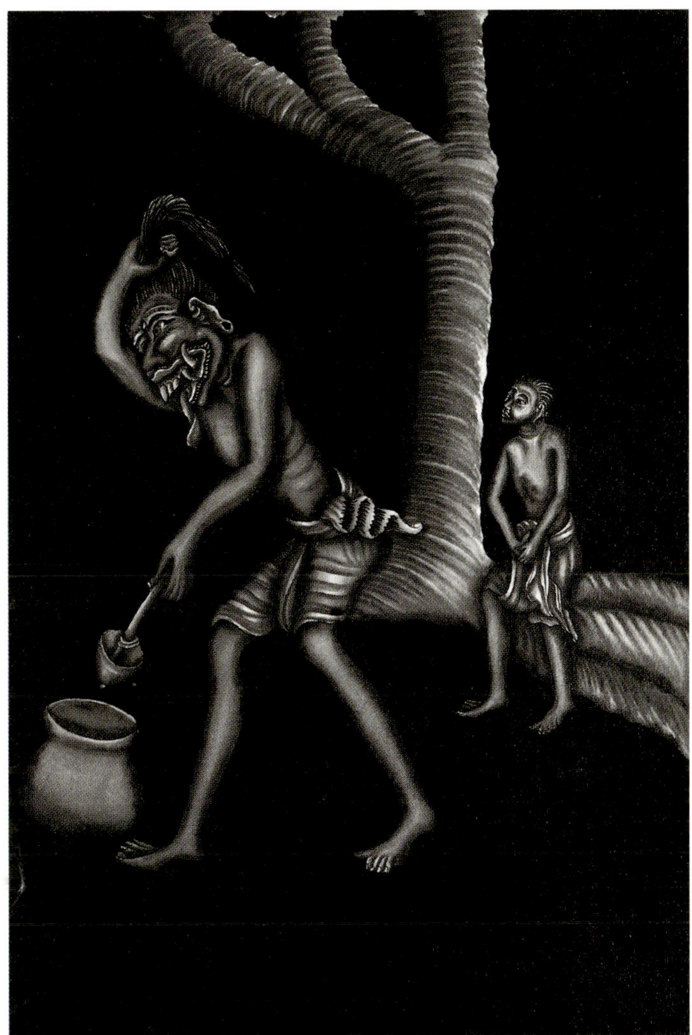

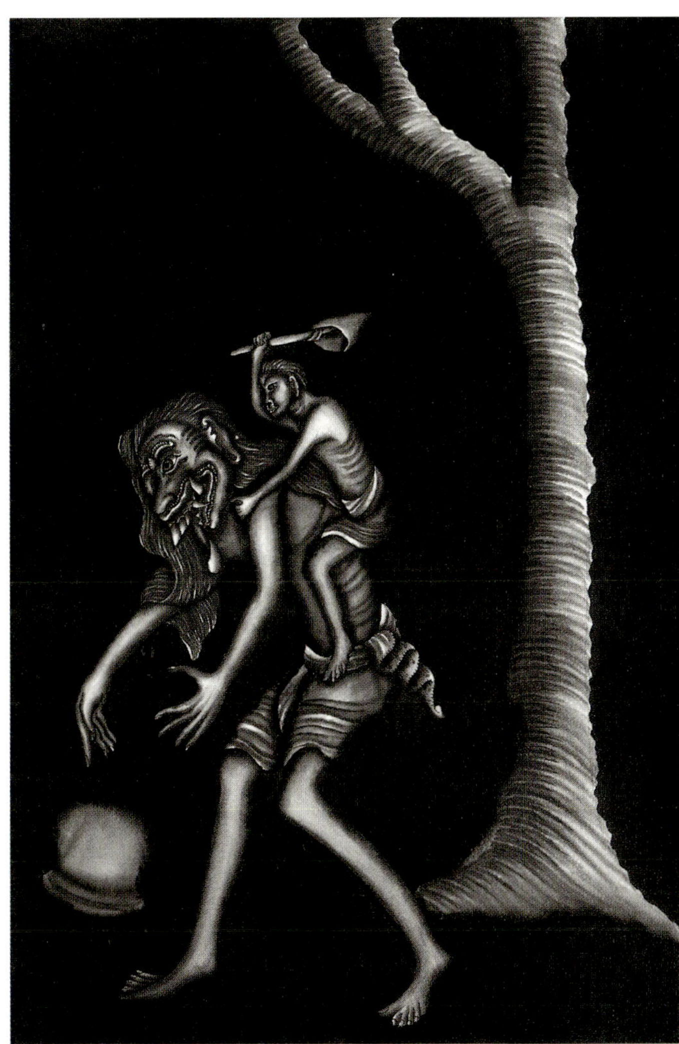

A Dream about Attacking a Sorcerer (léyak)

(dream 8, November 1, 1937)
Ida Bagus Madé Togog

I was just walking under a tree and I saw a woman in *léyak* form washing her hair. "Hey! who're you? So tall and terrifying!" I asked but she didn't answer. "What are you doing here, washing your hair in the middle of the night?" She still didn't say anything. So then my belly was angry because she didn't answer. "Who are you not to answer when someone asks you a question?" I said as I tied up my sarong between my legs [an act of getting ready for fighting or heavy work]. And then I grabbed her dipper from her and climbed up on her back and hit her and hit her—and then it was morning.

Here Togog directly confronts a malevolent *léyak*, a woman who can transform herself into various demonic forms to afflict people with sickness and death. It is unclear whether he defeated her or not. Washing one's hair is usually done in a stream. Only priests *(pedanda)* would have water brought to them in their house yard to wash so as not to risk the polluting actions of fellow bathers. This suggests that Togog dreamed of a *pedanda* who was also a *léyak*.

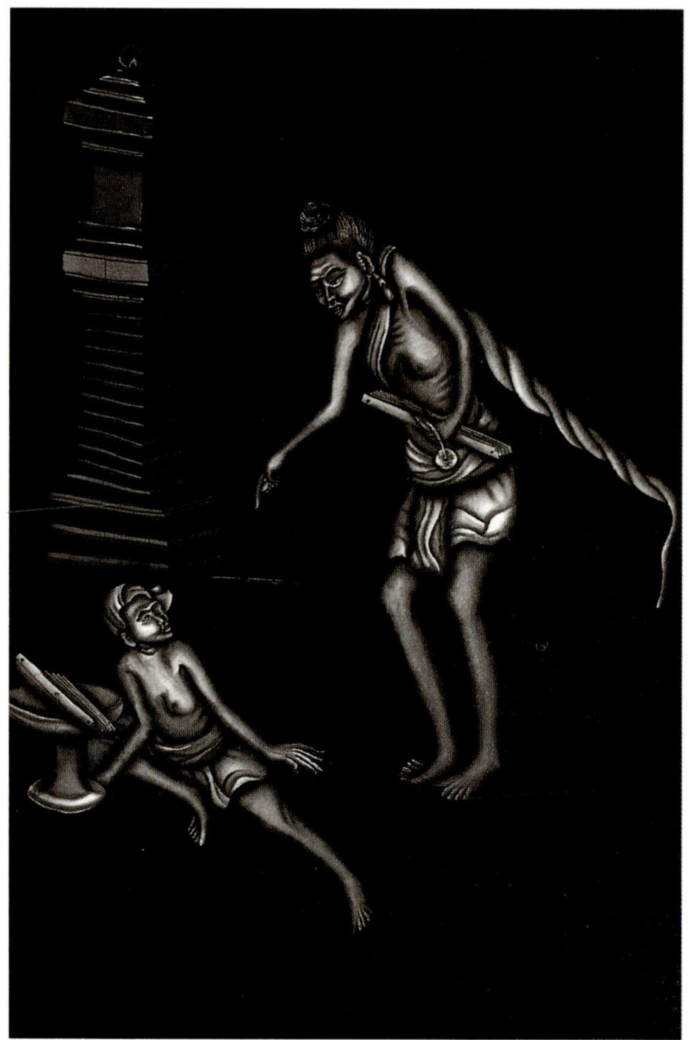

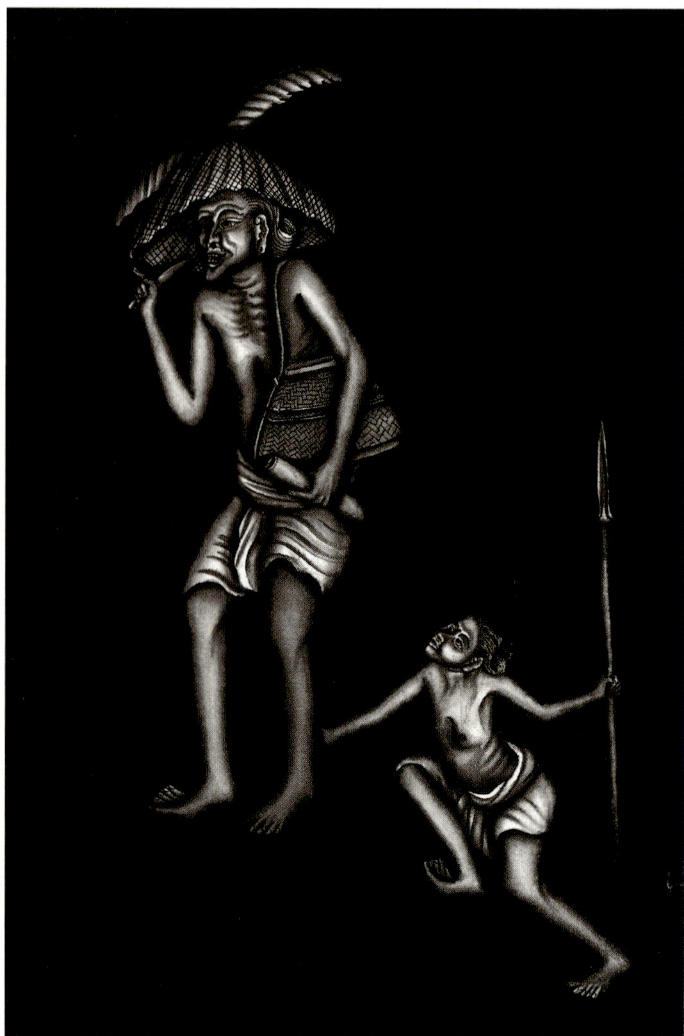

A Dream about Mystical Learning

(dream 17, November 27, 1937)

Ida Bagus Madé Togog

In this dream Togog sits down near an altar, presumably within his family temple, in the hope that he will be given the spiritual aid he needs in order to study a mystical handbook. This sort of learning is usually assumed to be intended for combating sorcerers and other dark beings. The person of ambiguous intent and form who appears is understood to be the spirit of the altar. In the first scene the spirit appears dressed as a Brahmana priest, holding a *lontar* manuscript (the long rectangular object), while in the second scene he is a man in a straw hat who may also be a priest, for he carries a packet of betel-chewing ingredients and the tube for crushing them, the standard equipment of a priest. The object in his right hand may be a *lontar.* This being can both give and take away *sakti*, in the form of the *lontar* and the ability to understand it.

I said to myself, "Beh! I've been studying a long time, and I still don't know how to write. I'll go here next to this altar and study." So then I chanted a hymn—I read it just right—just as well as in a recital session.

The writing said: "Ana sira ratu dibia rengon." [This is the first line of the *kekawin* Ramayana, "There was an excellent and famous king. Listen!"][10]

And then a priest was there, and he said, "Why are you studying that! You won't get anything out of that!" And then he gave me another book *(lontar)*—"Study this one!"

So then I was going to take it from him but I hadn't yet—he held it out to me and said, "Study this one!" And when I was going to take it from him the priest disappeared.

"Was he a crazy *(buduh)* man? He said that . . . but then he didn't give it to me. It must be a clever trick," I said to myself.[11]

So then I picked up a spear—"He must think that I'm not angry!"—and he'd taken my own *lontar.* Where had he gone? I went looking for him.

"Oh! There's that man!" But he had changed his appearance. The first one wasn't wearing a straw hat.

And then I grabbed his leg.

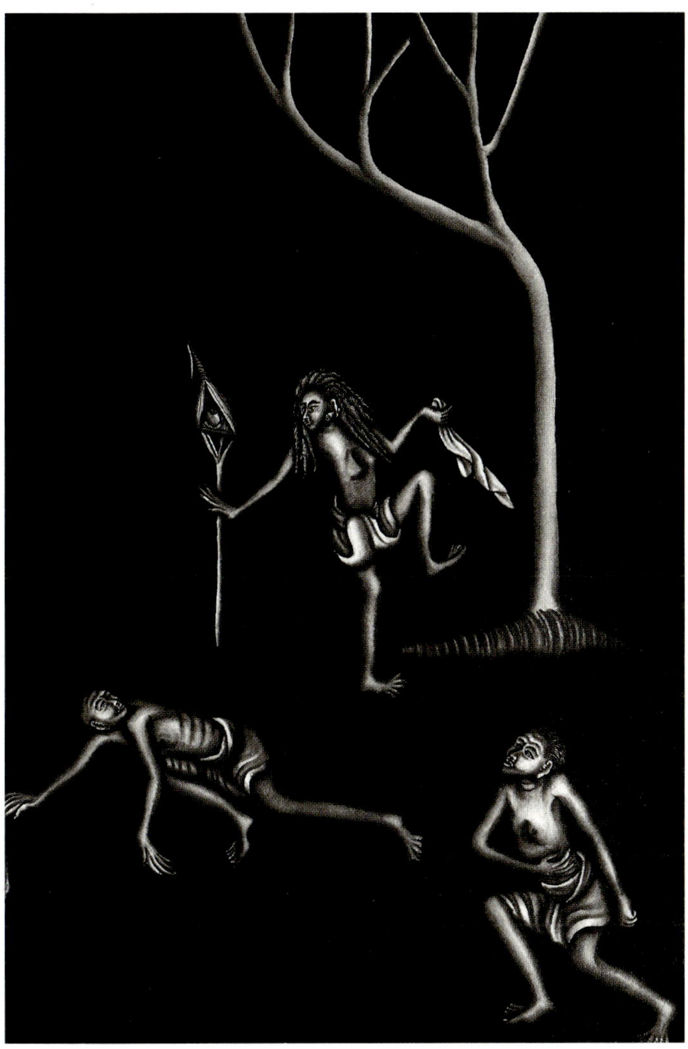

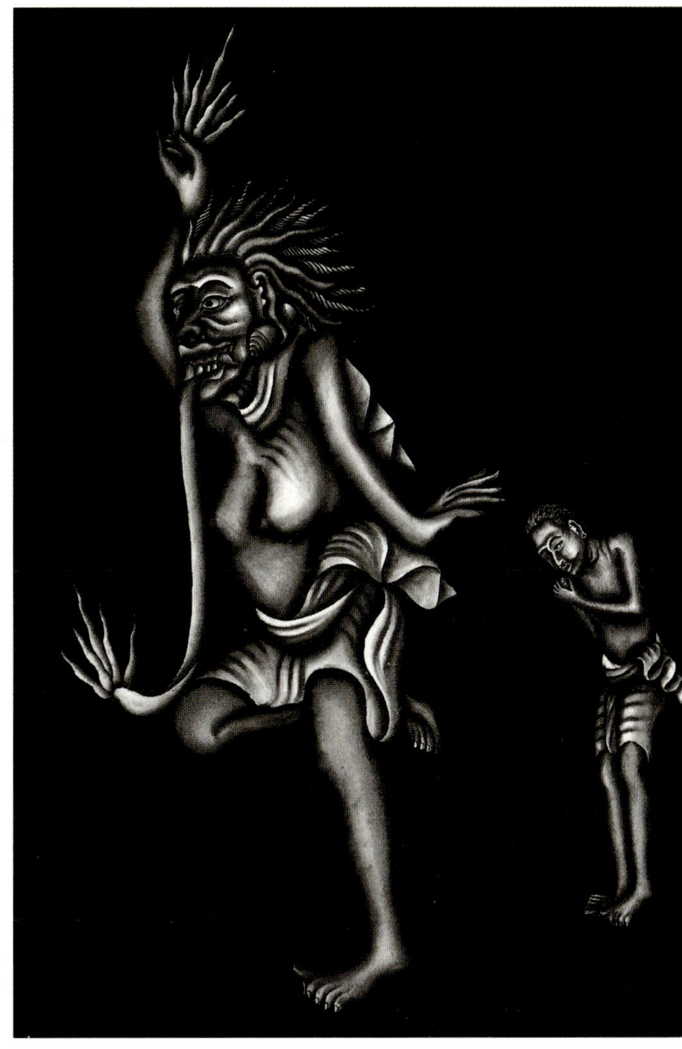

A Dream about a Sorcerer

(dream 20, January 4, 1938)
Ida Bagus Madé Togog

"Who's that shouting outside?" I asked my wife, but she didn't answer. I jumped up and ran out. I saw near the irrigation ditch across the road a person running and crawling at the same time.

"Who's that running there?" I said.

"What, it's me! There's a sorcerer transforming herself *(anak nglekas)* over there!" he answered.

"Where is she? If you run away she might chase you and eat you up! She's really a human being too!" I said. So then I looked closely and it was true. She was just on the point of changing form. "Peh! If she runs after me, I'll be dead. It's so dark!" I said.

So then I hid behind a food stall. That's how it was. [Left: Togog identified the figure at bottom right as himself.]

"I know many spells *(mantra)* for catching sorcerers *(léyak)*, very many," I said to myself. By then she had completely changed her form. "Now, I'll say the spells all mixed up together," I said. If a person says a spell and closes up his nose the *léyak* can't see him. [Right: The dreamer is on the right, standing in a position for saying a mantra.]

But I didn't get to speak the mantra at all because I woke up.

Togog's posture in the second picture, saying the mantra against the *léyak*, is the same as that in his picture of the master of *sakti*, Mercukunda, on page 82.

Terror, Violence . . . and Courage

Most of Togog's dreams contain images of terror, but they also depict courage. Interestingly, Togog does not report on his feelings in his texts, leaving one to guess at them. But repeatedly the dreams embody violent conflict of various sorts, as do many of his pictures. And in the face of these terrifying encounters, the dreamer stands up and fights back. In dreams 8 and 20 he attacks a *léyak*, and in dream 17 he valiantly goes after the priest who has stolen his book from him. Similar images of confrontation and response to threat appear in other dreams. As with his pictures, the dreams seem to express a persistent worry, or perhaps excitement, about danger.

Togog's dreams suggest something further: that the artist may have had a strong longing to become, himself, a master of *sakti*, to be one of those who can successfully overcome the unseen dangers that lurk everywhere. This is evident in dream 17, in which Togog studies the magical lore, and in dream 20, in which he attempts to conquer a *léyak* with his own mantra.

Was Togog alone among his fellows in dreaming of personal mastery of *sakti?* Could the many pictures that others made of battling demons have had the same sort of inner relevance to each of their makers? There is no independent evidence of the other picture makers' private concerns of the sort given us by Togog's dream accounts. However, from what I have learned about their lives, few had at the time any interest in becoming a healer. Three younger painters, years later, studied the magical writings (as Togog was doing at the time of making these pictures): Sanoer, who later became a priest *(pedanda);* Bala, who might have been headed in that direction but died too soon; and Baroe, who in fact became a healer *(balian)*. But in the late 1930s, all three were only in their early teens and had not begun such studies.

Whether or not they were actively imagining themselves as healers, they were all caught up in the daily talk about—and practical dealings with—the beings of the unseen world. This talk, simultaneously conventional and improvisational, clichéd and novel, still pervades much of Balinese conversational, ritual, and dramatic life. Its terms are not generalized but painfully particular and circumstantial, except in the dance-dramas, and even there each performance is taken as alluding to real people and immediate afflictions they have caused.

These ideas about *sakti* and the beings that wield it stir up feelings of anxiety and even terror, but they also provide grounds for courage. They define the dangerous, but simultaneously suggest the ways to defeat it, at least temporarily. Courage is necessary for commanding *sakti*, but this mystical potency also engenders courage. When, in this book, I speak of "fear" and "courage," I am talking about Balinese *representations* of emotions, implicit or explicit, as an aspect of their general view of the world and its beings, not hypothetical emotions said to be characteristic of the Balinese.[12]

Most Balinese, however, including the picture makers, were not (and still are not) at all like Togog. For all their preoccupation with sorcery, they were not concerned with becoming themselves masters of *sakti*, but rather with finding protectors against and healers of the devastation caused by the unseen beings out there waiting to do something terrible to them. In a world teeming with invisible beings and powers, human and nonhuman, including the masters of *sakti* themselves (many of whom are in mortal combat with one another), caution and the search for protection are the most prudent stance.

It takes unusual courage to be among the movers and shakers in this world. On the human side, masters of *sakti* are kings, sorcerers, healers, diviners, and priests. On the nonhuman side, masters of *sakti* are what might be referred to in English as "deities" (but each of these has a demonic potential), together with a large number of spirit servitors and followers. In these perpetual wars the advantage of one is always the disadvantage of another.

Many of the elements of this cluster of ideas about *sakti* have been dismissed by some Western scholars of Bali as simple beliefs in "witchcraft" or "black magic" and thought to concern primarily individual matters of love and hate.[13] But other writers, including myself, consider the ideas presented in this book as a key to Balinese understandings of the world.[14] To understand the talk about *léyak* as parallel to the medieval European pursuit of suspected witches as heterodox devil-worshipers, or as analogous to African notions of involuntary compulsions that disrupt village harmony, driven by cancerlike organic growths on one's heart and kidneys, is to reduce the *léyak* idea to only certain of its components and to ignore its grounding in more general Balinese notions about the human condition.

A major impediment in Western understanding of Balinese thought is the long and pervasive Christian tradition that defines "religion" as central and serious, and "magic" as peripheral and trivial. Magic in these terms is the use of mystical techniques for individual, nefarious goals, as against worship which, also immaterial, is oriented toward more-than-personal communal and beneficent goals. Magical beliefs are seen as fragmentary and particular, while religious beliefs are coherent and general. In this Western discourse of magic versus religion, some of the Balinese ideas concerning *sakti* are understood as "witchcraft" and have been dismissed as unimportant.[15]

The term "master of *sakti*" can be translated as "witch" or "sorcerer," but at the cost of reducing and trivializing the idea. If one states that the common village priest or the kings of Bali are "sorcerers," the statement sounds odd and denigrating because of the negative and trivializing connotations of the English word.

Rather than being fragmentary "superstitions," I believe that these ideas about sorcerers, and the other haunting shades found in the pictures and stories of the Batuan painters, are part of a "religious" conception of human life that is large, general, and inclusive as well as being vivid and pressing. This conception appears to lack coherence and, sometimes, logic, but in fact the whole set of notions implies a rejection of coherence as a major characteristic of the universe and of human knowledge of it. But this does not make it less significant.

Those descriptions of temple ceremonies by Western writers that focus on moments in which the "gods" are addressed and that omit or downplay the complementary moments when the "demons" are placated, give only part of the story. These beings, no matter what they are called, can act malevolently as well as benevolently. Balinese temple rituals,

I have come to believe, are best understood as procedures for accessing *sakti* in order to persuade these spiritual beings not to destroy the vitality and fertility of the temple congregation and its lands, to hold off those who cannot be so persuaded, and to bless the congregation with the strength to continue to oppose them. The success of these rituals requires mastery of *sakti* by the priests and the necessary assistance of the entire congregation in a highly practical series of communications with the forces of the unseen world.

Most Western writers assume that the Balinese view of the cosmos is firmly ordered and harmonious, and that human beings must attempt to imitate and therefore bring about that order again in this world. For these writers, the main aim of temple rituals and much else in Balinese culture is to prevent a sinking into chaos, which is the absence of order.[16] Mantras and prayers, and much ritual imagery, evoke sets of spatial oppositions: the direction of the mountain versus the sea, the direction of the rising sun versus its setting, high versus low, and interior versus exterior. These writers take the spatial oppositions (called by one writer "cosmic antipodes") as descriptions of the "cosmic order," either actual or desired. But in fact they are not descriptions but verbal forms that a master of *sakti* uses to call toward himself the *sakti* needed to defeat his opponents.

All of this sheds light on the claims made by kings and lords in nineteenth-century Bali. Aided by their entourages of priests and magically endowed generals, and by their inherited and otherwise acquired sacred regalia, these kings were seen by the Balinese as the potent guardians of their realm's well-being. As long as they were indeed potent, they were supported by the populace. What they were guardians *against* has not been specified in scholarly studies of the Balinese state, but in my view, it was a crowd of rival masters of *sakti*.

Insignia of royalty and divinity are interchangeable in Balinese ceremonies. The picture of a temple procession on page 24 shows the gods transported in regal sedan chairs, accompanied by parasols, banners, and men with spears. In the nineteenth century, the kings were carried in precisely the same way. See also the picture of Durga coming over the sea (page 96) for a similar pictorial statement of equivalence between kings and deities.

All these beings, human and nonhuman, royal and divine, were seen as engaged in competitive combat with one another, like the sorcerers and the *léyak* of the pictures on pages 87 and 88. War, in this view, not serene order, is the normal state of the cosmos, and the human world. Conflict is not evidence of chaotic breakdown of the cosmos, but the fundamental characteristic of life.

The Balinese world is one in which the many elements are never harmoniously united, in which there is no single all-encompassing principle, no way of comprehending the whole. It is a universe of fluctuating, flowing, shifting forces, which can sometimes be commanded by certain human beings, the masters of *sakti*, who momentarily and precariously can draw some of these forces together into a strong local node of power, which will inevitably later dissolve again.

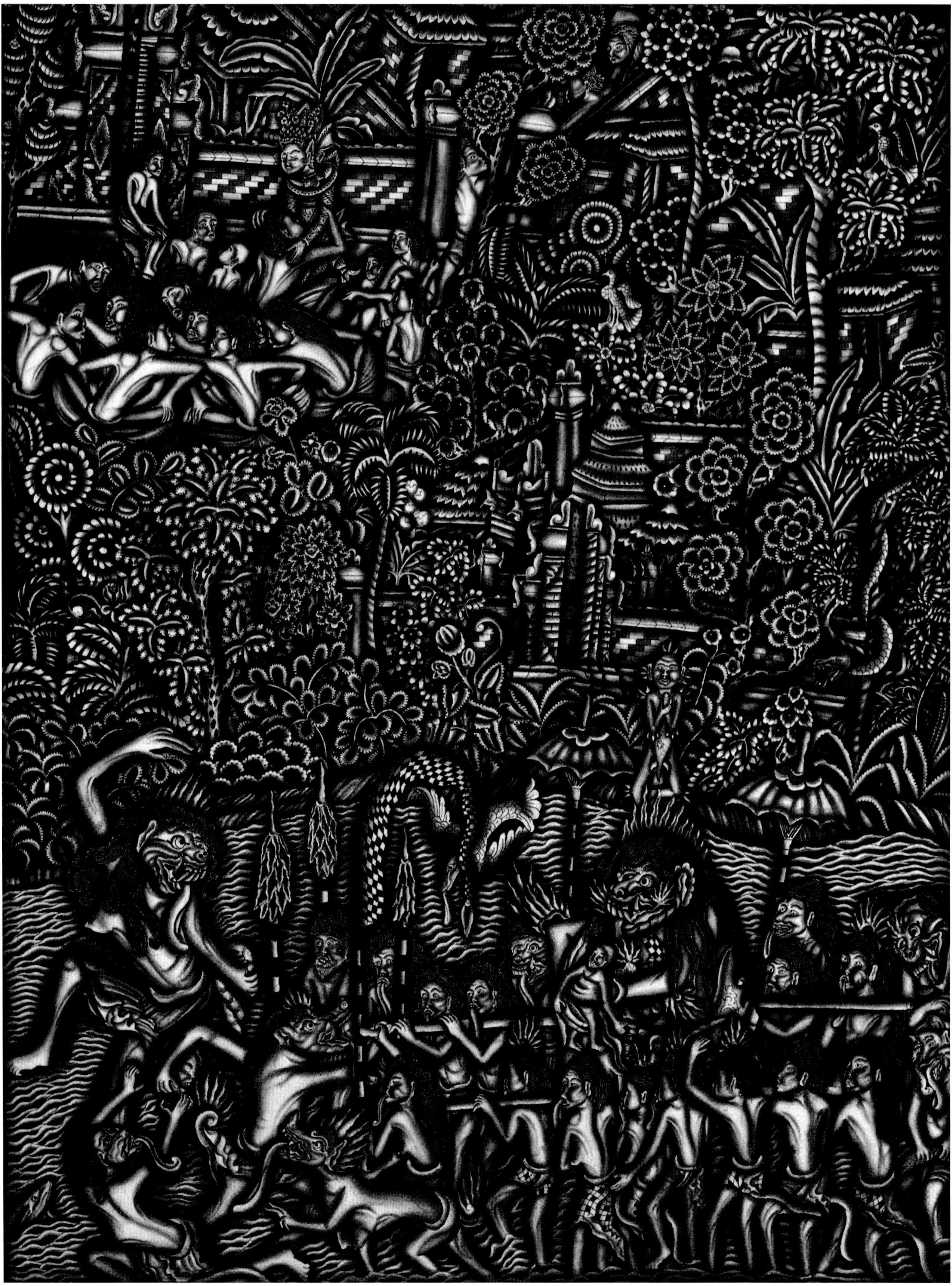

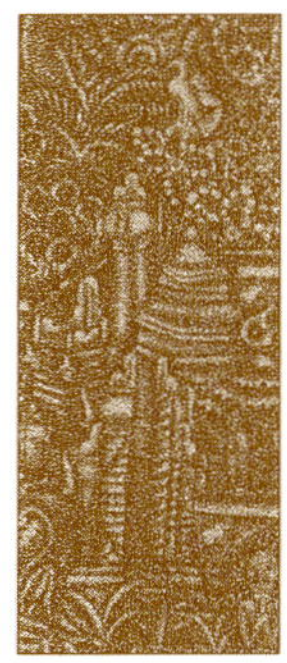

Crossing Cultures

Anthropologists, shuttling back and forth from one culture to another, are often beset with queasy feelings of being marginal or off balance. They move out of their comfortable natal world, where everyone speaks the same language, into a strange one where the talk and practices are unfamiliar. There, an awareness of the strangeness of their own ways gradually dawns, and with it an awkward, intense sensitivity to the way their own selves may look to their new neighbors. On return, the anthropologist, infused with a heightened awareness, feels out of place at home as well. The culture crosser who writes ethnographies sometimes expresses that ambivalence, but in obscure ways through word choice and metaphor.[1]

Those in the host country who go out of their way to meet foreigners, who engage with them for any length of time, may experience a similar, but perhaps less insistent, sense of unease and self-consciousness. Both sides have become mirrors for one another. The Batuan painters' crossover pictures, like the anthropologists' and travelers' texts, may also betray a sense of watching one's self observing and being observed. The picture makers were caught up in a situation in which the two cultures met, where there were many mirrors with which they might look at themselves. Their pictures were constantly pushed toward the margins of their culture.

Considered trivial by both parties—by Westerners because they are tourist art and not of our tradition, by the Balinese because they are tourist art and not of their tradition—it is astonishing that, under the circumstances, these pictures (or at least some of them) are so serious in their import, so central in their meanings to Balinese culture. In this book I have explored these deeper significances, selecting pictures and themes that probe toward the centers of Balinese culture. Much more could be said about their other aspects.

Some of the Batuan painters revealed a sense of the reflexive implications of their work, of an awareness that the viewers they were painting for were foreigners looking at the pictures as slices of "Bali" made by "Balinese." For instance, on the back of one picture (page 74) Djata wrote—in Malay, the language of foreigners—"A Meeting of *Léyak* in Bali." His phrase "in Bali" is a telltale sign that he was addressing a person from the outside.

The Ratu Macaling picture on page 67 provides another instance of the awareness that the picture was made for the eyes of a stranger. The painter (or someone for him) wrote on the back of this picture in Balinese, in a schoolchild's hand: "This is Ratu Macaling, a evil spirit of this village since the olden times." This last clause, "since the olden times," with its indirect reference to the possibility of change in Bali, is clearly directed to a foreigner. In both examples, there may be allusion to the idea that outsiders do not believe in these beings, or may not know about their enduring prevalence in Bali.

Five painters, Tibah, Baroe, Tjeta, Tjeti, and Sawa, made some pictures that can only be called ethnographic reports. These were detailed depictions of particular named rituals, showing, for each one, the kinds of offerings made, the special participants, and necessary acts. An example is Tibah's *Harvest Ceremony* (page 28). These pictures were made only during the three months of the anthropologists' stay in Batuan, and must have been a direct response to their own study of the anthropologists filming and taking notes on cremations and other rituals. Mead and Bateson did not specifically request illustrations of these rituals. One person made drawings of the steps in weaving. Two painters, Tjeti and Baroe, also produced a series on children's games, which they elucidated to Bateson, who wrote down the names and rules. These must also have been a response to Bateson and Mead's close attention to children's activities as they studied how Balinese children learn their culture's ways.

The complement of an awareness of self is a concern with the presence of foreigners. Oddly, other than Ngéndon's picture of Bateson and Mead, only one picture in the entire collection has a foreigner in it, a strange hybrid produced by the

OPPOSITE: *The Demonic Deity Betari Durga Comes from over the Sea to Bring Epidemic*
Ida Bagus Ketut Diding

In this scene, Betari Durga crosses the sea in royal splendor on a palanquin surrounded by her entourage of demonic spirits. Banners, parasols, and spearmen are the traditional accoutrements of royalty. From her head and elbows comes fire, a symbol of *sakti*.

The painter Diding told Bateson that Betari Durga comes to Bali from over the sea every dark of the moon, bringing epidemics. In the picture she carries an infant that presumably she is going to eat. At top and center the artist identified two major village temples, a *pura dalem* and a *pura puseh désa*. In front of one of them, a ritual is being performed to placate these beings. Floating above Durga is Cintia, who the painter said is "Durga's god."

In the upper left corner, in front of the temple gate, a young girl dances, held high by a young man. She is a *sanghyang*, or sacred dancer. In front of her, with naked torsos bent toward one another, is a chorus of *kecak* singers who perform a placatory dance intended to persuade malevolent spirits to leave the village.

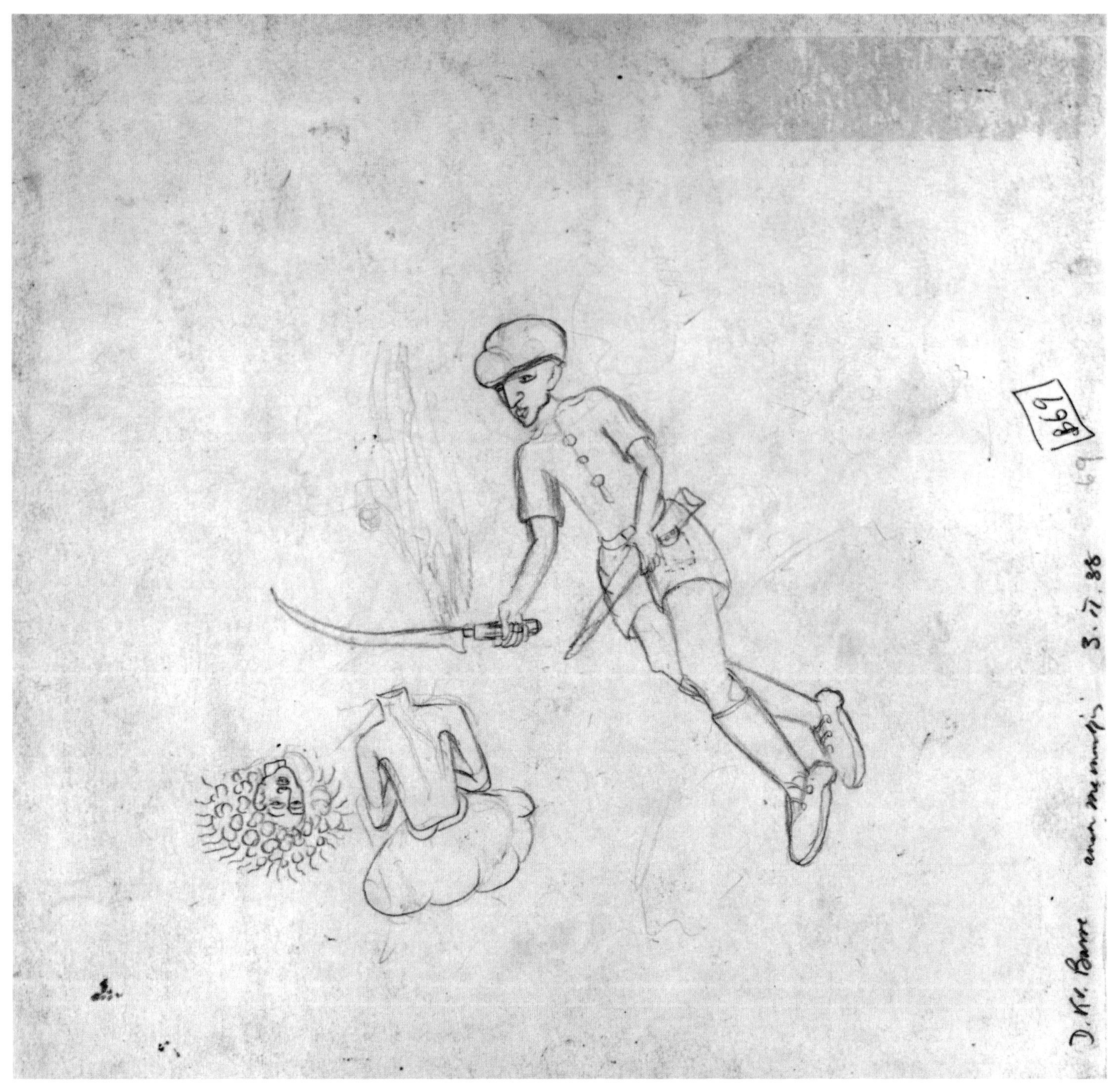

A Dutch Soldier Cutting off a Balinese Man's Head
Déwa Ketut Baroe

This unfinished drawing shows a man in Western clothing of the sort that Dutch soldiers and policemen wore, standing above a seated Balinese man and cutting off his head with a great sword. The Balinese man is a master of *sakti*, as indicated by his posture, hair, and dress, the scarf around his waist signifying respect for the beings he is addressing.

crossing of pictorial traditions. It is a simple sketch of a man in the uniform of the Dutch police (shorts, shoes, shirt, and peaked cap) slicing off the head of a seated Balinese holy man.

The sketch was rejected, unfinished, by its maker and never sold. It survived only because its reverse side was used for another picture. Why it was discarded, and why there are no other drawings showing Westerners may be explained by the widespread but unstated taboo in tourist art against non-traditional subjects. The Balinese recognized that the outsiders did not want to see themselves or the modern things they were bringing to Bali in the pictures they bought. Yet this picture does not show a uniformed Dutchman in the way they were ordinarily encountered in Bali at that time, standing guard before the Resident's office or at the police station. Here he is swinging a long traditional sword, a weapon of *sakti*, and in the manner of shadow puppets, is cutting off the holy man's head. It seems as though Baroe has presented Balinese-Dutch relations within the frame of ideas about *sakti*.

Does this puzzling, discarded picture give a clue to a suppressed theme of resentment against Dutch overlordship? The picture here implies a fear of Dutch violence, but how legitimate can this inference be? If there were such resentment, it had not yet been articulated into nationalist movements in Bali, although within the next decade it would be, with the painter Ngéndon leading the attack in Batuan.

The idea that this violent scene (and the pictures that do not explicitly show Westerners) could be covertly expressing wishes for eviction of the foreigners is, to me, entertainable but in the end cannot be substantiated. That would be the same sort of interpretation as that of Mead and Bateson's psychological functionalist reading of the "Rangda and Barong play" as expressing Balinese unconscious feelings toward their mothers and fathers. My own feeling is that these pictures should not be read as projections of repressed desires or fears, since the kind of supporting information needed for evaluation of such theories, the sort that psychiatrists and psychologists assemble for each person and each expressive act, is largely missing here. Without such necessary contextual confirmation, almost anyone's guess is as good as another's. It is easy to launch many striking, but similarly insupportable, interpretations of the uses these pictures had for their creators—as expressing repressed eroticism, diverted status pride, or the like. We cannot really know what psychological processes may have been at work, or what personal associations have been drawn together into each of these pictures and stories.

The picture by Diding at the head of this chapter shows a powerful fusion (to, perhaps, the level of confusion) of Western and Balinese notions about Bali. Bateson noted that the painter told him that the picture shows how "every month at the dark of the moon, Durga comes from over the sea to Bali and causes epidemics." This is a very peculiar statement, since Balinese do not talk of Durga coming over the sea every month, but rather of Ratu Macaling (see page 67). It is an even stranger thing to say, in that Ratu Macaling does not come "every month at the dark of the moon," but rather, in the Batuan area, the demon Ratu Macaling and his minions come nearly every night during the entire period from November through May.

Also anomalous in this picture is the ritual of placation Diding shows. It is a *sanghyang* dance, performed by little girls in trance accompanied by a male chorus, but in Batuan, in such circumstances the *rejang* dance is performed (see pages 26–27). To make matters even odder, the male chorus shown is not the smaller traditional one; rather, their uniform bare backs (almost a sort of costume) suggest that the scene is of a tourist dance called the *kecak*, which had been created only recently. The *kecak* was contrived out of a chorus that accompanied the sacred *sanghyang* dancers, but was made into a spectacle by costuming the men identically and having them sit formally in a circle facing one another, thus giving them a more picturesque look than usual. Perhaps the use of an image from a tourist dance is the key to the picture's interpretation.

It is as if, in making this picture, Diding put together a conglomeration of unrelated ritual notions and motifs from stories, together with a tourist dance, as things appropriate to the "conversation" he was having with the foreigners Mead and Bateson. He lived next door to both Togog and the household where the anthropologists lived and had ample opportunity to observe them in their research into Balinese rituals and to hear their persistent questioning about Balinese customs.

This picture has always made me uneasy, since it thwarts my anthropologist's desire for truth, for authenticity in the reports that informants make. It makes me wonder uncomfortably whether Diding invented his myth, and whether the picture is a parody, a tongue-in-cheek send-up of the tourist-anthropologists in their earnest and presumptuous ignorance. I think of the reference to "coming from over the sea": is this a covert allusion to the anthropologists, Mead and Bateson? I think of the parallels to Ngéndon's picture of them crossing the water between Bali and New Guinea (page 4).

Perhaps in introducing the image of the tourist dance, Diding was reaching for something familiar to the outsiders through which to convey the general meaning of such placatory rituals. Perhaps in speaking of "Durga," a name with Indic resonances that outsiders often know better than its Balinese equivalents (for Balinese rarely use the name Durga at all), he was attempting to adapt his speech and his picture to something they could better understand.[2]

On the other hand, perhaps Diding felt released through this bicultural genre to take a flight of imagination and explore in figurative ways matters of *sakti* that were important to him. Note the odd placing of the Cintia figure just above Durga's head. Sanghyang Cintia is a very serious being about whom one should not make jokes. Representing the highest god of all, Cintia takes prominent place in a ritual performed by shadow puppet masters at the beginning and end of every performance. Cintia's presence gives solemnity to Diding's picture.

In the end, it seems best to see this picture, and the others in the collection, as serious, creative work made within bicultural circumstances. Whether or not any of these pictures attain the privileged Western label of "art," they are not so far off center as to have lost their balance, nor their sense of rightness within Balinese culture of the 1930s.

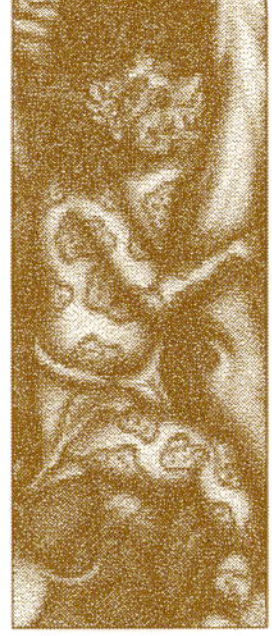

Painters' Profiles and Selected Works

Following are biographical notes on the major Balinese artists in the Bateson-Mead Collection and those of their works that are in this book or the exhibition *Images of Power.* **Boldface** page numbers refer to illustrations in the text.

Much of the information is from interviews designed by Gregory Bateson and Margaret Mead and carried out by their research assistant, I Madé Kalér, in mid-1937.

Bala, Ida Bagus Madé

The son of a high Brahmana priest couple who were also farmers, Bala went to the new Dutch elementary school for five years and could speak and write Malay. He was in his early teens when he made the pictures in the Bateson-Mead Collection, and had been drawing for several years. He was taught by Diding, and worked with Siring and Blatjok. Bala visited the Western artists Spies and Bonnet and watched them paint. He said that he was asked to make a picture of boys swimming, which was a favorite subject of Spies' young Balinese protégé, Sobrat, from Ubud, the center of tourist art. Bala was a member of Pita Maha, the artists' cooperative set up by Spies and Bonnet. He had been to a movie once, and had visited the government hospital in Denpasar. He made fifty-one pictures in the collection, many of which were small copies of sorcerers' talismanic figures. Bala died in 1942.

Looking for Crickets under a Stone at Night and Uncovering a Demon **(68),** December 2, 1937
Ink on paper, 8.25 × 9 in., B 19

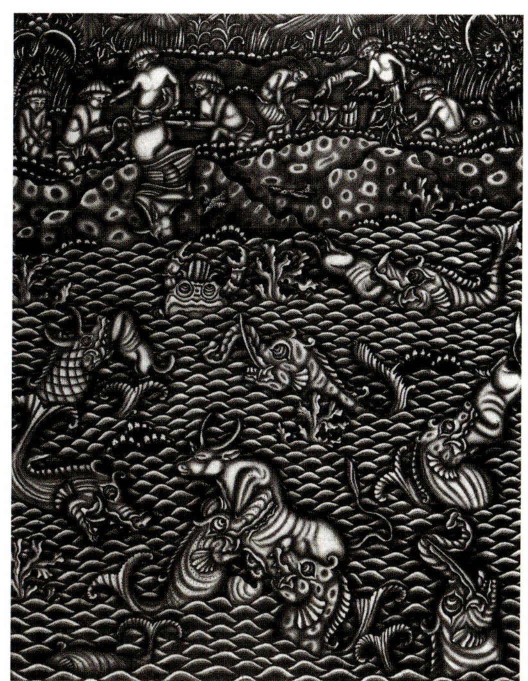

Propitiation during a Time of Drought,
February 21, 1939, Ink on paper, 20 × 15 in., B 53

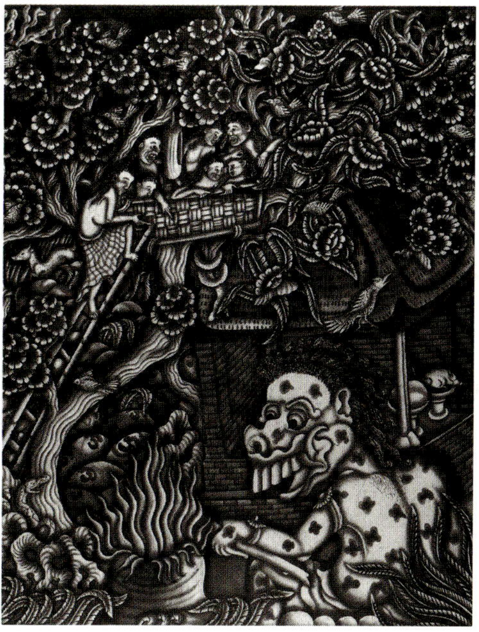

The Story of the Seven Maidens Lost in the Forest, March 10, 1938
Ink on paper, 19.5 × 15.5 in., B 52

Bala, Ida Bagus Madé *(continued)*

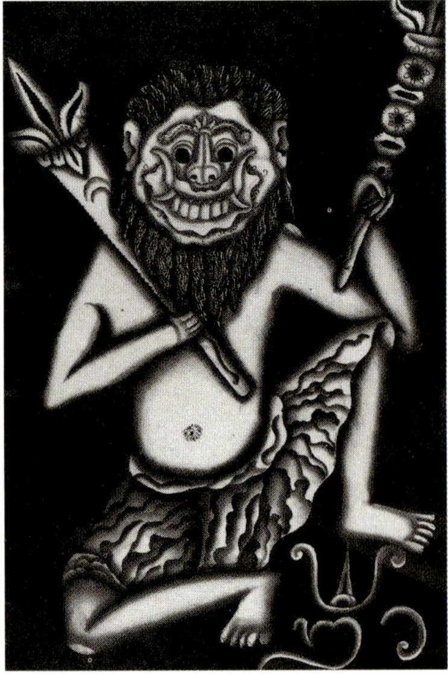

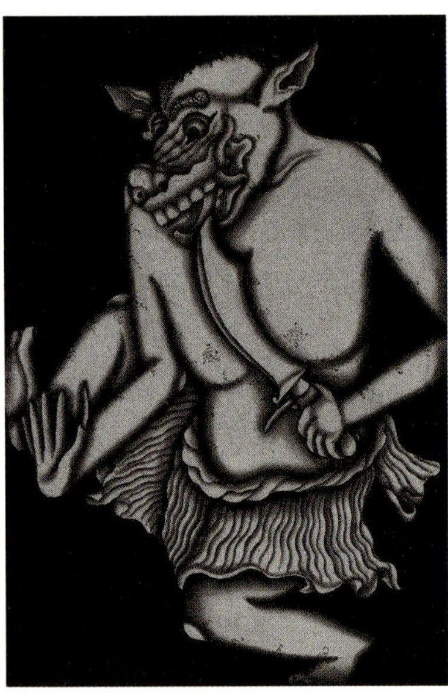

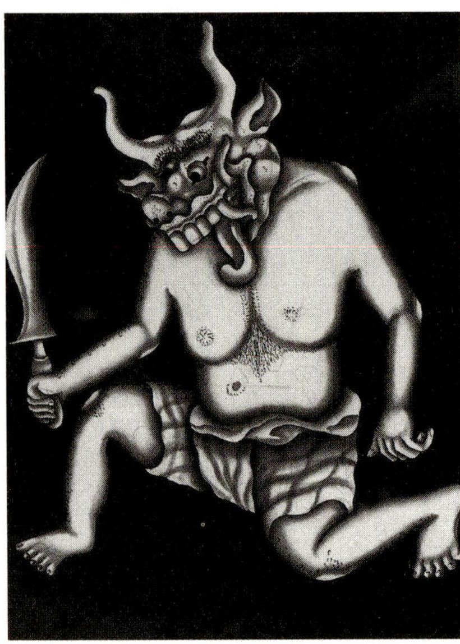

ABOVE: *Sorcerer's Talismanic Drawings of Disease Demons*, February 2, 1938
Ink on paper; set of 3, each 15 × 10 in., B 20–22

Baroe, Déwa Ketut

Baroe was only about eleven years old when he made pictures for Bateson and Mead. At that time he had recently started to paint, and some of his first pictures of children playing, made with Tibah, are in the Bateson-Mead Collection. He said he had not met any Western painters, although he sold pictures in the Neuhaus' shop on the beach at Sanur. He was not at the time a member of the artists' group, Pita Maha. Baroe had about three years of Dutch elementary school and could speak Malay. He danced in the *gambuh*. His father died when he was about eight, and his mother managed the family fields. Twenty-six of his pictures are in the collection. He went on in postwar years to make many pictures in the prewar style. In later life he studied classical Balinese and became a healer *(balian)*.

A Dutch Soldier Cutting off a Balinese Man's Head **(98),** February 3, 1938
Pencil on paper, 9.5 × 9.75 in., B 69.1

Sorcerers (léyak) *Eating Stillborn Babies* **(71),** February 10, 1938
Ink on paper, 10 × 9.5 in., B 78

Blatjok, Ida Bagus Putu

When these pictures were made, Blatjok was about twelve years old and had been drawing about a year. He was taught by Tjeta and never met any Western artists, although he sold pictures in Denpasar and Sanur, centers for tourist art. He was not a member of Pita Maha, the artists' cooperative established by Spies and Bonnet. Blatjok's parents were dead. He was very poor and spent time as a migrant harvester on a coffee plantation in the mountains. A distant relative was a Brahmana priest. Blatjok was illiterate but spoke a little Malay. There are thirteen pictures by him in the collection.

Cremation Preparations Observed by Sorcerers (léyak) **(80),** November 23, 1936
Ink on paper, 12.75 × 18.75 in., B 90

The Story of the Great Sorcerer Basur **(59–61),** September 23, 1937
Ink on paper, 7.75 × 7 in., B 95; 6.75 × 5.5 in., B 96; 7.75 × 7.25 in., B 97; 7 × 5.5 in., B 98; 6.75 × 5.25 in., B 99; 7 × 5.5 in., B 100

Dadoeg Kajoean, Déwa Nyoman

Dadoeg was probably about twenty-five years old at the time of making the pictures for the anthropologists, but he was not interviewed by Mead's assistant, Kalér. He was not a member of Pita Maha, the artists' cooperative. Dadoeg was primarily a musician, which may account for the fact that he made only seven pictures in the collection. There is evidence in his pictures that he had some training in cutting out and painting shadow puppets. In the postwar period he was an important musician. His son became a fine painter in the late 1970s.

The Story of the Prince Who Was Born as a Water Buffalo **(62)**, October 7, 1937
Ink on paper, 18.75 × 13.25 in., B 183

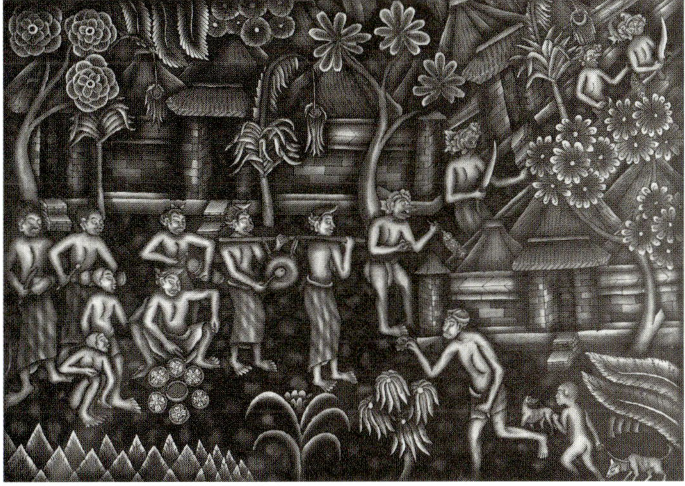

Youthful Wandering Performers, April 27, 1937
Color, 10 × 13 in., B 180

Dajoeh, I

Dajoeh was a minor member of the picture-making group, who may have been quite young during Bateson and Mead's stay in Batuan. He made only four pictures in the collection.

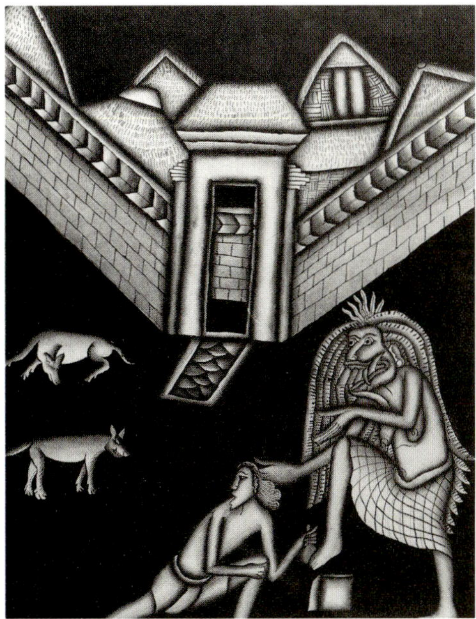

Sorcerer Aiding a Thief by Putting Everyone to Sleep, April 3, 1937
Ink on paper, 12 × 9 in., B 102

Diding, Ida Bagus Ketut

About twenty-two years old at the time of making the pictures in the collection, Diding probably had been painting since 1935. His teacher was Ngéndon, and he in turn taught Bala. He met Spies and Bonnet, watched them work, and brought them work for their criticism. He was a member of the group they founded, Pita Maha. One of the Western artists suggested that he make a picture like Djatasoera's of the *endé* ritual in Karangasem.

Diding had not been to school but could speak a little Malay. He played in a gamelan orchestra and danced in the *gambuh*, and was the only artist interviewed who said that he had been possessed and gone into trance. His father was dead, and he had no land to work. He and his wife supported themselves by painting, raising chickens, and dyeing cloth. They had no children. Sixteen pictures by Diding are in the collection.

Battle among Sorcerers (léyak) **(87)**, August 14, 1937
Ink on paper, 18 × 13 in., B 108

Death Ritual: Bathing the Body and Paying Last Homage to the Deceased **(33)**, October 20, 1936
Color, Ink on paper, 14.25 × 18.5 in., B 123

The Demonic Deity Betari Durga Comes from over the Sea to Bring Epidemic **(96)**, February 24, 1938
Ink on paper, 24.5 × 18.25 in., B 120

The Sorcerer Queen Takes Rangda Form and Causes Death and Moral Dissoluteness **(76)**, August 20, 1937
Ink on paper, 22.5 × 18.5 in., B 109

Djata, I Madé

About fifteen years old at the time of making the pictures in the collection, Djata had been painting about two or three years. He said that he was self-taught but had watched Ngéndon at work. He visited the homes of the Western painters Bonnet and Spies, and showed them his work for criticism. He was a member of their group, Pita Maha. Djata was the son of a very poor carpenter. He had not been to school but could speak a little Malay.

Djata was an apprentice to a shadow puppet maker in Batuan, Déwa Putu Kebés, and the details of the headdresses and clothing in his drawings are taken from puppets. He was also close to Ngéndon, who demonstrated how to draw rounded human bodies, especially nudes. In 1948 Bonnet appointed Djata teacher of art in a short-lived artisans' school established by the colonial government in Batuan. In the 1980s Djata was still painting, in much the same style as these pictures. His son also became a fine painter in the late 1970s. Djata produced twenty-seven pictures in the collection.

A Meeting of Léyak **(74),** February 17, 1937
Ink on paper, 19.25 × 14.25 in., B 338

The Mythic Hero Bima Battling the Guardians of the Other World **(56),** November 2, 1937
Ink on paper, 21 × 18.5 in., B 134

Play Performance of a Baris Melampahan: The Story of Radén Laksmana **(46),** with Ida Bagus Putu Sentoelan and Déwa Kompiang Pasek, August 25, 1937
Ink on paper, 19.7 × 18.5 in., B 340

Self-Portrait **(v),** March 1938
Ink on paper, 11 × 9.5 in., B 138

"You Can Destroy but Can You Bring Life Back?" **(79),** with Ida Bagus Putu Sentoelan, August 25, 1937
Color, Ink on paper, 24.5 × 20 in., B 711.15

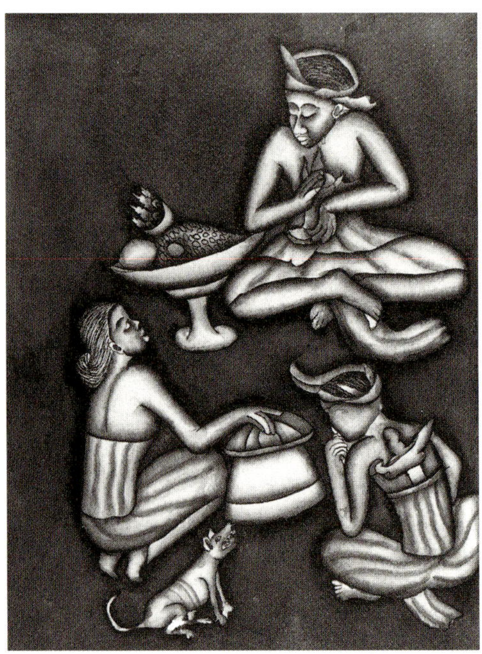

A Man and a Woman Consulting a Healer,
September 9, 1937
Ink on paper, 8 × 6 in., B 352

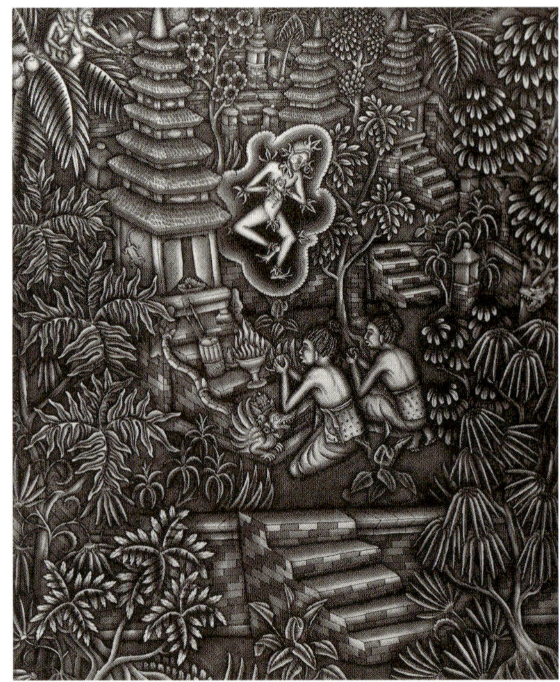

The Myth of Sang Kul Putih and the First People in Bali, December 2, 1937
Ink on paper, 19.5 × 16.5 in., B 135

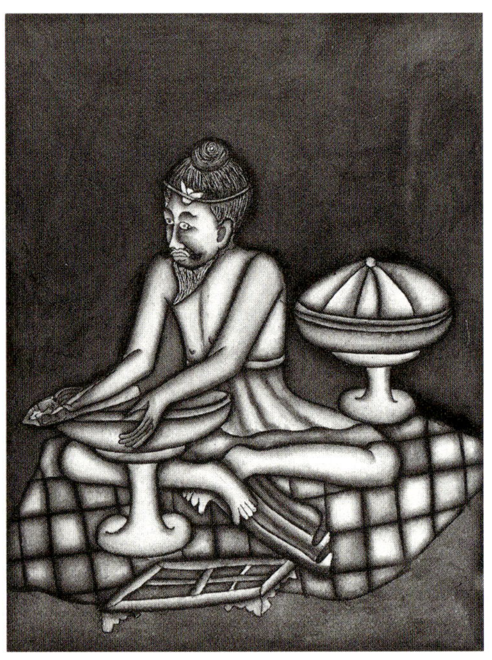

A Priest Making a Face for an Image of a God,
September 6, 1937
Ink on paper, 8.5 × 6.5 in., B 347

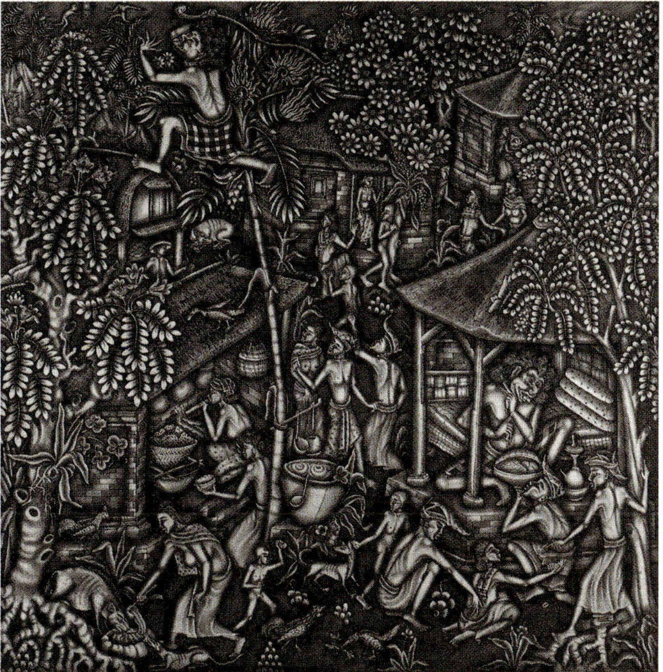

A Sorcerer Demonstrating His Powers, February 21, 1937
Ink on paper, 18.75 × 19 in., B 139

Djatasoera, Ida Bagus Madé

Djatasoera was Mead and Bateson's favorite artist, and one of his pictures was published by Bateson in an article on "Style, Grace, and Information in Primitive Art," under the name of Djatisoera. Mead and Bateson filmed him at work and collected nearly all the pictures he made during their research period. Nineteen of his pictures are in the collection.

About twenty-three years old at the time of making these pictures, Djatasoera had been painting about three or four years, having started with the first Batuan painters, Ngéndon, Togog, and Tjeta. He often went to the homes of Spies and Bonnet, and gave them work to be criticized. He said that once a foreigner asked him to make a picture of a landscape, and another asked him to make a copy of a traditional Balinese cloth painting.

Djatasoera had not been to school but spoke Malay. He danced in the *gambuh* and played in the tourist orchestra, the *genggong*. Djatasoera's father, a farmer, died when he was about twelve and left the family no land. Djatasoera worked as a migrant laborer in the coffee plantation in the mountains several times. Although he came from a Brahmana family, neither he nor anyone in the family was involved in ritual work. In 1937 he was married to his third wife (the first two marriages ended in divorce). After World War II, Djatasoera went into nationalist guerrilla combat against the Dutch government with Ngéndon, was captured, beaten severely, and died in prison in 1948.

Amad Defeated by Seroja's Magic Snake **(ii)**,
October 3, 1938, Ink on paper, 15 × 19.5 in., B 154

Cremation: Ritual Grinding of the Ashes after the Burning **(38)**,
September 17, 1937
Ink on paper, 13.5 × 18.5 in., B 147

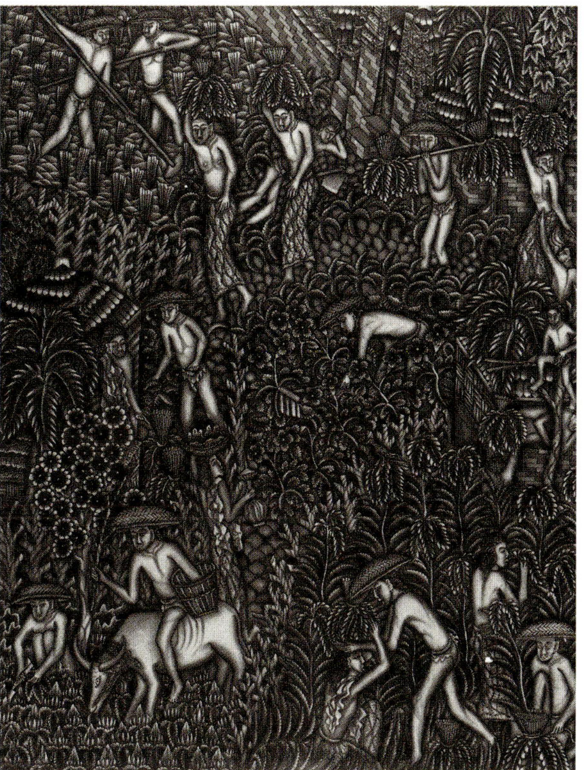

The Agricultural Round, December 2, 1937
Ink on paper, 19.5 × 15 in., B 150

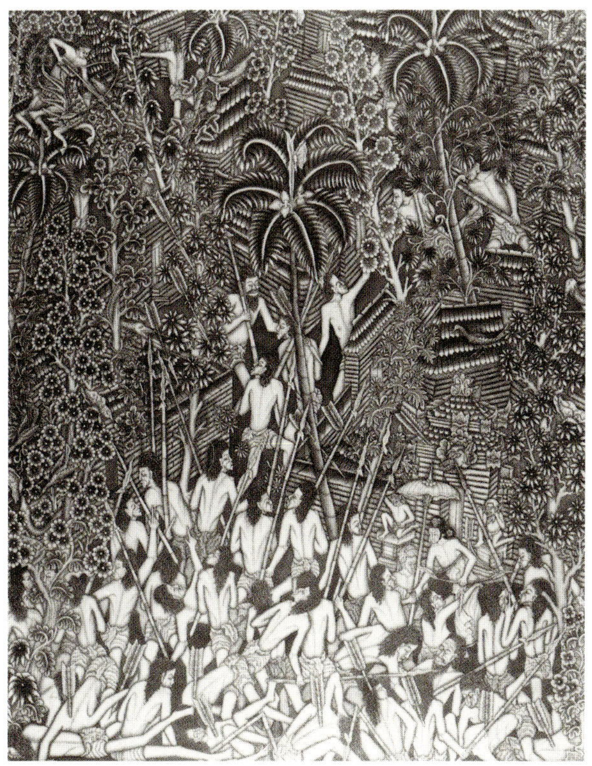

The Battle between Amad and Seroja, June 19, 1939
Ink on paper, 26 × 20.5 in. B 157.2

Cremation: The Start of the Procession **(35)**,
August 28, 1937
Ink on paper, 18 × 14 in., Collection of Lois Bateson

Djatasoera, Ida Bagus Madé *(continued)*

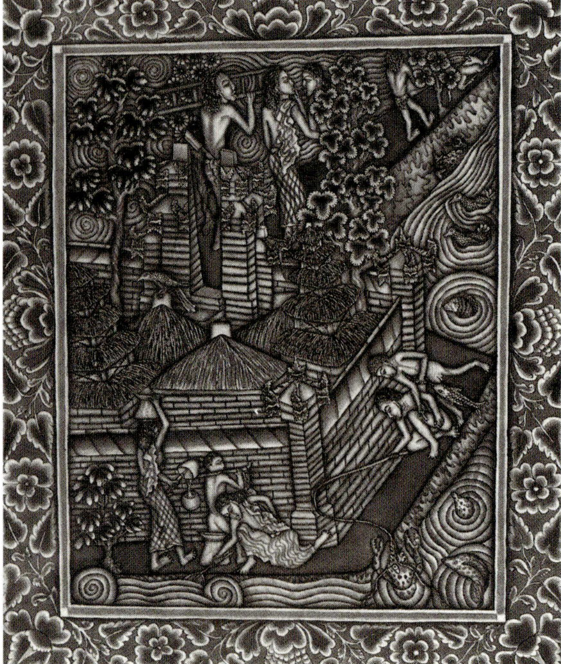

Fetching Water and Fishing next to a Temple,
March 10, 1938
Ink on paper, 11.5 × 9.5 in., B 155

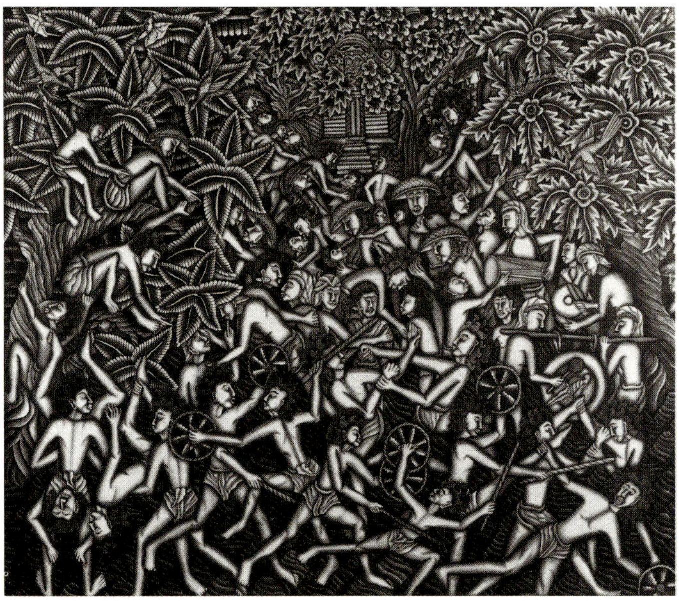

Ritual Battle (endé), June 4, 1936
Ink on paper, 19.5 × 22 in., B 140

Kandel Roeka, Déwa Kompiang

Also known as Déwa Kompiang Roeki, Kandel was about twenty-two years old at the time of making the Bateson-Mead pictures. His father was a fairly well-off farmer, and they both worked in the fields. He had never been to school and could not speak Malay.

Kandel had been painting for almost four years and had been taught by Ngéndon. He said he had been to the homes of Spies and Bonnet but never showed them work for criticism, nor was he ever given a commission to paint a certain kind of picture for them. He played in the gamelan orchestra and was a fairly accomplished dancer in *gambuh* and *baris.*

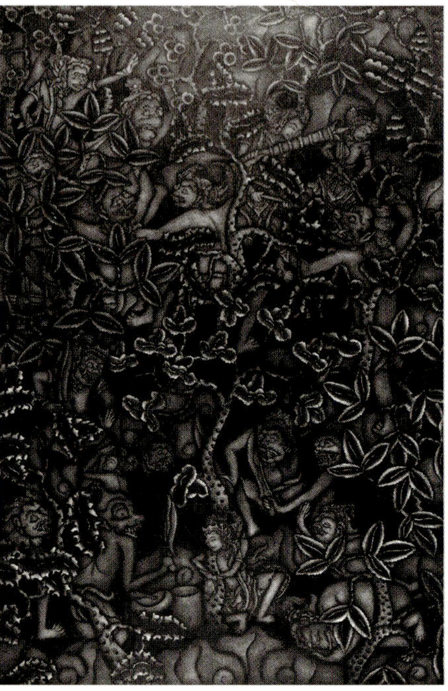

Battle Scene from the Bratayudha Myth,
November 4, 1937
Ink on paper, 19 × 29 in., B 320

Keteg, I

Keteg came from the same neighborhood as Ngéndon and learned how to make pictures from him. He was a close relative of Tombelos. Because he was not interviewed by Kalér, not much is known about him. He continued to make pictures in the postwar period.

Procession to a Temple **(24),** February 3, 1938
Ink on paper, 18.25 × 22.25 in., B 201

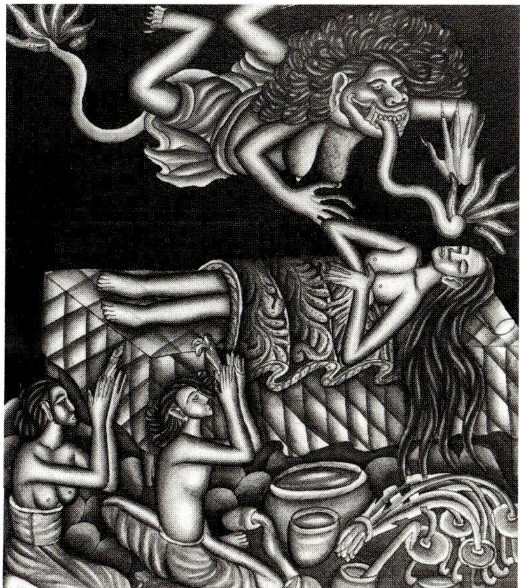

Funeral Ritual and a Hovering Sorcerer,
November 4, 1937
Ink on paper, 7.5 × 6.5 in., B 195

Lambon, Désak Putu

The only woman painter in the collection, Lambon was about fifteen years old at the time of Mead and Bateson's research. She had been introduced to painting by Ngéndon when she was only about twelve. Her father, Déwa Putu Kebés, was a highly skilled craftsman who made leather shadow puppets, costumes, and masks. He was, however, very poor, and he persuaded Ngéndon to teach his daughter. During part of 1936, when her family lived in the beach-side village of Sanur, Lambon came to know the Belgian resident artist, Theo Meier. Meier had considerable contempt for Spies and Bonnet, apparently a mutual feeling. According to Mead's notes, Meier encouraged the painters he knew to stop putting "all those leaves" in their pictures, as Bonnet had taught them to do. Lambon did a number of line drawings without the heavily filled-in black background common in Batuan. Her work was often more naturalistic as well, even more so than Ngéndon's. This difference in style was not due to her femininity, since very similar pictures were made by a young male Batuan artist, Ida Bagus Ketut Togog (not in this book).

The precise and accurate details of the costumes in Lambon's pictures come from her long experience in making dance headdresses under her father's tutelage. The buildings and gateway in her pictures are exact replicas of those in her own home, where the dance headdresses were often kept. When Mead visited it, the headdresses were hanging exactly as they are in *Costuming Up.*

Lambon had never visited Spies or Bonnet, nor was she a member of their artists' cooperative group, Pita Maha. She went to school for three years and could read and write Malay. In 1939, on a return visit, Mead noted that Lambon had married and stopped painting, but Batuan people in the 1980s said that she continued to paint in postwar years. She died in the late 1970s.

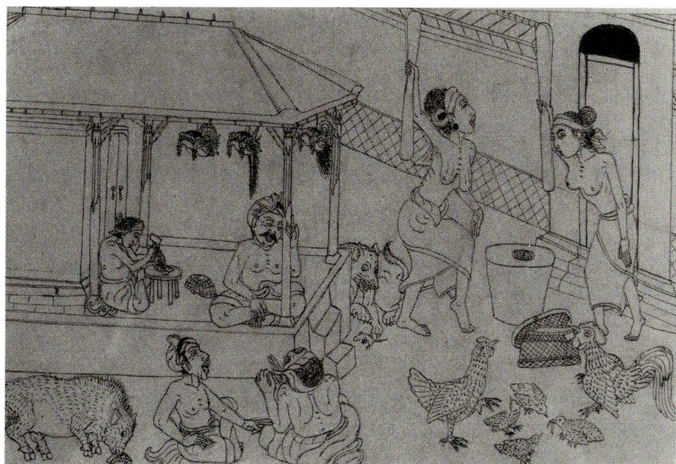

Discussing Preparations for a Dance-Drama Performance,
September 30, 1937
Ink on paper, 8 × 12 in., B 215

Birth **(69),** October 7, 1937
Ink on paper, 10.25 × 12.5 in., B 217

Costuming Up before a Dance-Drama Performance **(43),**
October 1, 1937
Ink on paper, 8.25 × 12.75 in., B 216

Mokoh, Ida Bagus Madé

Mokoh may have been only a child in 1937. He was the grandson of priests. Little more is known about him since Kalér did not interview him. He produced three pictures in the collection. Two are less skillful than B 245, which may be incorrectly attributed to him.

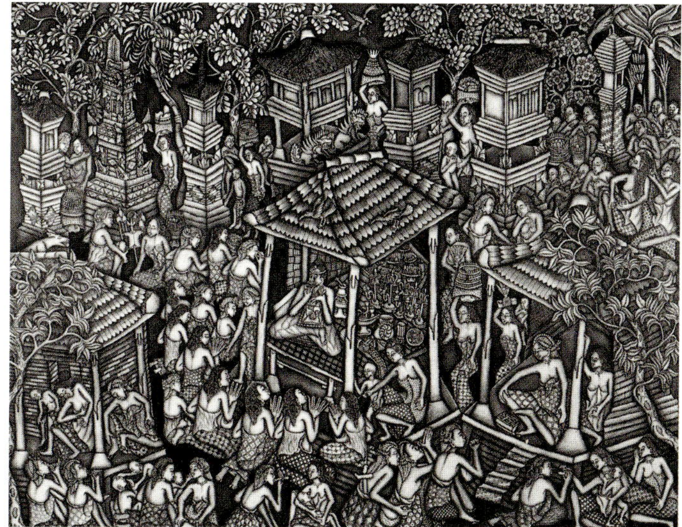

Cremation: Blessing the Offerings, February 10, 1938
Ink on paper, 19.5 × 24 in., B 245

Ngéndon, I Ketut

One of the first from Batuan to start painting in about 1933 or 1934, along with Togog, Djatasoera, and Tjeta, Ngéndon learned his skill from his cousin, Patera, who was the first to contact the Westerners Spies and Bonnet. In addition to painting and woodcarving, Patera organized dance troupes and orchestras for tourist performances, and after he died in 1935, Ngéndon took over that role. By the time Mead and Bateson began collecting, Ngéndon was not making many pictures. He taught a large number of the Batuan people. Nine pictures by him are in the collection.

According to Kalér, Ngéndon had been to school for five years, could read, write, and speak Malay and some Dutch and English. He frequented the homes of Westerners and was a member of Pita Maha, the artists' cooperative set up by Spies and Bonnet. At one point he was Spies' favorite Batuan painter.

His father was a moderately well-off farmer, and his mother an active merchant. During the Japanese occupation he went to Java to study painting and learned nationalist ideas, which he brought back to Bali. After the Japanese surrendered, Ngéndon became a local leader in the nationalist struggle against the returned Dutch colonial presence but was captured and executed in 1948.

Goodbye and Good Luck to Margaret Mead and Gregory Bateson **(4),** March 1938
Ink on paper, 18.5 × 15 in., B 711.14

Landscape with Women Bathing in Sacred Spring **(14),**
February 21, 1939
Ink on paper, 19.5 × 15 in., B 254

The Tiger in the Forest, c. 1934–1936 **(13),**
Color, Ink on paper, 18.5 × 13.5 in., Leiden University, Bonnet Collection, Br. 135–78

Pasek Gindjing, Déwa Ketut

Pasek Gindjing was the older brother of Pasek Malén (below) and only a child in 1937. He was not interviewed by Kalér.

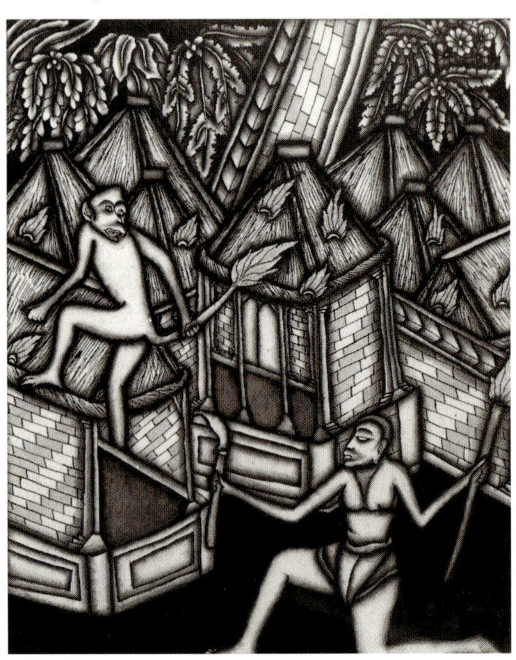

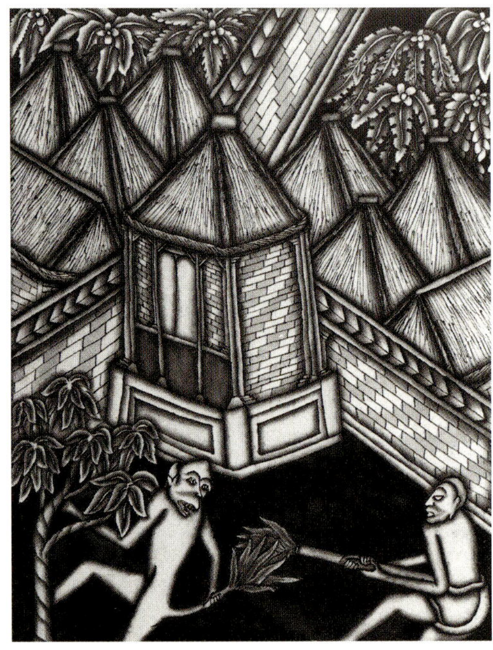

Anoman Setting Fire to the Palace of Rawana,
November 22, 1936
Ink on paper; set of 2, 8.75 × 7 in., B 266;
9.5 × 7.5 in., B 268

Pasek Gindjing, Déwa Ketut *(continued)*

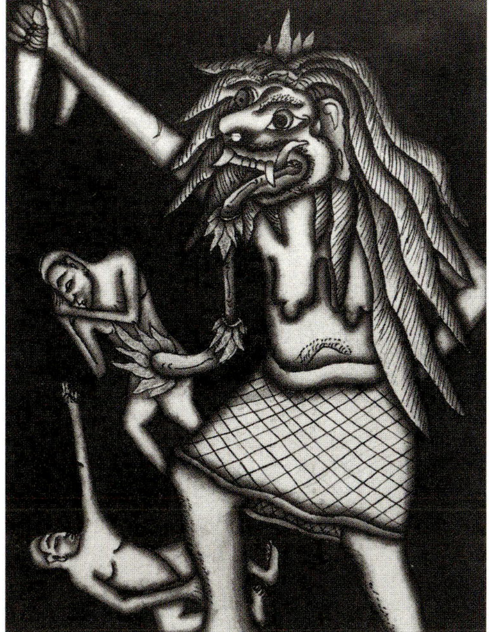

Sorcerer in the Form of Rangda the Witch, November 22, 1936
Ink on paper, 6.7 × 5 in., B 267

Pasek Malén, Déwa Kompiang

Pasek Malén was the younger brother of Pasek Gindjing (above) and only a child in 1937. He was not interviewed by Kalér.

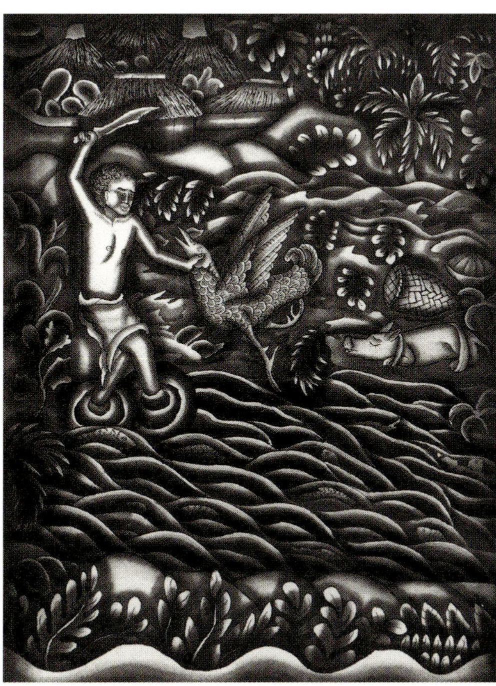

The Story of Belog and the Bird, March 28, 1937
Ink on paper, 11 × 8.5 in., B 272

Pasek Malén, Déwa Kompiang *(continued)*

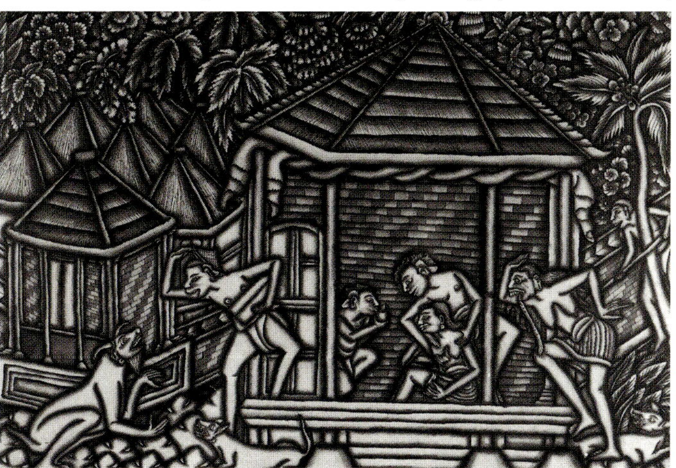

Woman in Childbirth Surrounded by Sorcerers (léyak), January 17, 1937
Ink on paper, 18.5 × 12.75 in., B 270

Pateh, I Ketut

Little is known of Pateh, as he was not interviewed by Kalér. His name is listed as a member of Pita Maha, the artists' co-operative. He may have also painted under another name.

Performance of an Arja Play **(41)**, June 2, 1936
Ink on paper, 13.75 × 18.5 in., B 279

Poedja, Ida Bagus Nyoman

Poedja was one of three brothers, all of whom painted. The other two were Ida Bagus Ketut Togog (represented in the collection but not in the book or exhibition) and Ida Bagus Nyoman Lanoes. Poedja was not interviewed by Kalér. He has three pictures in the collection.

Festival Preparation in Village Household **(29)**, February 3, 1938
Ink on paper, 18.5 × 18.5 in., B 283

Poerna, I

Poerna was not interviewed by Kalér, and nothing is known of his life. Two pictures in the collection are by him.

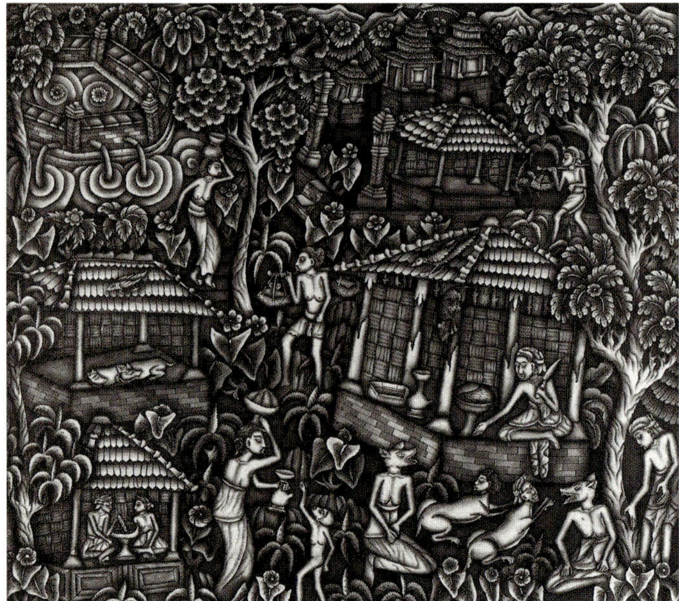

The Tale of the Transposed Heads, June 20, 1937
Ink on paper, 19.5 × 17 in., B 287
The story was dictated by Ida Bagus Putu Boen.

Rai, Ida Bagus Ketut

About thirteen years old at the time of making the painting in the collection, Rai had been producing pictures less than a year. He learned from either Tjeta or Tjeti. Rai went to school for three years, could read, write, and speak Malay, and also played gamelan and danced in the *gambuh*. He never met Spies or Bonnet, and was not a member of their collective, Pita Maha. After World War II, he became a peddler and also a shadow puppet master, but only performed the simpler ritual *wayang lemah*. Eight pictures by Rai are in the collection.

A War among Sorcerers **(88),** August 21, 1937
Ink on paper, 18.75 × 14.5 in., B 410

Reneh, I

Reneh may have been about twenty-five in 1937. A picture collected by Bonnet was dated 1933, so it appears he was one of the first group of Batuan painters. He was a member of Bonnet and Spies' group, Pita Maha. Reneh was not interviewed by Kalér.

Reneh was a fine professional dancer and was also a shadow puppet maker. He did not make many pictures. There are five by him in the collection.

A Cockfight at a Temple **(30),** with Déwa Wayan Kandel Débel, September 30, 1937
Ink on paper, 18.75 × 14 in., B 357

Cremation: Taking the Body from Its Bed **(34),** January 30, 1937
Ink on paper, 13.5 × 18.5 in., B 308

A Fight with a Demon in the Rice Fields **(66),** December 1, 1936
Ink on paper, 10 × 13.75 in., B 307

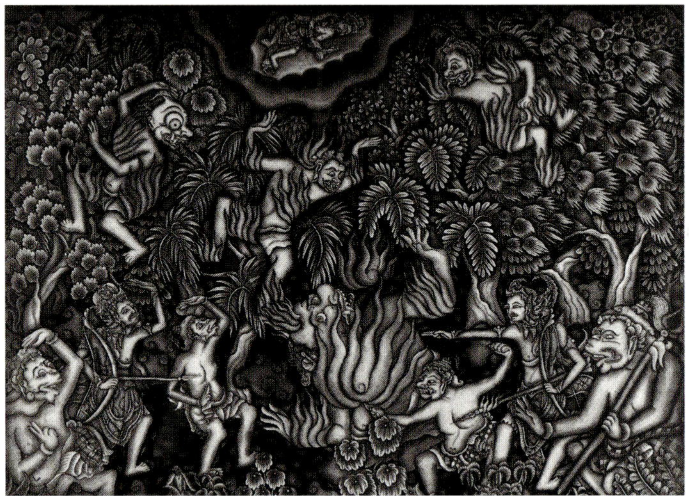

An Episode from the Bratayudha War, August 21, 1937
Color, Ink on paper, 14 × 19.5 in., B 309

Sanoer Tampi, Ida Bagus Nyoman

Sanoer was about twenty years old at the time that he made paintings for Bateson and Mead. He was the son of Brahmana priests and often helped his mother with priestly ritual duties. He later became a priest himself. He had learned to paint soon after the first group of Batuan artists, perhaps in 1934 or 1935, from his older brother, who did not produce many pictures. He had met Spies and Bonnet, and once brought them a picture for criticism. He was a member of the artists' collective, Pita Maha. Sanoer was quite poor and never went to school, although he could speak a little Malay. He produced thirty-four pictures in the collection.

Sorcerer's Talismanic Images **(86),** September 30, 1937
Ink on paper, each 8.5 × 6.5 in., B 467, B 469–B 471

Temple Festival **(26–27),** November 20, 1936
Ink on paper, 10.75 × 34.5 in., B 711.20

Sasak, Ida Bagus Nyoman

Sasak learned to paint along with his two brothers, Sawa (below) and Ida Bagus Wayan Gedé (not included in this book). All three began to paint pictures about when Mead and Bateson started collecting, so most of their pictures were made with less than a year of experience. None of them met Spies or Bonnet, and they were not members of Pita Maha. They sold most of their pictures to Bateson and Mead

At the time of making the pictures Sasak was about twenty-four years old and was married to a woman with two children of her own. They were very poor and lived off his woodcarving and painting for tourists, harvesting coconuts, and her weaving. He played in the gamelan orchestra for the *gambuh*. Sasak did not go to school and could not speak Malay. Fifteen of his pictures are in the collection.

The Battle between Grantang and the Ogre Benaroe **(55)**, March 3, 1937
Ink on paper, 18.25 × 11.5 in., B 402

Sawa (Semawa), Ida Bagus Ketut

Sawa was the younger brother of the artist Sasak (above). He was not interviewed by Kalér. At the time of the making of the pictures in the collection he was married. He danced in the *gambuh*, and later in *arja* dramas. He later became a long-distance merchant, bicycling into the mountains to buy garlic, which he sold in Denpasar. He once accompanied Togog to visit Mead and Bateson in their mountain village, Bayung Gede, to sell them pictures. Seventeen pictures by Sawa are in the collection.

Cremation: At the Burning Ground **(36)**, August 30, 1937
Ink on paper, 18 × 14.75 in., B 424

Performance of a Gambuh *Play* **(42)**, December 1936
Ink on paper, 18.75 × 14 in., B 413

The Tale of Little Képét **(48)**, December 16, 1937
Ink on paper, 18.25 × 14 in., B 426

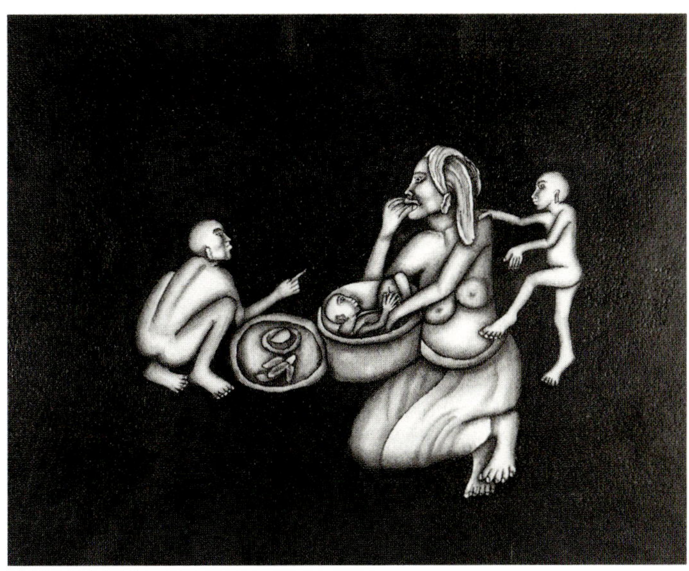

Bathing a Baby, July 30, 1937
Ink on paper, 9 × 7.5 in., B 425

Sawa, Ida Bagus Ketut *(continued)*

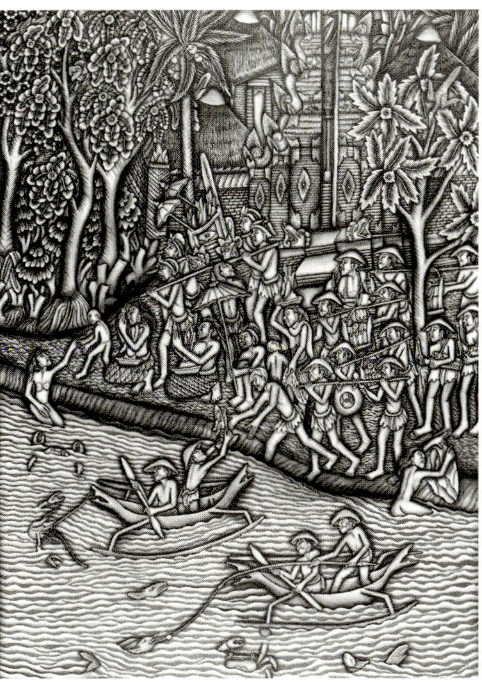

Cremation: Farewell at Seashore, April 3, 1937
Ink on paper, 23.5 × 17.25 in., B 421

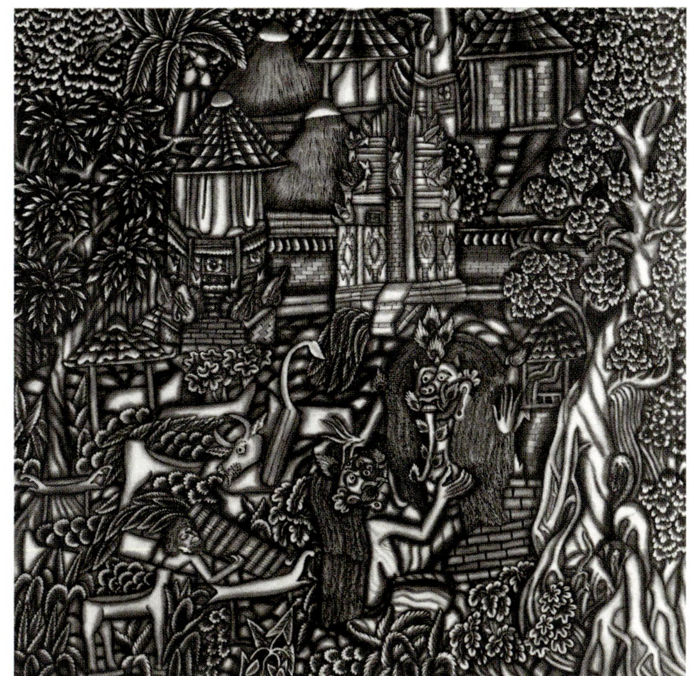

The Story of the Cunning Brahmana Scholar, August 14, 1937
Ink on paper, 19.5 × 20 in., B 422
Story dictated by Ida Bagus Teroewi

Siring, Ida Bagus Ketut

Siring was not interviewed by Kalér, and nothing is known of his life.

The Demon Ratu Macaling Brings Disease and Disaster Every Year in the Rainy Season **(67)**, November 4, 1937
Ink on paper, 9 × 7.5 in., B 439

Tantra, Ida Bagus Putu

Tantra was the younger brother of Ida Bagus Madé Togog, from whom he learned to draw. He was about twenty-one years old in 1938, already married, and had one child. He must have started painting around the time that Mead and Bateson arrived in Bali. Tantra did not meet any foreigners and was not a member of the artists' collective, Pita Maha.

Like his brother, Tantra was very poor, their father having died when he was about twelve. He did not go to school and could not speak Malay. For some time he worked as a migrant laborer on coffee plantations in the mountains, and it is known that he danced in the *gambuh*. Tantra died young. Seventeen pictures by him are in the collection.

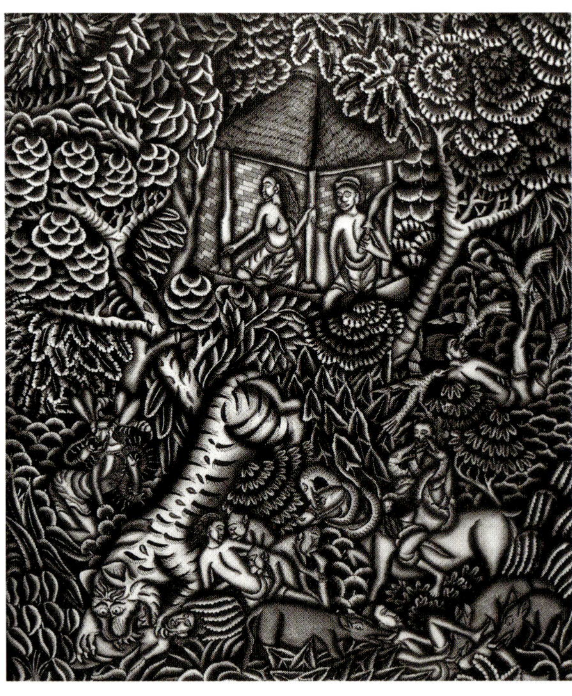

Defeat of the King Who Tried to Take the Dukuh's Wife from Him, July 28, 1937
Ink on paper, 17.7 × 15.5 in., B 481

Tibah, Ida Bagus Madé

About twenty-one years old at the time the collection was formed, Tibah had been painting almost as long as Ngéndon and Togog. He was a son of a fairly well-off peddler who had a shop selling tourist carvings. His older brother often peddled pictures in Denpasar and Sanur. Tibah did not go to school but could speak a little Malay.

Tibah was taught painting by Ngéndon, who lived nearby. He visited the homes of the Western painters Spies and Bonnet. They taught him to study his pictures from a distance and sometimes corrected his work. He was a member of Spies and Bonnet's artists' group, Pita Maha. Tibah continued to paint after the war, and in the 1970s opened a large art shop. He made twenty pictures in the collection.

Harvest Ceremony **(28)**, November 4, 1937
Ink on paper, 18.5 × 13.75 in., B 506

The Tale of the Two Sisters Bawang and Kesuna **(51)**, April 27, 1937
Ink on paper, 18 × 28.5 in., B 503

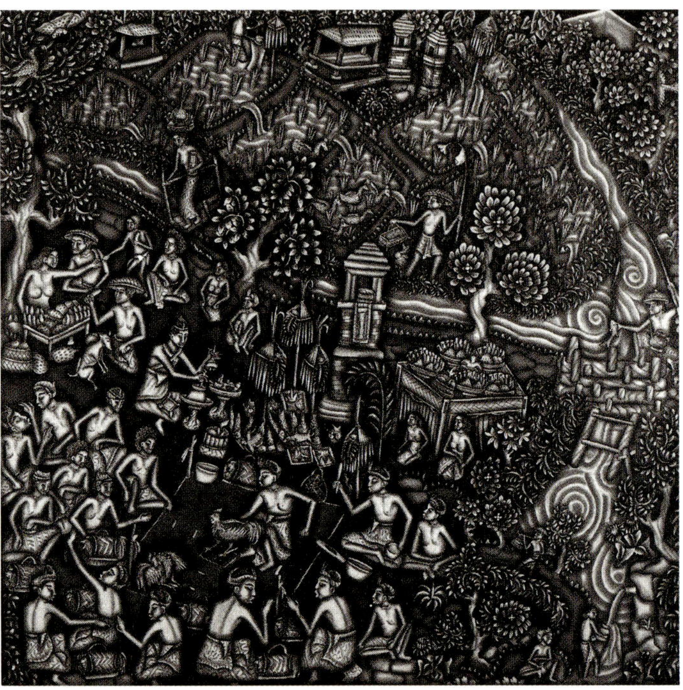

Cockfight at the Ritual Opening of a New Irrigation Dam, January 22, 1938
Ink on paper, 20 × 20 in., B 514

Tibah, Ida Bagus Madé *(continued)*

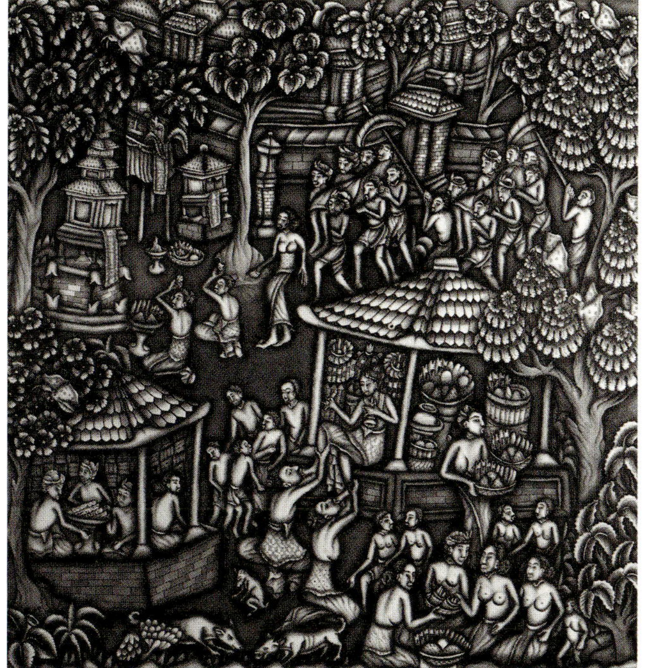

A Man and Wife Are Consecrated as Priests, December 24, 1937
Ink on paper, 16.5 × 16 in., B 513

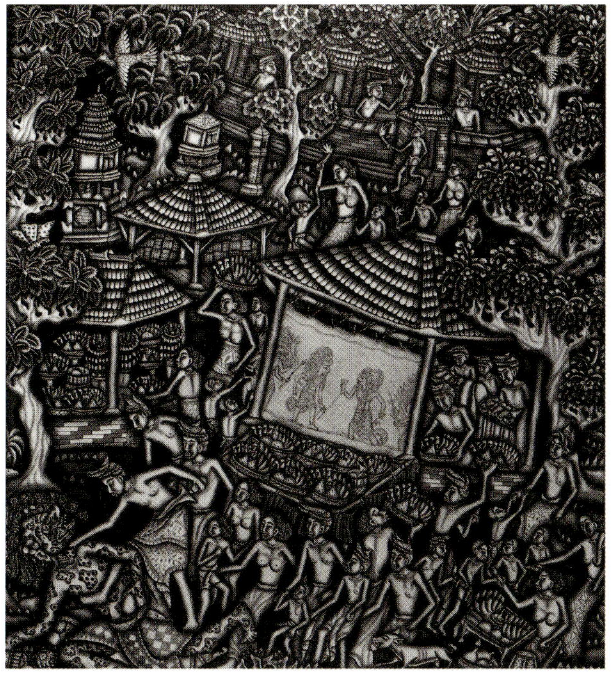

Shadow Play Performance, December 2, 1937
Ink on paper, 18.2 × 16.2 in., B 508

Tjeta, Ida Bagus Nyoman

Tjeta was the younger brother of Ida Bagus Teroewi, the head man of Batuan and the host of Mead and Bateson. Tjeta was about twenty-two years old when he began painting. At the time, he was married but had no children yet. His father was a renowned dancer and organizer of performances, who also painted cloth for dancers' costumes and funeral shrouds. Tjeta assisted with that work and also danced in the *gambuh*.

Tjeta, who learned to paint from Togog, was among the first Batuan painters. He did not go to school but could speak Malay. He often visited the Western artists in Batuan, watched them use colored paint and pastel, and brought them his pictures for criticism. Once he tried to copy a picture from a magazine. He produced twenty-nine pictures in the collection.

Balinese "Witches" **(16)**, December 2, 1937
Ink on paper, 13.75 × 12 in., B 536

Epidemic **(64)**, November 4, 1937
Ink on paper, 14.5 × 12.5 in., B 535

A Sorcerer (léyak) *Transforms Herself* **(72–73)**, February 2, 1938
Ink on paper, each about 8 × 6 in., B 543–B 548

Tjeti Raka, Ida Bagus Nyoman

Tjeti was a neighbor of Togog. He was about twenty years old at the time of Bateson and Mead's stay and was married but had no children. His father, a ritual specialist, was very poor. Tjeti had worked as a migrant laborer on a rubber plantation in the mountains. He was taught to paint by Tjeta several years before the time of Kalér's interview. Tjeti said he had visited the homes of the Western artists in Batuan once or twice, but never showed them his work for correction. Nor was he a member of the cooperative, Pita Maha. Fifty-five pictures by Tjeti are in the collection.

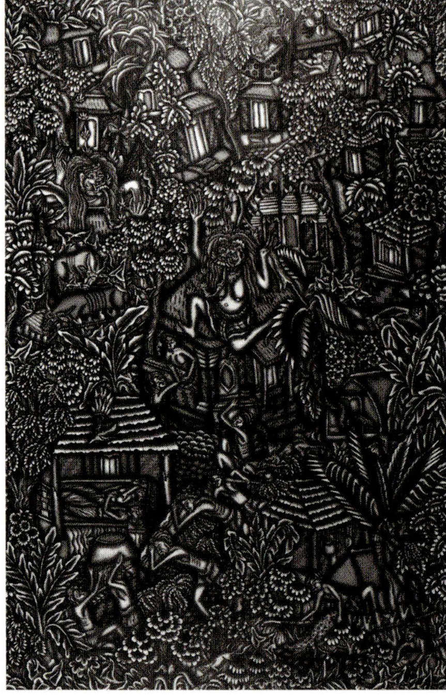

Sorcery and Thievery, April 26, 1937
Ink on paper, 30 × 20 in., B 563

Toeplan, I Madé

Little is known of Toeplan, as he was not interviewed by Kalér. According to Bonnet, Toeplan died in 1938. He made four pictures in the collection.

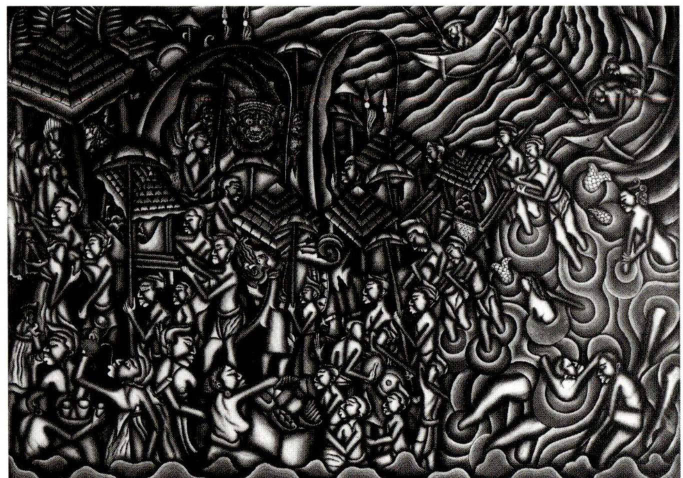

Cremation: Final Release of Spirit in the Sea, October 20, 1936
Ink on paper, 15 × 20 in., B 596.1

Togog, Ida Bagus Madé

Togog was a leader in the group of Batuan artists, in painting, in teaching painting to others, and in selling pictures. He was also one of the oldest, about twenty-five in 1937, was married and had one child. His father had died when he was twelve years old, and his mother supported him by selling foodstuffs. His grandparents had been priests. His wife was a weaver and a ritual specialist.

Along with Ngéndon, Togog was among the first to learn to paint, about two and a half years before Mead and Bateson arrived. He had painted designs on dancers' costumes and knew how to write classical Balinese on palm-leaf manuscripts. He was also a ritual specialist. Togog often visited Spies and Bonnet, watched them work, and tried to copy Bonnet's work and a picture from a magazine. He showed them his own work for criticism, and was a member of their artists' collective, Pita Maha. Togog spent some time as a migrant farm laborer, planting coconut trees and working in a coffee plantation in the mountains.

Togog assisted Bateson in checking the attributions of the paintings. He made eighty-three pictures in the collection.

Attack on Calon Arang, the Queen of the Sorcerers **(20)**, June 2, 1936
Ink on paper, 14 × 14 in., B 624.1

Calon Arang Story **(78)**, January 17, 1937
Ink on paper, 16.75 × 27.75 in., B 638

The Mythic Sorcerer Begawan Mercukunda and the Spirits He Can Invoke and Create **(82)**, September 7, 1937
Ink on paper, 13.5 × 21.75 in., B 668

Sorcerer's Talismanic Image **(21)**, November 1936
Ink on paper, 17.75 × 7.75 in., B 631

The Story of Amad and Mohammed Killing the Men in Iron Armor **(53)**, February 21, 1939
Ink on paper, 28 × 18.25 in., B 685

The Story of the Demon Who Pretended to Be a Priest **(22)**, April 8, 1937
Ink on paper, 22.25 × 18.5 in., B 645

The Story of Truna Tua Stealing the Clothes of the Sky Nymph **(12)**, June 3, 1936
Pencil on paper, 14.5 × 8.5 in., B 684

A Dream about a Tree with Dagger Leaves **(90)** (dream 6), September 7, 1937
Ink on paper, 15 × 9.5 in., D 8–D 9

A Dream about Attacking a Sorcerer (léyak) **(91)** (dream 8), November 1, 1937
Ink on paper, 15 × 10 in., D 11–D 12

A Dream about Mystical Learning **(92)** (dream 17), November 27, 1937
Ink on paper, 15 × 10 in., D 31–D 32

A Dream about a Sorcerer **(93)** (dream 20), January 4, 1938
Ink on paper, 15 × 10 in., D 37–D 38

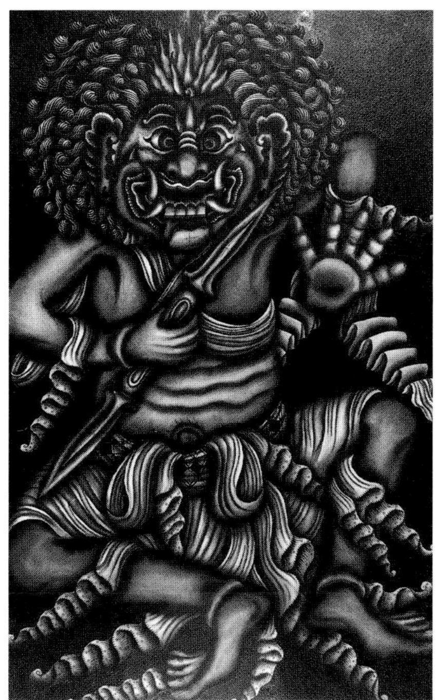

The Demonic Form of a Deity
(God of the East),
September 16, 1937
Ink on paper, 22 × 13 in., B 671

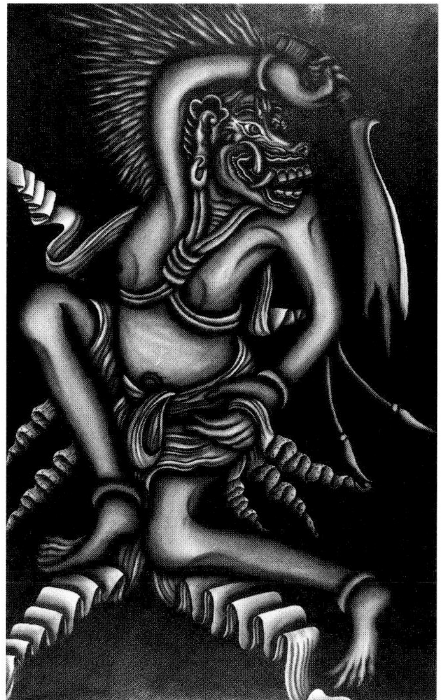

The Demonic Form of a Deity
(God of the West),
September 16, 1937
Ink on paper, 21 × 13 in., B 670

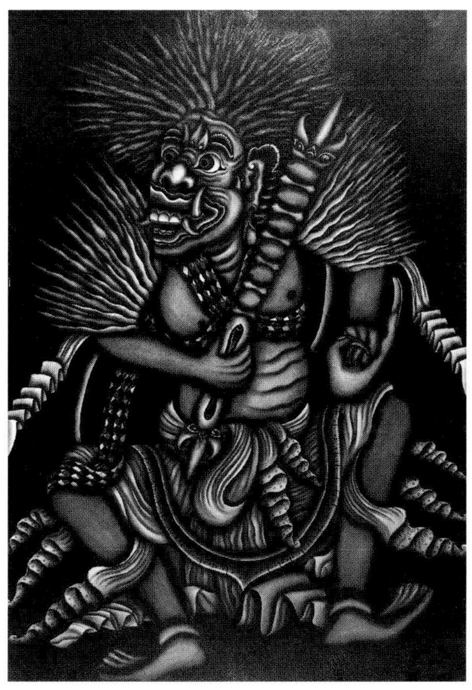

The Demonic Form of a Deity
(God of the South),
September 16, 1937
Ink on paper, 21.75 × 14.75 in., B 672

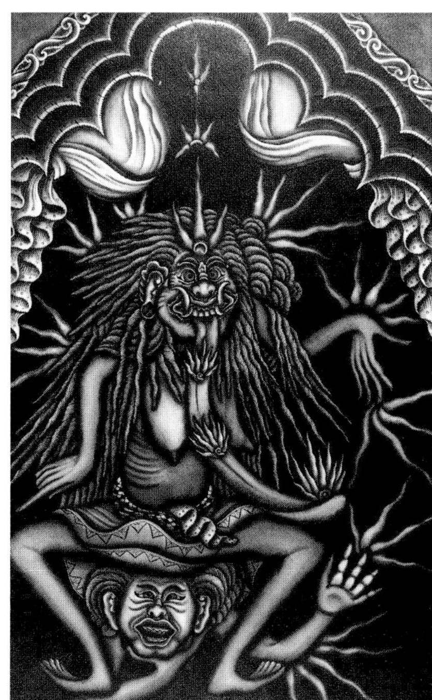

The Sorceress Semiring Seated on the
Head of a Human Victim,
September 1, 1937
Ink on paper, 21 × 12.75 in., B 667

Togog, Ida Bagus Madé *(continued)*

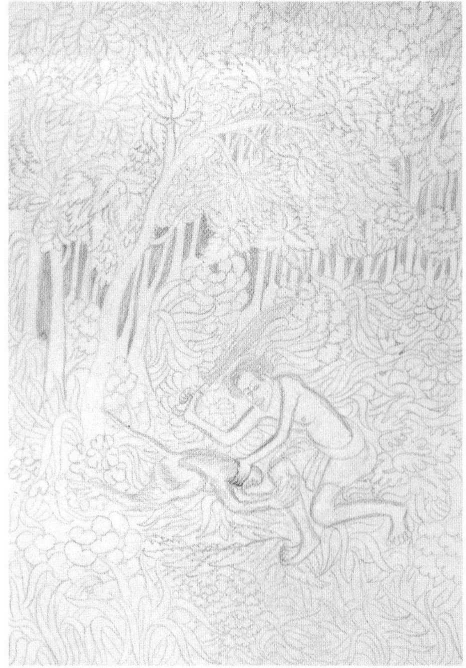

Penciling

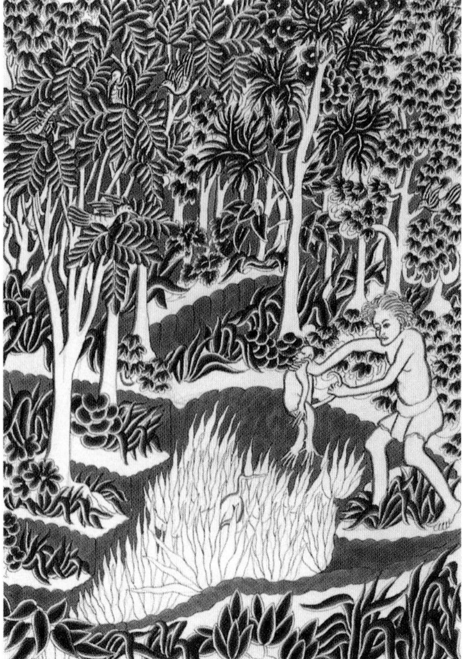

Applying ink-wash for shading

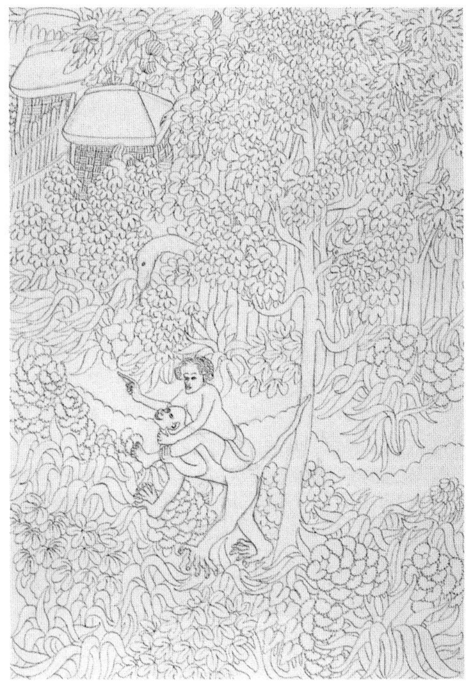

Inking in lines

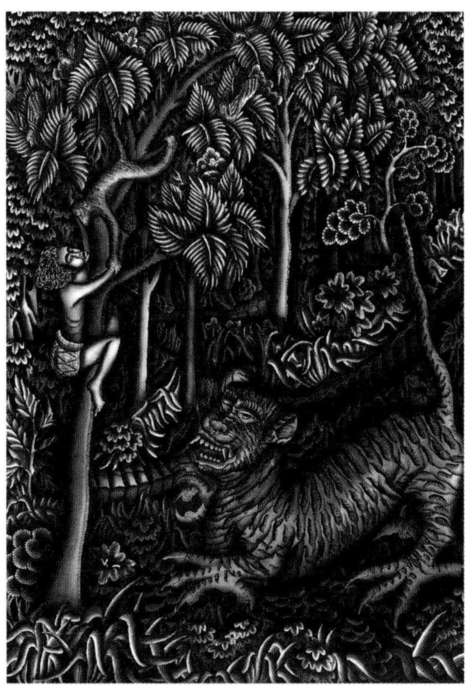

Completed picture

Demonstration of Steps in the Making of a Picture (The Story of Papaka, the Tiger, and the Monkey),
September 13, 1936
Ink and pencil on paper; set of 4, each about 14 × 10 in.,
B 623.1a–B623.1d

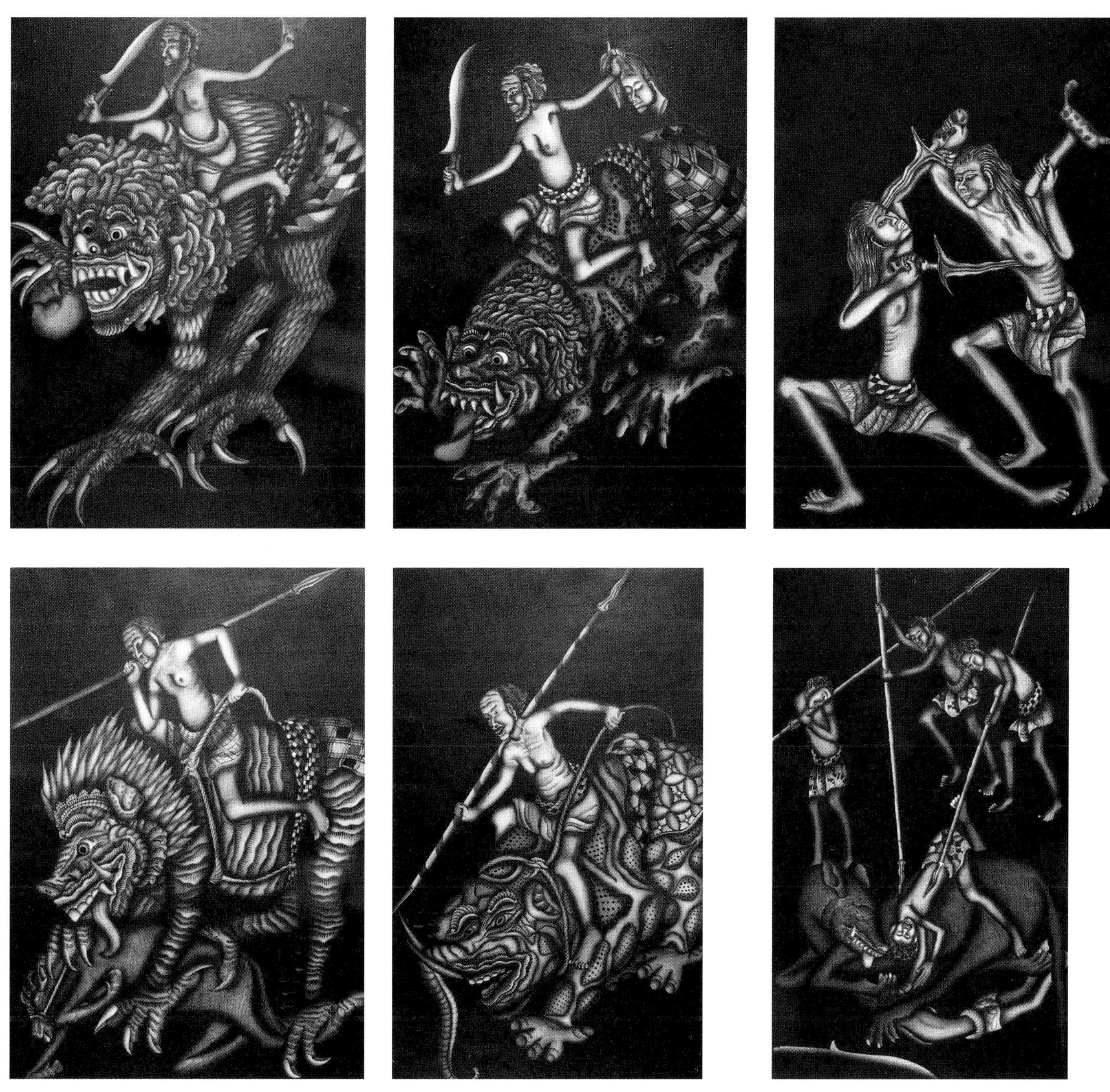

The Victory of King Rangga Lawé, September 13, 1936
Ink on paper; set of 8, each about 14 × 10 in., B 619–B 622, B 625, B 627–B 628, B 642 **(57–58)**

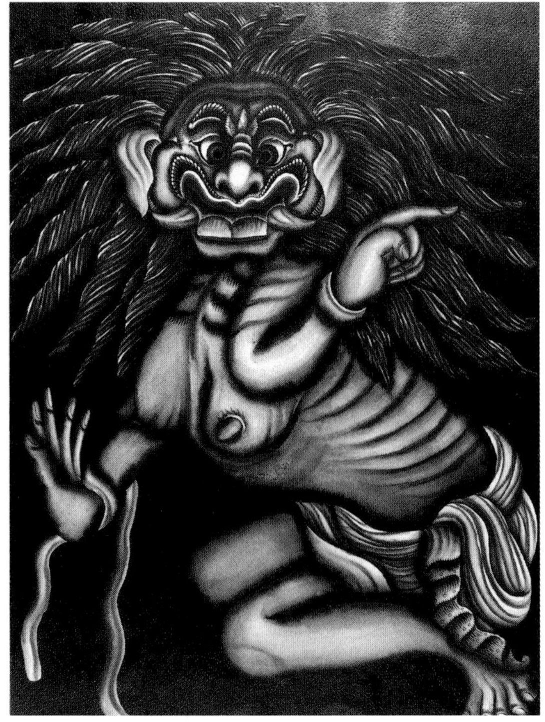

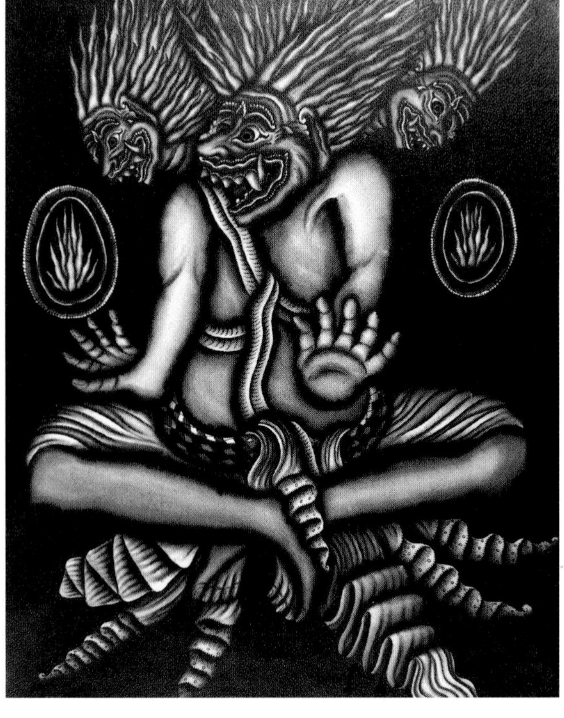

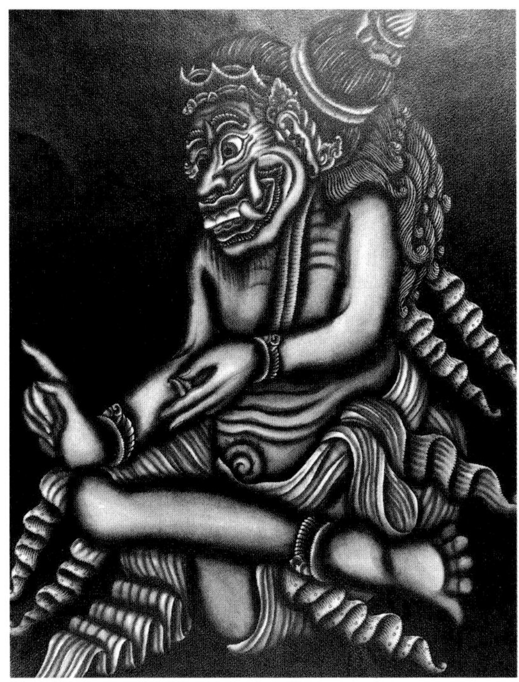

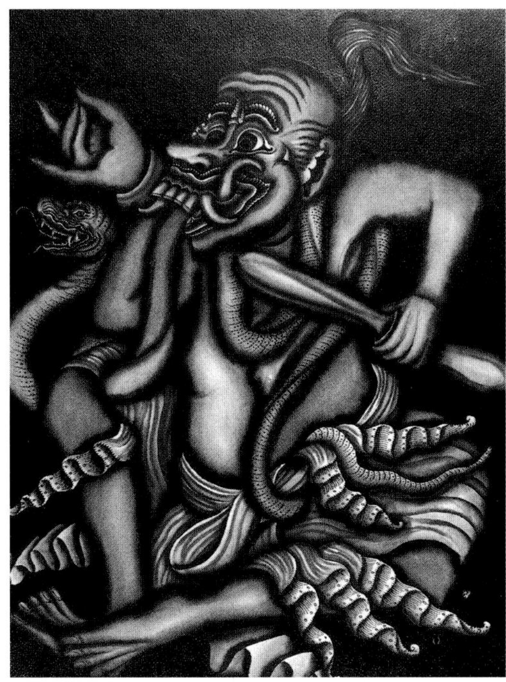

ABOVE AND OPPOSITE: *The Making of a Mythic Sorcerer,* November 1, 1937
Ink on paper; set of 7, each about 18 × 14 in., B 673–B 679 **(84)**

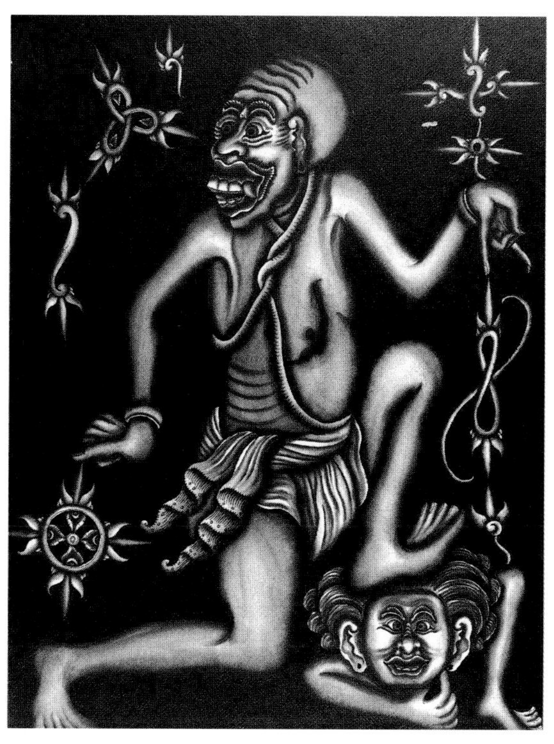
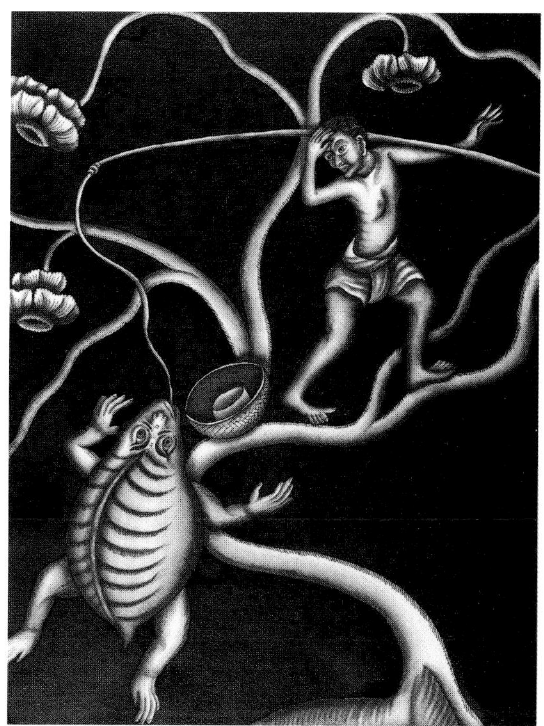
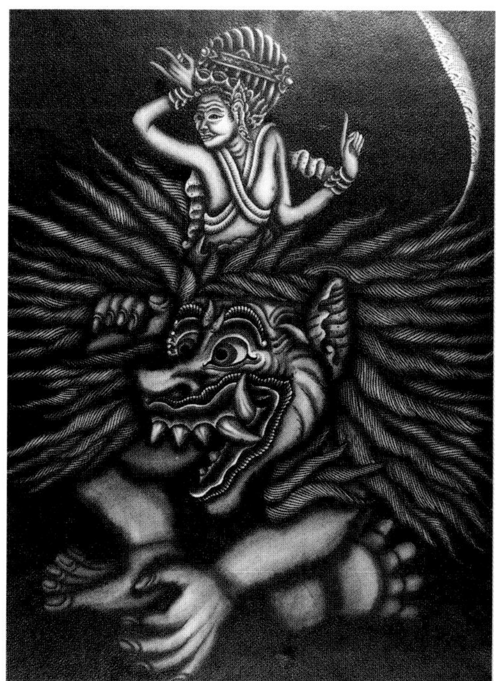
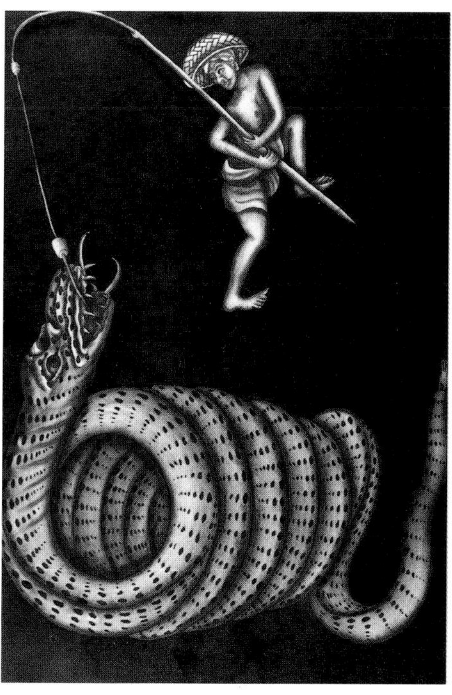

ABOVE: *A Dream of Fishing* (dream 4), September 1, 1937
Ink on paper; set of 2, 16 × 11 in., D 4–D 5

Tombelos, I

About fifteen years old in 1938, Tombelos had been drawing since about 1934 or 1935. He was taught by Ngéndon. His father, a poor stonecutter, was dead. Tombelos did not go to school but could read and write Balinese. He was a close relative of Ngéndon.

Tombelos had visited Spies and Bonnet, who taught him how to use ink and offered criticism of his pictures. He was a member of their artists' group, Pita Maha. There are twenty-three pictures by Tombelos in the collection.

Rejang *Temple Dance* **(40),** August 27, 1937
Ink on paper, 13.25 × 18.25 in., B 701

Two Players from a Baris Melampahan **(44–45),** with I Taweng, April 28, 1937
Ink on paper, 8.5 × 5 in., B 495; 8.75 × 5 in., B 496

Village Market **(15),** February 25, 1939
Ink on paper, 18.25 × 14.5 in., B 711.38

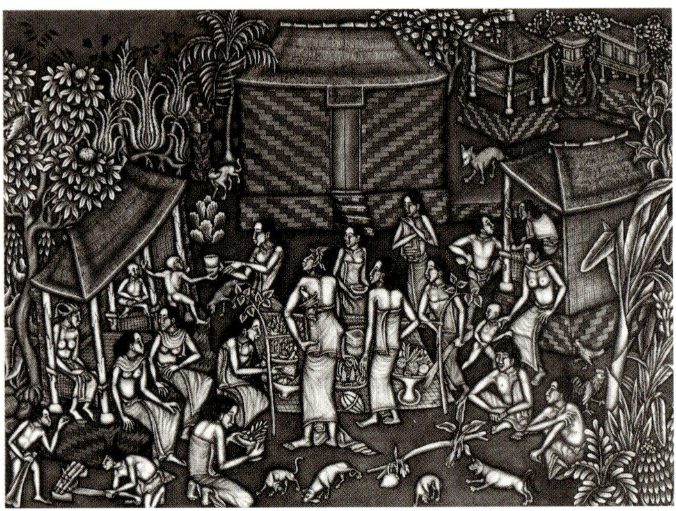

Wedding Ritual, February 3, 1938
Ink on paper, 15 × 19.5 in., B 705

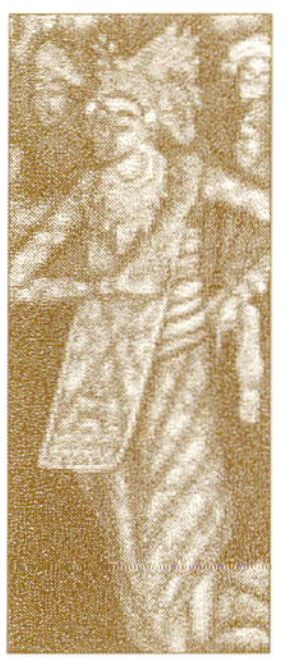

Notes

Introduction

1. From their first month in Bali until their last, Mead and Bateson were in frequent contact with the painters, who came to them wherever they were living in Bali to proffer their wares. The anthropologists decided in the first month to make a side study of the painters of Batuan and to interview each painter about each work. During their first year in Bali, they lived in the mountain village that was the focus of their study, but steadily purchased and annotated the pictures from Batuan. During the second year they primarily lived in the court town of Bangli, but set up a house in Batuan and lived there for about two months.

Bateson and a Balinese assistant, I Madé Kalér, made over two hundred pages of notes on the pictures bought, recording each painter's comments and stories in his own words. In addition, Mead and Bateson designed a lengthy questionnaire that was used by Kalér to interview twenty-three of the main artists. They were asked about their economic life, education, experience with foreigners, how they learned to make pictures, and how they usually marketed them.

Ten of these major painters were still alive in 1981 when I went back to Bali to work with them. I lived in Batuan in the home of Déwa Ketut Baroe, one of the youngest of the 1930s artists. Our house was just around the corner from his good friend, Ida Bagus Madé Togog, who was perhaps the most important of the Batuan painters, and I came to know him well. I had been in Bali in the 1950s, but had not made any attempt to study Balinese art, traditional or modern. In my 1980s research, which added up to an intermittent residence of more than two years in Batuan, it was the arts, both plastic and performed, that occupied my attention. In addition, I put together a socioeconomic history of Batuan, a history of the dance-drama in Batuan, and a close study of the architecture and carving of Batuan's many temples. Most of the first ten months were spent learning Balinese, but during that time I also interviewed both Baroe and Togog at length about their lives. I subsequently interviewed repeatedly, in Balinese, a number of other surviving picture makers, including Djata, Widja, and Tjeta.

I attempted many times in the 1980s to get various Balinese, including the artists, to elucidate and evaluate these pictures from the 1930s, but was constantly frustrated by the fact that there is no customary Balinese way for talking about pictures that corresponds to Western discussions about aesthetics and cultural analysis. They were also uniformly reluctant to express criticisms of the work of still-living artists (for example, Togog, Djata, Baroe, Sawa, Sanoer). Some stressed a desire to know the stories, many of which were strange to them. Aside from a few technical comments about draftsmanship, general "neatness," and the lack of color, most comments were about content rather than aesthetic value. All, however, were hesitant to make general interpretations about the burden of any picture on the grounds that since spiritual beings manifest themselves in myriad ways, the certainty of our knowledge of them and the stories about them are always a little suspect; therefore one can never be entirely sure of the "underlying" content or meaning of a picture. For these reasons, I have been forced to employ more indirect research strategies, piecing together fragmentary clues about the paintings' contents from Bateson's notes on the explications of the picture made by the artists just after completing them.

In this present book, intended for a general audience, I have not had space to go into the kind of detailed presentations of my findings that I would like. A subsequent volume, addressed primarily to scholars, will elaborate, substantiate, and further speculate on the materials presented here. At times, here, I have treated as certainties propositions which are more properly discussed as problematic, and which will be dealt with more completely in the other book.

2. I am aware that if a Balinese had written this book, he would have made a different selection and stressed other themes. Certainly, if more than one Balinese interpreted these pictures, many different readings of them would result. For the paintings, taken as a whole, present many facets of Balinese thought. However, each picture retains the traces of its maker's hand and eye, and can, however mutely, express protest or affirmation to what I as a distant outsider have said about it. To further allow the pictures to "speak for themselves," I have presented here as many of them as is practicable, and in my translations and summaries of the accompanying texts stayed as close as possible to the speaker's original words. The Balinese did not title their works, and I have taken the liberty of contriving more elaborate and informative titles. When the painter did not dictate a text, Bateson sometimes provided fragmentary notes, which I have summarized and extended.

3. For general introductions to Balinese culture, see Lansing 1983 and Ramseyer 1977.

Chapter 1: Inventing an Art—Both Balinese and Western

1. Bateson and Mead 1942; Bateson 1973b.

2. A. A. M. Djelantik, in his *Balinese Paintings* (1986), p. 36, states that "The Batuan painters, however, . . . originally all painted in the *wayang* style. . . ." This, however, is not so. There are only a few paintings, one by Ngéndon and several others by Reneh, that show knowledge of shadow puppets or paintings in the Kamasan manner. All but a few were not yet twenty and had no training at all.

3. For introductions to Balinese traditional art, see Forge 1978, Holt 1967, and Ramseyer 1977.

4. Ramseyer 1977, p. 72, caption 72.

5. Ibid., caption 73.

6. Ibid., caption 71.

7. Ibid., p. 105, caption 136.

8. Ibid., p. 89, caption 108.

9. Ibid., caption 107.

10. See Bateson and Mead 1942, pp. 64–65; Vickers 1991.

11. de Zoete and Spies 1973.

12. Roh 1925, pp. 81–82.

13. See Darling 1980.

14. This information comes from Margaret Mead's field notes, Margaret Mead Archives, Library of Congress, Washington, D.C.

15. It is unclear from the available evidence just which language, Malay or Balinese, Belo and Spies spoke customarily. Balinese were accustomed to speak Malay with all foreigners, and probably preferred it, because Malay, at least as it was spoken by foreigners, had no strong status markers in it. Balinese are highly sensitive to the rude errors that foreigners make when attempting to speak Balinese. However, both Spies and Belo certainly understood a great deal of Balinese, for they report stories and explanations which could only have been given them in Balinese. Belo always had a Balinese secretary who had been to school and knew Malay, who could serve as an interpreter for her. Belo apparently advised Bateson and Mead to do the same, and to work in Balinese from the very outset of their research.

16. For more details, see H. Geertz 1991b.

17. For further information on possession, see Belo 1960 and Connor, Asch, and Asch 1986.

18. The film is "Trance and Dance in Bali."

19. This story is part of the Aji Darma cycle, according to Adrian Vickers (personal communication).

Chapter 2: The Everyday World of (Mere) Appearances

1. In this chapter and subsequent ones, when I speak of "Balinese" beliefs and customs, I base my remarks primarily on my own experience, in Batuan and elsewhere in Bali, and on the published literature. However, there is high variation on specific terminology, customs, and even ideas among different Balinese localities. Nonetheless, I hope that I have identified certain underlying cultural conceptions that play important parts in the lives of most Balinese.

2. Kraus 1920, Covarrubias 1956.

3. For more information on the custom of *ngarap*, or fighting over the body on the way to cremation, see Connor 1979. Patsy Asch has made a film, as yet unreleased, using the Bateson-Mead footage together with some footage and a commentary by Anthony Forge, called *Ngarap: Fighting Over a Body.*

4. A full history of drama in Bali has yet to be written, but a number of special studies are moving in that direction. See especially Bandem and deBoer 1981; Bandem 1983; de Zoete and Spies 1973; Hinzler 1981; Hobart 1987; Picard 1990, 1992; Vickers 1986; and Zurbuchen 1987.

5. See the description of *gambuh* in de Zoete and Spies 1973, pp. 134ff. The illustrations in their book are photographs by Spies of the Batuan troupe in front of Pura Désa Batuan (identified by the carvings). They show the recently completed stonework of the temple and what look like new costumes.

6. de Zoete and Spies 1973, pp. 169–174.

7. See Holt 1967, p. 184, for another rendering of the *baris* by I Tupelen (Toeplan) of Batuan. The picture is in the Bonnet collection in Leiden.

Chapter 3: The Magical Story World

1. No one yet has made an extended study of such storytelling. Some texts exist, notably the large collection in the Kirtya van der Tuuk, which was drawn on in articles by Jacoba Hooykaas-van Leeuwen Boomkamp (1960a and 1960b) and Gusti Ngurah Bagus (1976a and 1976b) among others. However, these texts are reports of stories rather than the fully developed and quite dramatic performed versions that are given in an actual storytelling session. For this distinction between

reports and performances of stories, see Hymes 1981 and Bauman 1986.

2. The great number of stories that were told to Bateson and Mead is evidence of the pleasure the Balinese must have had in telling tales. This refutes a Western stereotype that Balinese pay little attention to the plots of the dramas, a stereotype repeated by Mead and Bateson.

3. The original texts, typed in Balinese by Kalér together with Bateson's occasional interlinear translations of difficult words (often into other Balinese words) and explications, are in the Margaret Mead Archives of the Library of Congress in Washington, D.C. Since they were slowly dictated to someone writing them down, rather than told at normal speed to an enraptured audience, they lack some of the verve (and perhaps the detail) of real storytelling performances. Some of the painters were much poorer storytellers than others and were content with presenting a mere outline of the plot or an identification of the main characters. I've chosen here some of the more complete and expressive ones.

4. The term *sakti* is a root term in Balinese, and in this form it resembles an English adjective, since it concerns an attribute of action, energy, or persons. When referring to a more generalized and abstract notion about *sakti* it takes the form of *kesaktian* and is closer to an English abstract noun.

The word *sakti* is not commonly used in everyday speech. It is replaced by euphemisms, or by more specific terms such as *pandéstian* (the capacity to change one's form) or *nglekas* (to transform oneself into an evil demon) or *ngléyak* (to transform oneself into a *léyak*, or "witch").

Someone with such powers, whom I refer to as a "sorcerer" is sometimes called a "person of *sakti*" *(anak sakti)*. (The term *anak* means in Balinese "person," not "child," as it does in Indonesian. It is not gendered.) Both men and women are capable of acquiring *sakti*. The art of healing in Bali requires the power to harm, although most healers or priests are thought not to use that evil potency except for healing by frightening away the afflictor. Healers are called *balian*, which derives from the term *bali* or *wali*, sacral power, which is the same or similar to *sakti*. While priests *(pedanda* and *pamangku)* are not usually spoken of as having *sakti*, it is understood that their long spiritual training and their knowledge of mystical lore play a great part in guaranteeing the efficacy of their rituals. Many of these priests are also healers.

On *sakti* and political power, see Anderson 1972, C. Geertz 1980, Wiener 1994, and Errington 1989.

5. For Balinese conceptions of and institutions of kingship, see C. Geertz 1980; Wiener 1994; Schulte Nordholt 1988, 1991; and Vickers 1989.

6. de Zoete and Spies 1973, pp. 145–146. I have modernized the spelling.

7. de Zoete and Spies 1973, pp. 143, 273, 275.

8. For an extended study of this story and its illustration in temple carvings and shadow play performances, see Hinzler 1981.

9. See Vickers n.d. For a set of photographs of the Kerta Ghosa paintings, redone in 1960, see Pucci 1985.

10. This is the story called "Mantri Wadak" that was used in the *gambuh* performances in Batuan, according to Adrian Vickers (personal communication).

Chapter 4: The Real World of Dangerous Powers

1. The dialogue between the spirit speaking through the medium, Jero Tapakan, and her clients is a good example of the process of mutual construction of increasingly specific explanations of the causes of the death of a young boy. See Connor, Asch, and Asch 1986, chapter 7.

2. For a comparable set of ideas, see J. Favret-Saada (1981), who shows that Breton peasants felt that overt talk about specific witches would "catch" the speaker into a tight net of reprisals and counterreprisals.

3. Some specific cases are given in Ann McCauley's Ph.D. dissertation (1984); Wikan 1990; Connor, Asch, and Asch 1986; and Barbara Lovric's Ph.D. dissertation (1987).

4. The term *"banjar"* has been adopted by the Indonesian government to signify the smallest administrative unit of the government. Consequently, in many villages there exist two institutionalized groups, the *banjar dinas*, or governmental unit, and the *banjar adat*, the group with religious duties. Sometimes both have exactly the same membership, but Balinese are never unclear about the difference between them.

5. For an account of an actual stoning to death of a man suspected of being a *léyak* by the entire membership of a *banjar*, see de Kat Angelino 1921.

6. Materials on the Calon Arang, associated stories and plays, and the rituals within which it is performed can be found in Bandem and deBoer 1981, de Zoete and Spies 1973, and O'Neill 1978. Most accounts of the story of Calon Arang are based on the text presented and translated by Poerbatjaraka 1926. It is puzzling why none of the many scholars who have written about Calon Arang have used or published a different and later text of the tale.

Many of the Batuan pictures were identified by Bateson as "Calonarang," but they are not accompanied by narrative texts. This omission I believe was because once Mead and Bateson had transcribed one version, they did not realize that the Calon Arang story is really many. The one text of the story in the Mead-Bateson field notes is a text composed by Kalér early in their field work. It contrasts with almost all the rest of their texts, which were dictated by local people to Kalér. Bateson and Mead thought of the Calon Arang story as a pervasive fundamental myth that was always told or performed in the same way. In accordance with the assumption that the Calon Arang is the same story in everyone's mind, a version from a man from Singaraja (where Kalér came from) would be the same as one from Gianyar. Other writers (e.g., Bandem and deBoer) have made this same assumption.

The Calon Arang is in fact a collection of related stories, with many linked episodes, and may have the form of a main "stem" story with many lesser "branch" plots, much like the Panji and the Parwa stories in the shadow play. Some alternative versions can be mined out of de Zoete and Spies 1973, pp. 101–102, 105–109, 116–122, 122–124, 124–125, 125–133, 284–285.

7. See O'Neill 1978 for another version of the Calon Arang story.

8. The account that I give here is based on that of de Zoete and Spies 1973, pp. 116–118, together with the translation of an early (probably late nineteenth century) text by Poerbatjaraka on which the former was based.

9. The terms *rangda* and *barong* as used by the Balinese themselves are puzzling. They do not really refer to specific spiritual beings, but rather to types of masks. Sometimes Balinese may appear to use the terms as the names of spiritual beings. But, I believe, they have come to do this through their conversations with foreigners as a way of condensing a much more complex way of thinking and speaking.

Rangda means "widow" and is an indirect way of referring to the "Widow of Dirah" or Calon Arang in the play. However, the mask may be used to signify other personages in other plays, as is shown in some of these pictures. On the other hand, even when these masks are not given particular personalities in performances, each mask is revered for itself. Many Pura Dalem have *rangda* masks kept on high altars, which are given offerings, and each is spoken of as a specific being with a personal honorific title such as Jero Gedé. But since stating someone's name in an ordinary conversation is rude, implying both familiarity and command, the name is not normally uttered. To call the mask "Rangda" is a compromise, which allows discussion with foreigners who cannot understand the circuitous locutions that proper politeness requires. Thus there are a host of local beings who are all referred to as Rangda but who in fact have diverse identities. In ritual, of course, the movement of transformation requires a certain kind of generalizing, and the nonlocal deity, Durga, is invoked and is thought to enter the mask. Jane Belo has discussed this issue at length in her book *Rangda and Barong* (1949). "*Rangda*," as the joining of that term and the mask, is a signifier, which can be applied to a whole range of signifieds, from a *léyak* to Durga, from a sorcerer to other gods in their fierce transfigurations.

The term *barong* appears to mean, at base, a certain type of mask. The term is used for a number of masks other than the one foreigners associate with the term—the Chinese-dragon-like mask which the Balinese call the Barong Két. Other *barong* masks represent various animals: for instance, the Barong Macan (tiger *barong*), the Barong Bangkal (wild-boar *barong*), and the Barong Asu (dog *barong*). In the late nineteenth century, the Barong Két replaced most of the others (see Bandem and deBoer 1981). Another kind of *barong* represents not animals but human beings. These are the Barong Landung, or tall *barong*. All of these are involved in propitiatory rites of one kind or another. The beings that enter *barong* masks, like those that enter the *rangda*, are of many kinds. They are specific to each particular mask and are given personal names. As with the *rangda* masks, the beings that enter them have both a local identity (most *barong* are considered guardians of their village) and also a nonlocal connection (to Siva, I believe).

10. Bateson and Mead 1942; see also C. Geertz 1973b.

11. The masks are also said to want to go out for a walk *(melancaran)* or to go visiting *(malawangan)*. This last word derives from the term for "doorway" and refers to the door-to-door visiting of the mask and its entourage. The *rangda* mask is not taken visiting in this way (see Lovric 1987).

12. See Belo 1949, pp. 28–29. Bandem and deBoer state that around 1890 the Calon Arang story was first dramatized, in the Batubulan area of Gianyar province. It may have been subsequently that the *barong* was brought in to directly oppose the *rangda*.

13. See de Zoete and Spies 1973 for examples of *barong* plays; also Eiseman 1990, chapters 26 and 27.

14. This quote is from Bandem and deBoer 1981, p. 139. It is similar to, but more elaborate than, what Balinese have told me that *rangda* says. Bandem and deBoer give an excellent description of a Calon Arang performance, stressing all its paradoxical qualities and intense feelings of danger, as also do de Zoete and Spies. Many Balinese may interpret these shouted challenges as aimed not merely at *léyak* but also implicitly at all malicious spirits and sorcerers in the vicinity.

15. See Bandem and deBoer 1981, p. 139, for this interpretation.

16. Some scholars writing on Bali have conveyed the impression that all "high" gods are good and all "low" demons bad, suggesting that the practice of malevolently intended sorcery is fueled by the powers of "lower" spiritual beings only. See especially Swellengrebel 1960 and Ramseyer 1977. In fact, Calon Arang goes to the high goddess Durga to ask for power, and Durga is a transformation of Uma, the consort of Siva, the highest god. In a lesser example, the ritual performed by a woman who wants to have the powers of a *léyak* is aimed both at the "higher" beings (the offerings made up on the shrine) and at the "lower" beings (the offerings provided on the ground). This double directedness is true of all Balinese rituals.

17. Other ritual dramas also employ such a transformation as a central move. One example is the performance of Sida Karya, a masked figure brought out at the end of a *topéng pajegan* performance, which itself comes near the end of a ritual festival. A *topéng pajegan* is a one-man act in which the actor puts on a series of masks and acts out a story, usually from the early history of the local ruling dynasty. The actor must go through a number of special purificatory and dedicatory rites, and the performance is considered a necessary element in the larger ritual in which it appears. The final mask taken on is Sida Karya, an old man with bright eyes, a smiling, bucktoothed mouth, and large bushy white mustache and eyebrows. He enacts an odd comic dance in which he alternately throws coins on the ground (which the awaiting children then grab up) and threatens to kidnap the children. His performance may end with his actually sweeping up one of the children, carrying him into the inner temple, or near it, putting the child down, and then making solemn obeisance to the gods of the temple. He is said to be a form of the demon Kala, and his act dramatizes the submission of the demon and his transformation into a being of beneficent attitudes toward the congregation (see Hooykaas-van Leeuwen Boomkamp 1961, p. 38, for this interpretation of Sida Karya).

Another example of a malevolent being transformed into a benevolent one comes from the Klungkung region, the demon Ratu Macaling, who in most of Bali is a feared epidemic-bearing monster. However, one of the early kings of Klungkung conquered him, and as a result Ratu Macaling and his huge army are the servitors and guardians of the kingdom of Klungkung (Wiener 1994).

A further example is the ceremony called Eka Dasa Rudra, which was performed in 1963 and again in 1979 at the temple of Besakih. I quote from Stephen Lansing (1983): "Rudra is an ancient Indian war god, probably pre-Vedic, whose name means 'Howler' in Sanskrit. In Balinese Hinduism, Rudra is identified as Siwa, the supreme deity, in his most terrible demonic form. Eka Dasa Rudra ('The Eleven Rudras') conceive of the god as divided into 11 shapes and distributed in space to pervade the entire macrocosm at the points of the compass and the center, zenith, and the nadir. Eka Dasa Rudra, then, symbolically represents the chthonic or destructive powers at large in the Universe" (p. 130). The ritual itself was intended to reorient these destructive forces, in fact to transform them into creative life-giving beings. "This transformation was symbolically portrayed in two drawings placed in the center of the enclosure: the first showed the god Siwa springing out of the demon Kala, the second showed the goddess Uma springing out of the demoness Durga" (p. 141).

18. Despite the fact that the Calon Arang story plays a very important part in the pictures made by the people of Batuan in the late 1930s, it is not the only story used to give meaning to propitiatory rituals, nor are *léyak* the only dangerous powerful beings that such rituals combat. In other ritual dance-dramas other kinds of masked personages and possessed dancers perform similar but not identical functions. See Lovric 1987, Bandem and deBoer 1981, and de Zoete and Spies 1973. It is important not to take Calon Arang as "the central plot" of Balinese imagination, as Bateson and Mead did. Not only is its popularity relatively recent but it is strong only in the Gianyar region, that is, the area in central Bali where Batuan and Ubud lie.

Chapter 5: Masters of *Sakti* Powers

1. Lovric 1987, p. 180. This thesis is a fine and detailed account of Balinese notions of *sakti*. See especially chapter 6 on *balian*. See also note 4 in chapter 3.

2. For a discussion of healers in general and a portrait of a divining healer, see Connor, Asch, and Asch 1986. See also for other examples McCauley 1984 and Ruddick 1986. For a study of suspicions of witchcraft, see Wikan 1990.

3. Another incident of combat among sorcerers, said to have occurred in 1976, is given in Bandem and deBoer 1981, p. 131.

4. Margaret Mead Archives, Library of Congress, Washington, D.C., Kalér notes.

5. The film is "Isle of the Demons," made by Walter Spies and Victor Baron von Plessen in 1931. The novel is *Life and Death in Bali* (also titled *A Tale from Bali*), by Vicki Baum, first published in German in 1937.

6. For an example of a person who became a healer after such dreams and visions, see Connor, Asch, and Asch 1986 and its accompanying films.

7. The temporal correlation between Togog's "*sakti* dreams" and his "*sakti* pictures" (i.e., those paintings that were not illustrations for his dreams, but which have content related to *sakti* matters) is as follows: Togog had made a number of what might be called *sakti* pictures in the year before Mead and Bateson asked him to paint his dreams. On August 24, 1937, Bateson asked him to report his dreams, and two days later he brought in the first paintings. His sixth dream, dated September 7, 1937 (page 90), was done at the same time as a picture of the sorcerer Mercukunda standing, invoking demons (page 82). On September 21 he brought in six very large pictures of demons associated with sorcery (not illustrated). There followed a long period when he made no pictures at all, during which time he may have been sick with malaria or preoccupied with a major cremation. On November 1 he brought in dream 8, of his attacking a *léyak* washing her hair (page 91), together with a set of other pictures of *léyak* (not illustrated). On November 7 he brought in the set of seven pictures that I have titled *The Making of a Mythic Sorcerer* and dictated the story that goes with it (page 84). None of Togog's paintings after that date concern matters of *sakti*, although his dreams continued to have such content for two months more.

8. Togog's dictations of his dreams were usually some days after the dream-experience itself, since he delivered them in bunches. The dream pictures (all 16 × 11 inches) were numbered and dated by Bateson and Kalér consecutively as Togog brought them in. The stories, dictated at first to Bateson and later to Kalér, were keyed to the dates of the pictures. Most dreams were accompanied by two pictures. I have given numbers and titles to the dreams. I have slightly shortened Togog's texts in translating them, but have stayed as close to his wording as I could.

9. The artist used the term *pengiwa* for sorcerer. It refers to the source of his competence: on the "left side" *(kiwa)*. The left hand of a person is the hand of pollution. Some Balinese interpret *pengiwa* to refer to a kind of spiritual writings, or to a special way of reading them.

10. I am indebted to Adrian Vickers and Raechelle Rubinstein for this identification and translation.

11. Vickers pointed out that the use of the term *buduh* might indicate that Togog meant a man who was "crazy" with *sakti* (personal communication). See especially Connor, Asch, and Asch 1986, p. 249, for a case of *buduh*, or as Connor translates it, "blessed madness," preceding the acquisition of healing powers.

12. Bateson and Mead in their book *Balinese Character* (1942) present a complex hypothetical model of the "character" of the Balinese, based on the premise that the people of every nation, ethnic group, or culture have common personality configurations due to commonalities in their early childhood experiences. This premise, popularly held among many still today, has been rejected by anthropologists since the 1960s. The rejection was in response to a series of systematic studies of the personalities of individuals, which showed that there was always such a high variation in psychological functioning of the members of a society, no matter how small, that generalizations of "national character" could not be made. Such generalizations are close to ethnic stereotypes and, like them, do not stand up to careful validation.

A serious critique of Bateson and Mead's *Balinese Character* has been made by Jensen and Suryani 1992. They particularly attack, in their (caricatured) version of Bateson and Mead's "conclusion," the idea that "fear, instilled through child-rearing practices is the basis of Balinese character" (p. 129). However, the two psychiatrists accept Bateson and Mead's premise that a "Balinese character" *can* be described, and attempt to replace it with another hypothetical personality type.

13. Those who have dismissed "witchcraft" as a minor and individual matter include the following: Mead and Bateson in their "Ethnographic Note on Bali" in *Balinese Character* distinguish "witchcraft" from "normal religion," following, I suspect, advice from Spies and Roelof Goris, whom they met in Bali. Covarrubias, doing research for his *Island of Bali* at the same time, and also reflecting the common Western ideas about Bali, also treated witchcraft apart from Balinese religion. Belo in her book on *Rangda and Barong* does not even mention the relation of "Rangda" to witchcraft and sorcery. Hooykaas in *Religion in Bali* doesn't mention witchcraft at all. Swellengrebel in his influential introduction to English translations of prewar Dutch research does not mention witchcraft or sorcery. Clifford Geertz leaves witchcraft beliefs out of his paper on "Person, Time and Conduct" (1973c) where it would have been very appropriate, but mentions it in passing in his paper on the Balinese cockfight (1973d) as "inverses of what might be called their person beliefs." In *Negara* he does not mention sorcery, *léyak*, or witchcraft, but places *sakti* near the center of his analysis. However, he sees *sakti* only as an aspect of royal power. Barth, in *Balinese Worlds*, discusses sorcery as "yet another tradition of knowledge that is salient in Balinese lives and social relations" (p. 249) and thus separate from and competing with other "traditions" (Islam, Bali-Hinduism, traditional kingship and caste ideas, and the modern sector) among which Balinese select to follow in different life circumstances.

14. The late Barbara Lovric, in her unpublished Ph.D. dissertation (1987), which is an invaluable study of Balinese con-

ceptions of illness and healing, set in a detailed study of a *balian*'s handbooks, places ideas of *sakti* and sorcery as central in Balinese thought and discusses at length their relations to Indic Tantrism.

James Boon, in *Affinities and Extremes*, following Lovric, points out the importance of "Tantrism" in Bali. Despite his warnings not to objectify and essentialize any cultural phenomenon, Boon calls these Balinese cultural notions "Tantrism" and makes a further comparison of them with Indian notions that, at least according to him, are often set within an orthodox/heterodox frame. This leads him to see these ideas of sorcery and healing in Bali as heterodox oppositions to more orthodox positions. He warns that "neither work on peripheral specialists nor interpretations of Tantric dimensions of court-sponsored arts (Ramseyer 1977, Worsley 1984) indicates a full-fledged philosophical doctrine, or even counterdoctrine, devoted to topsy-turvy ingestion of female juices and consorts' semen. Rather, Tantric features are dispersed across the conversation of cycles in Balinese rituals" (Boon 1990, p. 163). In my view, these features are indeed dispersed throughout Balinese rituals, although they are not opposed to other "orthodox" doctrines, but are all part and parcel of one another. Boon does not discuss connections to Balinese kingship notions.

Unni Wikan centers her book *Managing Turbulent Hearts* (1990) on fears of witchcraft and sorcery. She is the first writer on Bali to probe deeply in interviews on how Balinese speak about their inner emotional lives, and in doing so, discovered these fears to be central. Most people who have spent time in Bali are made aware of the importance of witchcraft fears and suspicions in Balinese life but have not written about it.

Margaret Wiener, in *Visible and Invisible Realms* (1994), directly introduces the problem of whether Balinese kings were seen as sorcerer-healers. Based on the most complete, and most Bali-centered, account of Balinese discourses concerning events surrounding the past kings of Bali, Wiener sets an image of the king as sorcerer against a historically later image of the king as accessing the highest powers in the cosmos. To my mind these are probably not historically distinct, and certainly not contradictory.

15. See my article, "An Anthropology of Religion and Magic" (1975).

16. The strongest statement of this position is by Swellengrebel (1960). Clifford Geertz, in *Negara* (1980), with a number of cautious qualifications, seems to agree.

Chapter 6: Crossing Cultures

1. James Boon, not only in *Affinities and Extremes* (1990) but also in *The Anthropological Romance of Bali 1597–1972* (1977), has brought to our attention and deftly probed the double-edged effects of "crossing cultures" on texts by travelers, as well as on rituals, myths, and artworks within Bali itself. See also Clifford 1988.

2. Jane Belo stated that in the 1930s Balinese rarely mentioned Durga (1949, p. 23).

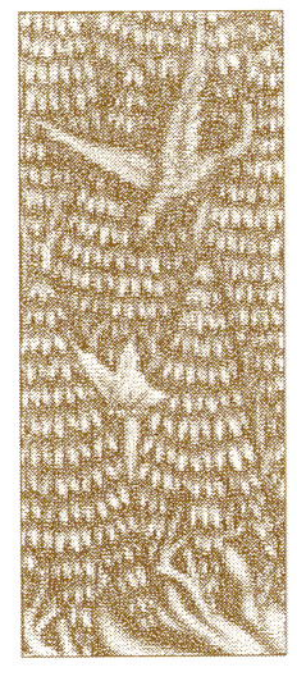

Glossary

anak: person, human being

anak nglekas: a person who can transform the self through mystical powers

anak sakti: a person with mystical powers

arja: a dance-drama genre

Arjuna Wiwaha: a mythical tale of the godlike hero Arjuna

arya: a role of a princely warrior in the dance-drama *gambuh*

atma: soul or soulstuff

balian: healer or sorcerer

banjar: hamlet or neighborhood; unit within village *(désa)*

banjar adat: a unit within a village of traditional form

banjar dinas: a unit within a village which serves as the smallest governmental organization

bantén: offering

baris: a dance form depicting an ancient warrior

baris melampahan: a dance-drama genre, in which all the heroes wear the costume of the *baris*

barong: mask and costume of a certain legendary animal

Brahmana: name of a cluster of clans who have priestly status

Brahmana Buda: name of a cluster of Brahmana clans

Brahmana Siva: name of a cluster of Brahmana clans

buta: demon

buta sungsang: a demon whose head points down and whose feet point up toward the sky

condong: a role in the dance-drama representing a servant woman

dalem: inside; used as a title of a king

désa: village

detya: demon of a tree, river, or other locality

gambuh: a dance-drama genre

gamelan: Balinese orchestra, consisting primarily of xylophone-like instruments

gamelan gong: the largest type of Balinese orchestra

gantian: a type of Balinese folk-tale

gedong: a fully enclosed Balinese domestic building

jogéd: a kind of dance

kawi: classical literature, poet, and, by extension, God

kecak: a kind of dance for tourists, sometimes called the "Monkey Dance"

kekawin: a kind of classical poetry

kesaktian, kesaktén: mystical power

kidung: a kind of classical poetry

kris: a kind of dagger

leluhur: ancestral spirits, gods

léyak: a sorcerer who transforms himself into demonic form, causes death, and eats corpses, especially those of newborn babies

lontar: manuscript of palm leaf, scratched with knife, and rubbed with soot so that the letters stand out

Mahabarata: classical epic myth

malawangan: to go from door to door

mapajar: term for the speech of spirits speaking through possessed persons; to put on a sacred dance of *barong* or *rangda*

mapamit: to take leave; name of ceremony at death

masolah: to dance

mebakti: to pray

melampahan: to travel; to walk; to tell a story

melancaran: to travel; to visit

meréh: to transform oneself through mystical powers

mudra: ritual gesture

ngarap: to grasp; to carry the litter or tower with a corpse; to violently mishandle a corpse

nglekas: to transform oneself through mystical power

ngléyak: to transform oneself through mystical power into a *leyak*

niskala: invisible; the invisible world of spirits, gods, and demons

nyekah: major ritual after cremation

odalan: annual temple ritual

pamangku: priest of a temple, usually a commoner

pamurtian: potent transformation of a deity or person

pandéstian: knowledge of mystical power

panggung: temporary altar scaffolding outside a temple during rituals

pasupati: to give mystical power; name of Siva; name of arrow of Arjuna

pedanda: high priest of Brahmana descent

penasar: role in dance-drama; clown who is director and interpreter of the classical speeches of nobles in the play

pengiwa: person who has mystical knowledge of a malevolent sort

pura: temple

Pura Dalem: temple of the village near the graveyard

Pura Désa: temple of the village

Ramayana: classical epic myth

ramé: busy, crowded, full of life

rangda: a form of mask of a witch-like woman

rebab: a kind of string instrument

rejang: a kind of sacred dance of placation

sakti: mystical power

sakala: visible, ordinary life

Satria: name of cluster of clans of noble status

Siva, Siwa: the high god, Shiva

suling: flute

tapa: to meditate

tonya: demon of river, rock, tree, or other locality

topéng: a kind of masked dance

topéng pajegan: topéng dance when performed entirely by one person

tukang bantén: specialist in making complex offerings

wali: sacred

wayang: shadow play

wayang lemah: shadow play when performed in daylight with no screen

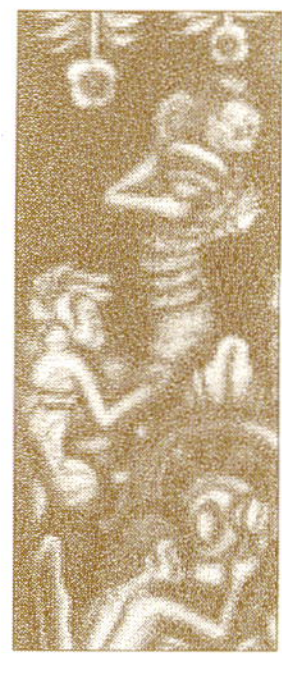

Bibliography

Anderson, Benedict. 1972. "The Idea of Power in Javanese Culture." In *Culture and Politics in Indonesia*, ed. Claire Holt. Ithaca: Cornell University Press.

Bagus, Gusti Ngurah. 1976a. *Si Kaya dan Si Miskin dalam Dongeng Bali* (The Rich Man and the Poor Man in Balinese Folktales). Singaraja, Bali: Balai Penelitian Bahasa.

——. 1976b. *Baju Bidadari yang Tercuri dalam Dongeng Bali* (The Stolen Blouse of the Sky Nymph in Balinese Folktales). Singaraja, Bali: Balai Penelitian Bahasa.

Bandem, I Madé. 1983. *Ensiklopedi Tari Bali* (Encyclopedia of Balinese Dance). Denpasar, Bali: Akademi Seni Tari Indonesia.

Bandem, I Madé, and Fredrik Eugene deBoer. 1981. *Kaja and Kelod: Balinese Dance in Transition.* Kuala Lumpur: Oxford University Press.

Barth, Frederik. 1993. *Balinese Worlds.* Chicago: University of Chicago Press.

Bateson, Gregory. 1973a. "Bali: The Value System of a Steady State." In *Steps to an Ecology of Mind.* 1949. Reprint, London: Granada Publishing Co.

——. 1973b. "Style, Grace and Information in Primitive Art." In *Primitive Art and Society*, ed. Anthony Forge. London: Oxford University Press.

Bateson, Gregory, and Margaret Mead. 1942. *Balinese Character: A Photographic Analysis.* New York: New York Academy of Sciences.

Bauman, Richard. 1986. *Story, Performance, and Event: Contextual Studies of Oral Narrative.* Cambridge: Cambridge University Press.

Belo, Jane. 1935. "The Balinese Temper." *Character and Personality* 4, no. 2 (Dec.). Also in Jane Belo, ed. *Traditional Balinese Culture.* New York: Columbia University Press, 1970.

——. 1949. *Bali: Rangda and Barong.* New York: J. J. Augustin.

——. 1953. *Bali: Temple Festival.* Locust Valley, N.Y.: J. J. Augustin.

——. 1960. *Trance in Bali.* New York: Columbia University Press.

——. 1970. Introduction to *Traditional Balinese Culture*, ed. Jane Belo. New York: Columbia University Press.

Belo, Jane, ed. 1970. *Traditional Balinese Culture.* New York: Columbia University Press.

Bonnet, Rudolf. 1936. "Beeldende Kunst in Gianjar." *Djawa* 16.

——. [1953?]. "A New Era, A New Art." In *Bali: Cults and Customs*, ed. R. Goris. Djakarta: Republic of Indonesia.

Boon, James. 1977. *The Anthropological Romance of Bali: 1597–1972.* Cambridge: Cambridge University Press.

——. 1990. *Affinities and Extremes.* Chicago: University of Chicago Press.

Clifford, James. 1988. *The Predicament of Culture.* Cambridge: Harvard University Press.

Connor, Linda. 1979. "Corpse Abuse and Trance in Bali: The Cultural Mediation of Aggression." *Mankind* 12, pp. 104–118.

Connor, Linda, Patsy Asch, and Timothy Asch. 1986. *Jero Tapakan: Balinese Healer.* Cambridge: Cambridge University Press.

Covarrubias, Miguel. 1956. *Island of Bali.* 1936. Reprint, New York: Alfred A. Knopf.

Darling, John. 1980. "The Context of Bali." In Hans Rhodius and John Darling, *Walter Spies and Balinese Art.* Amsterdam: Tropical Museum, 1980.

de Kat Angelino, P. 1921. "De Léak op Bali." *Tijdschrift voor Indische Taal-, Land-, en Volkenkunde* 60, pp. 1–44. Bataviaasch Genootschap van Kunsten en Wetenschappen.

de Roever-Bonnet, H. 1991. *Rudolf Bonnet: Een zondagskind* (Rudolf Bonnet: A Sunday's Child). Amsterdam: Pictures Publishers.

de Zoete, Beryl, and Walter Spies. 1973. *Dance and Drama in Bali.* 1938. Reprint, Kuala Lumpur: Oxford University Press.

Djelantik, A. A. M. 1986. *Balinese Paintings.* Singapore: Oxford University Press.

Eiseman, Fred B., Jr. 1990. *Bali: Sekala and Niskala.* Vol. 1. Berkeley: Periplus Editions.

Errington, Shelly. 1989. *Meaning and Power in a Southeast Asian Realm.* Princeton: Princeton University Press.

Favret-Saada, J. 1981. *Deadly Words.* Cambridge: Cambridge University Press.

Forge, Anthony. 1978. *Balinese Traditional Paintings.* Sydney: Australian Museum.

Galestin, Th. P. 1962. Introduction and annotations to *Hedendaagse Kunst van Bali.* Utrecht: Centraal Museum.

Geertz, Clifford. 1973a. *The Interpretation of Cultures.* New York: Basic Books.

——. 1973b. "Religion as a Cultural System." In Clifford Geertz, *The Interpretation of Cultures.* New York: Basic Books.

——. 1973c. "Person, Time and Conduct in Bali." In Clifford Geertz, *The Interpretation of Cultures.* New York: Basic Books.

——. 1973d. "Deep Play: Notes on the Balinese Cockfight." In Clifford Geertz, *The Interpretation of Cultures.* New York: Basic Books.

——. 1980. *Negara: The Theatre State in Nineteenth-Century Bali.* Princeton, N.J.: Princeton University Press.

Geertz, Hildred. 1975. "An Anthropology of Religion and Magic." *Journal of Interdisciplinary History* 5, no. 1.

——. 1991a. "A Theatre of Cruelty: The Contexts of a Topéng Performance." In *State and Society in Bali*, ed. Hildred Geertz. Leiden: Koninklijk Instituut voor Land-, Taal-, en Volkenkunde.

Geertz, Hildred, ed. 1991b. *State and Society in Bali.* Leiden: Koninklijk Instituut voor Land-, Taal-, en Volkenkunde.

Geertz, Hildred, and Clifford Geertz. 1975. *Kinship in Bali.* Chicago: University of Chicago Press.

Hinzler, H. I. R. 1981. *Bima Swarga in Balinese Wayang.* The Hague: Martinus Nijhoff.

Hobart, Angela. 1987. *Dancing Shadows of Bali.* London: KPI Ltd.

Holt, Claire. 1967. *Art in Indonesia: Continuities and Change.* Ithaca, N.Y.: Cornell University Press, 1967.

Hooykaas, C. 1973. *Religion in Bali.* Leiden: E. J. Brill.

Hooykaas-van Leeuwen Boomkamp, J. H. 1960a. "The Changeling in Balinese Folklore and Religion." *Bijdragen tot de Taal-, Land-, en Volkenkunde* 116.

——. 1960b. "The Myth of the Young Cowherd and the Little Girl." *Bijdragen tot de Taal-, Land-, en Volkenkunde* 117.

——. 1961. *Ritual Purification of a Balinese Temple.* Amsterdam: N. V. Noord-Hollandsche Uitgevers Maatschappij.

Hymes, Dell. 1981. *"In Vain I Tried to Tell You"—Essays in Native American Ethnopoetics.* Philadelphia: University of Pennsylvania Press.

Jensen, Gordon D., and Luh Ketut Suryani. 1992. *The Balinese People: A Reinvestigation of Character.* Oxford: Oxford University Press.

Kamus Bali-Indonesia (Dictionary Balinese-Indonesian). 1989. Denpasar, Bali: Dinas Pendidikan Dasar, Propinsi DATI I BALI.

Kraus, Gregor. 1920. *Bali.* The Hague: Folkwang-Verlag.

Lansing, J. Stephen. 1983. *The Three Worlds of Bali.* New York: Praeger.

Lovric, Barbara. 1987. "Rhetoric and Reality." Ph.D. diss., University of Sydney.

McCauley, Ann. 1984. "The Cultural Construction of Illness in Bali." Ph.D. diss., University of California, Berkeley.

Mead, Margaret. Field notes by Margaret Mead, Gregory Bateson, and I Madé Kalér (1936–1939). Margaret Mead Archives, Manuscript Division, Library of Congress, Washington, D.C.

——. 1939. "The Strolling Players in the Mountains of Bali." In *Traditional Balinese Culture*, ed. Jane Belo. New York: Columbia University Press, 1970.

O'Neill, Roma Sisly. 1978. "Spirit Possession and Healing Rites in a Balinese Village." Master's thesis, University of Melbourne.

Picard, Michel. 1990. "'Cultural Tourism' in Bali: Cultural Performances as Tourist Attraction." *Indonesia* 49.

——. 1992. *Bali: Tourisme culturel et culture touristique.* Paris: Editions L'Harmattan.

Poerbatjaraka, R. M. Ng. 1926. "De Calon Arang." *Bijdragen voor Taal, Land en Volkenkunde van Nederlands Indie* 82.

Pucci, Idanna. 1985. *The Epic of Life.* New York: Alfred van der Marck Editions.

Ramseyer, Urs. 1977. *The Art and Culture of Bali.* Oxford: Oxford University Press.

Rhodius, Hans. [1964?]. *Walter Spies: Schönheit und Reichtum des Lebens.* The Hague: Boucher.

Rhodius, Hans, and John Darling. 1980. *Walter Spies and Balinese Art.* Amsterdam: Tropical Museum.

Roh, Franz. 1925. *Nach-Expressionismus, Magischer Realismus, Probleme der neuesten Europäischen Malereien.*

Ruddick, Abby. 1986. "Charmed Lives: Illness, Healing, Power and Gender in a Balinese Village." Ph.D. diss., Brown University.

Schulte Nordholt, Henk. 1988. "Een Balische Dynastie: Hiërarchie en Conflict in de Negara Mengwi, 1700–1940." Ph.D. diss., Vrije Universiteit te Amsterdam.

——. 1991. "Temple and Authority in South Bali: 1900–1980." In *State and Society in Bali*, ed. Hildred Geertz. Leiden: Koninklijk Instituut voor Land-, Taal-, en Volkenkunde.

Swellengrebel, J. L. 1960. Introduction to *Bali: Studies in Life, Thought, and Ritual*, ed. W. F. Wertheim et al. The Hague: W. van Hoeve, Ltd.

Vickers, Adrian. 1986. "The Desiring Prince: A Study of the Kidung Malat as Text." Ph.D. diss., University of Sydney.

——. 1989. *Bali: A Paradise Created.* Victoria, Australia: Penguin Books.

——. 1990. "The Amad Story by Ida Bagus Madé Togog." In *Donald Friend's Bali.* Sydney, Australia: Art Gallery of New South Wales.

——. 1991. "Ritual Written: The Song of the Ligya or the Killing of the Rhinoceros." In *State and Society in Bali*, ed. Hildred Geertz. Leiden: Koninklijk Instituut voor Land-, Taal-, en Volkenkunde.

——. N.d. "The Kerta Ghosa, Art, Ritual and Power in a Balinese State," unpublished manuscript.

Wiener, Margaret J. 1994. *Visible and Invisible Realms: Power, Magic and Colonial Conquest in Bali.* Chicago: University of Chicago Press.

Wikan, Unni. 1990. *Managing Turbulent Hearts: A Balinese Formula for Living.* Chicago: University of Chicago Press.

Worsley, Peter. 1984. "E 74178 (An Analysis of a Balinese Painting of a Ramayana Episode)." *Review of Indonesian and Malaysian Affairs* 18.

Zurbuchen, Mary Sabina. 1987. *The Language of the Balinese Shadow Theater.* Princeton: Princeton University Press.

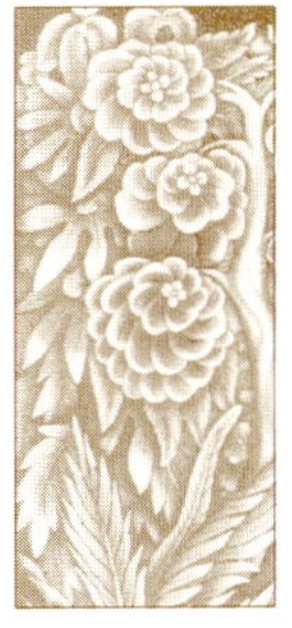

Index